Cyprus Before History

Cyprus Before History

From the Earliest Settlers to
the End of the Bronze Age

Louise Steel

Duckworth

First published in 2004 by
Gerald Duckworth & Co. Ltd.
90-93 Cowcross Street, London EC1M 6BF
Tel: 020 7490 7300
Fax: 020 7490 0080
inquiries@duckworth-publishers.co.uk
www.ducknet.co.uk

A catalogue record for this book is available
from the British Library

ISBN 0 7156 3164 0

Typeset by Ray Davies
Printed and bound by CPI Antony Rowe, Eastbourne

Contents

Contents

Contents

6. Cyprus in the Late Bronze Age

7. Epilogue: The End of the Bronze Age

List of Illustrations

List of Illustrations

Figures

List of Illustrations

List of Illustrations

List of Illustrations

Acknowledgements

I am grateful to my colleagues in the Department of Archaeology, University of Wales, Lampeter, for providing me with such a stimulating environment in which to prepare my text. In particular I want to thank Brian Boyd (discussion of early farming communities), Paul Rainbird (island archaeologies) and Mike Walker (radiocarbon dates). Carole MacCartney, Stuart Swiny and Trevor Watkins read sections of the manuscript and made helpful suggestions. My father, John, has read vast chunks of the manuscript and offered useful comments. I am particularly grateful to Denise Druce for preparation of the illustrations. These have been adapted from a variety of sources, acknowledged individually. My thanks go to Deborah Blake at Duckworth for her patience and advice concerning the preparation of the manuscript.

A number of colleagues and friends have kindly shared information, ideas and offprints, and have given me permission to use illustrations. In this respect I would like to thank Bill Andreas, Sophia Antoniadou, Paul Åström, Jacqueline Balensi, Celia Bergoffen, Diane Bolger, Stephen Bourke, Lucilla Burns (Fitzwilliam Museum), Joanne Clark, Nicolas Coldstream, Lindy Crewe, Trude Dothan, Kathryn Eriksson, Peter Fischer, David Frankel, Michael Given, Liz Goring, Sophocles Hadjisavvas (Cyprus Museum), Naomi Hamilton, Nicolle Hirschfield, Maria Iacovou, Vassos Karageorghis, Priscilla Keswani, Anne Killebrew, Bernard Knapp, Bill Manley, Sturt Manning, Sophie Marchegay, Ami Mazar, Meg Morden, Christine Morris, Karin Nys, Danielle Parks, Eddie Peltenburg, Ellie Ribeiro, David Rupp, Pamela Russell, Kylie Seretis, Nancy Serwint, Sue Sherratt, Joanna Smith, Alison South, Andrea Swinton, Laina Swiny, Gordon Thomas, Ian Todd, Adrian Turgel, Panayiotis Voilas, Marguerite Yon.

I am indebted to the archaeologists I have worked with in Cyprus over the years, on various excavations and in museums, for their friendship and exchange of ideas, many of which have come to fruition in this book. I am particularly indebted to everyone at CAARI, especially Vathy, to Andreas Savvas and the staff at Larnaca Museum, and to the villagers at Kalavasos for making me welcome and greatly facilitating my research. My family have always provided support for my fascination with Cypriot archaeology and encouragement for this book, which is affectionately dedicated to them.

L.S.

Abbreviations

BSC	Black Slipped and Combed ware
EBA	Early Bronze Age
EC	Early Cypriot
EIA	Early Iron Age
HBW	Handmade Burnished ware
KCU	Khirokitia Culture
LBA	Late Bronze Age
LC	Late Cypriot
LH	Late Helladic
MC	Middle Cypriot
MM	Middle Minoan
MNI	minimum number of individuals
PC	Philia Culture
PPN	Pre-Pottery Neolithic
PPNA	Pre-Pottery Neolithic A
PPNB	Pre-Pottery Neolithic B
PreBA	Prehistoric Bronze Age (EC and MC periods)
RP	Red Polished ware
RP(P)	Red Polished (Philia) ware
RPC(P)	Red Polished Coarse (Philia) ware
RW	Red on White ware
SCU	Sotira Culture
WP	White Painted
WP(P)	White Painted (Philia)
WPWM III	White Painted Wheelmade III

The Island of Cyprus

... Cyprus is a very suitable field of archaeological action. Being an island, not only its geographical but also its cultural boundaries are fixed. It is not so large as to render it impossible to obtain at least a general view of its ancient remains by means of some years of systematic excavations. From its geographical position Cyprus was destined to play an important role in ancient history. It served as a connecting link between the Orient and the Occident, its culture was exposed to various waves of influence ...'[1]

A review of the archaeology of Cyprus is long overdue and increasingly pressing given the quantities of excavation and survey data generated in recent years. Ongoing research has allowed the development of a refined chronological framework against which the material record should be assessed. Moreover, the increasing sophistication of theoretical concepts informing interpretative analysis necessitates review of the archaeological debate.[2] In particular, issues concerning the initial colonisation of the island and its earliest human occupation have been challenged. Moreover, the previously poorly understood transitional period between the Chalcolithic and the Bronze Age has been the focus of detailed discussion, in particular issues of demic diffusion (population movement) versus acculturation. Ethnicity, identity and acculturation remain at the forefront of the debate concerning the final stages of Bronze Age occupation on Cyprus. This book is concerned with the prehistoric foundations of Cypriot culture, from the earliest evidence for human activity on the island to the end of the Bronze Age. It aims to critically review the major issues and debates that currently are being played out in the archaeological literature. The cut-off point is the interface between the Bronze and Iron Ages; a period characterised by significant social, cultural and economic disruptions both internally in Cyprus[3] and throughout the wider East Mediterranean.[4] Although important new data is emerging for the Iron Age occupation of Cyprus, the nature of the evidence falls outside the remit for this book. The first millennium BC marks major transformations in the social and economic structure of the cultures of the East Mediterranean,[5] and in this period Cyprus moves from pre- and proto-history into the annals of charted historical records.

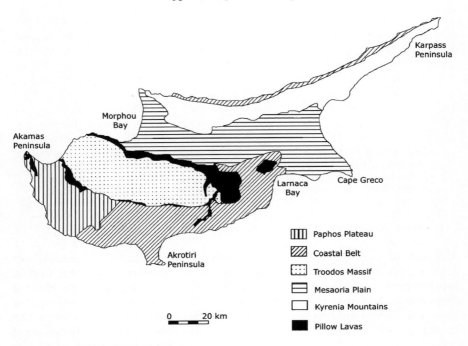

Fig. 1.1. Geological map of Cyprus.

Geography

The geographical location and physical landscape of Cyprus have had a distinct influence on the development of human societies on the island from the earliest period of occupation down to the present day. Cyprus occupies a strategic position at the eastern rim of the Mediterranean basin, in effect acting as a stepping stone between the Asiatic and European landmasses. Surprisingly, therefore, the earliest periods of settlement are characterised by apparent isolation from the surrounding cultures of the East Mediterranean,[6] and it is not until the second millennium BC that the island was fully integrated within the exchange networks between the Near East, Egypt and the Aegean.

Cyprus is the third largest island in Mediterranean, with an area of 9251 km^2 (Fig. 1.1). Internally there are four major geographical zones: the Troodos massif in the south, the Pentadaktylos (Kyrenia) mountains in the north, between these the Mesaoria plain, and the low-lying coastal belt. The Troodos massif is an upland formation of largely infertile, igneous rocks, reaching a height of 1950 m at Mt Olympos (Mt Khionistra). This mountain range is the remains of an ancient seabed of the Upper Cretaceous period (formed 85 million years ago), thrust up from the ocean floor in the Mesozoic era.[7] The Troodos massif covers an area of 3200 km^2, dominating the landscape in the southwest of the island (see Plate 1). The upper reaches comprise igneous rock – gabbros and diabase – surrounded by a ring of pillow lavas in the lower zone. Although the pillow lavas are very infertile, this zone contains sulphide ore bodies, most notably the rich Cypriot copper resources.[8] The lower reaches of the Troodos are formed from sedimentary limestone of Miocene date.[9] The Troodos massif is also one of the main sources of serpentine (a metamorphic rock) – the characteristic green picrolite that was used extensively during the Neolithic and especially the Chalcolithic period for the manufacture of small artefacts such as pendants and figurines. As a result of erosion substantial quantities of picrolite are found in the riverbeds of the Kouris and Dhiarizzos, which were presumably the main focus of procurement activities in antiquity.[10] The extent of human settlement and use of the Troodos massif in antiquity is unclear, but there is considerable evidence for exploitation of the copper resources from the beginning of the Bronze Age, in the later third millennium BC. Earlier archaeological activity, including the Cyprus Survey and the excavations at Apliki,[11] illustrates economic and settlement activity in the foothills of the Troodos. More recent excavations at sites such as Marki[12] and Sanidha,[13] together with extensive survey by the Sydney-Cyprus Survey Project,[14] are beginning to explore more fully the evidence for early human habitation and exploitation of the mountainous region of the Troodos.

The Kyrenia (Pentadaktylos) range is a precipitous ridge running west to east parallel with the north coast. It is formed primarily of sedimentary rocks (re-crystallised limestone and dolomite). To the north the coastal strip is very narrow, but is well watered by perennial springs, and communication between the north coast and the central plain is via three main mountain passes.[15] Physically, the Kyrenia mountains dominate the central lowland plain, the Mesaoria. The Mesaoria (see Plate 2), which lies between the Troodos and Kyrenia mountains, is a flat plain composed of Pleistocene sands, marls, gravels and conglomerates, interspersed with older formations of chalk and gypsum, overlain by recently deposited alluvium. It is watered by several seasonal rivers. In antiquity the Mesaoria was covered by dense forest, but today it is largely deforested and is used for grain production. The mountainous interior and dense forest coverage would have greatly impeded internal communication, but even so the island is characterised by cultural homogeneity from the earliest period of human settlement until the time when the island was incorporated into the Hellenistic and Roman worlds.

The coastal belt is low lying, although there are low cliffs that plunge into the sea, especially along the southeastern coast near Cape Greco and in the southwest between Kourion and Paphos (see Plate 3), developing inland in the southwest into a largely impassable limestone plateau. Indeed, during antiquity the extreme southwest of the island was more easily approached by sea. The mouth of navigable rivers, such as the Pediaios, probably served as inland harbours for sites such as Enkomi, but these have long since been silted up.[16] A characteristic geographical feature in the southern coastal zone is the salt lakes fringed by salt marshes in the Akrotiri peninsula and at Larnaca. The outcrop of sandstone and marl comprising the Akrotiri peninsula originally formed a separate island, possibly until as late as the Roman period.[17] The coastal area around Salamis and Morphou is also wet and marshy and would have been malarial in antiquity. Moreover, the high water table and saline soils of this area were less suitable for agriculture. It has been argued, however, that the increasingly dry climate during the second millennium BC might have improved conditions in the eastern Mesaoria, hence the apparent rise in population in this region during the Middle Cypriot (MC) and Late Cypriot (LC) periods.[18]

Flora and fauna

As an oceanic island, Cyprus was never connected to the mainland by a land bridge, even at the maximum extent of sea regression during the Pleistocene.[19] Consequently, the endemic fauna and flora on the island were sea-borne, and the species present in the Holocene were either sea-borne or introduced by human settlers.[20]

Myres proposed a threefold division of the ancient landscape of Cyprus: marshy areas in the central lowlands, dense coniferous forest in the mountainous regions, and a 'belt of parkland, composed in varying proportions of deciduous and evergreen shrubs, with rich meadow fringing the fens' in the intervening areas.[21] It has been suggested that this landscape relates closely to the phytographical zones still evident in the island's flora.[22] During antiquity Cyprus was heavily forested and timber was used extensively in architecture, the copper industry and ship-building.[23] The unusually high incidence of fallow deer (*Dama mesopotamica*) in the LC faunal assemblages of western Cyprus testifies to extensive woodland coverage in this region up till the later second millennium BC.[24] Pine forests, comprising Aleppo pine (*Pinus brutia*) and cypress (*Cupressus sempervirens*), still make up the largest natural habitat of wild flora on the island, in particular covering the Troodos mountains and the Akamas peninsula in the west.[25] Isolated stands of endemic cedar (*Cedrus libani* ssp. *brevifolia*) survive in the Troodos massif, in the area of the Paphos Forest.[26] Also common in the Troodos Forests is the endemic evergreen shrub, the golden oak (*Quercus cypria*).[27] Much of the island today is covered by maquis and garigue of anthropogenic origin, which have become predominant habitat types due to the destruction of the pine forests and overgrazing.[28] Species include the wild olive (*Olea europaea*), pistacio (*Pistacia lenticus*), terebinth (*Pistacia terebinthus*), juniper (*Juniperus phoenicea*),[29] and the widespread *Cistus creticus*, the source of laudanum.[30]

Small pockets of endemic plants survive in a narrow coastal belt, in rocky areas and in the rare wetland areas.[31] The modern landscape of Cyprus has evidently been shaped over the millennia by intensive human activity and the distribution of flora differs vastly from that encountered by the earliest colonists and their Neolithic and Bronze Age descendants.

Cyprus is a stepping stone between the African, Asian and European landmasses and as such is a stopover for migratory birds, most notably the flamingos present at Larnaca Salt Lake during the winter months. A very different picture emerges, however, for the mammal population. Given the paucity of the island's fossil record, the Cypriot biostratigraphy is incomplete, but it appears that only five mammals succeeded in breaching the water barrier between the Asiatic mainland and Cyprus prior to the Holocene: *Phanourios minutus*, *Elephas Cypriotes*, two types of murid (mouse) and a soricid (shrew).[32] The extreme dwarfism of the pygmy elephant and pygmy hippopotamus reflect the limited gene pool of these species and thus are a stark testimony to the rarity of such water crossings by these land-based species. Likewise, there is no extant evidence that humans made the crossing before the Holocene, in contrast to the evidence for maritime exploitation of other Mediterranean islands, such as the Cyclades, in the later Pleistocene.[33] It certainly appears that the relative remoteness of Cyprus was a significant barrier to both human and animal colonisation and that this was only effectively breached with increasing maritime technology and expertise on the part of the human populations early in the Holocene. The endemic large mammals (the pygmy hippopotamus and pygmy elephants) died out at the interface between the Pleistocene and the Holocene, in a pattern apparently replicated in other large Mediterranean islands.[34] The current debate focuses on the role played by human populations in these extinction horizons in Cyprus and the other Mediterranean islands.

Swiny[35] lists ten species of mammal that are present on the island today: moufflon (*Ovis orientalis*), fox (*Vulpes vulpes*), hare (*Lepus capensis*), rat (*Rattus rattus*), shrew (*Crocidura russula*), hedgehog (*Hermienchinus auritus*), two types of mice (*Mus musculus, Acomys dimiadiatus*),[36] Persian fallow deer (*Dama mesopotamica*) and wild boar (*Sus scrofa*). The large mammals are not endemic to Cyprus, but were introduced by humans during the early Holocene. This process of colonisation and introduction of domesticates is currently under review, and excavations at Parekklisha-*Shillourokambos* have pushed it back to the period of domestication in the Levant during the Pre-Pottery Neolithic B (PPNB).[37]

'A mischievous pastime'

Cyprus lay beyond the circuit of the Grand Tour during the seventeenth and eighteenth centuries, and knowledge of its past was limited to references in biblical and classical sources. The island was particularly renowned as the birthplace of Aphrodite/Venus and the centre of her ancient cult. Early western European travellers to Cyprus in this period were primarily interested in the 'Holy Land' and only visited the island en route between Europe and the Levant. In effect, the rediscovery of the antiquities of Cyprus dates to the mid-nineteenth century when the island was still under Ottoman control. This was the period of western colonial expansion in the Middle East and rivalry between the major western powers was characterised by 'archaeological' exploration and the acquisition of ancient 'treasures' to furnish the recently established national museums in London, Paris and Berlin. Initial interest in Cypriot antiquities was framed within an orientalist perspective, the emphasis being on the island's Phoenician heritage.[38] This reflected the scholarly traditions of the time, which were grounded in a thorough knowledge of biblical and classical sources. Moreover, in the nineteenth century Cyprus was regarded as exotic and oriental, as illustrated by representations of the island by European travellers, most notably those of Edouard Duthoit.[39] In the absence of standing monuments of a clearly classical tradition, this perspective was translated to the antiquity of Cyprus, which was placed firmly within an eastern framework; 'ancient Cyprus duly became Oriental, primitive and subservient'.[40]

In 1844 a stela of Sargon II was discovered in the remains of ancient Kition (modern Larnaca), together with a number of silver-gilt cups with figured relief decoration. The Berlin museum purchased the stela, and one of the cups was presented to the Louvre, where it was housed in the newly established Assyrian collection.[41] These finds were contemporary with the rediscovery of the palace of Sargon II at Khorsabad, and clearly placed Cyprus within an oriental cultural sphere, illustrating her close links with the Assyrian empire. The island was considered to be a fertile hunting ground for studying the Assyrians and Phoenicians who were gradually re-emerging from obscurity at this time. In 1850 Honoré d'Albert, duc de Luynes, acquired a bronze tablet with an inscription written in the Cypro-Syllabic script, which had been found the previous year at Dhali (ancient Idalion), and is now housed in the Cabinet des Médailles, Paris. The script, used to write the Cypro-Arcadian dialect of ancient Greek spoken on the island during the Iron Age, was deciphered in the 1870s. A small number of inscriptions written in the Cypro-Syllabic script remain undecipherable. These have been attributed to an unknown language spoken on the island in antiquity, belonging to the indigenous inhabitants of the island – denoted Eteocypriot in the archaeological literature.[42]

From the 1850s a number of French explorers visited the island, acquiring antiquities that today furnish the Cypriot collection in the Louvre.[43] Chief amongst them was Melchior de Vogüé, who visited the island in 1862 and completed the first systematic study of the island's antiquities.[44] De Vogüé's main interest was epigraphic. Duthoit, who accompanied him, wrote that the purpose of the expedition '... is to gather suitable material for the study of the Phoenicians, anything concerning their history, art, customs etc',[45] but it was also to acquire curiosities and ancient treasures. De Vogüé's expedition brought to light a number of important Iron Age limestone votive sculptures from Golgoi, Malloura, Paphos and Arsos, and numerous terracotta figurines, which today form the core of the Cypriot collection in the Louvre.[46] Most spectacular was a gigantic stone vase from the summit of the acropolis at Amathus.

The primary focus of nineteenth-century antiquarian interest in Cyprus was the many tombs that honeycomb the Cypriot landscape and the precincts of her ancient sanctuaries. Indeed, by the end of the nineteenth century at least 77 Cypriot sanctuaries had been identified and explored to some extent.[47] The tombs and sanctuaries were largely viewed as a source of 'treasures', primarily coins, inscriptions, terracotta figures and limestone sculpture, to furnish the museums in the west. In contrast, the architectural remains were largely ignored, possibly partly because the Cypriot monuments displayed nothing of the grandeur of the temples of Greece and Rome. In 1867, however, Sir Robert Hamilton Lang conducted the first systematic excavation of a Cypriot sanctuary at Idalion, recording the extent and depth of excavation, a topographical plan and some contextual data concerning associations of finds within the *temenos* (sacred precinct).[48] Lang's excavations mark the first methodical attempt to examine the ancient Cypriot remains within a cultural-historical perspective.

The most flamboyant and colourful figure amongst the early explorers was Luigi Palma di Cesnola, American consul to Cyprus from 1865, during the last years of Ottoman rule. During his stay on Cyprus Cesnola systematically explored the island, emptying large numbers of tombs and 'excavating' several Iron Age sanctuaries.[49] Many of the finds, in particular the fine limestone statuary, were subsequently transported back to New York where they were purchased by the city to form the nucleus of the collection of the Metropolitan Museum.[50] Cesnola's exploration of the sanctuaries was influenced by the work of his contemporary, Lang, at Idalion. Although he did not discuss his excavation techniques in the same detail as Lang, Cesnola did describe the architectural setting and examined the sculpture in some sort of context. Most notably, he attempted to create a sacred landscape — exploring the location of the sanctuaries and their relationship with nearby tombs and settlements.[51] Unfortunately, Cesnola's accounts of his discoveries were coloured by his desire to surpass Schliemann's discoveries at Troy, resulting in his fabrication of the discovery of the so-called 'Treasure of Curium'.[52] Although Cesnola's methods are to be criticised, even within the context of the formative stages of the discipline of archaeology at the end of the nineteenth century, his discoveries were widely disseminated around the museums of London, Paris, New York and Boston and served to bring Cyprus to the attention of scholars in its own right, rather than simply as a hunting ground for Assyrian and Phoenician treasures.

Despite the seeming flood of antiquities from the island during the mid-nineteenth century, the Ottoman rulers had implemented strong legal controls to restrict their export.[53] In 1878 Cyprus passed from Ottoman rule into the British Empire, but the Ottoman antiquities laws were maintained. Archaeological exploration greatly intensified during the period of British colonial rule, under the close control of British government officials. Excavation was a popular, privileged pastime for colonial officials and wealthy private individuals,[54] and excavation permits were closely guarded. Nonetheless, important discoveries were made during this period, laying the foundations of subsequent archaeological research on the island. In 1883 the Cyprus Museum was established to house and display the many antiquities that were being uncovered. Between 1879 and 1894 Max Ohnefalsch-Richter (a German journalist) was entrusted with carrying out official excavations on behalf of the British government. He excavated hundreds of tombs and numerous sanctuaries throughout the island, and in 1883 the British Museum acquired a number of terracotta and stone sculptures from his excavations at the sanctuary of Artemis at Achna. Ohnefalsch-Richter's excavations were exemplary for the time. He employed new techniques and carefully recorded the results, making detailed topographical plans (recording the sanctuaries stone by stone), and photographs and drawings of sculptures. He published his results in 1893, in *Kypros, the Bible and Homer*.[55] In this work Ohnefalsch-Richter completed the first comprehensive study of Cypriot sanctuaries and ancient cult practices, observing patterns in architecture, spatial organisation, the sacred landscape, votive practices and sacred iconography.[56]

In 1887 The Cyprus Exploration Fund was formed in London, with the purpose of promoting interest in the antiquities of Cyprus. Possibly the most significant project conducted under the auspices of the Fund was the excavation of the sanctuary of Aphrodite at Paphos,[57] directed by E.A. Gardner, some of the finds of which were presented to the British Museum in 1888. Between 1893 and 1899 the British Museum conducted a series of excavations on the island, most notably the LBA cemeteries at Enkomi, Kourion, Hala Sultan Tekke, and Maroni,[58] but also the later Iron Age and Roman cemeteries at Kourion and Amathus.[59] One third of the material was kept by the recently formed Cyprus Museum but the rest of the material was brought back to London, where it forms the core of the collection exhibited in the Leventis Gallery. These excavations were primarily concerned with the retrieval of fine objects for display in the British Museum and were frequently little more than a treasure hunt pitting the landscape. Despite the very great advances in archaeology at the end of the nineteenth century, the British Museum excavations are remarkable for their apparent disregard for new excavation techniques. Little account was taken of the burial context, the number of burials and grave goods that were of limited appeal to museum exhibitions, primarily the more mundane undecorated pottery. This was in very stark contrast to the classification of Cypriot burials that Sandwith had presented to the Fellows of the Society of Antiquaries as early as 1871 (published in 1880), which examined the tomb architecture, burials and grave goods as a unified assemblage.[60] The British Museum excavations, however, are significant in that they illustrate an important shift in the emphasis of Cypriot archaeology. While the earliest explorers had primarily viewed Cyprus as oriental, intrinsically linked to the Assyrians and Phoenicians, the British Museum expeditions were more explicitly framed within a classical, hellenic perspective.[61] The choice of sites was strongly influenced by later historical sources, as was the interpretation of the finds. Most significant was the emphasis on the island's 'Mycenaean heritage' – an aspect which became integral to the archaeological discourse of the twentieth century. Indeed, some of the finest examples of Mycenaean pictorial vases, many of which are on display in the British Museum, were recovered during their excavations on the island.

Possibly the most influential of the archaeologists to work on Cyprus in the late nineteenth and early twentieth centuries was John Myres, Wykeham Professor of Ancient History at Oxford between 1910 and 1939. Myres was very much involved in the establishment of the Cypriot collection at the Ashmolean Museum, Oxford. His particular interest was the Bronze Age civilisation of the Aegean, especially Minoan Crete. He worked closely with Evans at Psychro cave and was one of many archaeologists to express an interest in excavating Knossos. As a young scholar Myres first visited Cyprus in 1894, working with the British Museum team at Amathus. In contrast to the antiquarian perspective of his contemporaries working in Cyprus, Myres approached Cypriot archaeology with the specific aim of reconstructing a cultural history from the archaeological remains. Together with Ohnefalsch-Richter, he wrote a catalogue of the material exhibited in the recently opened Cyprus Museum.[62] This account attempted to organise the material remains of ancient Cyprus into some sort of chronological order, and to correlate these remains with those of surrounding regions. In 1914 Myres published the *Handbook of the Cesnola Collection*, which strongly reflects his hellenic perspective on Cypriot archaeology. He was especially struck by the large quantities of Mycenaean pottery found on the island and argued for Mycenaean colonisation of the island during the Late Bronze Age – a theme that has become entrenched in the archaeological literature.[63]

The pace of exploration quickened during the twentieth century, with increasing emphasis on the application of archaeological techniques, namely careful recording and analysis of stratified sequences, context, and seriation.[64] Possibly the single most important archaeological project conducted on the island was the Swedish Cyprus Expedition, under the direction of Einar Gjerstad.[65] Gjerstad first visited the island in 1923, and undertook a careful study of the finds of a number of Bronze Age tomb groups,[66] along with stratigraphic excavation at three settlement sites.

This work resulted in his thesis, *Studies on Prehistoric Cyprus*, published in 1926. Between 1927 and 1931 the Swedish mission undertook excavations at 25 sites throughout the island, ranging in date from the aceramic Neolithic through to the Roman period. The material was divided between the Cyprus Museum and Sweden – one of the best Cypriot collections outside the island, comprising as it does material with a secure context. The mass of data accumulated was organised into a chronological sequence based on a complex seriation of the pottery. The detailed publication of the excavation data was achieved by 1937 and enabled Gjerstad to develop a cultural historical interpretation of the island's archaeological remains for the Neolithic, Bronze Age, Iron Age, Hellenistic and Roman periods. His influence is most evident in the development of the study of the Cypriot Iron Age.[67] Gjerstad explicitly framed his analysis to examine the role played by the island as an intermediary between the Orient and Occident; 'in effect, the mélange response to the clash between Orientalist and Philhellenic ideologies'.[68] Until recently this perspective has persisted in interpretations of the material – parallels with the Aegean or the Near East being emphasised according to scholars' academic preference.

The enactment of the Cypriot Antiquities Law and the establishment of the Department of Antiquities in 1935 reflect the increasing international prominence of Cypriot archaeology during the earlier years of the twentieth century. Megaw was appointed as the first director of the Department, and Porphyrios Dikaios (curator of the museum) became the first Cypriot director in 1960 when the island gained its independence. As curator and director, Dikaios conducted a number of important excavations, most notably at the Neolithic settlements of Khirokitia and Sotira, and the LC urban centre at Enkomi.[69] Together with Stewart, who excavated the Early Cypriot (EC) cemetery at Vounous,[70] Dikaios was instrumental in writing the cultural histories of the earlier prehistory of Cyprus.[71]

Archaeological research by Cypriot and international research teams has continued on the island at a furious pace. Following independence in 1960, the Department of Antiquities greatly encouraged the continued activity of foreign excavation teams on the island and in particular has fostered prompt publication of their results. The Turkish invasion and occupation of the northern third of the island in 1974, however, has had a dramatic impact on the practice of Cypriot archaeology.[72] Effectively this area lies beyond the remit of archaeologists working on the island, creating an apparent geographical bias. Although ample remains from the north of the island are available from earlier excavations, this bias is increasingly problematic as novel aspects of Cypriot archaeology are being explored in the southern part of the island.[73] This is particularly apparent for the recent discovery of early Holocene activity on the island and the appearance of the first farming communities in the tenth millennium BP.[74]

The practice of archaeology underwent fundamental changes in the later twentieth century. Excavations are problem-oriented and a number of scientific techniques have been developed. Chief among these are the rigorous retrieval and analysis of botanical and zoological remains and the application of a variety of chemical techniques to examine the material remains such as pottery and metal artefacts.[75] These new techniques have been applied with enthusiasm to the Cypriot prehistoric record. Regional survey has become increasingly important for exploring the use of the Cypriot landscape, in particular changing patterns in settlement use and settlement hierarchy.[76] From the 1930s Dikaios carried out a number of surveys for the Department of Antiquities, and between 1955 and 1959 Catling carried out further survey work, aimed at establishing changing patterns of settlement on the island during the Bronze Age.[77] More intensive, systematic survey has been increasingly used by archaeologists from the 1980s.[78]

Interpretation of the archaeological material is very variable. The cultural-historical approach is still favoured by most archaeologists, and Cypriot archaeology remains couched within a cultural evolutionary framework.[79] Most attention has focused on the ancient economy, namely issues of production and exchange (pottery, metallurgy). Anthropological perspectives, however, are gradually being applied to the Cypriot data.[80] These new approaches are most evident in the more recent excavation reports, which are more than simple records of context, stratigraphy and catalogues of material remains.[81] Instead, the archaeological data is explored within a rigorous analytical framework, examining various aspects of ancient Cypriot life.

Chronology

Relative chronology

The basis of the Cypriot relative chronology[82] is the indigenous pottery styles that were used on the island from the fifth millennium BC. The earliest attempt to organise the pottery into a chronological sequence was made by Sandwith, vice-consul in Larnaca from 1865.[83] He assembled the finds from Cypriot tombs into four main chronological groups or classes according to the predominant types of pottery. Class I comprised incised Red Polished vases (RP III), which Sandwith noted were associated with copper/bronze spearheads. Class II included the typical LC I Base Ring and Bucchero juglets, White Slip bowls, White Painted (WP) VI zoomorphic vases and a Yahudiyeh ware import, also associated with metal implements (of copper/bronze). Moreover Sandwith noted that this group of pottery was closely paralleled by pottery found in the Egyptian delta.[84] The third group, Class III, is typical of the Early Iron Age, the Cypro-Geometric and Cypro-Archaic periods. It comprised various forms of the White Painted and Bichrome wares, and Black Slip and Red on Black jugs.

11

The final group, dating to the Classical and Roman periods, is characterised by coarse pottery and a predominance of glass vessels. The Class IV tombs are frequently built of masonry and contain stone sarcophagi and *cippi* (circular stone columns bearing inscriptions). Although Sandwith recognised the broad chronological groups that the tombs belonged to, he did not actually categorise the pottery found in the tombs, organising it into a typological sequence.

Myres made the initial classification of the prehistoric Cypriot pottery styles according to various technical criteria, in particular the surface treatment.[85] Gjerstad further refined this pottery classification, using the large body of data generated by the excavations of the Swedish Cyprus expedition.[86] Although he retained much of Myres' original nomenclature, Gjerstad made a number of changes that have remained integral Cypriot ceramic studies. In addition to the identification of a number of new wares – such as the LC Monochrome and White Shaved wares – he organised the pottery into a chronological sequence according to changes in morphology and surface decoration. Gjerstad forced the Bronze Age pottery sequence into an inflexible tripartite scheme based on the Three Age system in vogue throughout northern Europe.[87] The EC period was defined by the predominant use of the RP ware (subdivided into four main categories, RP I-IV), the MC period was characterised by the continued use of the RP ware alongside the novel WP ware, and the LC period was identified by the appearance of the White Slip, Base Ring and Monochrome wares (Table 1.1). The periods are subdivided again within a tripartite scheme: EC I-III, MC I-III, and the most complex subphasing is for the LC period (LC IA, LC IB, LC IIA-C, LC IIIA, LC IIIB). In effect, Gjerstad constructed the chronological framework that is still employed by Cypriot archaeologists today.

There are several problems inherent in the construction of the Cypriot relative chronology, and this sequence has been called into question by a number of scholars.[88] Gjerstad's scheme was based entirely on the pottery recovered from mortuary contexts, with all the problems that entails. The tomb groups housed multiple inhumations and might be used over several generations, obscuring patterns of pottery use through time. There is frequent specialisation of wares and forms for specific inclusion in burial assemblages, and it is not always possible to correlate settlement and funerary ceramic sequences. These problems are particularly apparent with the RP sequence. This style of pottery was in use over an extremely long period (possibly up to 600 years),[89] and in many ways epitomises the cultural conservatism of the prehistoric population of Cyprus. Gjerstad's sequence was based on material primarily recovered from tomb groups from a restricted geographical zone in the north of the island. The MC settlement material recovered from Sotira-*Kaminoudhia*, Episkopi-*Phaneromeni*, Alambra, Kalopsidha, and Ambelikou-*Aletri*, cannot be tied in satisfactorily to the RP ceramic sequence.[90] Rather than the rigid class

Conventional scheme	Revised scheme (after Knapp 1994, fig. 9.2)	Scheme used in this book	Absolute chronology
	Early Prehistoric Period	*Early Prehistoric Period*	
	Akrotiri phase	Akrotiri phase	10,665 ± 25 BP
Neolithic/Chalcolithic			
		Early Aceramic Neolithic /Cypro PPNB	Late 10th-late 9th millennium BP
Aceramic Neolithic	Khirokitia Culture	Late Aceramic Neolithic	*c.* 8200-58/5500 BC
Ceramic Neolithic	Sotira Culture	Ceramic Neolithic	*c.* 5500-3900 BC
Chalcolithic	Erimi Culture	Early Chalcolithic	*c.* 4000-2500 BC
		Middle Chalcolithic	
		Late Chalcolithic	
Philia/EC-MC	*Prehistoric Bronze Age*	*Bronze Age*	
Philia	PreBA I	Philia	*c.* 2500-2350 BC
Early Cypriot (EC I-III)	Pre BA II	Prehistoric BA	*c.* 2400-2000 BC
Middle Cypriot (MC I-III)		Prehistoric BA	*c.* 2000-1700 BC
Middle Cypriot-Late Cypriot	*Protohistoric Bronze Age*		
MC III-LC I	ProBA I	MC III-LC I	*c.* 1700-1400 BC
LC IIA-C	ProBA II	LC IIA-C	*c.* 1400-1200 BC
LC IIIA- LC IIIB	ProBA III	LC IIIA	*c.* 1200-1050 BC

Table 1.1. Cyprus: chronological sequence.

divisions put forward by Gjerstad, based largely on morphology and decoration, Barlow instead proposes a technical subdivision of the RP ware, identifying two main types: a fine calcareous clay used to make decorative incised vessels, and a coarse non-calcareous clay used for cooking pots. A third type, made from a mix of both pastes, was used to make liquid containers. These types cut across Gjerstad's RP I-IV subdivisions.[91]

There is, moreover, the issue of site dislocation. Unlike the contemporary Near East, on Cyprus there are no *tell* sites with a continuous sequence from the Neolithic period down to the Bronze Age. Instead, in each period new settlements tend to be established on virgin ground and it is not always possible to establish the exact chronological relationship between different sites/phases. This is a problem that is all too apparent for the transitional period between the aceramic and ceramic Neolithic, the ceramic Neolithic and the Early Chalcolithic, and the Late Chalcolithic to Early Bronze Age/Philia facies.

Dikaios proposed an alternative cultural/chronological sequence for the earlier prehistoric period, identifying and naming the cultural phases

13

after type sites: the aceramic Neolithic he termed the Khirokitia culture, the ceramic Neolithic the Sotira culture and the Chalcolithic period the Erimi culture.[92] This sequence takes little account of cultural continuity, nor of internal regional variation,[93] and is particularly problematic for defining the upper and lower limits of the individual periods. This is particularly apparent for the Neolithic/Chalcolithic transition and the Chalcolithic/Early Bronze Age transition. In both cases the transitional material does not conform to the cultural sequence defined by Dikaios. They comprise either novel and unique elements or a mix of cultural elements of the preceding and subsequent phases. Moreover, recent excavations have shown the internal development of the aceramic Neolithic and the Chalcolithic periods to be far more complex than Dikaios' sequence would allow.[94] In effect Dikaios' sequence ascribes chronological significance to spatially defined cultural entities. Despite increasing awareness of regional variation in the Cypriot archaeological record, the treatment of cultural variation within a chronological framework, in a unilinear sequential paradigm, rather than in spatial terms persists. Ultimately this scheme obscures patterns of cultural continuity and change.[95]

Despite the recent publication of the settlements at Marki-*Alonia* and Alambra,[96] too few EC and MC settlements have yet been excavated to allow archaeologists to establish the Bronze Age sequence from stratified contexts. The MC period is defined by the appearance of the WP ware alongside RP pottery, but this scheme makes no allowance for regional variation and staggered adoption of new ceramic styles. Instead, at present the evidence for the distinction between the EC and MC periods is too limited. An alternative scheme has been put forward, which represents a deliberate break with the conventional tripartite system (Table 1.1).[97] This scheme divides the Bronze Age into two major phases, defined by both ceramic and non-ceramic traits:

- On the basis that it is difficult to identify any aspect of Cypriot material culture to be exclusively EC rather than MC, the prehistoric Bronze Age (PreBA) lumps together the EC and MC material.[98]
- The Protohistoric Bronze Age is defined according to the major socioeconomic developments apparent on the island during the later second millennium BC and significant transformations in the material record. Knapp proposes a tripartite division of the Protohistoric Bronze Age (ProBA) material. The MC III-LC I interface is lumped into a single transitional phase (ProBA I), the entire LC II period is designated ProBA II and LC III is termed ProBA III.

Although there are good grounds for amalgamating the EC and MC material, ultimately this system is as crude and cumbersome as that which it aims to replace. In the absence of a good stratified sequence, the identification of the prehistoric Bronze Age is as valid as the conventional

Cypriot EC/MC division. Indeed, as early as 1973 Catling noted: 'Were it not for the confusion that would certainly result, a case could be argued for apportioning MC I and MC II to the Early Bronze Age, and reforming the MC period from a combination of MC III and LC I.'[99] The subsequent identification of the LC period would be according to the appearance of Mycenaean imports, although this takes no account of internal economic differences. On the other hand, the broad tripartite subdivision of the protohistoric Bronze Age obscures social and technological development. There is certainly a case for re-assessing the LC material, and in particular for developing a ceramic typology that takes into account regional variation and which is more dependent on the local utilitarian wares. However, given the rapid pace of development during this period, the more detailed conventional chronology (LC I-III) is to be preferred over the protohistoric Bronze Age proposed by Knapp.

The chronological depth of Cypriot prehistory has been extended in recent years to the earlier Holocene (Table 1.1). In the late 1980s an epi-Palaeolithic phase of human activity was identified at Akrotiri-*Aeto-kremnos*, on the southernmost tip of the island, dating to the mid-eleventh millennium BP.[100] This has been termed the Akrotiri phase. Prior to these excavations, late Palaeolithic and early Holocene human activity on the island had not been substantiated.[101] More recently, excavations at Parekklisha-*Shillourokambos* and Kissonerga-*Mylouthkia* have identified an earlier phase of the aceramic Neolithic, which goes some way to filling the lacuna between the Akrotiri phase and initial Neolithic occupation of the island.[102] This earlier phase of the Cypriot aceramic Neolithic appears to be contemporaneous with the PPNB in the Levant. In the light of the discovery of an earlier phase of the Neolithic, Dikaios' terminology (discussed above), referring to the Khirokitia culture, has now been dropped. Peltenburg proposed naming the earlier phase of the Cypriot aceramic Neolithic the Cypro-PPNB, given its apparent parallels with the PPNB material in the Levant.[103] The accepted terminology, however, refers to the early aceramic Neolithic (the material from Parekklisha-*Shillourokambos* and Kissonerga-*Mylouthkia*) and the late aceramic Neolithic (the Khirokitia culture).[104]

Absolute chronology

The Cypriot absolute chronology has been calculated using two methods: cross-dating and scientific dating techniques. While there is a good series of radiocarbon determinations from sealed contexts for the earlier prehistory of Cyprus, there are fewer reliable radiocarbon dates from stratified and sealed contexts as we progress into the Bronze Age. Instead, the absolute chronology for the Bronze Age, in particular the LC period, has been calculated using correlations with dated material from surrounding regions.[105]

The earliest phase of human activity on the island is represented by the stone tools and hearths uncovered in a rock shelter at Akrotiri-*Aetokremnos*, apparently associated with bones of the endemic pygmy hippopotamus.[106] These deposits have been dated using 31 radiocarbon determinations, 29 of which are from sealed archaeological strata, to around $10,665 \pm 25$ BP,[107] within the chronological range of the Levantine Natufian culture. There is an apparent gap of around a millennium before the presence of the earliest farming communities is attested at Parekklisha-*Shillourokambos* and Kissonerga-*Mylouthkia*, in the late tenth millennium BP. The chronology for the aceramic and ceramic Neolithic and the Chalcolithic periods is derived from radiocarbon determinations. There are apparent gaps in this sequence and at present it is unclear whether these reflect genuine lacunae in the archaeological record, or whether they are an artefact of modern reconstruction – the transitional periods remaining elusive to archaeological retrieval techniques. The LC IIC phase has recently been dated to between *c.* 1340-1315 to $1200 \pm 20/–10$ BC using radiocarbon determinations from a number of sites throughout the island.[108] There were problems involved in the calibration of the radiocarbon dates for this period, due to an effective plateau in the calibration curve at this point.[109] Even so, it is interesting to note the very close parity between the traditional dates for the LC IIC-IIIA transition derived from Egyptian historical chronology and the radiocarbon dates.[110]

In the absence of a series of radiocarbon dates that can be tied into the relative chronology derived from pottery seriation, the absolute chronology for the prehistoric Bronze Age is determined by synchronisms with historically dated sequences from the neighbouring regions.[111] The basis of the absolute chronology for the Bronze Age in Syro-Palestine, Cyprus and the Aegean has until recently been the Egyptian calendrical sequence derived from king lists.[112] Usually cross-dating depends upon the presence of closely datable artefacts, frequently named objects such as scarabs or seals that can be tied into the Egyptian or Mesopotamian king lists, thereby providing a *terminus post quem* to a fixed calendrical date.[113] In the case of Cyprus, however, such objects are exceedingly rare and discussion tends to concentrate on the circulation of pottery, which at most can provide a *terminus post quem* to an archaeological phase.[114] Unfortunately, very few imported objects are found on Cyprus before the LC period. These include a Syrian Early Bronze III-IV jug from Vounous-*Bellapais*, which implies a date in the later third millennium BC for the EC period.[115] Other synchronisms are provided by rare Minoan imports, such as a Middle Minoan (MM) IA bridge-spouted jug from Lapithos Tomb 806A and a MM II cup from Karmi-*Palealona*.[116]

There is far greater evidence for correlations between Cyprus and surrounding regions by the later prehistoric Bronze Age and the MC III-LC I transitional period, based on increasing Cypriot participation in maritime trade and the circulation of Cypriot pottery around the East

Mediterranean during the second millennium BC. Particularly large quantities of MC pottery have been found in the excavations at Tell el-Dab'a in the Egyptian Nile Delta,[117] and these wares now play an pivotal role in the synchronisation of the major civilisations of the Eastern Mediterranean basin. Indeed, recently Merrillees has written that '... the classification, distinctiveness and distribution of [Middle] Cypriote pottery in the eastern Mediterranean during the second millennium BC have given it a chronological role',[118] one equalled only by Mycenaean pottery in the fourteenth and thirteenth centuries. Certain Cypriot wares are particularly important for establishing synchronisms, chief amongst them the WP (III-IV) Pendent Line style, and Proto White Slip/White Slip I. The WP Pendent Line style is one of the most common MC exports to Palestine, but the most important deposits are at Tell el-Dab'a, in strata F to D/3, peaking in stratum E/1.[119] This style was imported to Egypt during the MB IIB-C period, otherwise contemporary with the Egyptian Second Intermediate Period (SIP) between *c.* 1710 and 1560 BC.[120] This date is corroborated by the distribution of this ware in the Levant, most notably an incomplete juglet from Kültepe, Karum stratum Ib, and another piece from Alalakh stratum VIII.[121] The date of production and export of this later MC ware (MC II-III) can therefore be placed with some accuracy to the MB IIB-C period in the surrounding region. There are problems relating these dates to the MC deposits from Lapithos and Vounous in the north of the island. The Cypriot wares exported to Syro-Palestine and Egypt during this period (WP Pendent Line Style and WP Closed Line Style) were manufactured in the southeastern part of the island and were only rarely exchanged internally. Thus their occurrence in the northern cemeteries is extremely unusual. Consequently, the application of the absolute chronology based on the circulation of these wares to date the northern deposits is fraught with difficulties.[122]

Initial LC products (early White Slip I, WP V/VI, and Monochrome) are found in SIP contexts in Egypt and MB IIC contexts in Syro-Palestine, which indicates that the early phase of the Cypriot LBA (LC IA) correlates with the Egyptian SIP and final MB II contexts in the Levant.[123] The distinctive grey Yahudiyeh ware juglets with punctured decoration, which circulated around the East Mediterranean at the end of the MBA, can be used to support Manning's correlation of the initial LC IA period with the final MBA in Egypt and the Levant. Yahudiyeh ware juglets are found in MC deposits at Arpera-*Mosphilos* Tomb 1 and Morphou-*Toumba tou Skourou* Tomb V,[124] and also in LC IA deposits at Enkomi[125] and Morphou-*Toumba tou Skourou*, Tomb I.[126] The Yahudiyeh ware therefore mainly occurs in MC deposits in Cyprus, but is still found in early LC IA contexts, whereas in the Levant it is restricted to MB II contexts.[127] Moreover, LC IA material is found in mature Late Minoan (LM) IA contexts in Crete[128] whereas Manning argues that mature LC IB material does not reach the Aegean until the mature LM IB phase. These correlations illustrate that the early LBA phases throughout the East Mediterranean cannot be exactly synchronised. The initial stage of the Cypriot LBA is contemporary with the final phase of the MBA in Egypt and the Levant – the Hyksos period in Egypt – but corresponds to the mature LM IA period in Crete.

The absolute chronology for the LC period is largely constructed with reference to the Mycenaean sequence of the Greek mainland, itself based on synchronisms with the Egyptian historical sequence. The increasing occurrence of the highly distinctive Mycenaean pottery on the island from the fifteenth century, and more especially during the fourteenth and thirteenth centuries BC,[129] is the basis for synchronisation of the two sequences. Only small quantities of Aegean (Mycenaean or Minoan) wares reached Cyprus during the early phase of contact, but these provide a synchronisation between LC I and Late Helladic (LH) I-IIA, in the sixteenth and fifteenth centuries. The quantity of Aegean imports increases in LH IIB-IIIA:1, during the later fifteenth to early fourteenth centuries. These are found in LC IIA contexts in Cyprus. The main phase of importation dates to LH IIIA:2-LH IIIB, the late fourteenth and thirteenth centuries BC, corresponding to LC IIB-C.[130] These correlations are ultimately tied back to Egyptian historical dates. The most important fixed point for these dates is the deposit of mature LC IIB pottery at Amarna in Egypt, alongside LH IIIA:2 material. Amarna is important as it effectively had a very short life, being occupied between year 5 of the reign of Akhenaten and year 3 of the reign of Tutankhamun (*c.* 1349-1334 BC),[131] thereby fixing the LC IIB and LH IIIA:2 material to the late fourteenth century BC.

The value of pottery for calculating absolute dates has certainly been over-emphasised and the limitations involved in using ceramic sequences to construct a precise chronological framework are in fact manifold.[132] It is unclear how long pottery will remain in use subsequent to its manufacture and export and prior to its eventual deposition in the archaeological record. Moreover, it is necessary to demonstrate that the pottery was found in a sealed context. Instead, far too much emphasis tends to be placed on stray sherds with no secure context. The dates derived from Egyptian historical context in fact at most will only provide a *terminus ante quem* for an export horizon, indicating that the pottery must have been made and exported before a certain date.[133] These can only be used to estimate a possible horizon of contacts rather than a single fixed date. In fact, it is not possible to establish the internal chronology for the Cypriot Bronze Age without a series of stratified sequences from different parts of the island and a series of radiocarbon determinations from sealed contexts.

The Colonisation of Cyprus

Island archaeologies

One of the defining characteristics of Cyprus prior to the Bronze Age is its physical isolation and perceived cultural insularity. First and foremost, studies of the prehistory of Cyprus have emphasised its island status, and subsequent interpretations of its cultural traditions and socio-economic trajectory have been embedded within island metaphors of isolation, uniqueness, and enclosed biological and cultural systems.[1]

Biogeography and the perception of islands as 'natural laboratories',[2] the arena for biological and cultural speciation,[3] have informed island archaeology. John Evans in particular has advocated this approach within Mediterranean archaeology, emphasising several physical qualities of islands which lend them to detailed analyses of populations and culture change. Chief amongst these is the unquestionable fact that islands are surrounded by the sea,[4] thereby controlling or restricting interaction with other social groups, giving rise to the assumption that island societies are less likely to be affected by external contact resulting in arbitrary cultural and ethnic change.[5] Evans also suggests that these isolated island communities 'often display a tendency towards exaggerated development of some aspect of their culture ... [such as] erecting extensive ceremonial and religious complexes',[6] a characteristic that has been identified and examined within more recent literatures.[7] Patton specifically marries this theory to the distance : area ratio, noting that 'islands with the greatest degree of cultural elaboration ... are those which are both relatively large and relatively distant from the mainland'.[8] Cherry's 1981 and 1990 surveys of the Mediterranean islands focused on explanatory models of human colonisation, drawn from island biogeography.

Without the impulse of external contact, island societies are assumed to lose their dynamism and stagnate, as for example has been suggested for Neolithic Crete.[9] Specifically for Cyprus, Held comments that the Chalcolithic inhabitants 'pursued a subsistence strategy that remained technologically inferior',[10] the direct result of isolation, and a major factor which impeded social evolution and the rise of complex societies by a couple of millennia. Within this context of isolation and 'cultural retardation',[11] external factors are frequently sought as the explanation of culture change. Although these approaches have not been made explicit in later

Cypriot prehistory, they have informed the nature of the discourse. Most notably, major cultural shifts in the archaeological record are unquestioningly attributed to population movements, from Anatolia in the third millennium BC [12] and the Aegean at the end of the second millennium BC.[13] This tension between the insularity of prehistoric Cyprus and the wide-ranging economic and cultural links of Cyprus during the Bronze and Iron Ages reflects the dichotomy inherent in other Mediterranean islands, usually epitomised by Sicily and Sardinia. Some can be identified as cultural crossroads while others are culturally conservative.[14] Alternate views of apparent physical and cultural isolation emphasise the choice exercised by an island population whether or not to adopt an innovation.[15] Failure to keep abreast of the innovations current in contemporary mainland cultures might be dictated by a number of cultural factors, but need not indicate that the island culture was unaware of these developments. Indeed, Broodbank notes that deliberate archaising elements and the apparent loss of other cultural traits are common strategies through which island identities are created and sustained.[16]

More recent island archaeologies,[17] however, have moved away from approaches grounded in biogeographies and western geographical preconceptions, towards a more fluid interpretation of the multiplicity of island experiences, emphasising social context and human choice. These island archaeologies argue that islands, and concepts of isolation and insularity, are cultural constructs.[18] Frequently the sea, which Evans viewed as an isolating factor, is perceived to be a connecting medium,[19] 'a territory that expands horizons rather than reduces them'.[20] Rather than acting as an impediment to communication, the sea is 'the medium of all human intercourse from one region to another', uniting communities both conceptually and physically.[21] Instead, it might be argued that landlocked communities are more physically and culturally isolated than their counterparts scattered in a variety of islandscapes.[22] In some island clusters communities on the same island might be more physically and conceptually separate from each other than from other communities on neighbouring islands. In the context of the initial utilisation of island resources and the subsequent colonisation phase within the Mediterranean, it might be assumed that seafaring technologies were sufficiently advanced to counteract physical isolation imposed by the sea.[23] However, whether this skill was maintained alongside exploitation of marine resources has yet to be fully addressed for Cyprus during the Neolithic. There is a deafening silence within the archaeological record for external contacts subsequent to the initial colonisation of the island. This would appear to suggest the loss of a sustainable maritime technology, but might equally be interpreted as conscious choice on the part of the early inhabitants of Cyprus to maintain their distinctive identity.

Rainbird has criticised the emphasis on the exotic and the uncritical use of the rare to infer external communications, arguing that 'the benefit of easily identifying introduced items is in reality a function of "isolation", inasmuch as it seems implicit that these items will be rare and "exotic"...; this in turn means there is a lack of such items, and implies a lack of interaction'.[24] Broodbank, however, notes that the ease with which imports can be identified on islands need not be a factor of the insularity of the island or the rarity of these objects, but in fact 'is simply a function of the limited geological types of most islands, which often make it possible to identify non-local [artefacts] ... whether they be rare or, as is often the case, frequent'.[25] In this context, Helms'[26] discussion of the political use of the exotic (tangible goods and esoteric knowledge) is resonant, alongside her evaluation of the cultural construction of geographical distance and space. The exotic might well be incorporated within the construction of symbolic worlds, imbuing ideologies with an aura of prestige, but equally it might be deliberately ignored or excluded.

Island archaeologies that emphasise the social context have yet to be applied to the Cypriot material, but should prove fruitful in re-assessing the perceived level of the island's cultural retardation throughout much of its prehistory. In particular, such approaches should inform our assessment of the new and exciting evidence for early human activity on the island, and its eventual colonisation by migrant farming communities.

Endemic Pleistocene fauna

The fossil record of Pleistocene Cyprus is characterised by an extremely limited assemblage of palaeofaunas. As Cyprus is an oceanic island that was never joined to the Asiatic mainland it is believed that the endemic Pleistocene mammalian population reached the island by swimming or was carried over by driftwood. The animals that comprise the Neolithic and Bronze Age agricultural package – pig, sheep, goat, fallow deer (*Dama mesopotamica*) and cattle (*Bos*) – were introduced to the island during the earlier Holocene by human agency. Fossilised bones belonging to the endemic Pleistocene fauna are commonly found in cave deposits, and some 32 fossil beds have been confirmed.[27] According to local tradition these bones belonged to the bodies of Cypriot saints,[28] but studies by nineteenth-century zoologists correctly identified the bones as the remains of a dwarf species of hippopotamus (*Phanourios minor/minutus*). The other dwarf species represented on the island is the dwarf elephant (*Elephas cypriotes*). This is much less frequently represented in the fossil record, and Held suggests the elephant population was far smaller, the reasons for which remain to be explored.[29] The small size of the Cypriot elephant and hippopotamus is replicated in other island mammalian populations throughout the Mediterranean, such as those on Malta, Sardinia, Sicily and Crete, and appears to be an example of speciation or adaptation to specific insular conditions. Indeed, it is suggested that the reduction in size of the species is a function of a limited gene pool and will be inversely proportionate to the distance of the islands from the mainland, the so-called founder principle. Consequently, as Cyprus is the most insular of these islands, it might be expected that the *Phanourios* display greater morphological variation from the parent population.[30] There is no biostra-tigaphy for Cyprus, and the dwarf species represent the final stages of an evolutionary process that has yet to be documented in the fossil record.[31] The other species that succeeded in colonising the island and are repre-sented during the Pleistocene are two types of mouse and a shrew, al-though it is possible that these are later Holocene intrusions in Pleistocene deposits. A dozen genet bones from a Pleistocene fossil deposit at Kato Dhikomo likewise are believed to be intrusive, dating to the Holocene.[32] The Late Holocene faunal assemblage, in addition to the farming animals introduced in the Neolithic and Early Bronze Age, includes the fox (*Vulpes vulpes*) and Cypriot moufflon (*Ovis ophion orientalis*). It is believed that these were introduced by humans.[33] Generally, Cyprus is characterised by few colonisation episodes and the island's post-Pleistocene faunal assem-blage is anthropogenic in origin.

Attempts to reconstruct the habitat and behaviour of the Cypriot pygmy hippopotamus (Fig. 2.1) suggest that the species had developed the ability to traverse rough terrain and thereby had access to much of the island, although the steeper slopes of the Pentadaktylos and the Troodos probably

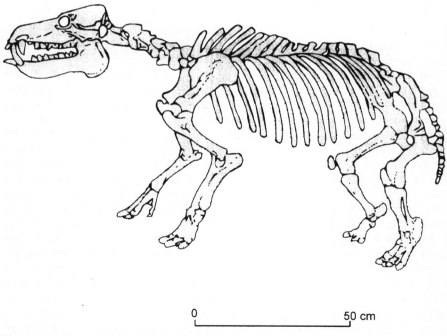

0   50 cm

Fig. 2.1. Skeleton of pygmy hippopotamus (*Phanourios minutus*).

acted as a natural barrier. The physical characteristics, especially the short legs, suggest that the species was better adapted to mountainous terrain than to swimming.[34] Proximity to a water supply is assumed to have remained vital, particularly given the coastal location of many of the fossil beds. Indeed, it has been suggested that the area around the salt lake of Akrotiri and the marshy plain around the Bay of Larnaca both provided a natural habitat or breeding ground.[35] Wear analysis of the dentition suggests a diet of weeds and shrubbery.[36] It is unclear whether the pygmy hippopotamus was a solitary or a group animal. A discrete group of extinct pygmy hippopotami found in a cave in Madagascar has been interpreted as evidence for a herd that had been trapped. However, it is not possible to extrapolate this to Cyprus, where the composition of the palaeontological sites appears to be the result of accretional deposition rather than herds.[37] The latest occurrence of the pygmy hippopotami and elephants appears to date to the Pleistocene/Holocene interface. Occasional finds of hippopotamus bones are reported at some aceramic Neolithic sites,[38] but it is generally accepted that the endemic faunas were extinct by the time the earliest agriculturists had colonised Cyprus.[39] The question remains whether human agency played a role in their disappearance from the faunal assemblage of Cyprus. Certainly the pygmy hippopotamus would have been a valuable meat resource which undoubtedly would have been exploited by humans.

Island colonisation and Cyprus

One of the most intriguing developments in recent years in Cypriot archaeology is the extension of evidence of human activity back to the epi-Palaeolithic. This is paralleled by similar developments in other Mediterranean islands, implicating human involvement in the extinction of insular endemic species throughout the Mediterranean archipelagos.[40] This early phase of human activity on Cyprus, the so-called *Akrotiri phase*, has provoked enormous discussion and remains controversial. The main focus of interest is twofold: first the date of the first appearance of humans on the island, and secondly the role that humans played in the extinction of endemic faunas at the beginning of the Holocene. The Akrotiri phase is equally important for the light it sheds on the issue of island colonisation within the Mediterranean during the early Holocene.

The islands of the Mediterranean were settled later than the surrounding continental regions, and until recently archaeological orthodoxy placed the earliest human activity on these islands within the Neolithic horizon.[41] Indeed, the Mediterranean islands have been used in arguments for demic diffusion of farming communities during the Neolithic, in direct opposition to the non-diffusionist models for the spread of the Neolithic that have been propounded for central and western Europe.[42] However, the picture of early island activity in the Mediterranean in general and Cyprus in particular has undergone substantial renegotiation in recent years, with repeated claims for a horizon of earlier pre-Neolithic activity on several islands. Kill-sites of endemic Pleistocene fauna have been identified on Mallorca and it is suggested that extinction of these fauna in the islands of the Western Mediterranean was anthropogenic.[43] Similar claims have been put forward in Cyprus for human involvement in the extinction of the endemic pygmy hippopotamus and pygmy elephant. Certainly, it has been clearly demonstrated that there was a clear overlap between humans and endemic Pleistocene fauna on several of the Mediterranean islands at the Pleistocene-Holocene interface.

Stanley-Price has discussed two alternate hypotheses for the establishment of human settlements on Cyprus during the early Holocene, both of which were primarily concerned with establishing the origins and date of the aceramic Neolithic farming communities of the so-called Khirokitia culture. Of these the *antecedent hypothesis* is relevant to discussions of the epi-Palaeolithic evidence. This allows for the possibility of a Pleistocene or epi-Palaeolithic landfall by humans on the island, but argues that any such landfall represents an abortive settlement phase, and did not mark the beginnings of a continuous cultural sequence on the island.[44] Securely stratified archaeological sequences with *in situ* anthropogenic artefacts from contexts that can be dated independently using radiocarbon are vital criteria for evaluating claims of early human activity.[45] As early as 1973 Watkins suggested that no Palaeolithic remains had been found on Cyprus simply because early researchers had a 'blind spot' concerning this material. To a certain extent this has been borne out by recent discoveries. There had already been some suggestion of human activity on Cyprus as early as the Palaeolithic prior to excavation of Akrotiri Site E.[46] These include the chipped stone *Ayias Mamas* assemblage from Khrysokou in northwest Cyprus, described as Upper Palaeolithic,[47] a series of early flint artefacts from three locations near Kyrenia,[48] flint artefacts from a fossil beach near the mouth of Moronou river, possibly pre-Neolithic/Middle Palaeolithic[49] and blade and flake tools from Tremithos valley, Ayia Anna-*Perivolia*,[50] believed to pre-date the aceramic Neolithic, possibly even as early as 12,000 BP. For the most part these have not met with general support.[51] Despite extensive archaeological research, the lack of culturally antecedent material underlying aceramic Neolithic levels and the lack of clearly diagnostic pre-Neolithic material from survey material contribute to a persuasive argument from silence.[52]

In assessing the evidence from Akrotiri-*Aetokremnos*, and from similar apparent kill-sites elsewhere in the Mediterranean, it is important to make a distinction between human use of island resources and actual settlement.[53] The earliest exploration of many of the Mediterranean islands is demonstrably much earlier than the first human settlement. This is illustrated for example by the exploitation of Melian obsidian from as early as the late Pleistocene,[54] although there is no evidence for human settlement of the Cyclades until the later Neolithic. Although maritime activity in the early Holocene Mediterranean implies knowledge of is-landscapes and communication routes, and a sophisticated maritime technology, Broodbank comments that there would, however, have been considerable variability in the purposefulness and range of different colo-nisation episodes.[55]

Pygmy hippos and early hunters?

A large deposit of extinct Pleistocene fauna, apparently in association with human artefacts, has been excavated at Akrotiri-*Aetokremnos* (see Fig. 2.2) – 'tantalising new evidence that raises more questions than it an-swers'.[56] The site was first discovered in 1961, by the son of a British serviceman stationed in the RAF Western Sovereign Base Area, who collected some chipped stone artefacts and bones, noted the site location and designated it Site E. The bones were subsequently identified as belonging to the endemic and extinct Cypriot pygmy hippopotamus, *Phanourios minor/minutus*.[57]

Akrotiri-*Aetokremnos* is located on the south coast of the Akrotiri pen-insula, the dominant geological feature of which is the salt lake. At one time the peninsula was a separate island, but it is unclear whether this

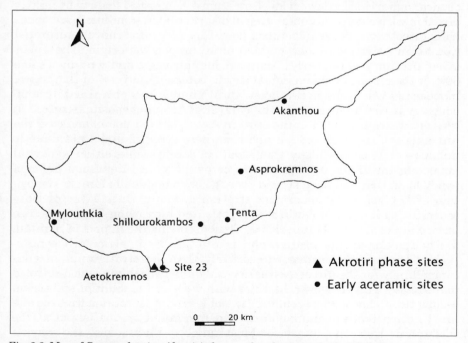

Fig. 2.2. Map of Cyprus showing Akrotiri phase and early aceramic Neolithic sites.

was contemporary with the occupation of Site E. Certainly as late as the Roman period the salt lake was open to the sea.[58] The site consists of a collapsed rock shelter situated on a flat bench on steep eroding cliffs *c.* 40 m above modern sea level. It is subject to significant erosion and much of the rock shelter has eroded into the sea below (see Plate 4). The extant shelter was very small, estimated to be less than 40 m^2.[59] Two distinct strata were clearly visible in the exposed section of intact sediment. The lower level comprised a thick deposit of bones covered by a thick ashy layer of burnt broken shells. Chipped stone artefacts were clearly embedded in the upper layer and initial radiocarbon dates taken from the exposed marine shell gave the remarkable date range of between 11,000 ± 100 BP and 3,700 ± 60 BP.[60] Excavations were undertaken to establish the relationship between the two layers, particularly whether there was any evidence for human co-habitation with the endemic pygmy hippopotamus, and to verify the date of this human activity. At the time of the discovery of the site it was accepted that the endemic large mammals had died out before the arrival of humans on the island.[61] It was hoped that excavations would reveal whether the bone deposits were the result of natural or human activity, whether the artefacts were *in situ*, and the relationship between the two.

Excavation revealed four major strata, two of which contained archaeological material. The lowest level, stratum 4, comprised loose ashy matrix mixed in with a dense accumulation of disarticulated semi-fossilised bones lying directly on the clean bedrock floor. The excavators have interpreted this as an intentional bone midden of anthropogenic origin. The upper layer, stratum 2, was clearly of cultural, human origin and contained some 60% of the chipped stone assemblage. In contrast, only 1% of the pygmy hippo bones was found in this layer, albeit numbering approximately 3000 bones. A discontinuous sterile sandy layer of Aeolian deposits (stratum 3) separated strata 2 and 4 in the eastern sector, but did not extend over the full extent of the rock shelter, and elsewhere strata 2 and 4 are directly juxtaposed. It seems likely that stratum 3 represents either a partial abandonment of the eastern sector, or possibly an intentional layer of sandy loam that had been spread over the bone midden before the deposition of hot ash. The uppermost stratum 1 was a thick layer of loose sediment with signs of disturbance, roots and burrowing. There are also large chunks of rock shelter, clearly demonstrating the impact of roof-fall.

The reading of this stratigraphic record has been particularly contentious. The excavators state categorically that the stratigraphy 'argues compellingly for the direct association of *Phanourios* (hippo) with cultural materials'.[62] This, however, has met with a certain amount of scepticism among the archaeological community, not least the contention that the site proves coexistence of humans and endemic fauna on the island at the Pleistocene-Holocene interface. Most notably, Bunimovitz and Barkai have argued that while the stone tools are indicative of human activity, they do not prove that this activity was exclusively responsible for the formation of the archaeological record. They maintain that only in stratum 2 is there any unequivocal evidence for human activity, and that contamination between the strata is responsible for mixing cultural remains with the bone bed in stratum 4 and similarly bones in the cultural deposits in stratum 2. They suggest erosion, tramping, pitting and 'grubbing' as possible causes for contamination between the strata.[63] However, while the exact role played by humans in the extinction of the Cypriot mini-megafaunas is still open to discussion, the archaeological integrity of the site and its place among the earliest of the insular Mediterranean archaeological locales is generally accepted.

A series of 31 radiocarbon determinations is available for *Aetokremnos*, 29 of them from sealed archaeological strata. These clearly demonstrate it to be the earliest archaeological site known on the island and among the earliest of the insular Mediterranean archaeological locales. With the exclusion of three surface dates and six contentious bone samples, the dates cluster together convincingly around 10,665 ± 25 BP.[64] Unfortunately the date of the site lies beyond the range of the dendrochronological calibration curve.[65] Even so, it is sufficient to place the use of the site within the chronological range of the Natufian culture on the Levantine coast, despite the lack of clear links between the Akrotiri and Natufian cultural assemblages.

An enormous assemblage of animal bones was recovered from *Aetokremnos*, totalling around 300,000 bones (Table 2.1). Although the animal remains were disarticulated, fragmentary and had been burnt, their preservation was excellent,[66] nor were they completely fossilised although petrification was setting in. The assemblage is dominated by remains of pygmy hippopotami (*Phanourios*), over 98% of the vertebrates represented at the site. In raw terms over 218,000 *Phanourios* bones were identified, including a number of complete skulls, and the minimum number of individuals (MNI) was estimated to be at least 505. All elements of the body are represented, suggesting that the entire carcass was processed at the site, the bones subsequently being deposited there in a midden. The *Phanourios* assemblage displays a number of unusual features.[67] It is simply the largest documented assemblage of pygmy hippo bones on the island; few of the other palaeontological sites known on the island have substantial quantities of bone.[68] Equally unusual is the extent of burning of the bones, up to 29% of the total assemblage.[69] The majority of the hippo bones were found in the lowest layer, stratum 4, which is thereby interpreted as a bone midden. However, although only 2% of the hippo bones were found in stratum 2 (clearly in cultural deposits) this actually represents a significant number of bones (3966). The huge numbers of hippo bones and the apparent evidence for human modification (disarticulation and burning) argue against the *Aetokremnos* assemblage being a natural

Fauna	Number and MNI	Context	Use
VERTEBRATES			
Pygmy hippopotamus (*Phanourios minutus*)	218,000+ bones MNI 505+ (98% of assemblage)	Stratum 4: 88% Stratum 2: 2% (3966 bones)	Food?
Pygmy elephant (*Elephas cypriotes*)	332 bones MNI 3	Stratum 4B	Food?
Pig: wild boar (*Sus*)	13 bones MNI 4	Stratum 2	Pelt/clothing?
Fallow deer (*Dama mesopotamica*)	4 bones	Stratum 2	Pelt/clothing?
Genet (*Genetta*)	2 bones	Stratum 4B	Commensal?
Mouse (*Mus*)	5 bones	Stratum 2 F10	Commensal?
Tortoise (*Testuda*)	25+ bones MNI 9-14	All strata, especially F3 in Stratum 4	Food?
Snake (*Viper lebentina*)	245 bones MNI 14-40	Stratum 2: 63% Stratum 4: 7.8%	Food?
Toad (*Bufo*)	1		
BIRDS (especially Great Bustard)	3207 fragments MNI 75+		Food?
FISH Grey mullet	1	Stratum 4	Food?
INVERTEBRATES			
Egg shell		Stratum 2	
Land snail	90		
MARINE INVERTEBRATES	73,365 fragments MNI 21,576		
Monodonta	20,750		Food
Limpet (*Patella*)	640		Food
Columbella	88	Stratum 2: 37.5% Stratum 4: 33%	Shell beads
Dentalium	49	Stratum 2: 63%	Shell beads
Conus	25		Shell beads
Crab	5	Strata 1 and 2	Food?
Cuttlefish	1	Stratum 4B	Food?
Sea urchin	1	Stratum 2	

Table 2.1. Palaeofauna: species represented at Akrotiri-*Aetokremnos* according to context and inferred use.

formation, and instead appear strongly to indicate human activity in the formation of the record.[70]

The pygmy elephant is less frequently encountered, and mainly in stratum 4B; an MNI of three is suggested.[71] The rare pig and deer bones[72] appear extremely unusual for an epi-Palaeolithic context on Cyprus, as this is far earlier than any suggested human movement of animals beyond their natural habitat, either domesticated or herded. However, the bones that are represented are largely phalanges and can be interpreted as the bones left in a pelt,[73] presumably brought over from the mainland by the humans using the rock shelter. These bones therefore are indicative of clothing rather than diet within the Cypriot context. Large quantities of snake vertebrae were found in stratum 2, a high percentage of which had been burned. It is suggested that these bones represent another element of the diet of the Akrotiri phase population.[74] The faunal assemblage is also important for the enormous quantity of bird bones – the largest such collection dating to the early Holocene in the Eastern Mediterranean, and the oldest bird assemblage on Cyprus.[75] The most commonly represented bird is the great bustard (*Otis tarda*). 18.5% of the bird bones were burnt. However, given the fragile nature of bird bones, it is probable that a far larger number of bones was burnt but did not survive. The high degree of fragmentation of the bones reflects the use of the rock shelter as a major activity zone, hence the bones were continually being trampled. For the most part the birds are aquatic species, or are from open or sparsely wooded landscapes, and the range of identified species indicates year-round occupation of the rock shelter by the human population. The bird assemblage illustrates changes in the Akrotiri economy, playing a more significant role by stratum 2, possibly because other food resources were becoming more limited. Akrotiri also boasts the largest collection of marine invertebrates so far excavated on Cyprus,[76] locally available from the rocky shores around the Akrotiri peninsula. For the most part this represents food debris, most typically *Monodonta* (around 96% of the assemblage). The human inhabitants of Akrotiri also consumed limpets (*Patella*), and possibly also cuttlefish, crab and sea urchins. The shellfish were either eaten raw, smashed open using igneous cobbles, or were roasted on fires.[77] Marine shells also had a decorative function: *Columbella*, *Dentalium* and *Conus* were all used to make shell beads.

The evidence for human activity at the site, other than that inferred from the faunal assemblages, comprises eleven features (the ephemeral remains of activity areas) and a discrete assemblage of artefacts. Typically the features comprise burned areas with a fill of igneous cobbles and artefacts such as chipped stone and ornamental shells, and are designated as casual hearths, presumably used for food preparation and cooking. Three such casual hearths were excavated in stratum 4 (F2, F3, F9; see Table 2.2). The concentration of intensively burned bone from F3 is more suggestive of a secondary use of the bones for fuel.[78] The stone-lined hearths (F6 and F7) are the most purposefully constructed. Other features include a concentration of marine shell (F5) in stratum 2, suggested as an area used for food preparation, for processing shellfish prior to cooking. Certainly the overall preponderance of cooked shell argues against consumption of raw shellfish at the site.[79] The bell-shaped pit (F8), cut into

Feature	Type	Stratum	Artefacts	Phanourios	Bird bone	Marine Shell
F1	ash heap/casual hearth area	2	chipped stone shell beads picrolite pendant igneous cobbles	●	●	●
F2	casual hearth	4B		●		●
F3	burnt bone concentration	4A-B	shell beads	●	●	●
F4	hearth, activity area	2	chipped stone shell beads picrolite pendant shallow mortar? igneous cobbles pumice	●	●	●
F5	shell concentration	2A	chipped stone shell beads	●	●	●
F6	casual hearth (stone lined)	1/2 + 2	chipped stone shell beads igneous cobbles fire-cracked stone	●	●	●
F7	casual hearth (stone lined)	2		●	●	
F8	bell-shaped pit	2/4	chipped stone	●	●	●
F9	casual hearth	4		●		●
F10	casual hearth	2		2 burnt bones	●	
F11	casual hearth	2	1 microflake (intrusive)		●	●

Table 2.2. Summary of anthropogenic features at Akrotiri-*Aetokremnos*.

strata 2, 3 and 4, has a dark ashy matrix suggesting a cooking function; however the fill contains little burnt food debris. Instead it might represent a storage facility or possibly was used for disposal. For the most part the range of activities associated with the rock shelter are associated with food preparation – from the initial dismemberment of the hippo carcass, to preparation and cooking of shellfish – and also deposition of the debris of these activities *in situ* on a midden.

A large number of artefacts was found at the site, for the most part in stratum 2, although some were found associated with features in stratum 4. These include a variety of chipped stone tools, ornamental shells, and occasional worked pieces of picrolite. The chipped stone assemblage has no clear affinities with either later Cypriot Neolithic toolkits or contemporary assemblages from the Levantine or Anatolian mainland. Even so, the formal retouched tools are characteristic of continental epi-Palaeolithic toolkits.[80] The diagnostic tool type of the Akrotiri toolkit is the thumbnail scraper (Fig. 2.3).[81] Other types include burins (Fig. 2.4), scrapers, flakes and retouched blades, and a small proportion (5%) of microliths. The materials used are locally available on Cyprus beyond the Akrotiri peninsula, indicating wider exploitation and knowledge of the Cypriot landscape. The predominant stone used is fine-grained Lefkara chert.[82] Small numbers of ornaments have been identified: six pieces of worked picrolite, apparently pendants, a worked *Phanourios* incisor, and quanti-

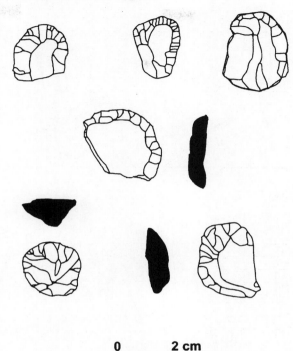

Fig. 2.3. Akrotiri phase thumbnail scrapers from Akrotiri-*Aetokremnos*.

0 ____ 2 cm

ties of ornamental shells, probably beads. These were made of *Dentalium*, *Columbella* and *Conus* shell. Other artefacts include a pierced disc of calcarenite[83] and a grooved beach pebble.[84] The latter might have been used in fishing as a net sinker.

Aetokremnos should probably be interpreted as a camp used primarily for intensive processing of a variety of meat resources: primarily pygmy hippo, but also marine shell and aquatic birds. It was not actually a kill-site as the animals would have been hunted elsewhere, possibly around the salt lake, and their carcasses subsequently brought back to the rock shelter. Within this scenario the absence of cutmarks has been criticised, as has the unsuitability of the toolkit, dominated by thumbnail scrapers, for processing pygmy hippopotami.[85] However, Simmons draws on ethnographic analogy to argue that butchering need not result in cutmarks and likewise that small tools are used in butchering large game.[86] The excavators suggest that the distribution of faunal remains between the strata reflects changing economic strategies throughout the use of the rock shelter. As the pygmy hippopotamus became scarcer the human population became increasingly reliant on other food resources, and consequently there is a dramatic increase in bird bones in stratum 2.[87] Likewise, the human population became increasingly dependent on other

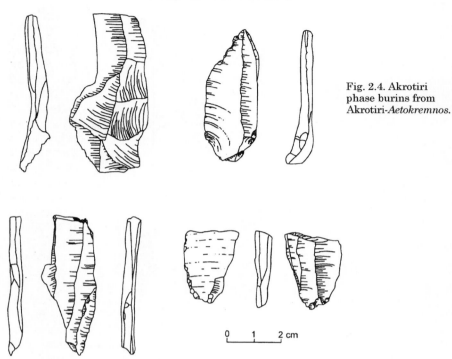

Fig. 2.4. Akrotiri phase burins from Akrotiri-*Aetokremnos*.

marine resources (shellfish). Certainly the site was well situated to benefit from a variety of food resources, although the abundant protein and energy/fat resources of the pygmy hippopotamus would have been the main attraction to the human population. Ultimately the excavators identify human activity as the cause of the extinction of endemic large fauna on the island, which they suggest led to the abandonment of the site and of Cyprus itself.[88]

Although epi-Palaeolithic activity has definitely been identified on Cyprus, the remains are too problematic to contextualise fully. We cannot place *Aetokremnos* in its landscape as nothing is known about other types of Akrotiri phase site used by this early population group. Although the use of local raw materials, such as chert and picrolite, suggests familiarity with the immediate environment around and beyond the Akrotiri peninsula, it is uncertain whether humans penetrated the island any further. Likewise, it is unclear whether the Akrotiri phase represents an abortive colonisation attempt or more sporadic, seasonal use of the island's resources by occasional visitors. Certainly, following the abandonment of *Aetokremnos*, there is a long hiatus in human habitation of Cyprus before the settlement of small farming communities and the colonisation proper of the island.

2. The Colonisation of Cyprus

The early aceramic Neolithic

The discovery of the Akrotiri phase creates a gap in the Cypriot prehistoric sequence between the earliest human activity on the island during the eleventh millennium BP and the arrival of the first agricultural settlers. The date of the initial colonisation of Cyprus by the Neolithic settlers and their point of origin has long been controversial.[89] The Cypriot aceramic Neolithic, the so-called Khirokitia culture, appears to erupt fully formed on Cyprus in the eighth millennium BP without an initial migrant stage, and already appears culturally divergent from possible parent cultures on the mainland.

The aceramic Neolithic is problematic on a number of counts.[90] First, there is the apparent time lag between the inception of the Neolithic in Cyprus and its supposed antecedents in the Levant. The calibrated radiocarbon dates for the aceramic Neolithic fall within the seventh millennium BC, whereas the earliest Neolithic in the Levant dates to c. 9300 BP (Pre-Pottery Neolithic B).[91] While the earliest Neolithic to flourish on Cyprus was aceramic, contemporary farming communities in the Levant and southern Anatolia had begun to use pottery receptacles. The question remains why the earliest farming colonists did not transmit this technology to Cyprus along with other elements of the economic and cultural package. Similarly, there is a divergence in toolkits, most notably the absence of projectile points, although with the posited extinction of the island's mini mega-fauna there was no indigenous large fauna, suggesting that projectile points might be a redundant element.[92] The apparent absence of cattle amongst the economic package introduced to the island is another puzzle, considering its importance in the mainland agricultural economies. Similarly problematic is the introduction of circular architecture to the island, although there is a marked tendency towards rectilinear architecture on the mainland. In comparison with the contemporary Neolithic cultures of the mainland the aceramic Neolithic appears to be culturally endemic, insular, and retarded; however, as Rainbird has noted in another context, the elements of choice and identity are important considerations in evaluating perceived cultural backwardness.[93]

Recent excavations have addressed several of the problems involved in assessing the origins of the Cypriot Neolithic, with the identification of an early Neolithic phase. These discoveries point to a common origin with the Pre-Pottery Neolithic B (PPNB) of the northern Levant, and this antecedent phase has consequently been termed the early aceramic Neolithic.[94] This phase has been identified at Parekklisha-*Shillourokambos*, Kissonerga-*Mylouthkia*, Ayia Varvara-*Asprokremnos*, Akanthou-*Arkosyko* (Tatlisu-*Çiftlikduzu*) and Kalavasos-*Tenta* (see Fig. 2.2).[95] The most important elements in the identification of this early and ephemeral phase of the Cypriot Neolithic are its characteristic lithic industry, unusual features in the subsistence economy, distinctive architectural types, and a suite of radiocarbon dates (Table 2.3) that are earlier than previously recorded for

Site	C-14 date (BP)
Kissonerga-*Mylouthkia*	9315 ± 60
Kissonerga-*Mylouthkia*	9235 ± 70
Kissonerga-*Mylouthkia*	9110 ± 70
Parekklisha-*Shillourokambos*	9310 ± 80
Parekklisha-*Shillourokambos*	9205 ± 75
Parekklisha-*Shillourokambos*	9110 ± 90
Kalavasos-*Tenta*	9240 ± 130
Parekklisha-*Shillourokambos*	8930 ± 75
Parekklisha-*Shillourokambos*	8825 ± 100
Parekklisha-*Shillourokambos*	8760 ± 80
Parekklisha-*Shillourokambos*	8725 ± 100
Parekklisha-*Shillourokambos*	8655 ± 65
Kalavasos-*Tenta*	8720 ± 400
Kalavasos-*Tenta*	8870 ± 500
Akrotiri Site 23	8684 ± 250
Kalavasos-*Tenta*	8480 ± 110
Kalavasos-*Tenta*	8020 ± 90
Kalavasos-*Tenta*	8010 ± 260
Kissonerga-*Mylouthkia*	8185 ± 55
Kissonerga-*Mylouthkia*	8025 ± 65
Parekklisha-*Shillourokambos*	8125 ± 70

Table 2.3. Radiocarbon determinations for the early aceramic Neolithic (after Todd 1985, table 1; McCartney 1999, table 1; Peltenburg *et al.* 2001, fig. 3).

the aceramic Neolithic phase.[96] The early radiocarbon determinations from Kalavasos-*Tenta* that have long proved problematic, lying outside the aceramic Neolithic range, can be readily integrated within the chronological limits of the early aceramic Neolithic. The late identification of this phase is largely due to the low visibility of its sites, which tend to be characterised by ephemeral architecture at best.

Settlement

Although the initial, colonising phase of the Cypriot Neolithic has been identified at only a small number of sites, it is possible to make some inferences as to the early use of the Cypriot landscape. For the most part the sites where early aceramic material has been identified lie in the coastal zone; however, there is evidence that these early farmers penetrated further inland. A small farming community was established at Ayia Varvara-*Asprokremnos*, lying on a low limestone ridge below the northeast foothills of the Troodos massif.[97] These sites illustrate the earliest documented forays by humans into the Cypriot hinterland. Presumably the subsistence strategy, specifically herd management or more probably hunting of fallow deer, would have required some negotiation of the wider landscape beyond the limits of the early settlements.[98] Knowledge and exploitation of indigenous Cypriot mineral resources is further illustrated by the range of materials used in manufacture of various items of material culture.

34

2. The Colonisation of Cyprus

The most important of the early aceramic sites to be excavated is Parekklisha-*Shillourokambos*, situated in southern Cyprus, 5 km from the present coastline. The excavators have identified five occupation phases, of which the three earliest relate to issues of colonisation by farming communities. The earliest occupation of the site (Early Phase A) is characterised by features in 'negative', ephemeral architectural remains that were dug into the *havara* bedrock (Fig. 2.5). These include cylindrical wells and basins,[99] and a series of ditches, post-holes and stake holes describing a trapezoidal and circular enclosures,[100] interpreted as possible animal stockades. The earliest architecture at *Shillourokambos* was wooden, but this appears to be exclusive to the initial occupation of the site during Early Phase A.[101] The earliest occupation phase at Kalavasos-*Tenta* (associated with the particularly early radiocarbon date) is similarly associated with wooden architecture. Subsequently, the occupants of *Shillourokambos* made use of boulders from the Troodos massif to construct the foundations of their houses. The remains of a possible kiln or hearth were found on the floor of a domestic structure (St. 63) in levels 1 and 1/2 (Early Phase B).[102] Similar 'kilns' are known from PPN occupation levels in the Levant,[103] but their use remains unclear.

The series of concentric circular structures (Structures 14, 17 and 36) crowning the summit of *Tenta*[104] date to the later early aceramic Neolithic phase, according to their radiocarbon determinations, which place them in the later ninth millennium BP (Table 2.3). These illustrate the crystallisation of the typical Cypriot aceramic Neolithic circular architectural form during the course of the early aceramic and the development of the building technology using stone and mudbrick. Recently, it has been suggested that their prominent location within the site topography, their elaborate ground plan, incorporating unusual features such as the radial cells, and the juxtaposition of smaller single-celled structures around the exterior wall recall the hierarchical arrangement of buildings at the PPNA site of Jerf el Ahmar in the Levantine corridor.[105]

Elaborate structures ensuring a water supply are the most remarkable element of the earliest architecture of the early aceramic Neolithic and mark an early adaptation to the particular environmental conditions of the island – specifically the rapid run-off of water and arid summer conditions.[106] In addition to the series of wells and basins at *Shillourokambos*, there are three wells at Kissonerga-*Mylouthkia* (see Plate 5). These comprise cylindrical shafts cut into the *havara* bedrock, which bell out towards the base and are equipped with foot- and hand-holes cut into the sides of the shafts. The wells tap small underground water courses and were located with great precision, suggesting that the well-diggers used some form of water divination.[107]

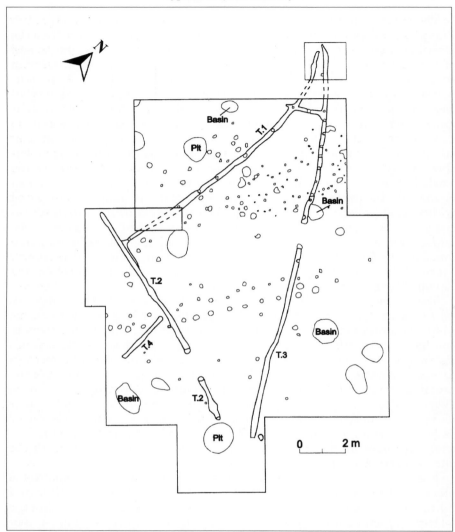

Fig. 2.5. Plan of the early aceramic Neolithic levels at Parekklisha-*Shillourokambos*.

Burial practices

The early aceramic levels at *Shillourokambos* give a few tantalising glimpses of the spiritual life underpinning this colonisation phase in the form of elusive funerary remains. The treatment of the dead is very different to anything documented for the late aceramic Neolithic, during which phase burial practices were formalised with single inhumations in pit graves beneath the floors of domestic structures. At *Shillourokambos* a single inhumation was made during Phase B within the fill of a large pit (F23). The body was placed on its left side in a contracted position and the burial was seemingly unfurnished. Also in the fill of the pit, pushed up against its wall, there was an isolated human mandible. Subsequently, during the Middle Phase, the pit was re-used as a rubbish pit, and the upper fill contained large quantities of rich meat-bearing bones, apparently the debris of feasting.[108] Kissonerga-*Mylouthkia* gives a further interesting insight into the treatment of the dead, which might illuminate the origins of the human population. The fill of Well 133 illustrates cultural activities that appear to reference the distinctive funerary practices of the PPNB in the Levant, in particular the emphasis on the treatment of human skulls.[109] The skull and upper vertebra of an adult male were found in the upper fill of the well, the skull demonstrating cranial deformation.[110] As the post-cranial remains were not recovered this suggests secondary burial focusing on discrete elements of the body, specifically the skull. The remains of four other individuals (skulls and other body parts, indicative of secondary burial) were found in the lower fill of Well 133. Three of the skulls were grouped with a macehead of pink conglomerate. An exceptional concentration of the complete unbutchered skeletons of sheep and goat were also deposited in the well, in the fill between the two burial layers. These animal remains, including at least eight immature sheep and twelve immature goats,[111] represent the removal from circulation of a valuable meat resource, which were not even consumed within the context of competitive feasting. As such, within the context of an early farming group, let alone a colonising group, this is a remarkable display of conspicuous consumption of a valuable wealth resource.[112]

Material culture

The chipped stone industry is one of the most distinctive markers of the early aceramic Neolithic and is particularly important for the light it sheds on the origin of the farming population that settled the island late in the tenth millennium BP. The toolkit used by this population is significantly different from that of both the Akrotiri phase and the later aceramic Neolithic. Instead it displays affinities with the tools in use on the Asiatic mainland during the PPNB (specifically the Early PPNB),[113] both in the technology employed and specific tool types. Together with the presence of some archaic PPNA characteristics, this suggests that knowledge of the chipped stone industry was transmitted to Cyprus early in the PPNB, where it subsequently developed independently.[114]

Large quantities of obsidian bladelets and flakes were found at *Shillourokambos*,[115] brought to the island from Cappadocia (Anatolia) in finished form. The quantity of obsidian imports can be defined as one of the qualitative markers for the early aceramic, since obsidian is found in only very small quantities on late aceramic Neolithic sites. Indeed, the occasional obsidian concentration at aceramic Neolithic sites such as *Troulli* I might indicate the presence of an antecedent PPNB phase.[116] Peltenburg suggests the development of an internal exchange network throughout the island during the early aceramic, local picrolite being procured in the south and exchanged for obsidian imports, possibly entering the island at the northern site of Akanthou-*Arkosyko*.[117] For the most part, however, the tools were made from local cherts. One characteristic feature, which places the Cypriot industry firmly within the sphere of the Levantine PPNB, is the naviform core reduction technology (Fig. 2.6: 1).[118] Also introduced in the early aceramic Neolithic was the opposed platform core reduction technique. The techniques were used alongside each other during the early aceramic phase, but, while the use of naviform cores declined, opposed platform core reduction continued to be used during the late aceramic Neolithic phase.[119]

Possibly the most distinctive element among the early aceramic toolkit is the projectile point. Two forms are represented, the elongated Byblos arrowhead (Fig. 2.6: 3) and the leaf-shaped Amuq arrowhead, both of which demonstrate clear ties with the mainland.[120] Various types of sickle blades with Levantine parallels are represented. Finely denticulated blades are found at *Mylouthkia*[121] and lunate segments at *Shillourokambos* (Fig. 2.6: 3). These composite elements were mounted into the haft at an angle, as is indicated by the oblique glossing of the silica sheen. The rare find of a deer antler haft shows the mounting intended for three aligned segments.[122] By the Middle Phase at *Shillourokambos* retouched segment blades (the sickle gloss parallel to the tool edge) replaced the lunate blades.[123] Sickle gloss (silica sheen) is clearly visible on the blades, indicating their function. This is supported by trace-ware analysis of a sample of the chipped stone tools, which suggests the harvest of green cereals.[124] The toolkit was supplemented by a variety of ground stone tools (pounders, querns and grinders), for the most part used in the preparation of cereals and other foodstuffs. A series of grooved stones decorated with geometric motifs might be net sinkers used in fishing. Maceheads are rare but are documented at both *Mylouthkia* and *Shillourokambos* in the earliest levels.

Throughout the early aceramic levels there is a clear line of development or change in the lithic industry, in particular varying exploitation of raw materials but also a perceived decline in the range of tools and in the technical skills of the tool workers. This is illustrated by a shift from fine high quality translucent cherts to coarser opaque cherts by the Middle Phase of *Shillourokambos*[125] and the eventual disappearance of projectile points. At present studies tend to emphasise an apparent decrease in direct contacts with the mainland, as is indicated by the decline in the number of obsidian imports, and the inception of the perceived Cypriot tendency towards insularity. However, a wealth of behavioural and cultural changes under-pinning these changes need to be explored as do the element of choice and the construction of a 'Cypriot' Neolithic identity.

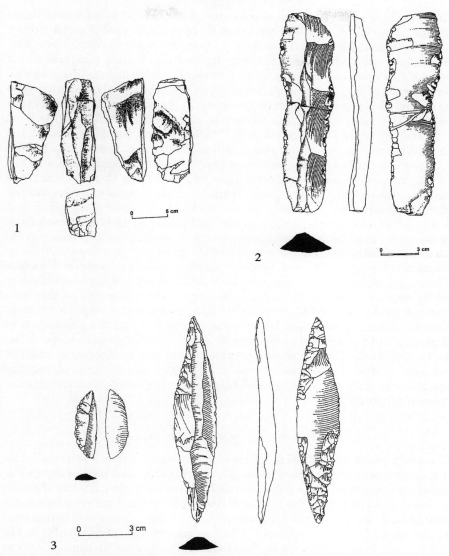

Fig. 2.6. Early aceramic Neolithic chipped stone assemblage from Parekklisha-*Shillourokambos*: (1) naviform core of translucent chert; (2) large blade of opaque chert; (3) lunate segment and Byblos point.

In the absence of pottery the neolithic population produced a variety of receptacles from stone (and possibly also from basketry and wood), but also made extensive use of pits and basins cut into the bedrock for storing food and water. Stone vessels comprise a series of limestone bowls and

shallow thick-walled basins. A specialised deposit of stone vessel fragments, believed to be the debris from their manufacture derived from a
surface dump, was found in Well 133 at *Mylouthkia*.[126] A large and
carefully made shallow basin (measuring 70-80 cm in diameter) was found
at *Shillourokambos*. This was made from local serpentine and the exterior
was decorated with a ribbed pattern. While the other bowls are believed to
have served a domestic function, possibly in the preparation and serving
of food, the excavators suggest that the more elaborate serpentine bowl
was not intended for domestic use.[127] These stone vessels stand at the
beginning of a peculiarly Cypriot cultural tradition, which reaches its
floruit in the late aceramic Neolithic, using harder volcanic stones.

The rich representational repertoire of prehistoric Cyprus[128] likewise
has its antecedents in the early aceramic. Two figural representations
were uncovered in the Early Phase levels at *Shillourokambos*. These
comprise an anthropomorphic plaster head and a feline head carved from
serpentine. The plaster head represents an inclining human face resting
on a cylindrical neck. The eyes are the only facial features depicted.[129] The
feline head was found in Well 66 and its facial features are clearly depicted.
The morphology of the carving suggests that it had been made specifically
to be mounted on a wall, which the excavators reference to the wall
fixtures from Çatalhöyük (Anatolia).[130] Although the evidence is extremely
elusive, it does offer some tantalising glimpses as to the ideology and
symbolism of the colonising farmers of Cyprus. Together with the emphasis on human skulls in funerary practices, this type of figurative artwork
appears to derive ultimately from the Asiatic mainland, implying the
transference of belief systems and cultural practices by the farming colonists of Cyprus.[131]

Noah's ark: early farming practices

The early aceramic Neolithic represents the earliest migration of a farming community within the insular Mediterranean, and indeed should be
numbered amongst the earliest spread of the Neolithic economy from its
foundation base in the Levant. The full complement of domesticated plants
and animals that form the subsistence base of this culture was introduced
to the island from the mainland. Whether the colonisation was effected in
a single crossing or successive crossings, the minimum distance of 69 km
from the mainland and the transference of semi-domesticated and wild
animals suggest that the colonists possessed a sophisticated maritime
technology. It is unclear whether the colonising population maintained
contacts with the parent culture on the mainland, although the apparent
insularity of the late aceramic Neolithic phase, and possibly also the
disappearance of important livestock from the economic package, might
argue for increasingly limited communications. The impetus for this colo-

nisation episode is unclear, but one possibility is the apparent environmental stress experienced by PPN communities of the coastal Levant.[132]

The absence of endemic species in early aceramic Neolithic bone assemblages clearly indicates their extinction between the Akrotiri phase and the Neolithic colonisation phase, as it is improbable that the early settlers would have ignored such an abundant protein resource. In contrast to the Akrotiri phase 'settlers', the early aceramic Neolithic population was not really exploiting the local marine resources. Marine invertebrates and fish and bird bones are rare. However, there is the possibility that these resources were utilised on a more localised basis, being consumed at specialised coastal sites that have not been identified, rather than being taken back to the main farming settlements. The full early aceramic Neolithic faunal repertoire comprises fallow deer (*Dama mesopotamica*), sheep, goat, pig and cattle. All of these, with the exception of cattle, form the typical faunal assemblage exploited by later Neolithic and Chalcolithic farming communities on the island. Other animals represented at *Shillourokambos* include dog, cat and fox.[133] The apparent stockades identified in the Early Phase levels at *Shillourokambos* would presumably have been used in herd management of semi-domesticated animals, giving a tantalising glimpse of the herding strategies of these early farmer/herdsmen.

The range of deer bones found at *Shillourokambos* indicates that the carcasses were processed away from the site. Taken with the age and sex ratios of the deer, this is suggestive of a hunting strategy rather than herding.[134] It is interesting to note that fallow deer was also introduced to a number of Aegean islands during the Neolithic. In Aegean contexts analysis of the bones implies a distance hunting strategy, and Halstead comments that deer are very unsuited to close herding because of their territoriality and violent male conflicts.[135] Sheep and goat bones illustrate culling of young males and also that the complete carcasses were processed on the site, implying that these animals were being bred.[136] Even so, the morphology of the skeletons is very suggestive, as they cannot be distinguished from the wild species, namely the Near Eastern moufflon (*Ovis orientalis*) and bezoar goat (*Capra aegagrus*). Although these animals are not fully domesticated (domestication has left no discernible modification of their skeletons), neither are they fully wild. They are in effect 'pre-domestic'. Pig bones are of the same type that is found at late aceramic Neolithic sites. The animals are significantly smaller than the wild boar found on the mainland (*Sus s. scrofa*) and are also smaller than earliest domesticated pig of the PPNB Syrian coast, indicating that the Cypriot pig was definitely domesticated from the earliest settlement phase. Most intriguing, however, is the presence of cattle bone, a situation that has required archaeologists to rethink the economic strategies of the earliest communities on the island. Cattle bones are found in Early Phases A and B at *Shillourokambos*, but disappear from the faunal assemblage by the Middle Phase. In this respect it is interesting to note that 1% of the animal bones from the later aceramic Neolithic settlement at Krittou Marattou-*Ais Yiorkis* are cattle.[137] At *Shillourokambos* all parts of the skeleton and all age classes are represented, indicating they were herded and processed on site. Although the cattle are large, they are slightly smaller than the wild aurochs (*Bos primigenius*) of the Early and Middle PPNB of the Levant and the earliest domesticated cattle found on the Syrian coast, implying that they belong to an early stage of domestication.

The range of animals exploited at *Shillourokambos* changes throughout the use of the site,[138] indicating changing subsistence strategies between the initial colonisation phase and the full settlement phase. In the earliest levels (Early Phase A) pig is predominant, possibly suggesting greater reliance on pig because there was initially greater expertise in pig rearing. Also pig would be particularly suited to a more forested environment, which we might expect in an initial colonisation phase. However by Early Phase B fallow deer dominates the faunal assemblage, possibly because the herds introduced by the initial settlers had become established. The transport of this non-domesticate to the island is particularly intriguing, illustrating the close control that the herder/hunters of the PPN exerted over animals. The introduction of the animal was partly economic and partly cultural, in that it ensured the provision of large game in the absence of endemic species to supplement the diet, and it perpetuated the ethos of hunting, which was probably strongly ingrained in the culture of the settlers. Whereas cattle represent 10% of the faunal remains in Early Phase B, they disappear during the Middle Phase and pig and caprines supplant fallow deer as the main meat resources. Simmons has suggested that cattle were kept at smaller specialised sites rather than larger Neolithic village centres,[139] but their ultimate disappearance from the Cypriot Neolithic economy has yet to be explained. The early aceramic Neolithic faunal assemblage is indicative of a more economically sophisticated Neolithic adaptation than that suggested by late aceramic Neolithic remains. Moreover, the animals represented are the same species and similar in form to those found at late aceramic Neolithic sites, allowing us to identify the early aceramic economy as the precursor of the later aceramic Neolithic economy. Despite the limited and ephemeral nature of the evidence for the early aceramic phase, it is evident that the farmers were ultimately successful in establishing a permanent presence and that they irrevocably altered the island's ecosystem.

The arable element of the economy can be inferred from the toolkit; in particular the sickle gloss on the composite blades suggests harvesting of plants such as cereals. Additionally, the range of pounders, querns and other stone tools and receptacles probably illustrates processing of these plant remains. This picture is supplemented by the well-preserved assemblages of charred plant remains found in the wells at *Mylouthkia*. These include wheat, barley, lentils, pistachio, and linseed/flax.[140] The high chaff content and high ratio of weed seeds are suggestive of the debris from cereal processing.[141] Despite the problems involved in distinguishing between domestic and wild forms, Peltenburg suggests that domestic wheat (einkorn and emmer) and barley are present at *Mylouthkia* during Periods IA and IB. There is evidence therefore that the three Neolithic founder crops were being cultivated on Cyprus from the late tenth millennium BP, not long after the domestication of cereals in the Levant.[142] There is little evidence that these taxa are native to the island; therefore the evidence points to the introduction of these cultigens by the early aceramic Neolithic farmer-colonists.

Migrant farmers

According to current understanding, before the introduction of the Neolithic economic package from the mainland during the PPNB there was no human population resident on Cyprus. The earlier Akrotiri phase was either an abortive colonisation attempt or possibly represents an initial exploration phase and sporadic use of the island's resources. Following the extinction of the indigenous mini-megafauna the island was abandoned for around a millennium before the arrival of the first farmers. Recent excavations suggest that the economic package, technical knowledge and symbolic values were introduced to the island from the Asiatic mainland (Anatolia or the Levant) during the ninth to eighth millennia BP. Given the explosion in evidence for early prehistoric human activity on the island it would be rash to assume that this material represents the earliest definite landfall of settlers on the island. The procurement of local mineral resources, especially picrolite, from the inception of this phase indicates to some archaeologists that the settlers had prior knowledge of these resources, possibly learnt from maritime groups active along the Levantine littoral.[143] Yet there is no evidence for the exploitation of these 'exotics' in Natufian and PPNA contexts, in situations analogous to the early exploitation of Melian obsidian in the Aegean from the Upper Palaeolithic.[144] Moreover, the hunter-gatherer group(s) of the Akrotiri phase also exploited the local mineral resources, including picrolite, suggesting that the early occupants of the island assimilated knowledge of the surrounding landscape and its resources (both mineral and food) fairly rapidly after their initial landfall.

Recent developments in our understanding of the initial genesis of farming and herding economies mean that models of Neolithic dispersal and migration are currently under review, and the Cypriot evidence has to be incorporated into this wider picture. One model describes the uneven spread of small communities of agro-pastoralists from larger parent communities.[145] This model recognises that the dispersal of the Neolithic did not occur smoothly in a steady continuum, but that instead there are apparent gaps between Neolithic populations – the geographical gap between the PPNB communities of the northern Levant and the earliest settlers of Cyprus being a case in point.[146] Recently, Peltenburg has suggested that a jump dispersal model best fits the evidence for the spread of the Neolithic to Cyprus, and as a corollary elsewhere in the region.[147] This model suggests movement over long distances, bypassing possible settlement locales, maybe because they were already settled by other hunter-gatherer groups (which would be more elusive in the archaeological record). The migrating communities would come into contact with other population groups and it might be expected that they would acquire knowledge of the surrounding regions in this way. This model would therefore allow the settlers of Cyprus to acquire knowledge of the island from coastal maritime-based groups. Indeed the earliest attested human activity on the island, at *Aetokremnos*, fits Cherry's suggestion of a pre-colonisation phase and Levantine maritime prospection. The absence of an indigenous population group resident on the island indicates that the transmission of the Neolithic to Cyprus represents demic diffusion (a population movement) rather than cultural diffusion (the transmission of ideas between human populations), much as has been suggested for the arrival of the Neolithic in Crete and the Cyclades.[148] Even so, there is clear evidence for the development of exchange networks and a common cultural experience linking the PPN communities of the Levant, and certain elements of the cultural repertoire link into this cultural horizon.[149] The reasons for the Neolithic expansion beyond the core of the Levantine corridor during the PPN are unclear, although population growth and demographic stress are possibilities, which would fit with a model of demic diffusion. Other possibilities include environmental stress, possibly exacerbated by human interference in the ecosystem necessitated by domestication.

Whether or not the remains at *Shillourokambos* and *Mylouthkia* represent the initial landfall of settlers, or were preceded by maritime prospection, or even an earlier settlement phase at present undetected, the farming communities established on the island during the ninth and eighth millennia BP are ancestral to the peculiarly Cypriot aceramic Neolithic. There is no need to posit a subsequent migration of farmers. Instead, the internal cultural trajectory over the period of a millennium resulted in the development of a very distinctive culture with few vestiges of its Asiatic origins. Instead, the major importance of these remains is that they show the expansion of human populations into the island to be contemporary with the phase of animal domestication on the mainland, thereby placing Cyprus centre-stage in the debate on neolithicisation, rather than representing a parochial off-shoot of little intrinsic interest to scholars working in the surrounding regions.

Early Farming Communities

The aceramic Neolithic

Origins

Before the discoveries at Parekklisha-*Shillourokambos* and Kissonerga-*Mylouthkia*, the aceramic Neolithic[1] (previously known as the Khirokitia culture or KCU, now referred to as the late aceramic Neolithic) was thought to represent the earliest successful human occupation of Cyprus by colonising farming communities, but its origins were uncertain. The aceramic Neolithic appeared to arrive fully formed on the island, with no apparent phase of internal development from the mainland parent culture. The genesis of the Neolithic in Cyprus is currently under review, but in the light of the new evidence from *Shillourokambos* and *Mylouthkia*, the introduction of a farming economy to Cyprus by human settlers in the late tenth or early ninth millennium BP has radically altered the discourse. One suggestion is that this was a migration of a human population in reaction to environmental stress on the Asiatic mainland.[2] This interpretation, however, has not met with total support by the excavators of *Shillourokambos*, who have sought to play down the apparent Levantine traits of the early aceramic Neolithic. Even so, the antecedents of the 'Khirokitia culture' have been identified, thereby answering one of the major problems in the earlier prehistory of Cyprus, providing a suitable formative phase for Stanley-Price's colonisation hypothesis.[3]

The late aceramic Neolithic dates to the seventh and sixth millennia BC (Table 3.1) and is characterised by distinctive settlements, material culture, economy, and presumably a shared social organisation. The aceramic phase of the Cypriot Neolithic was first identified in 1929 by Einar Gjerstad, on the island of Petra tou Limniti, off the north coast of Cyprus.[4] Subsequent excavations of small village communities throughout the island have illustrated the apparently insular and isolated characteristics of the Cypriot aceramic Neolithic, remarkably different from contemporary farming communities on the Asiatic mainland. Present interpretations emphasise the internal development of this culture, hermetically sealed from outside influence thereby losing many of the cultural and economic attributes of its early aceramic Neolithic antecedents and failing to acquire or assimilate innovations, most notably pottery production.

Site	Lab. code	C-14 date (BP)	Calibrated date (BC)
Khirokitia-*Vounoi*	Ly 4309	6230 ± 160	5479 – 4796
Khirokitia-*Vounoi*	Ly 4785	8850 ± 650	9816 – 6397
Khirokitia-*Vounoi*	Ly 4307	7930 ± 130	7140 – 6473
Khirokitia-*Vounoi*	Ly 4308	7470 ± 140	6530 – 6054
Khirokitia-*Vounoi*	Ly 4306	6310 ± 170	5558 – 4899
Khirokitia-*Vounoi*	Ly 4786	6590 ± 260	5932 – 4950
Khirokitia-*Vounoi*	Ly 3718	7930 ± 320	7549 – 6225
Khirokitia-*Vounoi*	Ly 4787	7070 ± 610	7353 – 4709
Khirokitia-*Vounoi*	Ly 3716	7000 ± 150	6109 – 5623
Khirokitia-*Vounoi*	Ly 3717	7700 ± 150	6840 – 6239
Khirokitia-*Vounoi*	Ly 3719	7540 ± 180	6774 – 6008
Khirokitia-*Vounoi*	St 415	7655 ± 160	6842 – 6214
Khirokitia-*Vounoi*	St 414	7515 ± 125	6574 – 6158
Khirokitia-*Vounoi*	BM 854	7442 ± 61	6430 – 6208
Khirokitia-*Vounoi*	BM 853	7451 ± 81	6441 – 6202
Khirokitia-*Vounoi*	BM 855	7308 ± 74	6265 – 6013
Khirokitia-*Vounoi*	BM 852	7294 ± 78	6264 – 5994
Dhali-*Agridhi*	GX 2484 A	7290 ± 465	7186 – 5319
Dhali-*Agridhi*	P-2768	7400 ± 60	6396 – 6092
Dhali-*Agridhi*	P-2775	7990 ± 80	7082 – 6647
Kalavasos-*Tenta*	P-2782	7600 ± 100	6595 – 6236
Kalavasos-*Tenta*	P-2555	7430 ± 90	6439 – 6158
Kalavasos-*Tenta*	P-2978	7400 ± 260	6774 – 5727
Kalavasos-*Tenta*	P-2784	7380 ± 100	6421 – 6057
Kalavasos-*Tenta*	P-2552	7250 ± 100	6264 – 5971
Kalavasos-*Tenta*	P-2550	7180 ± 90	6223 – 5876
Kalavasos-*Tenta*	P-2551	7140 ± 90	6209 – 5809
Kalavasos-*Tenta*	P-2783	7130 ± 410	6831 – 5298
Kalavasos-*Tenta*	P-2779	7120 ± 90	6113 – 5792
Kalavasos-*Tenta*	P-2553	7110 ± 90	6110 – 5774
Kalavasos-*Tenta*	P-2975	6970 ± 310	6431 – 5355
Kalavasos-*Tenta*	P-2977	6580 ± 290	6016 – 4901
Kalavasos-*Tenta*	P-2781	6300 ± 80	5390 – 5056
Kalavasos-*Tenta*	P-2549	5630 ± 260	5073 – 3941

Table 3.1. Late aceramic Neolithic radiocarbon determinations (after Todd 1985, table 1; Le Brun 1988, table 1; Lehavy 1989, table 6; Le Brun & Evin 1991, table 1).

Landscape and settlement

The Cypriot aceramic Neolithic is characterised by small village communities scattered throughout the landscape, though with a tendency to locate within the coastal zone (Fig. 3.1). There are, however, important inland sites such as Dhali-*Agridhi* and Kholetria-*Ortos*. There is very little evidence for intercommunications, though presumably the densely wooded and mountainous interior would have acted as a major barrier to movement overland. Limited exploitation of marine resources might argue against travel by boat around the island's coastline. Moreover, exploitation of fallow deer and indigenous mineral resources (chert, picrolite) argue for some movement within the landscape. Todd notes that Kalavasos-*Tenta* is located on a natural overland communication route, controlling movement

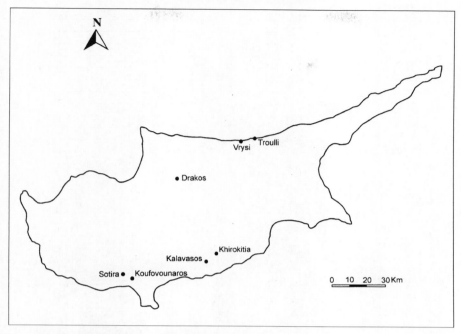

Fig. 3.1. Map of Neolithic settlements in Cyprus.

east-west along the coastal plain and north-south along the Vasilikos valley.[5] Likewise, the shared material culture throughout the island argues for some perceived common identity, although these are issues that have yet to be addressed in the literature.

Whether there was internal tension between the aceramic sites is also unclear. For the most part the settlements favour high ground or naturally protected locales, and it appears that security took precedence over immediate access to a water supply.[6] The first settlement at Khirokitia-*Vounoi* (Fig. 3.2) was enclosed by a pisé wall faced with stone on the west side, a structure originally identified by Dikaios as a road.[7] This wall remained in use until the settlement expanded beyond its boundaries and a second wall was then built, parallel to the first wall. The latter was 3 m thick, and was built of stone. Khirokitia was accessed via an elaborate entrance system. Two entrances to the village have been identified in Zone D. The earlier one is poorly preserved, destroyed by later buildings. The later entrance, however, is well preserved and comprises a stairway built inside a stone structure, leaning against the external face of the wall. The access route changes direction three times, which together with the narrowness of the stairway denotes controlled access into the village. *Tenta* (Fig. 3.3) was similarly encircled by a pair of concentric walls and an external ditch, although at a later stage the settlement expanded beyond this boundary.[8]

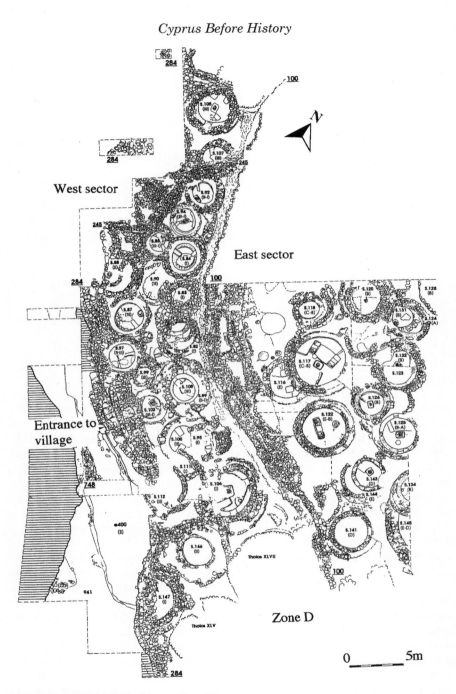

Fig. 3.2. Plan of Khirokitia-*Vounoi* (Zone D).

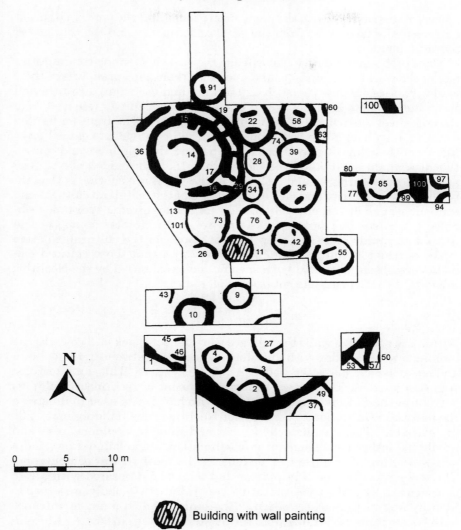

Building with wall painting

Fig. 3.3. Plan of Kalavasos-*Tenta*.

The aceramic villages thus appear to have grown up within a delimited enclosed area, and there is some evidence for control over entry and mobilisation of labour for large-scale communal building enterprises. It is assumed that these structures are defensive, and yet it is unclear what threat they were protecting themselves from. There is no evidence for violent destruction or deaths and there are no weapons in the cultural assemblage. The seemingly defensive aspect of settlement might indicate

49

unease or distrust between the population groups, but the perceived threat might equally have come from the wild landscape beyond the confines of the settlement.

More problematic is what knowledge these early farming communities had of the world beyond the island and what their perception was of their world. Exotics, or imports, such as obsidian and carnelian, are rare and the latter tends to be deposited in graves, being explicitly removed from the domain of the living. The rarity of these objects might argue for limited contacts, but there is the possibility that certain individuals gained prestige from their knowledge of the world beyond the sea and could control the dissemination of these exotics within the aceramic context.[9] The apparent backwardness and isolation of the Cypriot Neolithic is thought to illustrate insularity and lack of knowledge of the mainland cultures and contemporary cultural innovations. The failure to introduce ceramic technology, in particular, but also the preference for circular as opposed to rectilinear architecture, are viewed as evidence for the cultural isolation of the aceramic Neolithic. The alternative view, that these cultural elements are absent as a result of a specific choice exercised by the Neolithic inhabitants of Cyprus, has not been explored.

Domestic space

Within the enclosure walls the villages were densely packed. Typically, the buildings were circular with an internal diameter between 1.4 and 4.8 m and an external diameter between 2.3 and 9.2 m. This architectural tradition is in stark contrast to the development of rectilinear buildings current in the Levant,[10] and is one of the archaic traits used to illustrate the cultural retardation of the Cypriot Neolithic. The building materials are variable. These include limestone and diabase boulders, pisé and mudbrick, either used singly or in combination, stone foundations and a superstructure of mudbrick or pisé being the most typical combination. The walls were rendered in plaster and might be decorated with a red, ochre-based pigment. These paintings generally are too badly preserved to identify any motifs or decoration.[11] The buildings had a single entrance with two or three steps down onto the plastered living surface. At Khirokitia there is evidence that some of the houses had small openings or windows.[12] Traditional interpretations of the roofs show them to be domed, as was suggested by Dikaios, because of the internal curvature of the walls.[13] More recent excavations at Khirokitia, however, have demonstrated the roofs to be flat. Fragments of a roof were found in a structure destroyed by fire, allowing the excavators to reconstruct the construction method used by the aceramic Neolithic builders. A wooden frame was placed over the building, resting on top of its walls. Lying on top of this frame there were two crossed layers of reeds, which were covered by several layers of pisé and earth.[14]

Internal features include piers built of stone or pisé, usually thought to have a structural function, possibly to support a partial upper storey.[15] Peltenburg, however, argues that these are structurally redundant building elements, retained in Cypriot architecture as an archaising trait. He argues that these piers derive from pairs of pillars used in Syro-Anatolian architecture, which he suggests had highly symbolic connotations, as is indicated by their decoration with representations of human figures and animals.[16] The ephemeral traces of painted decoration on the Cypriot derivatives, the best preserved being a pair of figures with upraised arms on the central pier of Structure 11 at *Tenta*,[17] might imply the transmission of this symbolism to the island. Other internal installations appear to have a functional rather than symbolic purpose. These include platforms built up against the house walls, various types of hearths (circular, rectangular, made from limestone slabs or raised mud platforms), pits cut into the floor, (usually with a fill of ash or charcoal, pebbles, or animal bones), and a rectangular plastered basin.[18]

It is possible to make certain, limited inferences as to the internal social and household organisation and the use of domestic space. It is improbable that individual structures housed nuclear family units. Instead Le Brun reconstructs a group of several circular buildings grouped around an unroofed space or courtyard as the basic component of the household. The number of individuals that made up this household is unclear, as is the internal social structure – matrilocal or patrilocal, for example. Likewise, beyond positing an egalitarian community, the external organisation of the households remains elusive – how these groups worked together in the production of cereals, fishing, hunting and herding, and production of household utensils and toolkits. However, according to the arrangement of various installations within the household units posited by Le Brun, it is possible to reconstruct activity areas. Fixed querns set in a pebble paving are located in the courtyard, implying that food preparation, such as grinding grain, took place outside. However, cooking was probably carried out inside the houses, where a specific type of small rectangular platform hearth is found. Other hearths are found outside in the courtyard area.[19] Rubbish was deposited in the narrow passageways separating discrete household groups.[20] Large-scale storage of foodstuffs is difficult to illustrate in the absence of storage containers and bins, although the pits referred to by Dikaios are one possibility. There is evidence for a raised floor in the small Structure 34 near the summit of the hill at *Tenta* and Todd suggests that this was possibly used as a granary.[21] Water derived from springs nearby the settlements, but actual storage within individual households is uncertain, other than the plastered basin at Khirokitia. It is interesting to note that the effort expended in the construction of wells and cisterns by their early aceramic antecedents did not continue into the later aceramic Neolithic.

Although the construction of the village enclosure walls indicates some form of centralised control over use of space within the community, there

51

are no evident public or open areas for the community to congregate, nor is there any evidence for communal ceremonial activity. The relationship between the occupants of different households is difficult to assess. Forms of communal activity might be inferred from the effort expended in certain elements of the material culture, suggesting that competition took the form of display in personal adornment, or possibly competitive feasting using the elaborate decorated ground stone bowls. Todd suggests that there is some evidence for social differentiation within the architecture and settlement organisation at *Tenta*. The three large superimposed buildings (Structures 14, 17 and 36) that dominate the village by their prominent location on the highest point of the hill are likewise differentiated from other structures by their size, the complexity of their ground plan, incorporating unusual features such as the radial cells, and the unusual red plaster floor of Structures 17 and 36.[22] The actual function of these buildings is unclear. Very few artefacts were found *in situ* to allow reconstruction of particular activities, but the use of red plaster for floors was restricted, and might denote a building of special significance. The proximity of these structures to Building 11, where the wall paintings were found, is also instructive. This series of structures, however, might belong to the early aceramic Neolithic foundations of the site, as radiocarbon determinations place it in the later ninth millennium BP.[23]

Burial customs

The treatment of the dead is distinct from that identified during the early aceramic Neolithic phase and appears to have developed into a cultural norm, with a particular emphasis on the individual. This emphasis on the individual is similarly illustrated by the appearance of human figures as a typical element in the cultural repertoire, although not as an element deposited in graves.[24] The typical mode of burial, as attested at Khirokitia, was primary, intramural interment of individuals in pit graves beneath the house floors (Fig. 3.4).[25] Variant burial customs have been identified at *Tenta*, where only six of the twelve burials were placed in pit graves below the house floors. The others were placed in pits adjacent to a building, outside, or simply in the rubbish dumps between the buildings.[26] At Khirokitia, the body was usually placed on the right side in a contracted position and the degree of contraction was dictated by the age of the individual.[27] The orientation of the burial was variable, but illustrates differences in the burial rite according to the sex of the individual, particularly that there was considerably more variety in the orientation of female burials. Most burials lie on a northeast/southwest axis, but whereas male burials invariably were placed with their skull pointing to the northeast, the female burials might be oriented in either direction.[28] The burials, especially of males, might be covered by one or several stones. These might be shaped or rough boulders of andesite, or querns. The shaped stones and

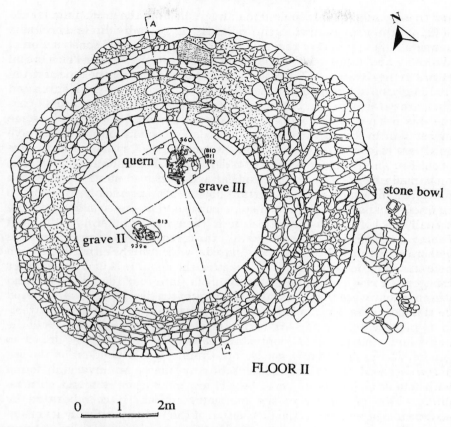

FLOOR II

0   1   2m

Fig. 3.4. Burials in Tholos XVII (floor II) at Khirokitia.

querns were most usually placed over the head, whereas the rough boulders might equally be placed over the legs or pelvis.[29] The belief system underpinning this practice is elusive, but the patterning involved indicates that it was intentional. Le Brun suggests that the practice implies an element of distrust in the wish to keep the dead separate from the world of the living.[30] If that were the case, however, we might expect it to be an integral element of burial ritual rather than associated with a select group. These burials are not differentiated by either the orientation of the burials or their range of grave goods. At *Tenta* there is some evidence for special treatment of the skulls of mature adult males.[31] In two cases the skulls were propped against a thin limestone slab against the wall of a building and covered with a second slab. In both cases the burials were placed not in a grave pit but adjacent to the wall of a building.

The limited space available within the house and the adjacent courtyard implies that a small number of mourners participated in funerary ritual,

53

and these were probably limited to individuals from the immediate house-hold. Again this indicates the prioritising of individuals and their immediate family, rather than the wider community. This construction of identities and social organisation is analogous to the Grotta-Pelos burial record in the Cyclades.[32] There is virtually no evidence for the type of ritual that might have accompanied these burials. Animal bones, deer, sheep and goat, are rarely found in burial deposits, suggesting that communal feast-ing was not a common element. However, there does appear to be some investment in the provision of grave goods for certain individuals. Grave goods are rare and individual burials were furnished with a limited range of objects. These include necklaces of dentalium shell and carnelian beads, tools made from bone or flint, conical and engraved stone of uncertain function, and stone vessels. Certain objects are specifically funerary in character, in particular spouted stone bowls and basins, which tend to be 'ritually broken',[33] possibly attesting to their use in funerary ritual and subsequent 'contamination'. Certainly, these receptacles were appropriate elaborate and visual containers of liquids, which might either have been poured as libations or consumed, toasting the dead. It is unclear whether the grave goods represent status symbols (in either life or death), and whether they were the personal belongings of the deceased or were offered by the mourners. Even so, the variable range of grave goods and invest-ment in individual burials argues for the development of the concept of the individual, and personal identity appears to be intrinsically linked to gender. The range of grave goods, for example, was dependent on the sex of the deceased. Carnelian and dentalium necklaces are invariably found with females. Similarly, stone vessels are more usually found with fe-males. This gendering of the mortuary context is corroborated by significant differences in the disposition of the body, specifically its orien-tation. The emphasis on the female burials – manifested by expenditure in grave goods and possibly also by certain forms of funerary ritual – might be expected in small, egalitarian subsistence communities. Female repro-duction was essential for maintaining the population, and given the apparent small size of the communities it is probable that exogamic relations would have played an important role. Consequently, we might assume a certain degree of mobility among the female population. The evidence for cranial deformation further illustrates the importance of women within these communities.[34] The custom was introduced to the island during the early aceramic Neolithic.[35] Presumably the characteristic deformation would have been a clear signal of group membership or identity, similar in purpose to the apparent tattooing of individuals, as in the EBA Cyclades.[36]

Material culture

The late aceramic Neolithic sites throughout the island shared a common material culture: typical elements include the chipped stone and bone

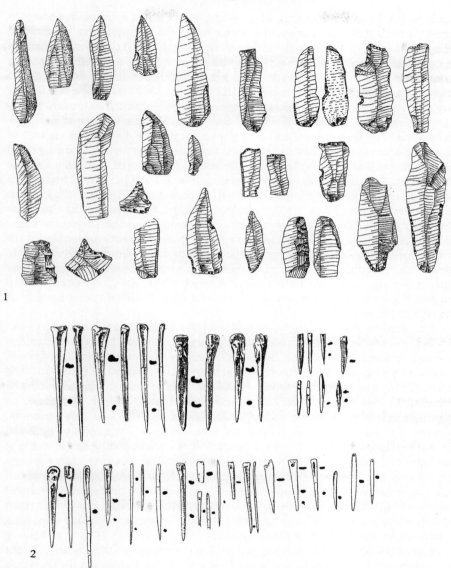

Fig. 3.5. Toolkit from Khirokitia: (1) lithics; (2) bone tools.

toolkits and the ground stone vessels made from volcanic rock. Although the antecedents of this material culture might be identified in the early aceramic Neolithic record, there are certain significant changes, which are perhaps most evident in the chipped stone assemblages (Fig. 3.5: 1).[37] The tools are primarily backed flakes or unretouched blades, some of which have sickle gloss along their cutting edge. Other types include notched and denticulated tools, burins, scrapers and rare perforating tools. The projectile point, such a distinctive element in the preceding phase, no longer formed an element of the Cypriot toolkit, implying a shift in hunting strategies. The tools are made from local cherts and flints, and obsidian imports are rare. This implies that the villages did not participate to any significant degree in the wide-ranging exchange networks that covered the Asiatic mainland, whether from choice or increasing insularity. Microwear analysis of the tools indicates that they were used for a variety of activities, such as harvesting cereals,[38] cutting reeds, wood-working, and scraping fresh skins. These reflect the varied economy of the late aceramic Neolithic, dependent on agriculture but also on meat, either hunted or herded. The toolkit was supplemented by bone tools (Fig. 3.5: 2). For the most part these were pointed tools,[39] such as perforators and fine needles (probably used to make basketry or for sewing), and fish hooks at Cape Andreas-*Kastros*. Ground stone tools include implements associated with food processing, specifically the preparation of cereals and other vegetable products, namely querns, pestles, mortars and grinders.[40] Another important element in the toolkit is the ground stone axe.[41] These indicate increased clearance of wooded areas, associated with intensification of agricultural production.

Possibly the cultural highpoint of the Cypriot aceramic Neolithic is the vessels carved from stone,[42] continuing a tradition already identified in the early aceramic period (Fig. 3.6: 1). There are numerous examples of these vessels, which are a distinctive marker of this period throughout the island. There are two main types, coarse vessels made from breccia or hard limestone, and fine vessels carved from soft limestone or diabase. The former comprises a series of large trays and basins. The finer vessels, frequently deposited with female burials, consist of a range of spouted bowls or basins, frequently with geometric decoration in relief (see Plate 6)[43] and the surface will be ground to a slight polish. Dikaios suggests that the forms are skeuomorphs, imitating basketry or wooden prototypes.[44] The spouted bowls, especially those with elaborate decoration, suggest some sort of cultural practice with an emphasis on liquids, possibly within the funerary arena, though mended examples suggest similar practices also took place within the living space.

There is increased emphasis on personal ornamentation, which might be interpreted within the context of an increasing emphasis on the individual. A variety of stones was used to make beads and pendants,[45] including imported carnelian and local picrolite. Dentalium shell beads are also found. The range of materials suggests some form of exchange network operating within the island and beyond, similar to that postulated for the early aceramic Neolithic.[46] A distinctive form of ornament made from picrolite comprises an open ring with a pointed protrusion, resembling a question mark, or with two protrusions (Fig. 3.6: 3).[47] Interpreted

56

Fig. 3.6. Material from Khirokitia: (1) stone bowls; (2, 4) engraved pebbles and conical stones; (3) stone ornaments.

by Dikaios as dress pins, their use is in fact uncertain; however, they were probably some form of dress ornament. The cultural repertoire includes a number of ambiguous objects: flat basalt pebbles with incised grid lines on one or both faces, and conical stones decorated with incised lines – a grid pattern on the base and chevrons on the sides (Fig. 3.6: 2, 4).[48] These were possibly used as tokens within a system of social storage, similar to that proposed for the Aegean in the Final Neolithic and EBA,[49] or within the exchange networks suggested for the Cypriot aceramic Neolithic. An alternative suggestion is that these geometric pebbles might have served as net weights.[50]

Representational art (Fig. 3.7 and Plate 7) is largely confined to three-dimensional figures carved from volcanic stone, with a single example of a human head sculpted from clay, which appears originally to have been mounted much as the feline head from *Shillourokambos*.[51] The range of subjects is almost exclusively limited to humans, which are represented in a wide variety of forms. Some are very schematic with only the body and legs indicated, others are more detailed, with the facial features indicated, especially those with discoid heads.[52] For the most part the sex of the figurine is not indicated, although there is a single example of an explicitly

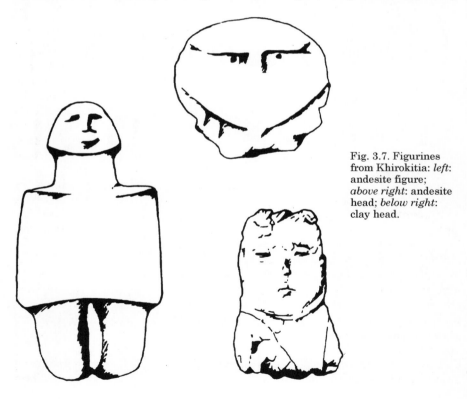

Fig. 3.7. Figurines from Khirokitia: *left*: andesite figure; *above right*: andesite head; *below right*: clay head.

58

female figurine from Khirokitia.[53] Even so, many of the figurines have a clearly phallic aspect. This ambiguity in human representation and gender is a continuing theme throughout the earlier prehistory of Cyprus, and presumably has important implications for social organisation. It is a distinctive element of the cultural repertoire of aceramic Cyprus, in marked opposition to the tendency towards representation of the female in contemporary Neolithic cultures on the mainland.[54] The profusion of figurines might reflect individuality as an increasingly important element in society, as is likewise reflected in the tendency for single primary inhumation. Recent studies of prehistoric figurines[55] have tended to debunk the 'mother-goddess' myth that has been perpetuated in studies of early representations of the human body, and instead have emphasised the importance of context for interpreting these objects. Within such a framework, it would appear that the aceramic figurines had very little symbolic, ritual import. They are almost invariably found in domestic habitation contexts, both inside houses and in the occupational debris outside.[56] Unfortunately, these figurines have not been examined for traces of wear and use, and their function remains elusive.

Economy: farmers, herders, hunters and fishers

The economic basis of the aceramic Neolithic communities that flourished on the island can be assessed using a wide variety of data. In addition to the direct evidence derived from analyses of the floral and faunal assemblages from recent excavations, it is possible to draw inferences for other aspects of the economy from the material cultural assemblage. This approach, contextualised within the parameters of the communities described above, suggests that the basis of the economy was agricultural, supplemented by herding, hunting and in some cases fishing. The organisation of farming and issues such as land rights are beyond reconstruction from the archaeological record. Estimates of the land used for agricultural purposes range from 20% at *Tenta* to around 50% at Khirokitia.[57] However, the clear identification of groups of households at Khirokitia and the emphasis on the individual might argue for individual households working their own fields. Alternatively, the limited evidence for group mobilisation in public architectural works and the architectural configuration of the summit of *Tenta*, with an apparent specialised storage building, might argue for some centralised group control of land. The agricultural technology would have been based on hoe agriculture at this stage, implying that the fields being worked were small and supporting the hypothesis of individual households working their own land. As Le Brun emphasises, agricultural production and associated activities were at the very core of the concept of the household at Khirokitia.[58]

The economic basis, both arable and animal, was relatively speaking homogeneous throughout the island, although there are some variations

59

	Khirokitia-Vounoi	Kalavasos-Tenta	Cape Andreas-Kastros	Ayios Epiktitos-Vrysi
CEREALS				
Einkorn Tr. monococcum	•	•	•	•
Emmer Tr. dicoccum	•	•	•	•
Bread wheat Tr. aestivum				•
Barley Hordeum sp.	•	•	•	•
Rye Secale cereale				•
Oat Avena sp.				•
LEGUMES				
Lentil Lens culinaris	•	•	•	•
Pea Pisum sativum	•		•	•
Chickpea Cicer arietium				•
Grass pea Lathyrus sativus				•
WILD FRUITS				
Pistachio Pistacia sp.	•	•	•	•
Fig Ficus carica	•		•	•
Olive Oleaeuropea var. Oleaster	•		•	
Vine Vitis sylvestris	•			•
Apple Malus sp.				•
Micocoulier? Cetis australis				•
OTHER SPECIES				•
Flax Linum bienne / usitatissimum			•	•

Table 3.2. Range of archaeobotanical remains recovered from Cypriot aceramic and ceramic Neolithic sites (after Le Brun 1996, fig. 1).

between individual sites, in response to local conditions or distinctions in local diet. The main cultigens identified are einkorn and emmer wheat, barley, lentils and small quantities of pea (Table 3.2).[59] These include the three founder crops that were introduced to the island during the early aceramic Neolithic phase.[60] Although there is no evidence for orchard husbandry at this early date, wild fruits such as pistachio, fig, olive and wild plum also formed part of the aceramic Neolithic diet. Archaeobotanical remains from *Kastros* include flax, although it is not possible to determine whether it was wild or cultivated. The importance of agriculture to the aceramic Neolithic communities is indicated by isotopic analysis of bones from burials at Khirokitia. These indicate that cereals form the core element of the diet.[61] Moreover trace wear analysis of flint tools suggests that they were used for harvesting cereals.[62] The increasing importance that cereals played in the aceramic Neolithic economy would have impacted upon the local environment. Intensive cultivation certainly would have necessitated some form of land clearance, as is evidenced by the large number of ground stone axes in the toolkit. Individual households processed cereals, possibly from their own fields, hence the typical arrangement of quern installations in the courtyard area.

The presence of flax among the archaeobotanical remains from *Kastros* is interesting, and might allow us to interpret evidence for clothing. Certainly there are examples of mineralised textiles, and the bone needles suggest that sewing was an important craft activity. The aceramic Neolithic is believed to pre-date the so-called secondary products revolution suggested for the fourth and third millennia BC,[63] and therefore it is unlikely that sheep and goat were being bred for their wool. This is supported by Barber's fundamental study of ancient textile manufacture in which she illustrates that plant fibres, such as linen derived from flax, are the earliest archaeologically attested textiles and, moreover, that the earliest sheep and goat domesticates were short-haired species.[64] Animal skins were also probably used to make clothing, as is shown by the use of chipped stone scrapers.

Faunal remains comprise the typical Cypriot prehistoric trio of sheep/goat, pig and fallow deer (Table 3.3), species that are present throughout the Neolithic and Chalcolithic periods, and which were introduced to the island during the early aceramic Neolithic.[65] By the late aceramic Neolithic sheep and goat were domesticated, whereas during the early aceramic Neolithic pig was the only fully domesticated animal in the economic package. Fallow deer probably continued to be hunted and played a significant role in the late aceramic Neolithic economy. At *Tenta* it comprised around 50% of the faunal remains recovered from the site, but

	Khirokitia-*Vounoi*	Kalavasos-*Tenta*	Cape Andreas-*Kastros*	Krittou Marattou-*Ais Yiorkis*	Ayios Epiktitos-*Vrysi*
DOMESTICATES					
Sheep/goat	49%	20%	34%	16.1%	51%
Pig	*c.* 20%	30%	31%	38.2%	11%
Cattle				1.2%	
HUNTED					
Fallow deer	31%	50%	35%	44.5%	38%

Table 3.3. Neolithic faunal assemblages.

more typically constituted around a third of the faunal assemblage. It is not known how deer was hunted, as projectile points are lacking from the toolkit, but it is possible that they set traps or used nets.[66] Certainly the ethos of hunting continued to be important to the aceramic Neolithic communities and the organisation of this activity, although elusive, would give significant insights into social organisation. Although the aceramic Neolithic settlements share the same basic economy, there are variations between sites, suggesting variable subsistence strategies, or possibly variable sampling strategies employed by the different excavators. There are also certain modifications in the exploitation of animal resources through time.[67]

Marine resources played a limited role in the economy of the community resident at Khirokitia; there are no fishing tools at the site and fish bones are rare.[68] If the population did exploit marine resources they did not bring these back to the settlement, although there is no evidence to suggest that they did not exploit and consume marine resources at the coast. This is in contrast to the evidence from *Kastros*, which appears in effect to be a small fishing village. The *Kastros* tool assemblage includes fishhooks, and marine shells are common at the site, especially *Monodonta* (topshells) and *Patella* (limpets). Other marine species attested at *Kastros* include crab, sea urchins and fish bones. For the most part fishing activities were directed towards coastal species, but other seasonal migrating fish, such as tuna, are also represented (36.5% of the assemblage).[69]

The end of the aceramic Neolithic

A recurrent theme in Cypriot prehistory is the apparent site dislocation between different cultural and chronological phases. This is partly due to the nature of site formation on the island and continually shifting patterns of occupation. Unlike the contemporary Levant, characterised by multi-period *tell* sites, in Cyprus archaeological sites tend to be occupied for culturally discrete periods and subsequently abandoned. Consequently, there is frequently little depth of deposit and there are apparent gaps in the stratigraphic record between the different archaeological phases. This problem is compounded by the limited range of radiocarbon determinations. Not only is there a discontinuous cultural sequence, there is also a limited chronological sequence. The problem is further exacerbated by the apparent reversal to archaeologically elusive settlements with ephemeral architecture during many of these phases of settlement shift. Even so, the current trend for identifying previously unknown archaeological phases would definitely underline the archaeological axiom that during the Cypriot prehistoric periods absence of evidence is definitely not evidence for absence. The economic, climatic and cultural reasons for this shifting settlement pattern and apparent decline at the end of discrete archaeological phases needs to be addressed more fully in the archaeological literature.

At around 5000 BC the aceramic Neolithic sites were abandoned and the associated culture disappears suddenly from the archaeological record. The sites were not destroyed violently, and neither human agency nor natural causes are evident for this abandonment. The absence of finds *in situ* on the floors of the buildings at *Tenta* suggests to Todd that the inhabitants had had time to collect their possessions before leaving the site.[70] The reason for the abandonment remains enigmatic, but was possibly the result of environmental or demographic stress. Certainly there is a significant hiatus in the archaeological sequence before the establishment of the ceramic Neolithic on the island around 4000 BC. Some archaeologists suggest that this break in the cultural sequence represents a real gap in occupation and depopulation of the island which was subsequently resettled *c.* 4000 BC, resulting in the establishment of the Cypriot ceramic Neolithic.[71] Others argue for continuity of settlement during this apparent period of abandonment.[72] The origins of the ceramic Neolithic are thus disputed, and both viewpoints are impeded by lack of clear evidence.

The ceramic Neolithic

Origins

There is an apparent gap of around 500-1000 years separating the ceramic Neolithic (Sotira culture) occupation of Cyprus from its predecessor, the aceramic Neolithic, during which time it is difficult to document human occupation on the island. The re-appearance of settlements indicative of an increase in sedentary population between *c.* 5000-3900/3750 BC (Table 3.4)[73] is characterised by several substantial cultural transformations. Most notable is the introduction of a ceramic technology to the island. This seemingly appeared fully formed with no development or learning phase, suggesting to some archaeologists that it was brought to the island by people who were fully aware of the plastic properties of clay, specifically how to form, decorate and fire vessels.[74] Other innovations include novel forms of architecture, settlement organisation and the organisation of domestic space, and changes in funerary practices. The origins of this culture are obscure and two distinct scenarios have been posited. The first of these argues for the arrival of a new population group on the island, bringing the new ceramic technology and architectural tradition. The alternate hypothesis argues for internal development on the island, and at the most cultural assimilation of the new traits.[75]

The migration theory effectively argues for an hiatus in occupation between the aceramic and ceramic Neolithic phases – although whether the island was completely deserted by the human population or whether it declined significantly in numbers and reverted to a more nomadic, archaeologically ephemeral lifestyle, is unclear. The colonisation hypothesis is largely dependent on the apparent defensive character of the ceramic

Site	C-14 date BP	1 standard deviation (BC)	2 standard deviations (BC)
Ayios Epiktitos-*Vrysi*	5389 ± 53	4330 – 4150	4350 – 4040
Ayios Epiktitos-*Vrysi*	5372 ± 92	4330 – 4050	4360 – 3980
Ayios Epiktitos-*Vrysi*	5360 ± 57	4330 – 4080	4340 – 4040
Ayios Epiktitos-*Vrysi*	5825 ± 145	4900 – 4510	5050 – 4350
Ayios Epiktitos-*Vrysi*	5740 ± 140	4780 – 4460	4950 – 4300
Ayios Epiktitos-*Vrysi*	5420 ± 80	4350 – 4150	4460 – 4040
Ayios Epiktitos-*Vrysi*	5355 ± 67	4320 – 4040	4340 – 4000
Ayios Epiktitos-*Vrysi*	5340 ± 95	4320 – 4040	4350 – 3970
Ayios Epiktitos-*Vrysi*	5330 ± 57	4240 – 4040	4330 – 3990
Ayios Epiktitos-*Vrysi*	5275 ± 47	4220 – 4000	4230 – 3980
Ayios Epiktitos-*Vrysi*	5255 ± 120	4230 – 3960	4350 – 3800
Ayios Epiktitos-*Vrysi*	5210 ± 85	4220 – 3940	4240 – 3790
Ayios Epiktitos-*Vrysi*	5360 ± 110	4330 – 4040	4450 – 3960
Ayios Epiktitos-*Vrysi*	3105 ± 130	1520 – 1160	1700 – 950
Ayios Epiktitos-*Vrysi*	5224 ± 78	4220 – 3960	4250 – 3800
Ayios Epiktitos-*Vrysi*	5290 ± 100	4230 – 3990	4350 – 3800
Ayios Epiktitos-*Vrysi*	5360 ± 110	4330 – 4040	4450 – 3960
Dhali-*Agridhi*	6415 ± 310	5600 – 4950	6000 – 4600
Dhali-*Agridhi*	5700 ± 100	4690 – 4400	4770 – 4350
Sotira-*Teppes*	5460 ± 110	4460 – 4150	4550 – 4000
Sotira-*Teppes*	5150 ± 130	4220 – 3780	4350 – 3650
Philia-*Drakos*	5720 ± 100	4690 – 4460	4780 – 4350
Kalavasos-*Tenta*	5460 ± 110	4460 – 4150	4550 – 4000
Kalavasos-*Pamboules*	5140 ± 110	4080 – 3780	4250 – 3700

Table 3.4. Radiocarbon determinations for the ceramic Neolithic (after Clarke 2001, table 1).

Neolithic settlements, implying unease with regards to the surrounding landscape,[76] and the novel cultural characteristics of the ceramic Neolithic. Dikaios suggested the Beersheban *facies* of southern Palestine as one possible source of the ceramic Neolithic,[77] but several aspects are lacking, namely ovens, churns, stone vases, cattle, metalwork, and ossuaries. Indeed, it is difficult to identify specifically foreign elements in the ceramic Neolithic, which moreover appears to lag behind contemporary developments in the Asiatic mainland cultures, such as the introduction of metallurgy. In favour of the migration theory is the apparent disappearance of the aceramic Neolithic followed by around 1000 years of apparent non-occupation by human groups and the subsequent appearance of the fully formed ceramic Neolithic. However, the recent developments in the earliest prehistory of Cyprus signal that we should be very cautious of forming hypotheses based on apparent gaps in the archaeological record. The alternative hypothesis is of local development. This is based on small quantities of ceramic material (Dark Faced Burnished ware: Fig. 3.8) found at certain sites apparently dating to the fifth millennium BC. Stratigraphically, the Dark Faced Burnished ware predates and is gradually replaced by the characteristic Broad Line Red on White ceramic style typical of the ceramic Neolithic. The occupation phase represented by this material might bridge the apparent gap between the aceramic and the

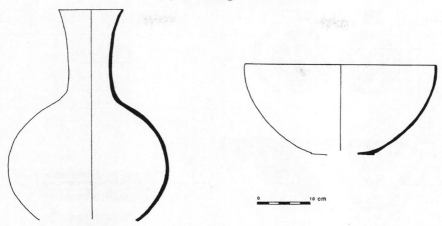

Fig. 3.8. Dark Faced Burnished ware pottery from Dhali-*Agridhi*.

ceramic Neolithic. Certainly, in favour of local development of the ceramic Neolithic is the apparent continuity in the economic basis, in particular exploitation of the 'Cypriot prehistoric trio' of sheep/goat, pig and fallow deer. If these innovations were introduced by newcomers, this population failed to introduce new breeds of livestock to the island. The continued absence of cattle is particularly striking in this respect.

The ceramic sequence

Although the chronological and cultural sequence has undergone substantial revision, the basic framework for the prehistoric period is that established by Dikaios.[78] The pottery typology that he developed for the Neolithic distinguished between the Broad Line Red on White style (Broad Line RW) from Klepini-*Troulli* Period II and the Combed ware typical of Sotira, interpreting the *Troulli* ceramics as antecedent in the sequence. The typology was subsequently refined following excavations at Ayios Epiktitos-*Vrysi* and Philia-*Drakos* A, by the University of Edinburgh. Watkins identified a new class of pottery at Philia-*Drakos*, Dark Faced Burnished ware, which he suggested should go in the gap between the final aceramic and earliest ceramic Neolithic. In effect he proposed a ceramic sequence beginning with the Dark Faced Burnished ware, which was superseded by the RW and which culminated in the Combed ware.[79] Sequential ceramic typologies form the backbone of the Cypriot cultural and chronological sequences of the Bronze and Iron Ages; however these have been criticised more recently in the archaeological literature, as they impose rigid systems that do not allow for continuity of ceramic styles between phases nor for regional variations.[80] The scheme developed by Peltenburg, following his excavations at *Vrysi*, responds to these shortcomings by

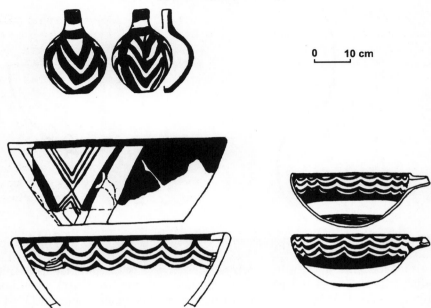

0   10 cm

Fig. 3.9. Red on White pottery from Ayios Epiktitos-*Vrysi*.

proposing that the differences in ceramics resulted from regional rather diachronic variation. According to the traditional sequence proposed by Dikaios and refined by Watkins, *Vrysi* should have predated the main phase of the ceramic Neolithic, as it was characterised by Broad Line RW (Fig. 3.9). However, the totality of the evidence from *Vrysi*, its settlement organisation, domestic architecture, and material culture, is broadly comparable to the material from Sotira-*Teppes*.[81] Moreover, the radiocarbon determinations (Table 3.4) place *Vrysi* firmly within the ceramic Neolithic sequence, contemporary with Sotira. Therefore, in a further modification to Dikaios' chronological sequence, the Neolithic Phase 1b (characterised by the Broad Line RW from *Troulli* II) was conflated with the Neolithic II (characterised by the Combed ware from Sotira). The apparent ceramic differences were attributed to regional variation. This main ceramic Neolithic phase was apparently preceded by the ephemeral phase identified by Watkins at Philia-*Drakos* and also at Dhali-*Agridhi*, and defined by its Dark Faced Burnished pottery.

Settlement and identity

The settlement pattern of the ceramic Neolithic resembles that of its precursor (see Fig. 3.1) in that it is largely concentrated around the coastal zone, although there are a number of inland sites, such as Dhali-*Agridhi*.

66

The mountainous regions (the Troodos massif and Kyrenia range) still appear to be beyond the range of human settlement. Moreover, the ceramic Neolithic has not been identified in the western part of the island, or in the Karpass peninsula. The characteristic settlement type is a small village (between 0.5 and 1.5 ha) located on high ground, most notably the type site Sotira-*Teppes*. There are also a number of smaller sites, characterised by substantial pitting but with no extant architectural structures, such as Kalavasos-*Kokkinoyia*, Dhali-*Agridhi* (Fig. 3.10), and Mari-*Paliambela*.[82] There is some occupation over earlier aceramic Neolithic settlements, at Kalavasos-*Tenta*, Khirokitia and *Troulli*,[83] but for the most part the settlements were founded on virgin ground. There was a 'defensive' aspect to settlement, indicated by their location atop defendable hills, as at Sotira and Klepini-*Troulli*, or on remote headlands, as at *Vrysi*. Settlements might also be protected by a circuit wall or ditch, such as Philia-*Drakos* and *Vrysi*.

The economic and social relationship between the various ceramic Neolithic settlements is unclear, but Clarke proposes three levels of social

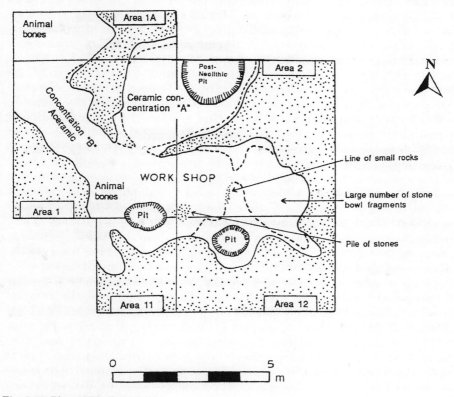

Fig. 3.10. Plan of Dhali-*Agridhi*.

relationship.[84] Clusters of sites are identified in certain areas, such as the Kalavasos cluster (including *Tenta*, *Pamboules*, *Kokkinoyia* and Mari-*Paliambela*). These, she suggests, belong to the same community, possibly with different sites serving different functional needs or being seasonally occupied within an itinerant, nomadic lifestyle. Such economic or seasonal variations need to be demonstrated archaeologically. The second group compares larger village settlements in close geographical proximity, such as Sotira-*Teppes* and Kandou-*Kouphovounos*, or *Vrysi* and *Troulli*. The relationship between these settlements is more uncertain. On the one hand they might be expected to be in direct competition over economic resources, on the other their proximity might indicate close cultural ties expressed through a common parentage, exogamic links and possibly mutually beneficial economic links. At the highest level there is the overall settlement pattern and the possibility of contact and interaction between distant groups, or alternatively cultural and economic isolation. These putative links might be explored through analyses of the material culture.

The ceramic Neolithic is characterised by an homogeneous material culture. Certain distinctive elements of the cultural repertoire – in particular common house types and the similar ceramic repertoire, the latter being indicative of shared patterns of food preparation and consumption – might argue for the creation of a common cultural identity,[85] which was distinct from extraneous identities beyond the island. This is also implied by shared economic practices and in particular the maintenance of the hunting ethos that is so characteristic of the Cypriot prehistoric period. The outstanding feature of this cultural standardisation is the probable difficulty of communication overland, through forested and mountainous terrain.[86] That this occurred, however infrequently, is indicated by the small-scale exchange of picrolite. Even so, the causes and dynamics of cultural cohesion during the ceramic Neolithic remain elusive. The probable economic catchment area of a village has been estimated to have a radius of around 3 km,[87] which would result in neighbouring settlements coming into contact with each other. However, hunting groups might have ranged far further afield in search of fallow deer. The population of any individual settlement has been estimated at around 500 individuals, implying that the ceramic Neolithic communities would have been dependent on exogamy for survival. However, such contacts might be expected to result in internal stress, hence the defensive aspects of the settlement. Consequently, within the overall cultural homogeneity of the ceramic Neolithic, there might be evidence for the expression of more localised cultural identities. This has already been expressed, to a certain extent, by Peltenburg's identification of regional variation in pottery styles,[88] and more recently Clarke has re-examined the pottery from the perspective of style. Clarke argues that there is significant enough variation in the range of decorative motifs within either the Combed ware or RW traditions between neighbouring sites to argue for the use of symbolic style as a means of expressing group identity. The choice of Combed ware versus RW, reflecting wider regional variation, might be attributed to an expression of emblemic style expressing more ingrained cultural differences between groups.[89]

Organisation of space

The configuration of settlement during the ceramic Neolithic is best illustrated by Sotira and *Vrysi*.[90] The settlement at Sotira (Fig. 3.11) occupied the plateau and southern slopes of a prominent hill that dominates a wide valley.[91] Most excavation concentrated on the plateau, uncovering a consistent pattern of settlement. The houses are free-standing and largely share the same orientation. Moreover, there is no discernible variation in house type, size or contents,[92] suggesting an egalitarian society with household-based activities rather than craft specialisation located within discrete areas of the settlement. There are two destruction levels at Sotira, one during Phase 1b and the other at the end of Phase 2.[93] During the earlier destruction level the houses were destroyed by fire, and the second appears to be the result of an earthquake.[94] The configuration of the site alters dramatically between the initial Phase 1, which is characterised by fairly sparse occupation and plenty of space between the houses, and the densely packed settlement plan of Phases 2 and 3, with houses packed together over the available space of the plateau.[95] Following the second destruction, the site was almost immediately reoccupied. No new houses were built but instead the debris on the house floors was flattened and the Phase 2 houses were re-used. However, a massive retaining wall was constructed along the northern edge of the plateau.[96]

Vrysi is located on a coastal headland, and in the excavated west area occupation was located in two sectors on either side of a ridge of undisturbed soil 3 m wide (Fig. 3.12). On either side of this ridge the configuration of the promontory was considerably altered by the human occupation, in particular the construction of massive hollows up to 6 m in depth. The houses were built into these hollows and were therefore semi-subterranean.[97] During the earliest phase of occupation the headland was protected by a defensive ditch cut through the southern sector. The architecture associated with this phase comprises simple timber constructions in the north sector associated with RW pottery. Soundings indicate that these are not the earliest habitations at the site.[98] The main occupational phase at *Vrysi* during the Middle Phase is characterised by contiguous structures built of stone and pisé constructed within the hollows. The space between groups of houses consisted of narrow winding passageways, wide enough for a single person.[99] There are continuous building episodes of houses, resulting in a rather columnar arrangement of buildings stacked on top of each other. A notable feature is the general continuity in terms of the use of space and internal arrangement of fittings between the

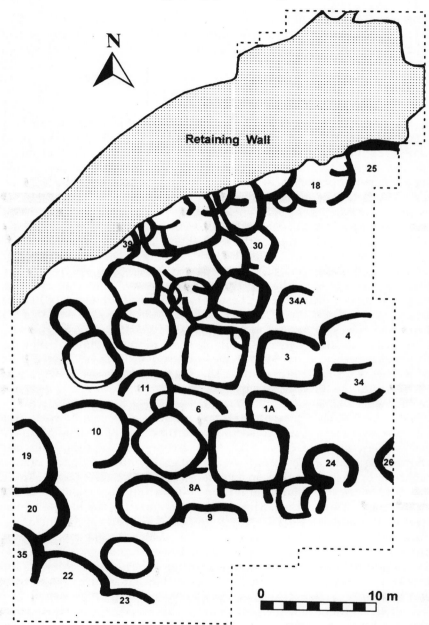

Fig. 3.11. Plan of Sotira-*Teppes*.

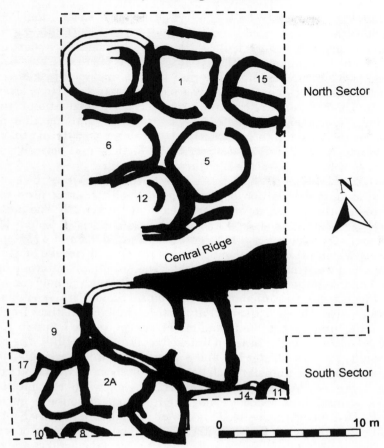

Fig. 3.12. Plan of Ayios Epiktitos-*Vrysi*.

different building phases.[100] The settlement configuration at *Troulli*, with its contiguous architecture, recalls that of *Vrysi*. Likewise, the site is located on a promontory.[101]

At neither site is there any open space suitable for public congregation, nor is there any unequivocal evidence for social hierarchy in the form of larger structures, which stand out from the norm in terms of construction, size or contents. Even so, Peltenburg suggests that there was a clear disparity between the northern and southern sectors at *Vrysi*, which was revealed through quantitative analyses of the buildings' contents.[102] The north and south sectors were separated by a ridge, which Peltenburg maintains acted as a natural barrier throughout the use of the site, effectively creating two distinct social groups. The northern sector was the older area of occupation, and Peltenburg notes that more artefacts were

71

recovered from the floors of the north sector buildings. In addition, Peltenburg notes the unique occurrence of apparent ritual equipment from
within the northern sector of the settlement. Particularly important is
House 1, which occupies a central position and is located in the longest
occupied part of the site. Here internal fixtures include upright stones
(interpreted as baetyls) in the northwest corner demarcated by a low wall
(Fig. 3.15: C).[103] Peltenburg concludes that there is a correlation between
the older, wealthier sector and ritual expression, implying that older
lineages were located in the northern part of the settlement and that this
group retained privileged access to ritual practices and actively maintained the exclusive character of the northern sector.

The central building (Hut Γ), in Area C at *Troulli* crowning the summit
of the promontory,[104] is one of the largest Neolithic structures so far
uncovered on the island, covering an area of at least 25m². The building
had post supports for the roof, and internal installations include three
querns and a bin feature comprising five upright slabs and a horizontal
slab, from which we might infer that preparation and storage of agricultural produce were important activities.[105] The prominent situation of the
building and its large size might indicate that this building held some sort
of significance for the inhabitants of *Troulli*, though its exact nature
remains elusive. House 7 (floor 2) at *Vrysi* is similarly distinct from the
surrounding architectural units and might interpreted as a building used
for central or communal storage of finished tools and foodstuffs. The house
was equipped with a plaster bin and a stone bin, but surprisingly lacked
the normal domestic utensils, such as querns, associated with food preparation. Even so, other finds were prolific, as were the mollusca,
archaeobotanical and archaeozoological remains. Peltenburg suggests
that these were beyond the basic needs of an individual household and
should be interpreted as communal storage.[106] The construction of retaining and enclosure walls at Sotira and other sites, and the hollows and ditch
at *Vrysi*[107] illustrate some form of mobilisation of labour, but the underlying mechanics are unclear. At present, the overall architectural indices of
the ceramic Neolithic are more indicative of egalitarian communities.

The household

Although there is a certain degree of inter-site variation in the actual
configuration of the settlements, they share the same basic architectural
unit, the ceramic Neolithic house (Fig. 3.13).[108] At Sotira these houses are
largely free-standing, whereas at *Vrysi* and *Troulli* the architecture is
contiguous. The typical house plan is square, with rounded corners. The
houses have only a single room and are one storey high. At *Vrysi* the houses
had an average floor space of 14.2 m², whereas at Sotira it is around 16 m².
The houses were built of mudbrick or pisé on a foundation of stones, and
the interior surface was plastered. Timber (pine) was used extensively, for

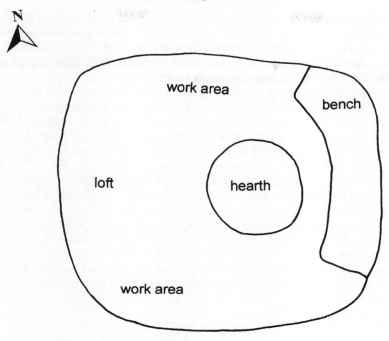

Fig. 3.13. Schematic *Vrysi* house plan showing activity areas.

posts to support the roof, for beams, and at *Vrysi* to brace the walls.[109] Flat roofs of reed and mud, similar to those at aceramic Khirokitia, and conical roofs are both attested.[110] There was a single entrance into the house, usually with a step down to the floor of packed clay or mud. Standard internal features and installations include prominent off-centre hearths, pisé or stone benches against walls, a corner area demarcated by a semi-circular wall, and earth-fast utensils in clusters.[111] Peltenburg suggests that these single hearthed structures were built explicitly to house single nuclear families of three to four individuals.[112] Stanley-Price, however, argues that the floor space was insufficient for even a nuclear family and instead suggests that complex households lived in groups of structures or subsidiary buildings grouped around a large structure.[113]

The density of artefacts and domestic installations recovered on the house floors of the various sites has allowed some reconstruction of the domestic use of space within these settlements. Peltenburg comments on the density of artefacts, hearths and domestic installations on the house floors at *Vrysi*, and suggests that these were largely given over to a range of domestic activities, such as the preparation of food, and household-based craft production. The actual living or sleeping space he suggests was probably outside the buildings, or inside in loft areas.[114] The repetition of the specific internal arrangement of furnishings is suggestive of an ideal-ised type of spatial organisation.[115] Clusters of portable artefacts are found against house walls, next to the benches, which might indeed have func-tioned as work platforms, suggesting that a variety of craft activities took place at the edge of the floor surface around the house walls.[116] Similar studies of the artefact assemblages at Sotira illustrate the household organisation of a variety of craft industries. Stanley-Price notes that pottery production was organised within the household. Specific indices for this activity include chalcedony pebbles, used to burnish the pot surface to its characteristic lustrous finish, and stone grinders used in the prepa-ration of the lumps of iron-rich ochre found in Houses 3, 5 and 7.[117] It is suggested that at Sotira the pottery was fired in large circular clay platforms, and Peltenburg notes the similarity in diameter of bowls and fire-pits at *Vrysi* and Sotira, suggesting that the pottery was somehow fired on these hearths in the houses.[118] Other household industries include production of chipped stone tools, picrolite and bone ornaments, and stone grinding. Stanley-Price argues that at Sotira these tend to be located in the large (older) structures in the centre of the plateau, and Peltenburg has noted a similar concentration of craft activities in the older northern sector at *Vrysi*.[119]

Material culture

The ceramic Neolithic is characterised by a standard range of equipment (Fig. 3.14), apparently produced within the household, with no apparent evidence for craft specialisation. Typical elements include limestone ves-sels, chipped stone tools, picrolite and bone ornaments,[120] ground stone tools such as pestles, mortars, rubbers, querns, and pierced discs inter-preted as spindle whorls, either for wool or more probably for plant fibres.[121] Axes, adzes and chisels are common,[122] indicating that woodwork-ing was an important craft activity. Moreover, such tools would be impor-tant for clearance of the dense woodland around *Vrysi* for arable purposes. These tools were found occasionally with grooved limestones, which Peltenburg suggests were used as whetstones for sharpening the blades.[123] A large number of picrolite ornaments have been uncovered at Kandou-*Kouphovounos*. These no doubt illustrate the inhabitants' privileged access to picrolite, which would have been procured from the nearby Kouris river. Also of interest at the site is a large deposit of unworked jasper pebbles.

The most characteristic feature of the material repertoire is the pot-tery.[124] The mode of production, using local clay beds and simple coil-made vessels apparently fired on open hearths, is consistent with household production. The range of forms is very limited and is common throughout the island. The repertoire comprises a series of hemispherical bowls (frequently spouted: see Plate 8), ovoid jugs/bottles (see Plate 9) with a nipple base, and hole-mouth jars, all made in the decorated wares. Shallow

74

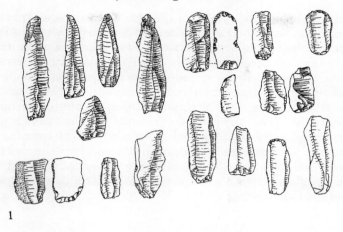

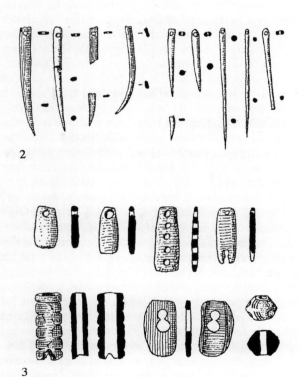

Fig. 3.14. Ceramic Neolithic cultural assemblage: (1) flakes; (2) bone tools; (3) bone and stone ornaments, from Sotira-*Teppes*.

trays with a pierced wall are made in the Coarse ware. This common pottery tradition flourished at all ceramic Neolithic sites, the only apparent distinction being the actual mode of decoration, either in the Broad Line RW or in the Combed ware style. The RW style is more characteristic of the northern sites and the Combed ware of the southern sites.[125] The former decorative style is characterised by the application of motifs in red paint on a white ground, and the latter by the application of red paint over the surface of the vessel and the use of a multi-toothed tool to remove this surface in straight or wavy parallel lines while still wet, creating a sort of ripple pattern. The regional variation first noted by Peltenburg has recently been developed by Clarke, who suggests that variations in the combinations of motifs are explicit examples of the use of style in the expression of group identity.[126]

Symbolic and spiritual expression

The cultural repertoire displays a deafening silence when it comes to the symbolic or spiritual aspect of ceramic Neolithic society. Particularly notable by their almost total absence are figurines, in stark contrast to the rich repertoire of ceramic anthropomorphic and zoomorphic figures from other Neolithic and Chalcolithic societies of the Eastern Mediterranean.[127] Two stone figurines, extremely schematic in form, are attested at Sotira and *Vrysi*[128] in domestic contexts (Fig. 3.15: B). Both figures are similar in form, possibly representing a schematic human (female?) body, the legs indicated by a vertical incision and the head by a constriction around the body. No facial features are represented. However, alternative readings of these figurines note their clear reference to male genitalia. Similar ambiguity is expressed in a limestone seated figure from Sotira-*Arkolies* measuring 16 cm in height (Fig. 3.15: A). Like the figurines from *Vrysi* and Sotira-*Teppes*, it is clearly phallic, but it also represents a figure in a seated birthing position, and other views, from the top, bottom, front and back, clearly represent both male and female genitalia. This ambiguity in representations of gender and sexuality are themes that become central to Chalcolithic representations of the body.[129] A schematic anthropomorphic limestone figurine, a rare picrolite figurine and a fragment of a clay figurine have been found in the settlement deposits at Kandou-*Kouphovounos*.

Enigmatic spiritual beliefs and ritual practices are indicated by the arrangement of a group of three stone pillars in the northwest corner of House 1 at *Vrysi*, within a clearly demarcated limestone kerb boundary. The pillars, one of which was clearly phallic (Fig. 3.15: C),[130] were wrapped in matting or possibly a woven cloth made from vegetable fibres, which survive as silicates. Domestic utensils (a pestle and grinder) were found with these pillars. The actual rituals associated with these stones are enigmatic, but the overall phallic nature of these representations suggests that fertility was a prime concern of the late Neolithic communities on

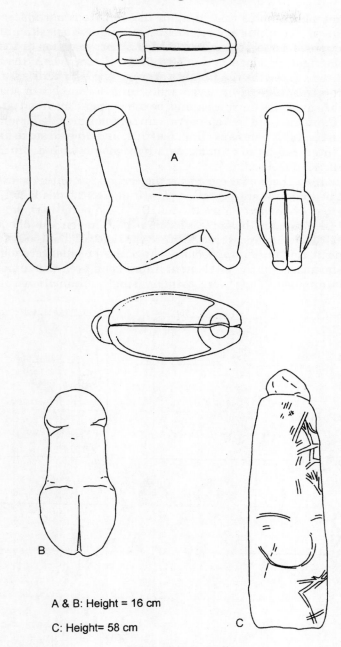

A & B: Height = 16 cm

C: Height= 58 cm

Fig. 3.15. Ceramic Neolithic symbolic material: (A) stone figurine from Sotira-*Arkolies*;
(B) stone figure from Sotira-*Teppes*; (C) carved stone pillar from Ayios Epiktitos-*Vrysi*.

Cyprus. Peltenburg notes that, despite the abundant portable material found *in situ* at *Vrysi*, this arrangement was unique, suggesting that it is not an example of domestic cult but defines House 1 as a special building. Likewise, Peltenburg suggests that House 5 at Sotira, where the figurine was found, was likewise a distinct structure with specialised ritual or ceremonial connotations.[131] A large subterranean complex of shafts and tunnels with multiple entrances and benches was excavated at Philia-*Drakos* A. Contents from this subterranean complex included quantities of animal bone, possibly remnants from feasting, and unused stone axes. The excavator interpreted the complex as a hypogaeum with a ritual rather than utilitarian purpose.[132]

Unfortunately the burial record for the ceramic Neolithic is extremely limited, impeding full interpretation of attitudes to the dead. Only twelve burials were excavated at Sotira (Fig. 3.16),[133] and none at *Vrysi*, suggesting that at the latter site burial was extramural. The remains of both adult and child burials were uncovered beneath the floors of a building in recent excavations at Kandou-*Kouphovounos*. At Sotira burials were found only on the eastern slope of the settlement, in an open area where household debris was dumped. They were primary single inhumations placed in

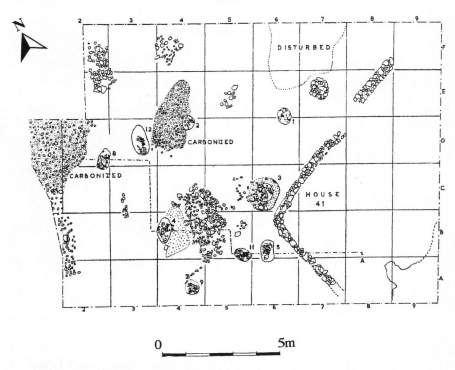

Fig. 3.16. Plan of Sotira-*Teppes* showing location of burials.

simple oval pit graves dug into a midden of ash, stone and animal bone. The bodies were placed in a contracted position on their side and covered by stones. There is no evidence that the burials were equipped with grave goods.[134] These remains indicate a desire to remove the dead from the habitation space of the living, in marked contrast to the burial of the dead below the floors of houses during the aceramic Neolithic, although they are still retained within the confines of the settlement. The juxtaposition of the dead with the settlement midden is particularly interesting. Ethnographic analogy demonstrates that space is laden with meaning and is culturally constructed, and also that attitudes to rubbish and death are culturally specific. The juxtaposition of rubbish and death, such as is evident at Sotira, is not simply a matter of chance but is a statement of cultural attitudes.[135] At Kandou-*Kouphovounos* the placement of the dead continued to be within the domestic structure, beneath the floor. The diversity of burial practices during the ceramic Neolithic bespeaks very differing attitudes to the dead throughout the island. The data is presently too limited to explore this in greater detail.

Economy

The evidence, largely from *Vrysi* but supplemented by Sotira, suggests a mixed economy with an agricultural basis, supplemented by herding and hunting of animals and exploitation of marine resources.[136] Direct evidence for cultivation of plants comes from *Vrysi*, and is represented by poorly preserved archaeobotanical remains from house floors and middens (Table 3.2). These indicate that the basic arable base derives from the aceramic Neolithic, although there are a number of new species being cultivated, namely bread wheat, rye, oats and chick peas. Pistachio, fig, olive, vine and apple probably represent exploitation of wild fruits rather than the development of orchard farming. The artefactual evidence from other sites supplements the floral samples from *Vrysi*, and allows us to interpret how these foodstuffs were incorporated within the late Neolithic diet. Flint blades with sickle gloss illustrate the harvesting of cereals, and from the large numbers of axes and adzes we might infer clearance of woodland in preparation of arable land. The decline in pig in the faunal assemblage similarly illustrates the move towards open farmland rather than wooded terrain immediately around the settlement. The abundant rubbers, querns, pestles and mortars were no doubt used in processing cereals and legumes. The absence of ovens implies that these foodstuffs were consumed as gruel rather than being baked as bread.

The faunal assemblage at *Vrysi* is well preserved but very fragmentary and comparatively sparse, suggesting that rather than creating middens around the settlement area the inhabitants tended to throw debris off the promontory into the sea.[137] It comprises the typical Cypriot prehistoric trio of sheep/goat, pig and fallow deer (Table 3.3). Unlike the agricultural basis, no new elements were introduced, which might suggest cultural continuity from the preceding aceramic Neolithic. Caprines (sheep and goat) are predominant, comprising 51% of the total faunal assemblage, whereas domesticated pig makes up only around 11%. The continued importance of fallow deer is indicated by the large quantity of deer bones, around 38% of the assemblage. There has been extensive discussion of whether these deer were hunted or whether the ancient inhabitants of Cyprus practised herd management.[138] However, the bones from *Vrysi* suggest that the deer were hunted and butchered at kill sites at some distance from the settlement, only the rich meat-bearing bones being brought back to the site.[139] Other animal bones from *Vrysi* include remains of five or six domesticated dogs, cat, fox and a number of reptiles, birds and rodents. The ubiquitous presence of spouted bowls in the ceramic repertoire indicates that the diet included an important liquid element, possibly that the caprines were being exploited for their milk products. This might be answered through lipid analyses of the sherd material. There is indirect evidence for textile production, specifically the identification of spindle whorls and needles. Although these might be indirect evidence for greater emphasis on sheep/goat at *Vrysi*[140] it is more probable that the early textiles were based on plant fibres, such as flax which was certainly being cultivated.[141]

Recently Clarke has argued against an agro-pastoralist economy for the ceramic Neolithic, instead preferring to interpret the economic evidence in terms of a more mobile lifestyle, following deer herds.[142] This is largely dependent on the large quantities of deer bones that have been retrieved from a number of sites, such as Philia, Sotira and Dhali-*Agridhi*. These suggest that fallow deer bones are predominant at a number of sites, although the quantities Clarke cites for *Vrysi* are erroneous and caprines are the predominant species. Moreover the retrieval techniques for the earlier excavations at Sotira might be questioned, and it would be dubious to base interpretations of the economy on these remains. For the other sites with high quantities of deer bone, and ephemeral architectural remains, there is the possibility that these represent specialised kill-sites. The importance of hunting and deer to the Cypriot economy should be emphasised. Indeed it continued to be an important element of the Cypriot economy well into the Bronze Age, at which point the agricultural basis of the economy is in no doubt.[143] Moreover, many elements of the settlement organisation and artefacts actually argue for a sedentary agricultural basis to the economy. The continuous occupation levels at *Vrysi* and Sotira are suggestive of sedentary communities, as are the artefactual assemblages with emphasis on woodworking tools for land clearance and tools for processing cereals. Likewise the introduction of pottery as a primary element of the cultural repertoire is suggestive of settled agricultural communities. On the other hand, the importance of hunting would require specific kill-sites and certain adaptations to a more mobile lifestyle in parallel to the farming villages, which might be reflected in the diversity of settlement types.

Marine species were also exploited by the community at *Vrysi*, as befits a small village located on a coastal promontory. *Patella* and *Monodonta* are the most commonly represented molluscs, comprising 76% of the total number of sea shells found.[144] Although the inhabitants exploited the marine resources from the coastal fringe there is no evidence that they actively fished the waters, as fish bones are infrequently represented in the faunal assemblages.[145]

The end of the Neolithic

Peltenburg has categorised the ceramic Neolithic as the establishment of sedentary farming communities on Cyprus, associated with an apparent increase in population.[146] The duration of occupation within the ceramic Neolithic villages and their chronological and cultural relationship with the subsequent Chalcolithic settlement of Cyprus have yet to be fully addressed. The various settlements of the ceramic Neolithic all appear short-lived, according to their stratigraphy, the depth of deposit and the corresponding radiometric evidence, which suggests a maximum duration of between 500 and 1000 years. The transition between the ceramic Neolithic and the subsequent Chalcolithic settlement of Cyprus is difficult to document fully for many of the reasons that bedevil the inception of this phase. There appears to be an island-wide abandonment of settlements, although given the limited radiocarbon assays for the ceramic Neolithic and the problems of synchronising developments across the island, it is impossible to say whether this abandonment was contemporaneous. Certainly at Philia, *Vrysi* and Sotira the excavators noted a break in the occupation of the sites prior to their abandonment, and at Sotira this was interpreted as evidence for earthquake damage. The radiocarbon dates for the subsequent Chalcolithic occupation of Cyprus suggest a hiatus of around 600 years, although there is still no adequate series of determinations for the Early Chalcolithic period.[147] The Early Chalcolithic remains from Kissonerga-*Mosphilia*, Period 2, have helped to close the gap, but there are still insufficient radiocarbon determinations to be sure of the exact chronological and cultural relationship between the ceramic Neolithic and the Chalcolithic periods. Certain features indicate cultural continuity, or at least that the antecedents of the Chalcolithic lie within the ceramic Neolithic. These include the ceramic tradition, the basic agro-pastoralist economy, especially the continued emphasis on hunting deer, and certain aspects of symbolic representation. Other features, most notably the substantial shift in settlement location, in particular the initial occupation of the southwestern reaches of the island, and the internal configuration of settlement and domestic space, suggest substantive shifts in social organisation and cultural traditions. The question remains whether the Neolithic-Chalcolithic interface represents an island-wide dislocation in settlement or whether there was uninterrupted development between the phases, with localised regional disruptions in settlement.

The cause of the abandonment of the ceramic Neolithic villages is unknown, but this settlement discontinuity, already seen at the end of the aceramic Neolithic, is one of the defining characteristics of the prehistoric Cypriot settlement record. To a certain extent it can be accounted for by the elusive, ephemeral nature of settlement during the transitional phases, which are difficult to detect archaeologically; however, this is descriptive rather than explanatory. Whatever the internal Cypriot impetus to settlement dislocation, be it economic or social stress, this still needs to be explored. Peltenburg has suggested that this discontinuity is a factor of 'communal fissioning', which he views as a social response to the excessive concentration of agricultural wealth and economic power in the hands of a select group in society, an internal levelling mechanism.[148] However, this does not seem an adequate explanation for the disruption to the earliest farming communities of Cyprus at the end of the aceramic and ceramic Neolithic periods.

The Age of Copper

Genesis of the Cypriot Chalcolithic

At the end of the ceramic Neolithic there was a major disruption to the settlement sequence on Cyprus. This is marked by the wholesale abandonment of the ceramic Neolithic sites and an apparent gap in occupation of around 600 years before the establishment of the Cypriot Chalcolithic period.[1] However, this scenario is based on a very limited series of radiocarbon determinations (largely from *Vrysi*) and limited understanding of the nature and extent of the earliest stage of the Cypriot Chalcolithic. A few sites throw some light on the nature of the transitional phase between the ceramic Neolithic and the Chalcolithic periods. These are attributed to the Early Chalcolithic phase, as many of its cultural features are antecedent to the full Chalcolithic, and are dated to around 4000-3500 BC by a series of radiocarbon determinations.[2] The transitional Early Chalcolithic period is characterised by ephemeral architecture, which reflects its transient nature. Yet it is also marked by a number of transformations that are critical in the formation and development of the subsequent culture and ideology of Chalcolithic Cyprus. These include a major shift in settlement pattern (Fig. 4.1) and concentration of occupation in the chalk lowlands of the southwest of the island and the development of a new ideological expression, illustrated by the figurines. The major innovation of the Early Chalcolithic period is the first attempts at copper metallurgy. The earliest copper artefacts, such as a chisel tip from Erimi and a hook from Kissonerga-*Mylouthkia*,[3] are extremely rare finds and were made using a simple hammered technology from native copper. Other innovations include more extensive exploitation of picrolite and the development of communal activities based around intensified agricultural production, such as increased storage facilities and communal cooking and feasting.[4] Other aspects, however, imply cultural continuity from the preceding ceramic Neolithic population, in particular the economy and household crafts such as pottery, which continues the Red on White tradition.

A notable feature of Early Chalcolithic sites is the lack of standing architectural remains. For the most part these sites are characterised by ephemeral structures, a change that has important implications for possible interpretations of settlement dislocation at the Neolithic/Chalcolithic interface. Abandonment of the Neolithic 'fortified' villages might indicate

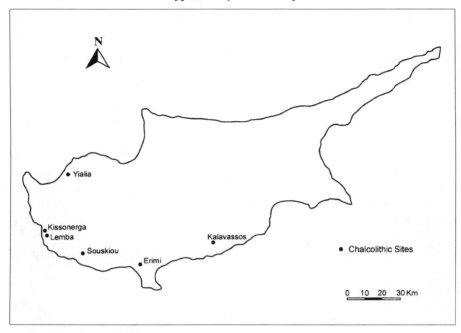

Fig. 4.1. Map of Chalcolithic settlements in Cyprus.

internal stress or population pressure, but intriguingly at such a time the population moved away from easily protected sites. More plausibly the shift in settlement and the changing settlement type reflect economic and social transformations,[5] the nature of which have yet to be identified. The architectural remains from the Early Chalcolithic levels are elusive, usually comprising shallow hollows, pits of varying size and postholes.[6] This suggests that the structures were flimsy, presumably built from organic materials such as timber, wattle and daub, which only survive in negative in the archaeological record. Some pits and hollows, with peripheral settings of posts to support a light covering, were apparently used as dwellings. Floor surfaces have been identified in some larger pits, interspersed with layers of debris, indicating that the use of a pit would change as it gradually became filled. No fixed internal furnishings have been identified, but it is possible to infer functional differences from the portable furniture (such as ground stone tools, pots, figurines) and other debris (building debris, animal bones, plant remains). For the most part the postulated shelters appear to have been mainly used as living/sleeping areas, and the majority of domestic activities were undertaken in the outside areas. The fill in F16 from Kissonerga-*Mylouthkia* represents the debris from craft activities. Finds included fine bone pins and awls, ground stone spouted bowls, mortars and pounders, ochre-stained jugs and stones,

84

and unfinished axes and adzes which were heat cracked. Some pits with evidence for substantial burning and containing fire-cracked stones were used as ovens. Other large bell-shaped pits were apparently used for large-scale storage of agricultural produce. Peltenburg suggests that during the Early Chalcolithic period the storage, preparation and consumption of food were communal activities,[7] in contrast to the household based organisation of society during the ceramic Neolithic.

The extent of the pitting at some sites is considerable: substantial subterranean features were identified at Kalavasos-*Ayious*,[8] including a complex of pits and shafts interlinked by tunnels in the northern part of the site (Fig. 4.2). These passageways, which were accessed by steps and had blocking slabs of gypsum, represent a considerable investment of labour, especially considering that the tunnels and pits were dug into the bedrock using stone tools. The large concentration of figurines found in these tunnels and pits indicates the special nature of the subterranean structure, possibly indicating a ritual function. The figurines were broken, possibly ritually as an inherent element in their use,[9] although it is possible that the figurines represent debris that had been broken elsewhere on the site. The tunnels and pits are significantly different from other features at the site, both in construction and contents, which indicates that they served some specialised function, possibly ritual associated

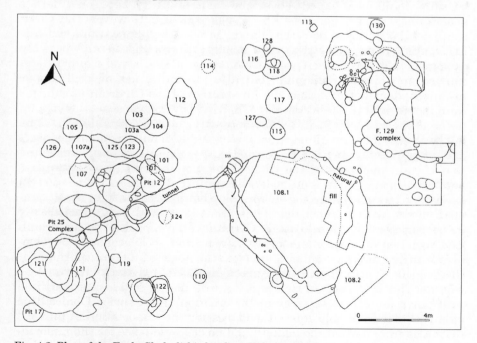

Fig. 4.2. Plan of the Early Chalcolithic levels at Kalavasos-*Ayious*.

with metaphysical chthonic beliefs.[10] There is, however, insufficient evidence either from Kalavasos-*Ayious* or from other Early Chalcolithic sites to explore this hypothesis fully.

The Middle Chalcolithic

Landscape and settlement

The appearance of a new architectural form (the Chalcolithic house) and novel burial practices heralds the Middle Chalcolithic period, dating to between *c.* 3500 and 2500 BC. This phase is characterised by intensification of production, as is evident in the greater diversity of artefact types – pottery, representations and ornaments. Survey and excavation reveal a large number of sites dating to this phase throughout the Cypriot landscape, but with a particular concentration of settlement in the chalk lowlands of the southwestern part of the island. The settlements are large unwalled villages with substantial architectural remains, and there is evidence for internal hierarchical organisation. Archaeological remains at the largest of the settlements, Kissonerga-*Mosphilia*, cover an area of ten hectares. The nearby sites at Lemba-*Lakkous* (Fig. 4.3) and Kissonerga-*Mylouthkia* are three and six hectares respectively. Several geographical barriers would have impeded overland communication between different geographical zones, not least the Troodos massif. However, the Chalcolithic villages throughout the island shared a common culture, indicating contact between settlements, mobility of population and possibly exogamic relations.[11] Increased exploitation of the island's mineral resources, in particular picrolite, but also the initial use of local copper resources, demonstrates that the inhabitants of the Chalcolithic villages were mobile within their landscape, moving beyond the coastal fringe up to the lower reaches of the Troodos massif. Continued exploitation of the fallow deer[12] likewise illustrates a reasonably mobile population base. Antlers were collected and transported back to the settlements, suggesting that certain members of the Chalcolithic population followed the deer herds.[13] Although there is no evidence for internal isolation, the island still appears to be cut off from the surrounding cultures of the East Mediterranean basin, with a subsistence base that is viewed as technologically inferior by some archaeologists.[14] Certainly, in comparison to the urbanised societies of the contemporary Levant and socio-economic developments during the third millennium BC in the Aegean and central Anatolia, Chalcolithic Cyprus appears to exhibit 'cultural retardation'.[15] It is unclear whether this is a result of isolation, cultural inertia and loss of maritime skills, or a deliberate strategy in the creation of a 'Cypriot' Chalcolithic identity.[16] There is only limited evidence for the importation of mineral resources from beyond the island[17] and no clear evidence for the importation of finished objects. While the Chalcolithic population did exploit

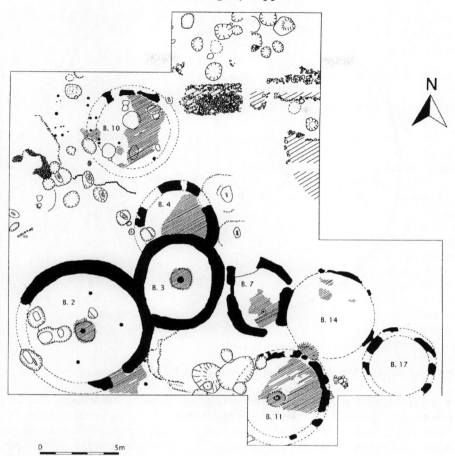

Fig. 4.3. Plan of the Chalcolithic settlement at Lemba-*Lakkous*.

marine resources, these are shallow-water species procured from the coastal zone and there is no evidence for deep-water fishing.[18] There is therefore no clear evidence that the Chalcolithic population possessed any real maritime skills, to enable it to come into contact with the inhabitants of the neighbouring regions.

The Chalcolithic household

The organisation of Middle Chalcolithic domestic space was substantially different from the preceding Early Chalcolithic period. Most notable is the construction of large substantial circular structures.[19] The typical Chalcolithic house has a circular plan (Fig. 4.4; Plate 10), and is built of pisé on

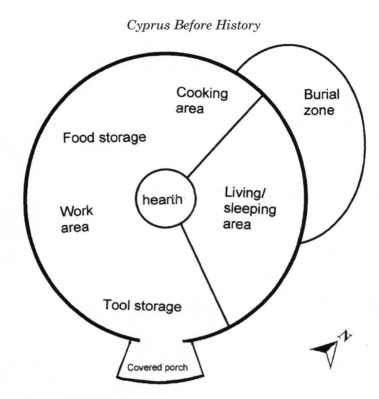

Fig. 4.4. Schematic Middle Chalcolithic house plan showing activity areas.

stone foundations. At the centre of the house there was a hearth and the roof was supported by a concentric ring of posts. The floors and walls were plastered. Internal partition ridges indicate increasing organisation of household space, with the definition of discrete work, storage and living areas, implying greater organisation of domestic activities. Analysis of the physical architectural remains at *Mosphilia* (Periods 3a and 3b) and the spatial distribution of the portable furniture indicates a standard use of domesticate space in the Middle Chalcolithic period, which was underlined by the configuration of the internal fixed furnishings.[20] The typical Chalcolithic house had a four-fold division. The focal point of the Chalcolithic house was the central raised platform hearth. The area to the right of the doorway was delimited by ridges, screens or posts and appears to have been used as the main living, eating and sleeping area. Greater effort was invested in the construction of this sector, in particular the construction of hard floor surfaces. Concentrations of silicates found against the walls of some houses have been interpreted as the traces of reed matting or bedding. Typically, the burials associated with individual houses were placed outside the walls around the living area, underlining the relationship between the living and the dead (the ancestors). To the left of the doorway was the work area also used for storage of tools, usually piled up against the wall behind the door. Opposite the entrance to the house was a cooking area, indicated by the remains of ovens, and it was also the area where the household stored its food. In a number of houses there is a concentration of figurines, including the 'Lemba Lady' (see below), at the interface between the living area and the food preparation area, which might indicate that this was an area of some symbolic significance. Particularly noteworthy is the deposition of the 'Ceremonial Deposit' recondite with birthing imagery in a pit in this 'liminal' zone in B994. Many of these features are new and illustrate changing social and economic organisation at the household level.

The overall character and mode of construction of the Chalcolithic house illustrates a more permanently settled way of life within the village. Another major change is a perceived shift away from communality, with an apparent emphasis on individual households. This is most apparent in the move away from communal storage facilities (illustrated by the disappearance of the bell-shaped pits) and communal preparation and consumption of food, to the location of these activities within the defined spaces of individual households. A more settled existence and increasing organisation of household activities is similarly reflected in the increasing investment of time and labour in the production of varied classes of portable objects, including a variety of utilitarian tools, a wider range of pottery containers, and representational 'art' possibly of ideological significance. Although most production appears to have been conducted at a household level, there is some evidence for craft specialisation, such as the pendant workshop identified at *Mosphilia* in B1547.[21] Bowls are particularly prominent in the pottery repertoire at Middle Chalcolithic *Mosphilia* and were probably used for serving food. The excavators suggest that these bowls illustrate a new emphasis on the presentation of food as an element of feasting[22] and reflect internal competition between households.

Settlement organisation

Excavations at *Mosphilia* have revealed important developments in the organisation of communal space during the Middle Chalcolithic (Fig. 4.5), which can be used to infer the emergence of social ranking as the population levels passed a critical threshold.[23] The development of the Chalcolithic house, with its stone foundations, indicates greater investment of time and labour, and as a corollary there is increased permanence of settlement. In the earlier part of the Middle Chalcolithic (*Mosphilia* Period 3a) households on the upper terrace were organised in pairs associated with discrete clusters of burials. Peltenburg suggests that this configuration reflects the development of property rights.[24] Of particular interest is the discussion of the relationship of the Middle Chalcolithic inhabitants with their Early Chalcolithic forebears, manifest in the architectural

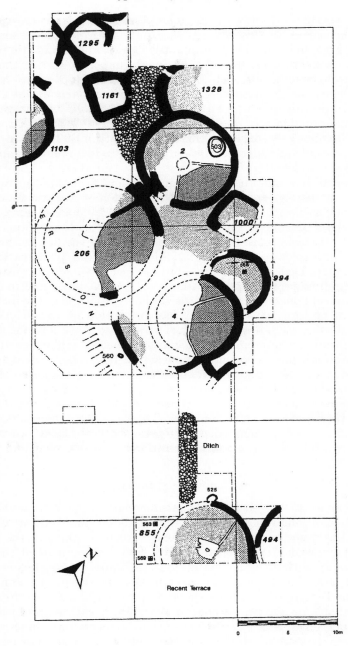

Fig. 4.5. Plan of the Middle Chalcolithic levels at Kissonerga-*Mosphilia* (Period 3b).

sequence of Building 1547.[25] The excavators suggest that the carefully defined storage area of the building was deliberately built over an earlier area of Early Chalcolithic storage pits in a conscious attempt at appropriation and manipulation of earlier habitation, specifically to claim property rights and to demonstrate control over agricultural production.

The major change in settlement organisation, however, dates to the mature phase of the Middle Chalcolithic (Period 3b), and is characterised by the development of internal settlement hierarchy. This phase marks the cultural zenith of the Middle Chalcolithic period, evident at *Mosphilia* by the dramatic increase in settlement size and the establishment of areas within the settlement that were used for particular activities. Pre-eminent amongst these is the so-called 'Ceremonial Area', a spatially discrete group of buildings that are also linked by their size, distinctive architectural form, and their prominent location within the settlement on a spur.[26] The buildings that constitute the Ceremonial Area are imposing structures, not least for their unusually large size,[27] but also for their fine, well executed architecture; the stone foundations are of specially selected calcarenites and the plaster floors are particularly thick and hard. The internal fixed installations, however, are typical of domestic architecture. Associated with the calcarenite buildings are more insubstantial small rectilinear structures, such as B1161, distinct from the typical Chalcolithic domestic architectural form. The Ceremonial Area is not only imposing in terms of architecture and location, but it is formally separated from the rest of the settlement by a wall to the south, a ditch to the north and an open space to the east. The Ceremonial Area is accessed from the north via a formal approach. The open area appears to have been a focus for communal ceremony, in particular competitive feasting. There is a concentration of earth ovens in this area and the surrounding calcarenite buildings have a concentration of highly decorated open bowls for serving food. The pottery contrasts with the utilitarian forms found at smaller households elsewhere within the settlement. The important ritual deposit of symbolically charged material, explicitly associated with the Middle Chalcolithic birthing ideology, is discussed below. The architecture of the Ceremonial Area, the provision of an open space apparently used for communal ceremonies and the controlled access all suggest some communal mobilisation of labour. Similar internal hierarchical organisation of space is evident at Lemba, with the spatially discrete location and inferred specialised function of Building 1.[28] The development in the use of space at *Mosphilia* illustrates changes in the organisation of Chalcolithic society, no doubt a factor of population growth. During the Middle Chalcolithic the population had increased, passing the critical threshold at which point formal social organisation becomes necessary.[29] During such a period of social re-ordering, it would be expected that there would be a marked increase in the use and manipulation of symbols,[30] which is manifest with the development of the symbolic complex of representational art in the Middle Chalcolithic.

Economy

The peculiar Cypriot economic adaptation, namely dependence on hunting or herd management of fallow deer, continued into the Chalcolithic period. Faunal remains from *Mylouthkia, Ayious* and Lemba (Period 1) indicate that deer was the primary meat resource in the Early Chalcolithic, although by the Middle Chalcolithic there was an apparent decline according to the evidence from Lemba (Period 2).[31] This apparent shift towards domesticated livestock suggests increasing intensification in the pastoral economy, although it might equally be due to increasing human population and settlement density reducing deer habitat, hence a decline in the deer population.[32] Even so, deer still remained a valuable meat resource as late as the latter part of the second millennium BC, as is indicated by the faunal remains from the LC settlements of Kition and Maa.[33] Alongside the decline in deer there is evidence for increased exploitation of pig. Faunal remains from Lemba (Period 1) and *Mylouthkia* suggest that during the Early Chalcolithic period pig made up one quarter of the meat diet, whereas by the Late Chalcolithic period (*Mosphilia* Period 4, Lemba Period 3) it constituted as much as a half of the meat consumed.[34] Goat was also extensively exploited in the Chalcolithic. Detailed analyses of these faunal remains suggest that an unusually high proportion of males were allowed to reach maturity before being slaughtered. The high ratio of males to females would be more typical of wool production than of meat or milk production; however there is no archaeological evidence for textile production in Chalcolithic Cyprus, and Croft considers that goat was not a suitable wool source. Instead, Croft suggests that during the Chalcolithic the maintenance of flocks with full-grown males was socially desirable.[35] Possibly these goats signalled wealth or had other symbolic meanings. Conspicuous consumption of these goats would have formed an element of competitive feasting. In the Late Chalcolithic hunting declines further and pig-rearing becomes a major occupation.[36]

Alongside hunting and stockbreeding, the Chalcolithic inhabitants of Cyprus practised agriculture, exploiting a diverse range of plants.[37] Cereals include barley, emmer, einkorn and bread wheat. Legumes, such as lentils, vetch and grass pea, were also exploited. The increasing importance of the agricultural basis to the Chalcolithic economy can be inferred from the ground stone tool industry, characterised by the plentiful querns, rubbers and mortars. The archaeobotanical remains from *Mosphilia* also include olive, grape, pistachio and fig, and might further elucidate the question of the third millennium BC development of orchard husbandry in the Mediterranean.[38] Murray, however, suggests that these were collected as wild fruits, together with capers and juniper berries, to supplement the diet.[39] The overall picture of the Chalcolithic subsistence economy is one of increasing intensification of human management of resources, especially herding and agriculture, alongside a gradual decline in the importance of hunting as an economic mainstay.

Pottery production

Pottery production remained a household industry, and pottery was used to make an increasingly diversified range of shapes, used to store and serve food. The Early Chalcolithic is characterised by the development of an island-wide pottery style, in contrast to the regionalism typical of the ceramic Neolithic. The Red on White (RW) Close Line style of the Early and Middle Chalcolithic developed from the RW Broad Line style typical of the northern sites of the ceramic Neolithic,[40] but with more intricate decorative schemes (Fig. 4.6). The range of shapes increased, with the appearance of coarse ware trays, flasks, tubular spouted bowls and the characteristic platter. The homogeneity of the Early Chalcolithic gives way to increased complexity in the Middle Chalcolithic – the height of the Red on White style. There is greater diversity in forms, decorative motifs and decorative syntax.[41] Although there is a common RW style throughout the island, the increasing complexity of decorative syntax and wider repertoire of motifs result in pronounced inter-site variation, which Bolger suggests illustrates local centres of production.[42] New shapes include deep bowls with lugs or spouts, hemispherical bowls and large storage jars (*pithoi*). The large variety of bowls was used to display, serve and consume food. Many of the fine decorated vessels were found in specialised buildings, such as B206 within the Ceremonial Area at *Mosphilia* and Building 1 at Lemba,[43] rather than within the domestic arena, implying the production of this style specifically for high status competitive feasting. The larger storage jars corroborate other archaeological evidence for intensified agricultural production in this period. The introduction of these jars in the Middle Chalcolithic period reflects the shift away from communal storage in pits during the Early Chalcolithic period and is a good illustration of how social changes will impact upon pottery production.[44]

Picrolite procurement and copper production

The Chalcolithic period is characterised by the development of complex ideologies and the first clear evidence for social inequalities. This is demonstrated by the very great increase in the exploitation of picrolite, used to make a wide variety of ornaments and figurative art. Picrolite procurement became an integral element of Chalcolithic society and was used to underpin the new ideological system. This blue/green stone was invested with symbolic connotations, and its dissemination in Chalcolithic society was restricted. Moreover, preference was given to unblemished stone of blue/green hue,[45] suggesting very careful and selective procurement practices. The extensive symbolic use of picrolite demonstrates the

93

Fig. 4.6. Red on White pottery from Kissonerga-*Mosphilia* (Period 3): (1) hemispherical bowls; (2) deep bowls; (3) spouted bowls; (4) bottle.

incorporation of a new colour into the Cypriot cultural and chromatic repertoire and signifies a major conceptual shift within Chalcolithic society.[46] The main picrolite sources are the Kouris and the Dhiarizzos river beds. The economic and social pre-eminence of Erimi and Souskiou is surely no accident, lying as they do at the point where these rivers are intersected by the main coastal route east-west across the island.[47] Studies suggest that picrolite procurement and production were not in the hands of craft specialists despite the very evident cultural value of this resource.[48] Instead, Peltenburg argues for decentralised production of picrolite ornaments and figurines, rather than the establishment of exchange networks and the movement of finished objects. Even so, the dissemination of picrolite within Chalcolithic society was strictly controlled and closely integrated within the developing symbolic system, with connotations of rank and status, which might argue for a more rigorous system of procurement and inter-site exchange.

Peltenburg suggests a link between the development of early metallurgy on the island and intensified picrolite procurement during the Chalcolithic period, noting that the distribution of the native copper ores would closely mirror that of the picrolite sources.[49] He argues that native copper would have been collected alongside picrolite, but that the collection of these resources was weighted towards the symbolically charged picrolite.[50] Despite the apparent scarcity of metal artefacts in Early and Middle Chalcolithic deposits,[51] it is possible to infer the use of copper to make tools from changes in the ground stone tool repertoire, in particular the appearance of thin flat axes and adzes which mimic metallic forms. Similar skeuomorphs that illustrate the symbiotic relationship between early metal artefacts and ground stone tools are apparent in the EBA repertoire in the Aegean.[52] This might bespeak more widepread copper production than can be discerned from the physical remains on Chalcolithic sites. In contrast to the early horizon of metallurgy in the Aegean, there is no evidence for the integration of copper objects within the symbolic system that was developing in Chalcolithic Cyprus. Final Neolithic and EBA metal objects in the Aegean were carefully curated[53] and deposited in culturally significant patterns, in cave hoards or in burials. Moreover, by the EBA the preferred metal type was the dagger.[54] This is in direct contrast to Cyprus, where the earliest copper artefacts were tools, which turn up in settlement contexts. The limited quantity of copper objects in Chalcolithic Cyprus is predicated by the very nature of the early consumption of copper on the island. It was used to make utilitarian tools that were employed within the settlement. Rather than its being carefully and consciously curated, the evidence implies continuous recycling of this new and precious resource.

Burials

There is very limited evidence for funerary ritual during the earliest, formative stage of the Chalcolithic. Two disarticulated skeletons were placed in a pit at *Mylouthkia*, together with deer bones, domestic refuse and figurine fragments.[55] No complete skeletons were found at *Ayious*, and it does not appear that any of the pits were cut specifically for a funerary purpose. However, some disarticulated human remains were found at *Ayious*. The incomplete and disturbed skeleton of a young child was placed in a shallow depression, two cranial fragments of an adult were found in a surface deposit, and the teeth of a child were found in a pit.[56] All this evidence suggests that during this transitional Early Chalcolithic phase there was no formalised location for the burial of the dead, either extra-mural or within the settlement area, at least that can be detected archae-ologically. However, the disarticulation of the skeletal remains suggests specialised funerary ritual, in particular manipulation of the physical remains.

The development of formalised and differential burial ritual is one of the major innovations of the Middle Chalcolithic. This is particularly illustrated by the 73 burial facilities excavated at *Mosphilia*, comprising the largest set of mortuary data for the Chalcolithic period on the island. For the most part adults were buried in cemeteries outside the settlement area, such as Souskiou-*Vathyrkakas*, whereas children were buried in pit graves within the limits of the settlement (Fig. 4.7).[57] This might suggest less investment in child burial, before the individual was fully integrated within society. However, child burials were richly furnished with an array of specialised goods, in particular dentalium necklaces with picrolite pendants, which might suggest that these individuals were valued in Middle Chalcolithic society.[58] Two Middle Chalcolithic grave types have been identified. Shallow oval pit graves, sometimes sealed with capstones, were used in the settlements.[59] The cemetery at Souskiou had larger shaft graves, which housed between one and three burials,[60] and recent excava-tions have revealed more complex, large funerary structures at the cemetery. Mortuary ritual was highly organised, complex and in some instances was multi-phased with evidence for both primary and secondary inhumations. During the initial stage of funerary ritual the body was placed in the grave in a flexed position on its right side.[61] A typical feature of Middle Chalcolithic funerary ritual was the re-use of graves over a long period of time for successive interments of members of the household or family group, with the shaft left open between burials. Earlier burials would then be exhumed to make room for the later inhumations, as there was not enough space to place the earlier bones to one side.[62] The concen-trations of disarticulated human bone found in settlement levels at *Mosphilia* may represent the secondary deposition of these human re-mains.[63] Although in most Chalcolithic settlements there was usually a very dense concentration of graves around the habitations, only two burials were found in the Ceremonial Area at *Mosphilia*. These are both secondary interments of adults, and the absence of child burials is particu-larly striking.[64] It is unclear what attendant ritual would have accompanied this practice, but exhumation, post-burial alteration of bod-ies and secondary burial were all important elements of Chalcolithic burial

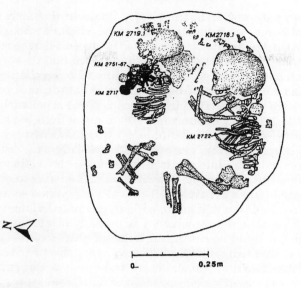

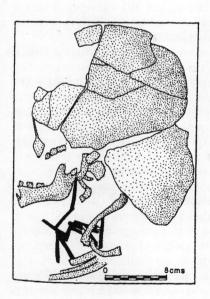

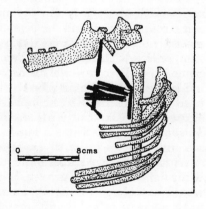

Fig. 4.7. Burial of two children in Grave 563 at Kissonerga-*Mosphilia*, insets showing dentalia associated with upper (left) and lower (right) burials.

practices, possibly a development from Early Chalcolithic funerary ritual. Animal and bird bones were found in the grave shafts at Souskiou and might be the remains of animal sacrifices to the deceased or feasting.[65]

At Lemba (Area I) there is an interesting association of burials with Building 1, which housed a large limestone figure (the 'Lemba Lady') (Fig. 4.8: 3).[66] Only the eastern part of Building 1 was extant, in a prominent position on the edge of the terrace in an area with no other architectural remains. In addition to its location some 100 m away from the habitation area, the architecture and finds of Building 1 were distinctive, indicating that it served a specialised function within the settlement. Although the floor plan was typical of Middle Chalcolithic houses, the walls were more substantially constructed and the internal segments were more clearly defined, with pebble-lined grooves that possibly supported a reed partition. Moreover, the building was large, with an estimated diameter of 6 m. As well as the limestone figure, which was possibly originally placed up against the wall, the building contained large quantities of Red on White pottery, such as storage jars, bowls and flasks, and a cache of stone axes. Immediately to the north of the structure there was a concentration of graves and there were two burials against the preserved terminals of the existing walls. The distinctiveness of Building 1 suggests that it was of ceremonial importance and had a funerary aspect. In particular, Peltenburg suggests that the picrolite birthing figurines that are typically found with Middle Chalcolithic burials, were smaller, portable versions of larger figures such as the limestone figure found in Building 1, and that these representations had a special funerary association.

Middle Chalcolithic burials were commonly equipped with a small number of grave goods. For the most part these grave goods are types that were commonly found in settlement levels, suggesting that everyday objects, possibly the personal possessions of the deceased or their close kin, were placed with the burials. Typical objects are pottery bowls and bottles. Some specialised ceramic forms were deposited in the graves at Souskiou, including a zoomorphic vase with a human head, which might have been used for specialised libation ceremonies. Other typical grave goods are dentalium necklaces with picrolite or bone pendants. Evidence from *Mosphilia* demonstrates a marked association between infant/child burials and necklaces with cruciform picrolite pendants (see Plate 11). Attrition on the necklaces indicates that these had been worn in life before being deposited in the graves. However, as Peltenburg notes, these objects would have been too heavy for infants and were therefore the personal possession of other family members, and so perhaps are indicative of inherited status. The iconography of the picrolite cruciform figurines refers to the act of childbirth, signalling a complex symbolism of fertility. Moreover, representational evidence demonstrates a strong association of this artefact type with women. Peltenburg suggests that only a select group of children and adults had access to these necklaces, and that they might represent markers of social rank and a means of defining the role of women and children in Chalcolithic society. They also appear to refer to exogamic relations with a network of inter-regional contacts associated with the procurement of picrolite over long distances and its restricted use for birthing figurines and pendants.[67] These social relations illustrate the status attributed to women and children in Middle Chalcolithic society, which is reflected in the mortuary record.

Representations and ideology

Chalcolithic Cyprus is a rich source of representational art (Fig. 4.8), which not only illustrates the development of ideology and belief systems but also throws light on gender relations. The development of the symbolic repertoire began during the Early Chalcolithic phase and is represented by the appearance of clay and stone figurines.[68] The development of figured representations indicates increasing interest in the human body at this time, especially in contrast to the limited representations from the ceramic Neolithic. The size and type of the figurines is variable. In contrast to the highly schematic figurines of the Neolithic, the Early Chalcolithic terracottas are more immediately recognisable as human, with individual features (fingers, toes and facial features, eyes and nose) indicated in greater detail, although the faces are still highly stylised. If depicted, the sex tends to be female. The terracotta figurines are decorated with elaborate painted motifs, possibly indicating body tattoos or referring to textiles. Goring notes that these motifs have the same source of inspiration as the Red on White ceramics, and suggests that the potters and figurine-makers are the same specialists.[69] Fantastic zoomorphic figurines have been identified at *Mylouthkia,* presaging the elaborate creations from Souskiou. Although the origins of the Chalcolithic figured representations are unclear, the evident skill inherent in the manufacture of both the terracotta and stone figures implies that these were not the earliest attempts but that the origins lie further back in time, possibly in another medium. The function of these figurines is elusive. At *Ayious,* they were mainly found in the complex of pits and tunnels in the north part of the site and apparently had been broken deliberately.[70]

By the Middle Chalcolithic an island-wide symbolic system with a rich repertoire of representations had developed.[71] Figures in a variety of media (ceramic, limestone, and picrolite) are a distinctive cultural marker of the Cypriot Chalcolithic. The representations are extremely varied in size, from schematised pendants measuring only a few centimetres in height, to small portable figurines between 5 and 15 cm high, to large figures standing some 40 cm tall. Many of the trends that began in the Middle Chalcolithic are further developed. There is increasing emphasis on the human form, illustrated by the position of the arms, the indication of gender (usually female) and particular emphasis on the facial features,

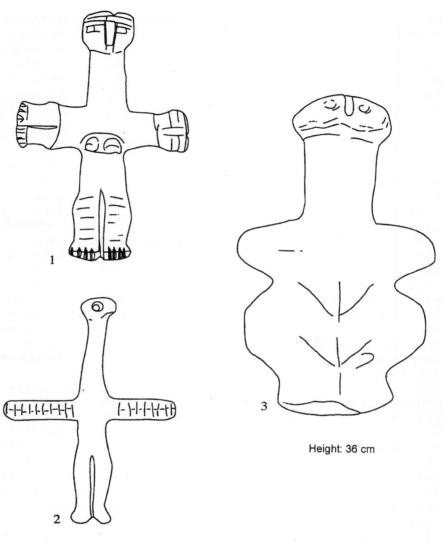

Scale 1:1

Height: 36 cm

Fig. 4.8. Middle Chalcolithic representations: (1, 2) picrolite cruciform figures; (3) limestone figure of female from Lemba-*Lakkous*.

although mouths are not usually depicted. Stone and terracotta figurines are depicted wearing jewellery, including explicit representations of anthropomorphic pendants, and the bodies of the terracotta figurines are richly decorated with painted motifs. The pendants, usually made from

100

picrolite, are in four main forms. The characteristic form is cruciform, but there are also squatting figures, schematic figures with a triangular body, and schematic plug-shaped figures. The cruciform shape, also used for figurines, depicts a birthing figure. The posture, squatting with outstretched arms, refers to the assisted position in childbirth in which the mother was supported under her arms.[72] Nevertheless, these picrolite cruciforms are in fact less frequently represented than figures in stone or terracotta, suggesting their limited circulation as prestige goods. There is greater variety in the form (posture and gestures) of the terracotta figurines. Some are shown standing, some seated and some squatting, all postures associated with childbirth.[73] In addition to the anthropomorphic representations there are a number of fantastic animals from the cemetery at Souskiou.[74]

There are multiple interpretations of the function and symbolism of figurines from various prehistoric cultures, and the Cypriot Chalcolithic material has added an important dimension to the reassessment of this class of material. Originally, the function of figurines was interpreted within an evolutionary framework of human society. This argued that earlier unstratified societies were characterised by matriarchies, but as society became more organised and stratified these matriarchies were replaced by patriarchies and as a consequence the social position of women plummeted.[75] It is frequently assumed that a woman's prime social role is reproductive, and this has been transposed to studies of figurines. Female figurines from early societies were viewed as evidence for matriarchy and/or a female-oriented cult based on fertility and sexuality. Most popular is the mother goddess interpretation, but in funerary contexts figurines are usually interpreted as concubines or servants of the deceased. Typical interpretations of the function of figurines therefore centre on religious or symbolic practices. They have been identified as cult objects (either representations of deities or votaries), charms or amulets possibly with apotropaic properties, but also as toys and pedagogic aids. Even so, it is unlikely that all figurines even from one culture group served the same function. In particular, the simplistic mother goddess interpretation is inadequate for prehistoric figurines, and their use in the identification of ancient matriarchies should be treated with caution. Contemporary figurine studies are more closely associated with feminist archaeology, which challenges androcentric views of the past. These studies prioritise the context, attributes and sex of the figurine, and stress the importance of use-wear analyses. Figurines are an important source of visual information on past social practices, such as body marking, dress, gender and identity, and have been used in discussions of the concept of individuality in antiquity.[76] The Cypriot Chalcolithic figurines appear primarily to have a funerary use as grave offerings, but they are also known from settlement contexts, suggesting that they were integrated within everyday life. Possibly these represent prized personal possessions that were buried with the deceased and might even have been closely identified with the creation of particular identities. An amuletic value cannot be dismissed, even within habitation contexts. However, the complexity of the representational material – the varied forms, the distinction between figurines and pendants, and varied find contexts – indicates a multiplicity of possible uses.

In addition to the smaller portable figurines there are occasional larger figures, usually measuring around 40 cm in height, which have been interpreted as cult images even though their exact function is unclear. Chief amongst these is the limestone statuette found in Building 1 at Lemba, the so-called Lemba Lady (Fig. 4.8: 3, see Plate 12). This figure is violin-shaped with rudimentary arms and legs and a schematic tilting-back face on a long neck. Attention is focused on the incised female genitalia and breasts; however the depiction of the head is rather phallic, and recalls the sexual ambiguity of the few human representations that have been recorded for the ceramic Neolithic.[77] The distinctiveness of Building 1 might argue for a ceremonial use and the limestone statuette obviously held some symbolic meaning, although there is no evidence that this was a cult statue and the object of worship.[78] The dense concentration of graves adjoining the north part of Building 1 suggest that the statuette had a funerary aspect. Even so, the emphasis on the sexual attributes of the figure and the ambiguous nature of this sexuality are more suggestive of fertility, a concern which would fit in with the Chalcolithic ideology centred on childbirth. Other large figures refer to the childbirth imagery prevalent in Middle Chalcolithic society. A limestone statuette from Souskiou is the largest Chalcolithic representation known to date from Cyprus (39.5 cm).[79] It replicates the canonical cruciform type and has clearly indicated breasts and carved motifs on the arms, possibly representing body tattoos. The famous picrolite figurine from Yialia stands at around 15 cm and is in the typical birthing pose with bent legs and outstretched arms (see Plate 13).[80] This piece is of exceptional workmanship and is usually viewed as a cult statue; given the complexity of function of the Chalcolithic figures this should not be accepted unquestioningly. However, these large figures might be seen as the focus of the Middle Chalcolithic ideology and the smaller figurines and pendants are probably portable representations of these figures.

Another large Chalcolithic figure (36 cm) was allegedly found at Souskiou.[81] This terracotta figure depicts a male seated on a stool very similar to the birthing stools from *Mosphilia*. He is resting his head in his hands, his head tilts back and his mouth is open in a grimace. The figure's torso and head are hollow for pouring liquid out from the penis and the figure might have been used in libation ceremonies. Although the seated male figure is unique in Cyprus, his face recalls the quadruped from Souskiou and the grimacing figure from the ceremonial deposit at *Mosphilia*, and it can be interpreted as another attention-focusing device with a ritual function. Some archaeologists have interpreted this as an ejaculating figure and a representation of male fertility.[82] Hamilton, however, counters this interpretation with an innovative reading of the figure's symbolism that attempts to contextualise it within the iconography of the Middle Chalcolithic period.[83] In particular she questions whether the figure is truly ithyphallic, noting that the penis is not the focus of the viewer's attention. Even so, the phallus was clearly indicated, from which we might infer that the sex of the Souskiou figure was important to its function. Instead, Hamilton suggests that the focal point of the seated male was in fact its grotesque face. She argues that the seated pose of the figure had a specific meaning within Chalcolithic symbolism and referred specifically to the act of childbirth rather than a more generalised concept of fertility, whereas a motif referring to male fertility had little relevance to the prevalent ideology. Hamilton suggests that the figure refers to the custom of *couvade*, which might range from taboos invoking total exclusion of males during pregnancy and parturition to rituals that involve imitation of childbirth. These customs are intended to divert the attention of evil spirits away from the woman giving birth and might be used to claim paternity. Hamilton's interpretation of the Souskiou figure emphasises the importance of childbirth in the small communities of Chalcolithic Cyprus. Certainly, the representational evidence in conjunction with the burial evidence indicates the elaboration of a complex ideology surrounding fertility and childbirth during this period.

A ceremonial deposit at Kissonerga-Mosphilia

A unique deposit of representational art was found in the 'Ceremonial Area' at Kissonerga-*Mosphilia*, which throws light on the symbolic system and prevalent ideology of Chalcolithic Cyprus and in particular the possible function of the ubiquitous figurines.[84] Underlying the wall of a large Middle Chalcolithic building (B994) was a rectangular flat-bottomed pit containing fire-cracked stones, pebbles and organic material together with over 50 artefacts of stone, bone, shell and pottery, in a matrix of ash and soil. This deposit was distinct from the usual domestic refuse found at the site, and moreover appears to have been deliberately deposited in the pit. The focal element of the deposit was a Red on White bowl modelled to resemble a typical Middle Chalcolithic house, complete with internal central hearth, segmented floor and pivoted door (see Plate 14). Bolger has suggested that the painted designs on the interior and exterior walls of the bowl might mimic wall paintings.[85] It is probable that these motifs conveyed symbolic messages as, prior to the final deposition of the bowl in the pit, the decoration was concealed by a layer of whitish clay, as though to 'kill' it or relieve it of its innate powers.[86] The house model contained (see Plate 15) ten stone figures, eight ceramic figures, a terracotta model of a stool, a triton shell and an anthropomorphic vessel with a grotesque grimace, which had been deliberately broken before deposition (Fig. 4.10: 3). The excavators suggest that the last is clearly an attention-focusing device, a typical attribute amongst prehistoric religious paraphernalia, and have commented likewise on the ceremonial or ritual use of triton shells within Levantine and Aegean religious contexts.[87] The stone figurines (Fig. 4.9) measure between 13 and 17 cm. These are very schematic representations and only two of the figurines are clearly sexed (female), although several have necks and heads modelled to resemble phalli, continuing a tradition of ambiguous sexuality in representations that began in the Neolithic. None of the stone figurines is freestanding; instead they were designed to be held in the hand. Indeed, Goring notes clear evidence of handling all over these stone figures, suggesting that they were held or rubbed as fetishes.[88] The terracotta figures are clearly female. Unlike the stone figurines, these are free-standing, more varied in posture and have elaborate painted decoration (Fig. 4.10). Some are standing, some are squatting and others are seated on stools. One seated figure was clearly giving birth, and was also depicted wearing a birthing pendant. Moreover there is an emphasis on the hips, buttocks, swollen stomachs, breasts and pubic triangle of these figurines, indicating a preoccupation

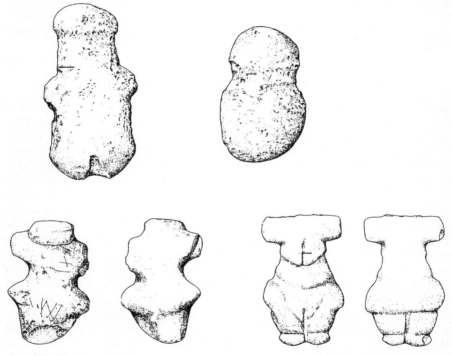

Fig. 4.9. Stone figurines from ceremonial deposit (Unit 1015) at Kissonerga-*Mosphilia* (Period 3b).

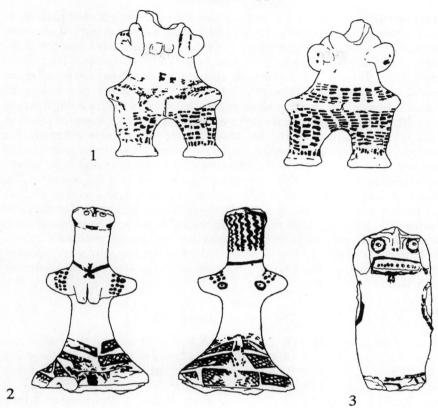

Scale 1:4

Fig. 4.10. Clay figurines from ceremonial deposit (Unit 1015) at Kissonerga-*Mosphilia* (Period 3b): (1) hollow figure of female; (2) birthing figure; (3) grotesque anthropomorphic vase.

with female fertility. The abrasion patterns on the terracottas indicate frequent handling. This wear is localised on the genitalia, breasts, buttocks and arms. Goring and Bolger suggest a specific didactic use of the pottery figures, to demonstrate aspects of pregnancy and parturition.[89]

The figurines from this deposit evidently all have connotations of fertility, more specifically of childbirth, and were probably used in rituals promoting female fertility. Within this context Bolger interprets the building model, which clearly mimics contemporary standing structures, as a model of a domestic birthing structure. The customs involved in the use of such a structure were associated with a number of taboos, rituals and customs surrounding childbirth.[90] Attrition, in particular around the door, indicates that this model was repeatedly handled like the figurines. The final deposition of the model and figurines, which were buried ritually in some form of deconsecration ceremony within a special part of the site, underlines their symbolic content. Particularly noteworthy are the desecration of the model and many of its contents and the absence of burials in this part of the site. The childbirth symbolism would have been of paramount importance in the small social groups that made up the communities of Chalcolithic Cyprus, particularly given their high infant mortality. The context of deposition within the spatially discrete Ceremonial Area is illuminating for interpreting the rituals surrounding fertility.[91] This area provided an arena for the performance of ritual in the open air, as well as a series of architecturally distinctive and functionally specialised houses of symbolic significance, most notably the so-called Red House. A large number of bowls were found in the Red House (B206), including vessels used for display in serving food, suggestive of ceremonial competitive feasting. It is difficult to establish a synchronic correlation between the two aspects of ceremonial life associated with this area – birthing ritual and feasting – but the evidence does appear to suggest the development of a complex ideological system and associated rituals during the Middle Chalcolithic.

The Late Chalcolithic

At the end of the Middle Chalcolithic the settlements of Lemba and *Mosphilia* were abandoned and left unoccupied for a period of around 200 years. There is a major dichotomy between the Middle and Late Chalcolithic occupation of Cyprus and it is unclear how the two phases should be culturally inter-related. The Late Chalcolithic is characterised by a series of major social, cultural and economic transformations, many of which foreshadow developments of the subsequent Cypriot Bronze Age. These changes are illustrated by the Period 4 occupation levels at *Mosphilia* and Period 3 at Lemba. Particularly important is the evidence for increasing extra-insular contact, especially with southwest Anatolia, which was the source of inspiration of many of the cultural transformations of the Late Chalcolithic. However, certain aspects of Late Chalcolithic occupation are suggestive of a degree of cultural continuity. Not least, the architectural tradition is derivative from the Middle Chalcolithic house type. Moreover, the reoccupation of earlier settlements, the remains of which were at least partially visible to the later inhabitants,[92] is in stark contrast to the radically new settlement pattern characteristic of the subsequent Bronze Age and might suggest reoccupation by the same population group. The changes of the Late Chalcolithic involve a major transformation in the organisation of space within the wider settlement and in individual households, novel patterns of preparation and consumption of food and drink, and changing fashions in dress. Innovations include faience disc beads and conical stones, possibly tokens (Fig. 4.11: 3, 4).

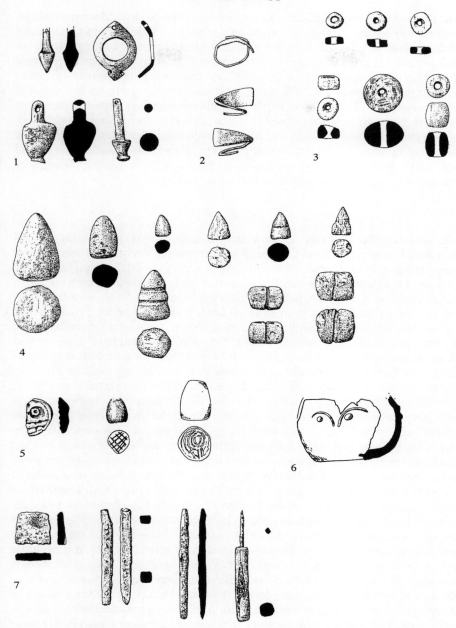

Fig. 4.11. Late Chalcolithic ornaments from Kissonerga-*Mosphilia*: (1) shell pendants; (2) copper spiral earring; (3) faience beads. Miscellaneous Late Chalcolithic artefacts from Kissonerga-*Mosphilia* and Lemba-*Lakkous*: (4) conical stones and grooved stones; (5) seal impression and stone seals; (6) relief 'face pot'; (7) copper tools – adze, chisels, awl.

There are also rare examples of stamp seals (Fig. 4.11: 5). Above all there was a shift in the underlying ideological system evidenced in the decline of figurative art, picrolite procurement and changing funerary ritual. As the period progresses there is an apparent shift away from communal activities, such as a decline in public works, the performance of ritual activities and communal feasting, and the maintenance of extramural cemeteries. The Late Chalcolithic is truly transitional between two very distinct cultural traditions: that of the island's prehistoric occupation, which reached its *floruit* in the Middle Chalcolithic period, and the very different lifeways of the Cypriot Bronze Age. Full assessment of this period will allow more refined interpretations of the socio-economic changes of the initial stages of the prehistoric Bronze Age.

Settlement

The stratigraphy and radiocarbon determinations from *Mosphilia* (Period 4) attest to a lengthy Late Chalcolithic occupation,[93] which the excavators have subdivided into two phases (4a and 4b) (Fig. 4.12).[94] In the earlier occupation phase only a small number of isolated structures have been identified, built over the long abandoned remains of the Middle Chalcolithic settlement. The principal structure of this earlier phase is the Pithos House (B3),[95] which has been interpreted as an elite structure, with a possible storage and redistribution function and with privileged access to prestige goods. The Pithos House was destroyed in a violent conflagration, and the Late Chalcolithic settlement that grew up over its ruins in Period 4b was radically different. Rather than the hierarchical organisation of settlement inferred for the Middle Chalcolithic period, which possibly continued into the Late Chalcolithic under the guise of the Pithos House, the final Chalcolithic settlement at *Mosphilia* was very different, not least for the lack of communal architecture. Instead of public works, maintenance of communal spaces and a focal point of activity or pre-eminent and prominent structures, *Mosphilia* (Period 4b) was divided into discrete habitation areas, three of which have been uncovered. These three zones appear to refer to small groups of households that were possibly connected through shared economic resources and social ties.[96] A group of smaller buildings was built over the remains of the Pithos House. These include a larger, more substantial structure (B86), which might have taken over some of the elite associations of the Pithos House. A second group of houses was built further to the south, arranged either side of and facing onto an east-west passageway. The third habitation zone lies at the southern limits of the excavation area, and comprises successive pairs of buildings. Peltenburg argues that this spatial arrangement closely mirrors the fractured nature of Late Chalcolithic society. By the final stage of the Late Chalcolithic, society had broken down into smaller groups of

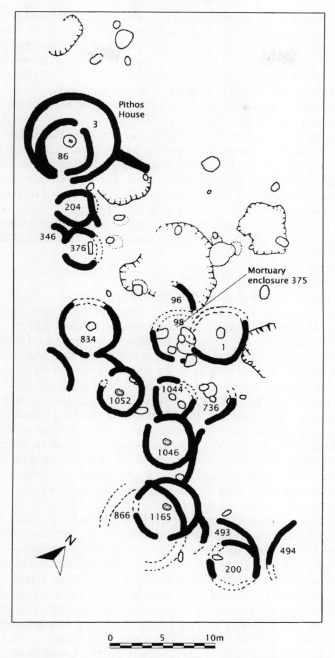

Fig. 4.12. Plan of the Late Chalcolithic levels at Kissonerga-*Mosphilia* (Period 4).

households that shared economic activities (agricultural and craft production) and were linked through close agnatic ties.[97]

Architecturally the Late Chalcolithic testifies to a certain degree of continuity from the Middle Chalcolithic, albeit with a number of salient differences. The basic architectural form, the Chalcolithic house, survived, albeit modified. The formal division of space within the house disintegrated with the disappearance of floor ridges and partition walls; the same basic range of domestic functions continued within the limits of the house, though there was less formal segregation of these household activities.[98] However, the central rectilinear hearth, focal point of the Middle Chalcolithic house, disappeared. The finer aspects of Chalcolithic architecture, such as the very hard plaster floors and the use of calcarenite as a construction medium, also disappeared.[99] The overall architectural continuity testifies to some degree of cultural continuity at least in the organisation of domestic space, albeit with modifications reflecting the very major transformations that typify the Late Chalcolithic period.

The Pithos House at Kissonerga-Mosphilia

Before the social fragmentation of the latter stages of the Late Chalcolithic period there is some evidence for the emergence of social complexity, which finds its physical expression in the construction of the Pithos House (B3) at *Mosphilia* (Fig. 4.13). Peltenburg identifies this house as 'a freestanding residence whose occupants possessed impressive wealth and control over productive labour'.[100] Specifically, he argues that the artefactual evidence points to a number of specialised activities taking place within the Pithos House. These include bulk storage of agricultural produce, possibly within the context of a redistribution centre, food processing, especially olive oil production, and specialised craft production, including copper metallurgy and the manufacture of prestige goods such as annular spurred shell pendants. There is a clear concentration of the new accoutrements of prestige symbolism within the Pithos House, including large numbers of conical stones (possibly used as tokens) and a cache of 47 stone axes and adzes. The annular shell pendants that were manufactured in the Pithos House are another prestige artefact used to express high status. Several pristine triton shells were also recovered from the remains of the Pithos House. The function of these shells is unclear, but a symbolic, ritual use might be inferred, which is corroborated by the association of a complete triton shell and the house model from the Ceremonial Area in Period 3. The unusual faunal assemblage also points to the high status of the associated residential group, specifically the large number of deer bones. Croft notes that in the Late Chalcolithic period deer hunting/herding had become a more marginal meat resource and that greater emphasis was placed on pig rearing.[101] The large numbers of deer bones from the Pithos House, therefore, might indicate that hunting had become a high status

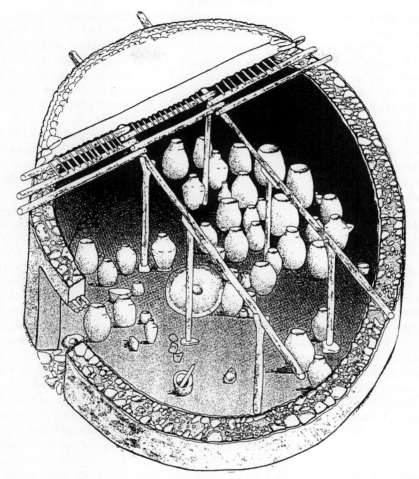

Fig. 4.13. Possible reconstruction of the Pithos House (B3) at Kissonerga-*Mosphilia*.

activity in the Late Chalcolithic period, controlled by the occupants of the Pithos House.[102]

Although the material remains recovered from this structure are exceptional, architecturally it conforms to the Chalcolithic tradition of domestic architecture and so it should probably be interpreted as a special residence. However, the distinctive material remains and the excavator's interpretations merit closer attention. Certainly there is evidence for large-scale storage, at a completely different order of scale to the provision for agricultural storage in any of the preceding periods. The large number of storage jars (*pithoi*) had an estimated capacity of 4000 litres and might indicate some measure of centralised bulk storage. Also found inside the

111

Pithos House was an accumulation of standardised bowls, which could be interpreted as units of measure for the redistribution of an agricultural surplus. In this respect, it is interesting to note the close association of these bowls and the quantities of small conical stones that might be interpreted as tokens for exchange.[103] The Pithos House might therefore exemplify a significant increase in bulk storage capacity and production of an agricultural surplus, which precedes the introduction of the cattle-plough complex to Cyprus in the Bronze Age.

More controversial is Peltenburg's contention that the residents of the Pithos House had privileged access to copper and olive oil. According to Peltenburg 'the twin pillars of Cypriot Bronze Age political and economic power ... were already exploited by LChal aggrandizers'.[104] There is some evidence for copper production within the building, in the form of ores, crucibles and finished copper artefacts, but at present the evidence for Chalcolithic metallurgy is too limited to construct models of production and control. The posited oil production is extrapolated from the suggested introduction of the Mediterranean polyculture (the vine, olive and wheat) to the Aegean subsistence base in the third millennium BC. Peltenburg suggests that certain elements within the Pithos House were explicitly associated with the production of olive oil, namely an olive press, a stone basin and the large storage capacity of the many storage jars.[105] Moreover, the massive conflagration that destroyed the house is attributed to the presence of large quantities of olive oil stored in the jars. In the Aegean it is suggested that the investment of time and labour required both for cultivation of the olive and for production of olive oil, would place this cultigen beyond the means of most households.[106] Instead, the olive and its products are intrinsically associated with emergent elites. However, in the Aegean it has been argued that there is no firm evidence for cultivation of the olive before the Late Bronze Age, nor any evidence that it would have been used as a foodstuff.[107] Hamilakis suggests that the initial use of olive oil was to make luxury perfumes and ointments rather than dietary.[108] At *Mosphilia* there is a similar dearth of concrete evidence for cultivation of the olive and oil production. The hypothesis rests on inferred evidence from the installations found in the Pithos House. However, given the problems inherent in the application of a model of the adoption of a Mediterranean polyculture in the EBA Aegean, it is perhaps unwise to extrapolate this model to contemporary Cyprus without any unequivocal evidence for olive cultivation.

Halstead's social surplus model,[109] developed in the context of the Aegean Bronze Age economy, might be more appropriate to interpreting the evidence from the Pithos House. Halstead argues that the growing Bronze Age population needed to develop increasingly complex economic strategies to guard against shortfall. In particular, there is evidence for increasing storage provision amongst these early farming communities. However, in the third millennium BC storage technology was insufficiently developed to ensure against sustained shortfall and additional strategies were necessary. Halstead suggests that the cultures of the EBA Aegean translated surplus into durable and convertible tokens, usually exotics imbued with high symbolic content and value, which could be exchanged during times of economic stress. Appropriate exchange objects included the marble figurines characteristic of the EBA Cyclades and high status metal goods.[110] In the Cypriot Chalcolithic context there is evidence for ever-increasing sophistication in storage strategies, from the bell-shaped pits of the Early Chalcolithic period, to the development of the large storage jars in the Middle Chalcolithic period. This process reaches its height in the Late Chalcolithic period, most notably with the large-scale storage facilities in the Pithos House. Moreover, this large-scale storage is associated with the introduction of tokens, a peculiarly Cypriot response to the modes of social storage.

Pottery production

One of the most marked discontinuities between the Middle and Late Chalcolithic periods is evident in pottery production (Fig. 4.14).[111] Use of the characteristic RW style declines dramatically, and it is replaced by a novel monochrome class of pottery. With the decline of the painted styles relief decoration becomes the main decorative mode. The main Late Chalcolithic pottery style, Red and Black Stroke-Burnished ware, was used to make a wide range of bowls – hemispherical, conical, and deep bowls – as well as hole-mouth jars, flasks and spouted bottles. The coarse painted ware was particularly popular for large hole-mouth storage jars. These stand up to 1 m in height, and might indicate the production of an agricultural surplus and possibly the beginnings of a redistributive economy.[112] Late Chalcolithic pottery production is characterised by experimentation in clays and slips, in contrast to the pottery industry of the earlier periods. Other aspects of Late Chalcolithic pottery illustrate technological advances in production skills, possibly indicating that the mode of production shifted away from individual households to more specialised production.[113] The thinner walls and harder fired clays denote increasing control over firing, as does the carefully produced red and black surface, an effect achieved deliberately using differential oxidising and reducing firing conditions. The potters were using new clay sources, indicating that the changes in production do not merely represent a change in fashion, but mark a substantial transformation in pottery technology. The introduction of a number of novel forms, in particular the spouted bottles of Anatolian inspiration, might suggest that some of these innovations were externally derived. The association of spouted flasks with a complex of basins and grinding equipment, as noted at Lemba-*Lakkous* in Building 7, is suggestive of beer production, to be drunk from these specialised liquid containers.[114]

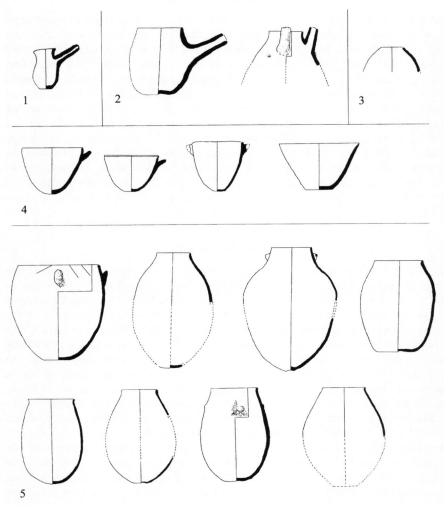

Fig. 4.14. Late Chalcolithic pottery from Kissonerga-*Mosphilia* (Period 4): (1) spouted jar; (2) spouted holemouths; (3) holemouth jar; (4) hemispherical bowls; (5) storage jars.

Metallurgy

There is some evidence to support the intensification of copper production at *Mosphilia* during Period 4, although this remains essentially small-scale. *Mosphilia* has the largest copper assemblage uncovered in any Chalcolithic settlement on Cyprus to date. This comprises a limited reper-toire of tools (chisels and awls) and there is no evidence for the ornamental use of copper, nor are there any weapons. This no doubt is partly due to

114

the context of use and deposition of the copper artefacts, which are only found in settlement contexts. Apparently copper was not used to make high status objects of symbolic content, hence its absence from funerary contexts and the perceived lack of curation of copper within the settlement. Excavations at *Mosphilia* have uncovered evidence for localised small-scale copper production during the Late Chalcolithic. Fragments of smelted copper were found on the floor of B834, and in B706 there was a very suggestive association of a lump of copper ore, an apparent crucible, and a pestle. A second crucible was found in the Pithos House. Moreover half of the copper objects from the site were found in the immediate area of the Pithos House.[115] Even so, the true impact of copper production on Chalcolithic Cyprus is difficult to assess from the physical remains.

Funerary ritual

Dramatic changes in funerary ritual and the breakdown of traditional burial customs underline the transformations between Middle and Late Chalcolithic society and in particular ideological shifts. Most notable is the introduction of a new, more elaborate type of burial facility, the chamber tomb (see Plate 16).[116] This comprised a vertical circular shaft leading down to one or two smaller sub-circular chambers. The shafts, which were dug down through earlier occupation levels, were not filled in after successive interments, suggesting that the burials were deposited in quick succession. Double burials are relatively frequent at *Mosphilia*. These include two males buried in Tomb 539, two females in Tomb 545, and a male and female in Tomb 505. Age continues to be the major determining factor in the choice of burial practices and tomb type. The new chamber tombs were used exclusively for adult burials, while children were interred in poorly defined pits or scoops, another new grave-type.[117] The child burials were single inhumations and had few grave goods. The excavators dismiss the possibility that these scoop graves were designed to hold secondary inhumations, noting that child burials are particularly prone to disintegration, hence the apparent disarticulation of the funerary remains. In the better-preserved burials, the skeletons are found *in situ* in the typical flexed position on their right side. Therefore there was a dramatic change in the treatment of child burials in the Late Chalcolithic period, comprising a shift from multiple inhumations, richly equipped with funerary furniture, to simple burials. This is echoed by the disappearance of the picrolite birthing figurines, which had been closely linked to child burials, indicating that the changing mortuary treatment is interlinked to the development of a new ideology in which children and childbirth played a very minor role.

The spatial configuration of the burials at *Mosphilia* might reveal significant details concerning the organisation of Late Chalcolithic society at the site, especially the apparent burial enclosure B375.[118] A series of

115

around ten postholes arranged in a double line describing an arc is all that remains of a flimsy enclosure, either a palisade or a timber, wattle and daub construction. Within the area enclosed by this palisade there were six graves but no domestic installations. There was also a polished rectangular platform, 20 cm high, aligned with the hearth in the adjacent Building 98. This enclosure is unique at the site and suggests the existence of a particular social group that chose to distinguish itself from the others by the creation and maintenance of a discrete burial plot. The excavators interpret this presumed group as a descent group, although it might equally refer to a non-agnatic social group. This builds on Goldstein's hypothesis that burial ritual, in particular the maintenance of a specialised bounded area for the exclusive disposal of the dead, is a means of affirming lineal descent from ancestors. Through this reaffirmation of ancestral ties the burial group thereby laid claim to rights over restricted resources, such as land, mineral resources and prestige goods.[119]

Alongside the elaboration of the mortuary facility, adults were buried with a larger number of grave goods. Despite increasing evidence for the development of copper metallurgy during the Late Chalcolithic period, metal grave goods are all but absent.[120] There is some evidence for the development of specialised funerary furniture during the Late Chalcolithic period, rather than the simple deposition of the personal possessions of the deceased and/or the mourners with the burial. This is best illustrated by the flat-bottomed jugs with elongated spouts, a frequent element in grave furniture, but a shape that was rarely found in settlement contexts. This vessel type also illustrates the introduction of new aspects of funerary ritual to the island, apparently from Anatolia, in particular the increasing emphasis on the use of liquids in funerary ritual.[121] Although the use of the chamber tomb and the burial enclosure might refer to the earliest stages in the emergence of social complexity in Chalcolithic Cyprus, Peltenburg notes that there is no real correlation between the use of chamber tombs and the distribution of prestige objects. However, certain elements of funerary ritual indicate increasing knowledge of the world beyond Cyprus, and appear to be integrated within Cypriot funerary ritual as prestige items which confer status through the medium of control of exotica and knowledge of distant places. In addition to the Anatolianising flat-bottomed, spouted jugs, there are faience beads, which were specifically restricted to richer burials. Control of land and agricultural produce and the development of a new redistributive economy were closely interwoven in the new ideology and prestige system of the Late Chalcolithic period. This is possibly reflected in funerary ritual by the presence of conical stones, apparently tokens, which accompanied female burials placed beside pottery containers.[122]

4. The Age of Copper

Emergence from isolation

One of the defining characteristics of the earlier prehistory of Cyprus is the island's apparent isolation from the neighbouring cultures of the East Mediterranean basin, whether this be from choice or a result of cultural inertia. Subsequent to the initial colonisation phase back in the tenth-ninth millennium BP, the first concrete evidence for sustained contacts with cultures beyond the island dates to the Late Chalcolithic period. This contact appears to have been at an esoteric cultural level, rather than direct trading contacts, and the only traded commodity that has been identified in Cyprus is the faience beads.[123] Even so, a number of the defining cultural traits of the Late Chalcolithic period can be demonstrated to be of southwestern Anatolian inspiration.[124] New elements include a stamp seal from Lemba,[125] new forms of ornamentation, such as shell annular pendants, copper spiral earrings and the faience disc beads, and possibly the introduction of textile manufacture (indicated by a RP spindle whorl found in a firm Late Chalcolithic context). The introduction of a new ceramic tradition to the island is a salient trait of the Late Chalcolithic period.[126] The monochrome tradition, which supplanted the Red on White style, is associated with new manufacture techniques and exploitation of different, non-calcareous clay sources. New shapes are introduced, most notably the spouted jug, as are new decorative techniques, namely ribbed decoration including a rare 'face pot' (Fig. 4.11: 6).[127] These changes illustrate technological transformations associated with the production of the pottery, and changing style and patterns of consumption, in particular drinking customs, all of which would have been integral to the negotiation of new identities. That this foreign influence was reciprocal is illustrated by the appearance of Red on White ware in EB II Tarsus.[128]

These innovations illustrate major social and organisational changes in Late Chalcolithic society, namely changes in diet, or at least in the consumption of food and drink, and fashion, both of which would echo shifting social identities. In particular, the changing styles of dress and ornamentation reflect a dramatic shift away from the prevalent 'birthing' ideology and patterns of picrolite procurement typical of the Middle Chalcolithic period. In the earlier part of the Late Chalcolithic period, there is clear evidence that the local elite controlled access to these exotics and the associated prestige activities (new styles of dress and feasting). There was a clear concentration of these foreign novelties in association with the Pithos House (B3).[129] Helms has convincingly demonstrated the political and ideological use of exotic materials and esoteric knowledge (including the practice of particular customs) from distant places in the construction of elite power bases.[130] This is precisely the dynamic in which the Late Chalcolithic material should be assessed. Peltenburg identifies two stages in this initial contact phase: the earlier stage, represented by the material from the Pithos House, is characterised by sporadic contacts very much controlled by the elite, whereas in the later phase this contact has intensified and is widely disseminated throughout Late Chalcolithic society.[131]

Transition to the Bronze Age

The Chalcolithic remains one of the most dynamic periods in the prehistoric settlement of Cyprus. This phase is characterised by a marked increase in settlement and population and increasing exploitation of the island's natural mineral resources. Alongside these changes, the characteristic representational art of the Middle Chalcolithic period illustrates a quickening of symbolic life, which might relate to increasing social complexity. The changes apparent in the organisation of society during the Late Chalcolithic in many ways serve to link the earliest prehistoric trajectory of Cyprus with the developments and the increasing pace of change in the subsequent Bronze Age. While some aspects foreshadow Bronze Age society, most notably the gradual incorporation of Cyprus within the maritime networks of the East Mediterranean, other aspects refer to the island's ancient, pre-Bronze Age heritage. The subsequent Bronze Age settlement of Cyprus, however, marks a profound break with the early prehistory of Cyprus. This is most evident in shifting patterns of settlement and greater exploitation of the island's copper resources, indicating greater exploitation of the Cypriot landscape. However, many of the changes are related to increased contacts with southern Anatolia, and no doubt had their origins in the Late Chalcolithic period.

5

Cattle, Anatolian Migrants, and the Prehistoric Bronze Age

An age of change

The transition from the Late Chalcolithic to the Early Cypriot period marks a major break in the cultural sequence of prehistoric Cyprus and is characterised by transformations in settlement and architecture, burial practices, domestic technologies and economy. There are, however, problems involved in defining the initial stage of the Cypriot Bronze Age and in particular trying to fit the material evidence into the somewhat rigid chronological and cultural system devised by Gjerstad. In particular, it is problematic defining any element of Cypriot prehistoric material culture as exclusively Early Cypriot as opposed to Middle Cypriot, and scholars have suggested that it is best to refer to the period in its entirety as the prehistoric Bronze Age.[1] This is largely due to the absence of stratified EC settlements and as a corollary the lack of a series of radiocarbon determinations (Table 5.1).[2] Consequently, the definition of the EC cultural repertoire is largely dependent on tomb material, in particular two cemeteries in the north of the island: Lapithos-*Vrysi tou Barba* and Vounous-*Bellapais*. The relative chronology is largely based on stylistic seriation of pottery from these cemeteries and absolute dates were derived from a few foreign correlations, most notably a Syrian Early Bronze III-IV jug from Vounous.[3] However, the tomb groups within these cemeteries are communal, used over several generations, thereby impeding the development of a refined chronology, and the identification of regional ceramic styles[4] compounds the problem. Therefore interpretations of the major social and economic changes that occurred during this period are fraught with difficulties, because of the problems involved in contextualising the cultural record both chronologically and spatially.

The remarkable changes in the culture of Cyprus at the transition to the Early Bronze Age are signalled by a shift in occupation, the new settlement pattern (Fig. 5.1) illustrating novel uses of the island's mineral resources, together with the introduction of new architectural forms indicative of new patterns of domestic organisation. Alongside these spatial changes there is a wholesale change in the island's material culture – the pottery, metalwork, textiles (illustrated by novel types of spindle whorls and possibly the decoration on figurines), symbolic representations and

119

Site	Provenance	Date BP	Calibrated date BC
Sotira-*Kaminoudhia*	Area A, room 1	3890 ± 90	2583 – 2066
Sotira-*Kaminoudhia*	Area A, room 7	3780 ± 90	2466 – 1932
Sotira-*Kaminoudhia*	Area A, room 7	3780 ± 90	2466 – 1932
Sotira-*Kaminoudhia*	Area A, room 7	3890 ± 100	2606 – 2049
Sotira-*Kaminoudhia*	Area A, room 4	3690 ± 100	2376 – 1783
Sotira-*Kaminoudhia*	Area C, unit 2	3840 ± 75	2480 – 2046
Sotira-*Kaminoudhia*	Area C, unit 2	3860 ± 75	2518 – 2062
Sotira-*Kaminoudhia*	Area C, room 8	3760 ± 75	2414 – 1943
Sotira-*Kaminoudhia*	Area C, room 8	3860 ± 80	2536 – 2055
Sotira-*Kaminoudhia*	Area C, room 17	3800 ± 75	2460 – 1990
Marki-*Alonia*	370 (EC)	3892 ± 39	2458 – 2290
Marki-*Alonia*	370 (EC)	3886 ± 42	2457 – 2286
Marki-*Alonia*	370 (EC)	3834 ± 42	2392 – 2197
Marki-*Alonia*	336 (EC)	3675 ± 118	2198 – 1886
Marki-*Alonia*	343 (EC)	3645 ± 95	2141 – 1878
Marki-*Alonia*	394 (EC III-MC I)	4394 ± 58	3141 – 2944
Marki-*Alonia*	763 (EC III-MC I)	3764 ± 50	2275 – 2046
Marki-*Alonia*	212 (MC I)	3480 ± 80	1888 – 1682
Marki-*Alonia*	212 (MC I)	3460 ± 90	1867 – 1631
Marki-*Alonia*	347 (EC III-MC I)	1038 ± 44	AD 957 – 1030
Alambra-*Mouttes*	Building III, room 19	3970 ± 90	2570 – 2310
Alambra-*Mouttes*	Building IV, room 13	3610 ± 60	2030 – 1830
Alambra-*Mouttes*	Building II, room 2	3500 ± 120	2010 – 1630
Alambra-*Mouttes*	Building IV, space 27	3440 ± 140	1920 – 1530

Table 5.1. Radiocarbon determinations for the prehistoric Bronze Age on Cyprus.

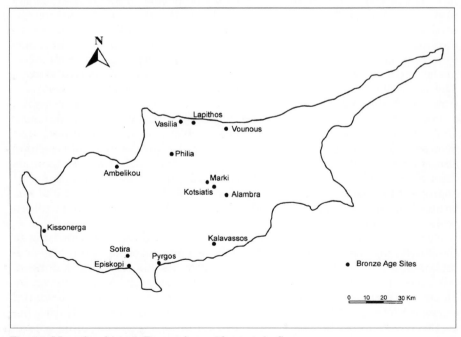

Fig. 5.1. Map of prehistoric Bronze Age settlements in Cyprus.

funerary ritual. There is clear evidence for an altered economy and a new religious expression. While the dynamics of this transformation remain largely undocumented, the most significant characteristic is a clear break in all areas of social and economic life.[5] Recent excavations at Kissonerga-*Mosphilia* have to a certain extent closed the cultural gap between the Late Chalcolithic period and the earliest phase of the Bronze Age. A number of elements of Period 4 foreshadow subsequent cultural developments, although the economy and much of the cultural repertoire remain firmly within the Chalcolithic sphere. In contrast, the poorly preserved final phase of the site (Period 5) is characterised by a number of so-called Philia elements, including Red Polished (Philia) pottery, cattle bones and pot burials, all of which signal the Cypriot Early Bronze Age.[6]

Characterising the Philia phase

The so-called Philia phase is crucial for understanding the transition between the Chalcolithic and EC period.[7] It is, however, poorly understood because of the paucity of the archaeological evidence. Dikaios interpreted the Philia phase within a sequential framework, as the initial phase of the Cypriot Early Bronze Age. An alternative interpretation was put forward by Stewart,[8] who viewed the material as a regional assemblage typical of the west of the island, which overlaps with the EC sequence represented elsewhere on the island. Most recently Frankel and Webb have suggested that while the distinctiveness of the Philia assemblage should be recognised there is insufficient evidence to indicate whether this distinctiveness denotes regional, cultural or chronological differences. Consequently, they prefer to term this phenomenon the 'Philia *facies*'.[9] Even so, their ensuing discussion of the Philia material inevitably involves placing it within a chronological and regional context.[10] Radiocarbon determinations for the Philia material are limited, but suggest a range between 2500 and 2350 BC.[11] The evident contacts with Anatolia during the late third millennium BC are of particular importance in unravelling the transformations of this period, in particular whether it should be seen in terms of demic diffusion (population movement), cultural interaction, or internal Cypriot development.

The Philia assemblage was first identified in the cemeteries of the northwest Mesaoria. Today Philia material has been identified at nineteen sites (Table 5.2) in the western, central and southern parts of the island, the majority clustering around the Ovgos valley, close to the island's copper resources.[12] This suggests a major dislocation in settlement between the Late Chalcolithic period and the earliest Bronze Age, particularly a decline in settlement in the western reaches of the island, in the area of the Ktima lowlands. The proximity of the sites with Philia material to the copper-rich regions of the island suggests that the exploitation of these resources played a significant role in the internal economy of these sites, as had been suggested by Stewart.[13] Characteristic elements

Site	Site type	Pottery	Other material
Bellapais-*Vounorouthkia*	Settlement/cemetery?	RP(P)	
Dhenia-*Kafkalla*	2 pit graves	RP(P), RPC(P), WP(P)	Biconical whorl 2 spiral earrings Stone bowl
Episkopi-*Bamboula*	Cemetery (Tomb 1)	RP(P), RPC(P)	Toggle pin
Khrysiliou-*Ammos*	Cemetery	RP(P), WP(P)	
Kissonerga-*Mosphilia* (Period 5)	Settlement/cemetery Chamber tomb? 2 urn burials	RP(P), BSC	Biconical whorl Spiral earring Pendant
Kyra-*Alonia*	Settlement	RP(P), RPC(P), BSC	
Kyra-*Kaminia*	Pit grave	RP(P), WP(P), BSC?	Spiral earrings Metal knives
Marki-*Alonia*	Settlement	RP(P), RPC(P), WP(P), BSC	Biconical whorls Spiral earrings Toggle pins
Marki-*Davari*	Pit grave (Tomb 6)	RP(P), WP(P) , BSC	Spiral earring
Marki-*Vounaros/Pappara*	Chamber tomb?	RP(P)	
Nicosia-*Ayia Paraskevi*	Pit grave (Tomb 7) Chamber tombs?	RP(P), RPC(P) ? WP(P), BSC	Biconical whorl Spiral earrings Pendants Stone beads Whetstones Metal knives
Philia-*Drakos* B	Settlement	BSC	
Philia-*Laksia tou Kasinou*	Chamber tomb Urn burial	RP(P), RPC(P), WP(P), BSC	Biconical whorl Spiral earring Toggle pins Pendants Knives & an axe
Philia-*Vasiliko*	Settlement	RP(P)	
Philia/Vasiliko-*Kafkalla*	Pit grave	RP(P), RPC(P) ? WP(P), BSC	Biconical whorl
Sotira-*Kaminoudhia*	Chamber tombs	RP(P), RPC(P)	Biconical whorl Spiral earrings Pendants Knife
Vasilia-*Alonia*	Cemetery		Axe & knife
Vasilia-*Kafkalia & Kilistra*	Pit grave Chamber tomb Urn burial?	RP(P), RPC(P), WP(P), BSC	Toggle pins Arm rings Knife, razor, spear Alabaster vases
Vasilia-*Loukkos Trakhonas*	Chamber tomb?	BSC?	

Table 5.2. Distribution of Philia material from sites in western and central Cyprus (after Webb and Frankel 1999, table 1).

of the Philia assemblage include its ceramic repertoire, the range of metal artefacts, in particular a distinctive range of copper and gold ornaments, shell and picrolite annular pendants and the biconical clay spindle whorls (Fig. 5.2). These elements, all of which are intrusive to the Cypriot cultural repertoire, are largely associated with burials, in pit graves, chamber tombs or urn burials, although occasionally they are found in settlements, associated with a novel type of rectilinear architecture.[14]

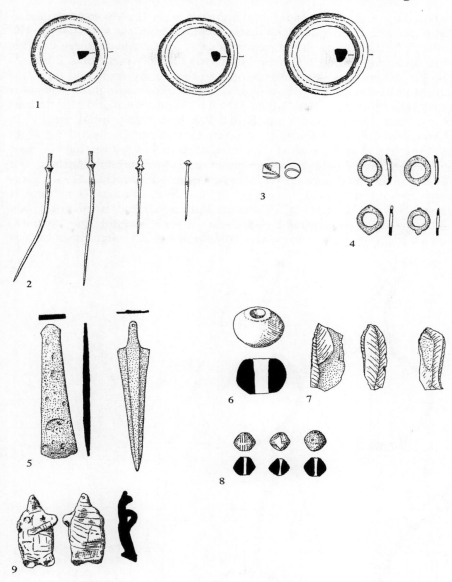

Fig. 5.2. Philia material: (1) bronze armbands; (2) bronze toggle pins; (3) bronze hair ornament; (4) shell and stone annular pendants; (5) bronze axe and bronze dagger; (6) stone macehead; (7) flint blades; (8) terracotta spindle whorls; (9) terracotta figure.

There was initially considerable confusion in the terminology applied to Philia pottery, in particular its distinctiveness from the wares of the EC period,[15] but following recent excavations at Marki-*Alonia* there is sufficient material to allow a clearer definition of the distinct Philia fabrics.[16] The Philia ceramics illustrate changes in technology, style and function, indicative of changing patterns of production and consumption. The main wares represented are Red Polished (Philia), White Painted (Philia), Black Slipped and Combed ware and Red Polished Coarse (Philia). RP(P)[17] is characterised by its uniformity of fabric throughout the island[18] and its good quality, evenly polished slip. This ware includes a distinctive class with irregular burnishing to make intentional patterns on the surface. The surface might be decorated with incised geometric motifs (zigzags, herringbone and chevrons), paralleled by the Early Bronze II pottery at Tarsus.[19] Typical forms (Fig. 5.3) include flat-based jugs with an ovoid body and cut-away spout, round-based flasks or juglets, amphorae, 'teapots', and a variety of bowls, some with a tubular spout. Although the pottery is

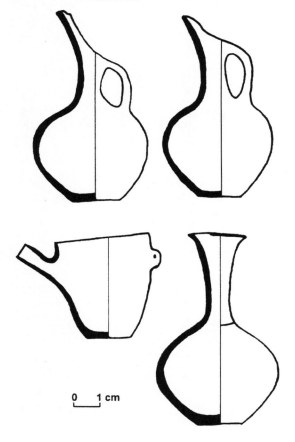

0   1 cm

Fig. 5.3. Philia Red Polished pottery from Khrysiliou-*Ammos* Tomb 1: two jugs with cut-away spout, spouted 'milk bowl' and bottle.

not a direct parallel to contemporary pottery from Anatolia, a number of features of the RP(P) pottery indicate its close Anatolian connections, in particular with Early Bronze II Tarsus. These include similar morphological and technological elements, such as the cutaway spouts, and the thrust-through handles.[20] The RPC(P) has a grittier more porous fabric and was used to make medium to large jars and cooking pots.[21] WP(P) is a minor ware, restricted to the Ovgos valley and also found at Marki.[22] This is characterised by decoration in matt red to brown paint. Motifs include vertical and horizontal bands, zigzags and wavy lines. There is a limited range of shapes, usually a deep flat bowl with a shallow spout. The BSC pottery appears to be related to the Red and Black Streaked Burnished ware from Early Bronze II Tarsus.[23] This has a characteristic surface treatment: the vessel was covered with a slip and burnished and then bands of the slip were scratched off.

The mould-made metal artefacts characteristic of the Philia material are a clear indication of the introduction of copper-working technology to the island, which is distinct from the occasional hammered tools of the Chalcolithic. Spiral earrings of copper or electrum and copper rings and armbands are peculiar to the Philia phase,[24] whereas other artefacts are types which continue in use throughout the prehistoric Bronze Age, although the Philia examples are distinctive. These include flat-tanged knives, pins with conical heads and flat axes.[25] Other metal types are indistinct from the prehistoric Bronze Age assemblage. Also peculiar to the Philia phase are picrolite and shell annular pendants with a pointed projection, and terracotta biconical spindle whorls with linear incised decoration.[26]

Cattle, copper and the economy

Chief among the transformations of the Philia phase (and the EC period) are the introduction of cattle[27] and intensified exploitation of the island's copper resources, both of which had a major impact on the subsequent development of the island's economy. Knapp suggests that the reintroduction of cattle to the island at the beginning of the Early Cypriot period enabled a major transformation in agricultural practices, namely a shift from hoe cultivation to plough agriculture. This would allow increased productivity, as larger areas of land could be cultivated through harnessing animal power. Alongside this transformation of arable practices, Knapp also argues that animals were no longer being kept purely for their meat, but that their secondary products (wool, milk and traction power) were at last being fully exploited.[28] It is not made explicit how these economic changes were instituted in Cyprus (or the wider East Mediterranean), in particular whether the spread of the cattle-plough farming complex and associated pastoral practices were a result of population movement or of the dissemination of cultural knowledge. However, the transportation of breeding cattle and the knowledge associated with new farming techniques, including the use of a plough and maintenance of a herd of cattle including castrated oxen, suggests that this economic transformation was far from simple.[29] The acquisition of such knowledge and the actual physical acquisition of a herd of cattle would have been powerful mechanisms for the construction of an elite, based on the control of wealth, new and exotic resources, and esoteric knowledge.[30] The adoption of this new farming economy would have had a very different impact on different households, as it is improbable that they would all have been able to afford the new livestock,[31] or even that these new breeding animals would have been made available to all households. Consequently, Manning suggests that from the very inception of the Cypriot Bronze Age there would have been a major disparity in wealth.

The economic implications of the adoption of plough agriculture are manifold, but Knapp suggests that these are supported by the archaeological record. Intensification of agricultural production had been indicated as early as the Late Chalcolithic period, with the development of bulk storage facilities at both Lemba and Kissonerga-*Mosphilia*[32] and in particular the cache of stone axes and adzes in the Pithos House, suggestive of forest clearance. The copper axes characteristic of the Philia assemblage might indicate further land clearance and intensification of agricultural production.[33] Similarly, the exploitation of other secondary products, such as wool, might be inferred from the biconical whorls.[34] The sudden *floruit* of mould-made copper artefacts indicates intensification of copper production on the island, and the introduction of cattle and equids and harnessing of animal traction (pack animals and possibly wheeled transport) would no doubt have facilitated the increased exploitation of the island's copper resources.

The Anatolian connection

Already by the Late Chalcolithic period there is evidence for increasing cultural contact with the communities of southern Anatolia, indicated by novel elements in the cultural repertoire such as stamp seals (at Lemba-*Lakkous* Period 3 and Kissonerga-*Mosphilia* Period 4). Occasional ribbed decoration on pottery (at Lemba) includes the rare example of a 'face pot'.[35] Peltenburg suggests that there is a specifically southwestern Anatolian influence on Late Chalcolithic pottery in the southwest of the island, which is distinct from the Cilician influence inferred for the Philia material.[36] The Anatolian parallels to the Philia assemblage – the pottery, ornaments and spindle whorls, and the novel, multi-roomed rectilinear architecture – are particularly striking and have been commented on by numerous archaeologists.[37] Dikaios originally attributed these affinities to an influx of Anatolian migrants or refugees fleeing the mainland at the beginning of the Early Bronze III, a period characterised by destruction horizons and apparent unsettled conditions.[38] However, as noted by Mellink, the close phase of contact appears to date to the late Early Bronze II period in Anatolia and there are no Early Bronze III traits among the Philia assemblage. Instead she emphasises the wide-ranging commercial contacts of Tarsus during the Early Bronze II period, preferring to interpret the Philia/Anatolian affinities in terms of economic contacts, in particular exploitation of the copper resources.[39] Although recognising the impact of Anatolian culture on Cyprus during this period, both Manning and Peltenburg have chosen to interpret these transformations in terms of internal development by the indigenous population, within the context of incipient elite groups participating in exchange networks with the communities of southern Anatolia. They suggest that these groups were able to exert control over the movement of luxury exotica within Cyprus, and the transmission of esoteric knowledge, including new farming techniques and the production and consumption of alcohol within the context of competitive feasting. In this context it is argued that cattle, ceremonial drinking and funerary display are all exploited as a means of developing and maintaining these exclusive new social groups.[40]

Alternatively, the changes associated with the Philia phase might be interpreted as evidence for a clear population movement from Anatolia. This is dependent on interpreting specific elements of material culture as markers of group identity or ethnicity, both the artefacts and their underlying technological, behavioural and economic connotations.[41] Pottery, for example, informs us as to the technological tradition of its producers, and the behavioural traditions and diet of its consumers. Changes in personal ornament and dress accessories might indicate changes in clothing, commonly viewed as a clear marker of group identity. In particular, it has been suggested that the transmission of new technologies over cultural boundaries is difficult to achieve without the movement of personnel and therefore that a suite of technological changes might signal the presence of a migrant population.[42] Webb and Frankel have identified a horizon of technological transformations which they interpret as evidence for a migration from Anatolia to the island at the beginning of the EC period and which incorporates the Philia material. These include innovations in ceramic technology, the introduction of copper mining and metallurgical technology, new farming techniques associated with the introduction of cattle, donkeys and the plough, new methods of textile production (spinning, weaving), and the introduction of new forms of food processing represented by the occurrence of low-walled baking trays and ceramic hobs.[43] Other cultural changes attributed to Anatolian migrants include pot burials,[44] rectilinear houses and a different use of domestic space. In comparison to the wealth of objects found on the floors of Chalcolithic structures, there are very few finds *in situ* on the floors of prehistoric Bronze Age houses, implying culturally determined innovations in the use of space and deposition of waste.[45] The changes in domestic arrangement, food preparation and in particular textile production are seen as evidence that this migrant population incorporated women,[46] but this gendered view of the organisation of household activities is extremely problematic. The emphasis on the technological aspect of the Philia/EC transformations illustrates its impact on ordinary household activities, implying that these changes were not specific to a select economic elite but had an impact on everyday life for the whole community. Webb and Frankel therefore attribute the social and economic changes inherent in the Philia material and EC period to the arrival of discrete groups of settlers from Anatolia, specifically targeting the island's copper resources.[47] Within this framework, they posit preliminary, sporadic contact during the Late Chalcolithic between Cyprus and EB II Cilicia, represented by the movement of small trinkets, followed by a phase of copper prospecting and initial settlement in western and central Cyprus, which is represented by the Philia material. The final phase of contact, during the EC period, sees Cyprus being assimilated within established international trading networks.[48]

Settlement and economy

There is a dramatic shift in settlement pattern in the prehistoric Bronze Age (see Fig. 5.1), concomitant with a substantial increase in the number of settlements. Even so, the 270 identified sites were not contemporaneous but subsume Philia settlements, EC settlements and MC settlements,[49] probably with increasing settlement density by the MC phase. This suggests a massive increase in population, which became possible in the Bronze Age with the harnessing of animal power and consequent increase in arable production. Many of the sites that have been identified are known only from their cemetery remains, but, as Swiny has stressed, every cemetery must be associated with and proximate to the contemporary settlement.[50] However, the living area was also clearly defined from the mortuary area. Clusters of settlements occur in particular geographic zones, such as along the north coast and around the northwestern foothills of the Troodos massif, especially at the interface of the arable land and the mineral-rich lower reaches of the Troodos.[51] Indeed, exploitation of the island's copper resources is seen as the prime mover in the development of Cypriot society in the Bronze Age.[52] Other than Lapithos on the north coast and possibly Vasilia, no coastal settlement has been identified, indicating that exploitation of maritime resources and maritime trade was not a high priority in the economy. Many of the settlements that have been identified through survey are seemingly large, between 15 and 20 hectares,[53] but it is probable that this represents a discontinuous settlement pattern with clusters of smaller habitation areas, such as farmsteads or small clusters of houses.[54] The location of the settlement was determined by access to a water supply (rivers, streams and springs) and arable land, emphasising the importance of the arable economy. Swiny notes a slight preference for plateaux with a commanding view, but also that this was a secondary concern. Indeed the apparent absence of settlements in commanding defensive positions or with enclosure walls or fortifications implies that defence was not an imminent concern of the island's inhabitants.[55] However, their determined avoidance of the coast might imply they distrusted the sea and, by extension, maritime peoples.

At the end of the prehistoric Bronze Age there is evidence for the development of fortified sites in the central Mesaoria plain and along the Karpass peninsula.[56] Traditionally these forts were viewed as defensive strongholds and refuges, reflecting presumed unsettled conditions on the island at the transition to the Late Bronze Age, either due to climatic conditions (drought), population pressure or external stimulus.[57] An alternative explanation emphasises the intensification of trade in Cypriot copper at this period, and suggests that the forts developed to control the movement of copper from the mines in the foothills of the Troodos to nascent urban centres on the coast, such as Enkomi.[58] Frankel, however, has noted that some sites are too large to be primarily defensive and suggests that these may in fact be large animal enclosures.[59] The character of settlement on the island certainly altered dramatically at the end of the prehistoric Bronze Age, reflecting profound economic and social transformations which will be explored in the following chapter.

Recent excavations have allowed archaeologists to draw some conclusions as to the changes in internal organisation of prehistoric Bronze Age settlements and the use of domestic space. The introduction of rectilinear agglutinative architecture (Fig. 5.4) marks a fundamental shift in the organisation of domestic space in Cyprus. Rectilinear structures are attested from the Philia occupation phase at Marki (see Plate 17),[60] and the accretive nature of the settlement architecture remains a constant throughout the prehistoric Bronze Age. The houses were built of mould-made mudbricks on low stone foundation walls, or had walls built entirely from stone.[61] The internal arrangement of the houses varies between the settlements and there is no uniform house plan.[62] Individual rooms are usually rectangular and vary in area between 2 m^2 and 30 m^2.[63] Inside the houses there are fixed elements, such as rectangular clay hearths, low benches built against the walls, pot emplacements and lime plaster bins (used either as mortars or jar stands). These are usually positioned against the walls or in the corners, leaving the central floor area free for a variety of activities.[64] Portable furniture includes a wide range of ceramics, coarse ware trays possibly used as griddles, jugs, amphorae and coarse ware cooking pots, clay hearth surrounds[65] and a large range of grinding and pounding equipment.[66]

Given the accretive nature of the architectural units, it is difficult to identify specific households. At Sotira-*Kaminoudhia* studies failed to identify discrete specialised activity areas.[67] Frankel and Webb, however, have been able to identify specific activity areas within the settlement at Marki.

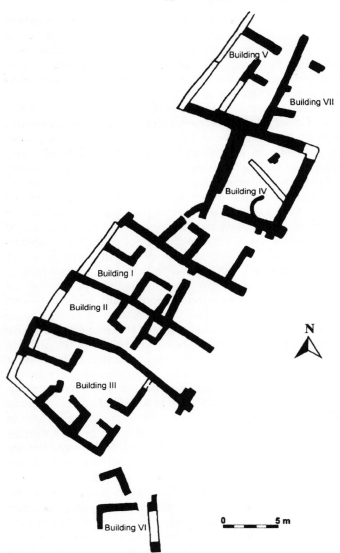

Fig. 5.4. Plan of
Alambra.

They identify specific areas for communal preparation of food, for cooking
and for textile production on the basis of the find spot of portable and fixed
furnishings found *in situ* on the floor.[68] In general, household activities
took place inside the buildings – incorporating areas for storage and
preparation of foodstuffs, cooking, spinning, and weaving. Other activities
that occur within the household include flint-knapping, and indeed
chipped stone tools continue to be a significant component of the toolkit

130

well into the prehistoric Bronze Age.[69] The floors were kept clean of debris from household and craft activities and refuse was removed from the immediate habitation area.[70] Ground stone tools, including pounders, hammers, querns, mortars, and axes, were also used in a variety of household activities, primarily associated with food preparation or agrarian activities.[71] Although some studies have emphasised household production of ceramics it seems more probable that this was beginning to move into the hands of specialists, albeit on a small scale. Certainly the limited excavations to date have failed to produce evidence for household production along the lines suggested for the ceramic Neolithic, and it was probably economically and technologically beyond the means of individual households to produce their own pottery.[72] The changes in metallurgy no doubt also entailed low level craft specialisation and the development of workshops either within individual settlements or at specific metal-working centres. Crucibles, indicative of metallurgical production, are found at most sites. The overall nature and organisation of the excavated settlements are indicative of small, egalitarian communities, with no apparent internal differentiation.

The economic basis was essentially agrarian. The large number of grinding stones, querns and pounders indicates the importance of cereals (and probably pulses) in the diet;[73] however there is very little primary evidence available. Wheat, barley, lentils and the olive are attested at sites on the south coast, the latter providing the first indication of orchard husbandry on the island. Grape pips and apple and pear seeds might substantiate this evidence for the development of orchard husbandry, but these seeds are too small to determine whether the plants were wild or domesticated. The best available evidence is from Marki-*Alonia*; it suggests that the major cultigens were those that had been exploited from the aceramic Neolithic. The staples were wheat and barley, supplemented by olives, grapes, pistachios, chickpeas and lentils. The major dietary change was the switch from the primitive einkorn and emmer wheat to bread wheat.[74]

There is more evidence for the development of the pastoral economy during the prehistoric Bronze Age (Table 5.3), which has most recently been supplemented by the excavations at Marki. Swiny suggests that cattle represent the major meat source at Sotira-*Kaminoudhia* and Episkopi-*Phaneromeni*, representing around one third of the faunal assemblage at both sites. Similar quantities of sheep and goat are also attested, and

Site	Cattle	Deer	Pig	Caprines
Sotira-*Kaminoudhia*	33%	20%	12%	36%
Marki-*Alonia*	23%	21%	5%	51%
Alambra-*Mouttes*	21%	23%	12%	44%
Episkopi-*Phaneromeni*	31%	11%	26%	32%

Table 5.3. Faunal assemblages from prehistoric Bronze Age settlements (values rounded up).

Swiny suggests that these were kept for milk production.[75] The possible importance of milk in the diet is inferred from the presence of spouted bowls; however these are not dissimilar to spouted bowls from earlier ceramic Neolithic and Chalcolithic pottery assemblages. Certainly it remains to be demonstrated that milk was a novel element of the diet and part of the so-called secondary products revolution suggested by Knapp.[76] At Marki,[77] sheep and goat represent around half of the faunal remains, while cattle and deer each comprise around 20% of the faunal assemblage. Croft comments that the cattle bones are a richer supply of meat than the sheep and goat bones that dominate the assemblage and estimates that the actual meat yield was a mere 13% for caprines as opposed to 57% for cattle. Moreover, the deer also yielded more meat, and is estimated to represent 16% of the meat supply at the site.[78] There is evidence for the introduction of a new species of goat at Marki, the screw-horned goat, probably from Anatolia.[79] Similar proportions of sheep/goat, cattle and deer are found at Alambra.[80] The other animal that was bred was the pig, which seems to have been of variable economic importance. Fallow deer continued to be hunted, and are represented at all the prehistoric Bronze Age settlements. The continuation of the hunting ethos is a common thread throughout Cypriot prehistory and serves to link the inhabitants of prehistoric Bronze Age Cyprus to their forbears of the Neolithic and Chalcolithic periods. The economic and ideological importance of hunting and of the newly introduced cattle is indicated by their common inclusion as decorative motifs on RP pottery, in contrast to the other quadrupeds being exploited on the island. However, the most significant aspect of the prehistoric Bronze Age faunal assemblage is the successful reintroduction of cattle to the island, exploited as a major meat resource and as traction animals for ploughing. Equids, either horses or donkeys, appear to be exploited as pack animals and have been identified at both Alambra and Marki.[81] A clay model of a donkey bearing panniers illustrates this economic function.[82] There are occasional horse burials at Lapithos.

Pottery production

The characteristic pottery of the prehistoric Bronze Age ceramic tradition is the Red Polished ware (Fig. 5.5). This includes a wide variety of fabrics and was used to make very different types of shapes. RP ware has a long currency in Cyprus and was used throughout the EC and MC periods. The vessels were manufactured by hand and might have incised decoration, usually geometric motifs, such as multiple zigzags and hatching. Vessels in this ware were commonly used in the settlements and were also typical grave goods. Excavations at two important settlements, Marki and Alambra, have done much to clarify the manufacture and use of this pottery. This new type of pottery is one of the major innovations of the Cypriot

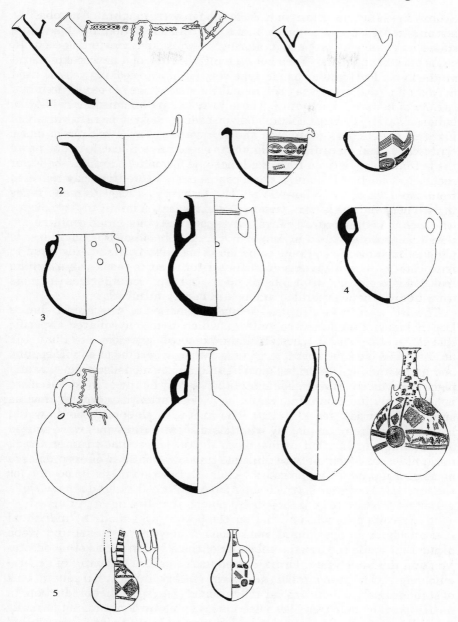

Fig. 5.5. Red Polished pottery from Vounous-*Bellapais*: (1) spouted 'milk bowls'; (2) small bowls; (3) amphorae; (4) cooking pot; (5) jugs.

Bronze Age, and the origins of this class have been sought in Anatolia.[83] It not only represents a major technological transformation, but also illustrates new ways of preparing, storing, serving and consuming food. In particular, Frankel and Webb note the introduction of a new cooking form at Marki – a low circular pan, a type very similar to cooking vessels used in Anatolia.[84] RP ware was used to make a wide range of vessels used in a variety of household activities. These include small hemispherical bowls, ladles, a variety of large spouted bowls, basins, cooking pans, a variety of jugs and juglets, jars, amphorae and storage vessels.[85] Two distinct fabric types have been identified at Alambra. These are a fine calcareous paste made from clays derived from the limestone formations around the lower reaches of the Troodos, and a dark, coarse paste made from clay collected from the area of the pillow lavas. The former was used to made fancy incised pots and the latter to make cooking wares. A mix of the two pastes was used to manufacture a range of jugs, jars and other liquid containers.[86] Small holes were drilled in some sherds, usually of bowls, from Marki to allow broken or cracked pots to be laced together. Other sherds seem to have been re-used as tokens and counters or in some cases as burnishing tools.[87] Figurines might also be mended, and repaired figurines and pots were frequently incorporated amongst funerary furniture.

The RP ware was also used to make a series of specialised shapes largely known from funerary contexts, which might have played a specific role in funerary ritual. These include zoomorphic vessels (see Plate 18), multi-bodied jugs and bowls, large jugs with exaggerated or double spouts, and bowls and jugs decorated with figured scenes modelled from clay and placed around the rim or shoulder of the vessel.[88] Many of these vases are not obviously functional but would have been attention-focusing devices suitable for ritual (see Plate 19). The jugs with elaborate spouts would have made a dramatic display when liquids (water or wine) were poured out, possibly in libation ceremonies. Morris notes that in later Greek antiquity *kernoi* (vessels with multiple cups) were used to offer samples of agricultural produce to the gods.[89] A similar function might be posited for the multiple bowl vases, which may have contained small quantities of a variety of produce to be incorporated among the offerings at a funeral.

It is a contentious issue whether the pottery was made by individual households or in specialised workshops.[90] However, Frankel and Webb argue that while the broad conformity of the style, in terms of its decoration and the basic vessel forms, served as a marker of identity (a general emblemic style), the overall nature of the pottery illustrates a general lack of standardisation more typical of household than specialist production. In particular they note that clay selection and preparation were not formally controlled, hence the very great variability in the different fabric types.[91] They assume that the pottery was a female household craft, but there is no real evidence to substantiate division of labour according to sex. Barlow, however, concludes that the skills inherent in the production of RP vessels and the high temperatures required to fire these vessels preclude household production and instead are indicative of the earliest steps towards ceramic specialisation on Cyprus.[92] The increased pyrotechnic skills of the Cypriot potters probably owe much to concurrent advances in metallurgical production.

The other main ceramic style of the prehistoric Bronze Age is the White Painted ware (WP), traditionally seen as the marker of the MC period (Fig. 5.6). At the MC settlement of Alambra-*Mouttes*, however, the ware represents less than 1% of the total ceramic assemblage.[93] This style is therefore a regional variant, one that appears more characteristic of the north and east of the island. Typical WP vesels are small juglets and bowls with linear painted decoration. Technical studies of the WP ware from Alambra suggests that the vessels were formed or finished on a tournette and were fired at a high and controlled temperature, suggestive of some form of ceramic specialisation.[94] Frankel, however, argues for household production of this style, specifically by women. Based on a detailed study of the decorative style of the WP ware, Frankel suggests that the island can be subdivided into a number of smaller regional groupings. Within these groupings he interprets the WP ware as a marker of identity (an emblemic style), and suggests that the transmission of specific motifs between the different groups is evidence for exogamic social relations between these groups.[95] That is to say that the movement of women between villages in different areas was the primary means of social interaction and cultural exchange, including the transmission of pottery styles. Certainly, due to their small size, prehistoric Bronze Age communities would be dependent on exogamy for survival, but whether ceramic production was a female activity within these communities has yet to be demonstrated. Instead, the transmission of decorative motifs might have been effected through the development of internal trade routes – the small WP juglets (or more probably their contents) representing a prized, luxury commodity. Certainly, by the end of the prehistoric Bronze Age these Cypriot juglets were widely exported around the eastern rim of the Mediterranean basin, suggesting that this commodity was equally prized by the surrounding cultures of Syria, Palestine and Egypt.[96]

Copper production

The extraordinary wealth of mould-made copper and copper alloy objects found in the major prehistoric Bronze Age cemeteries, especially on the north coast, testifies to the intensification of metallurgical practices on the island at the end of the third millennium and into the second millennium BC. This is in direct contrast to the relative paucity of metal artefacts from Chalcolithic sites, which were largely confined to a hammered technology. In conjunction with the expansion of settlement in the metalliferous zone around the foothills of the Troodos, this advance in metallurgy implies

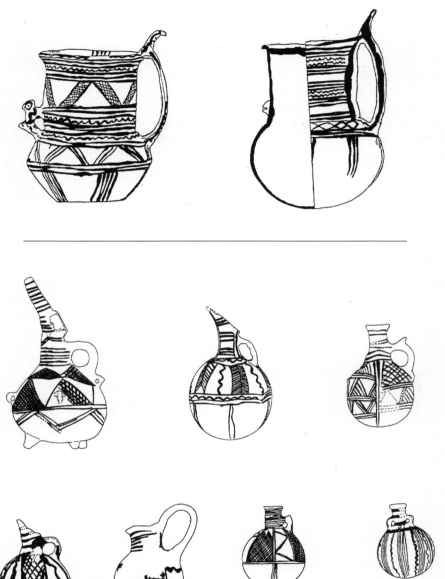

Fig. 5.6. White Painted pottery: *above*: tankards from Myrtou-*Stephania*; *below*: variety of juglets in the Williamson Art Gallery, Birkenhead.

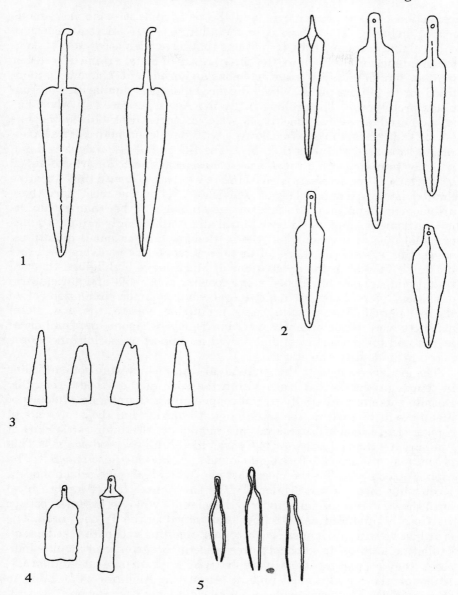

Fig. 5.7. Prehistoric Bronze Age metalwork: (1) daggers; (2) knives; (3) adzes; (4) razors; (5) tweezers.

extraction of local copper ores and the development of an indigenous copper industry. The advance in metallurgy is yet another aspect of cultural and economic transformations that have been attributed to Anatolian immigrants.[97] Even so, the actual range of metal artefacts is rather limited. Ten metal types (tools, weapons and ornaments) have been identified for the Philia phase, which display typological similarities to Anatolian prototypes.[98] The prehistoric Bronze Age repertoire as a whole has an increased range of artefact types, which comprise hook-tanged weapons (swords, daggers and spears), knives with developed midribs, flat axes, razors, tweezers and pins (Fig. 5.7). The EC metal assemblage is dominated by pure copper but there is use of arsenical bronze for artefacts such as daggers. Three artefacts from Alambra were alloyed with tin, indicating limited metal exchange beyond the island.[99] For the most part these artefacts are represented in funerary assemblages rather than within the few settlement contexts. At both Marki and Alambra only a limited range of metal objects was found in the settlement, and in small quantities, suggesting systematic re-use of metal artefacts, as they were used and broken.[100] Moreover, the excavations at Marki have highlighted the continuing importance of chipped stone tools in household and agricultural activities.[101] Metal appears not to have been in common circulation before the LC period. Rather than being utilitarian objects, the new metal artefacts were predominantly used in display (weapons, personal ornaments and toiletry articles) and served an important social function as markers of identity and status.

The evidence suggests that individual settlements were self-sufficient in copper production, at least within the zone of the Troodos foothills. Despite the site's proximity to the copper mines there is no evidence of metal production within the settlement at Marki,[102] but the occurrence of copper slag, crucible fragments and moulds at the later settlement of Alambra are ample testimony to Cypriot metallurgical production.[103] This is echoed by the crucible fragments found at Kalavasos-*Laroumena*.[104] The copper objects were for the most part alloyed with arsenic, which made a harder but more brittle artefact.[105] The tin bronzes from Alambra have been shown to be a foreign import to the island[106] whereas arsenical copper was locally produced using copper ores mined in the Troodos area. The crucibles were used for small-scale copper-smelting within the settlement, exploiting local oxidised copper ores, and the occurrence of moulds indicates that copper artefacts were likewise cast on site at Alambra.[107] Although the metallurgical finds in Area A at Alambra were found in clusters, there is no clear evidence for an actual metal workshop.[108] According to the excavator of the EC site of Pyrgos-*Mavrorachi*, there is evidence for a wide range of metallurgical activities, such as washing, smelting and casting.[109] In particular Belgiorno notes the presence of copper slag and has identified several structures that she interprets as furnaces for smelting copper.[110] Analyses of the slag from the site suggests that sulphide ores were being processed,[111] in contrast to Alambra where analyses suggested the use of oxidised ores. Some of these findings have been questioned by other archaeologists, and further corroboration is necessary.

Funerary ritual and feasting the dead

There were significant changes in burial practices at the beginning of the EC period, which were to have an impact on the organisation of funerary ritual during the Bronze Age throughout the island. Burial was extramural in large, formal, organised cemeteries usually located on the slopes of hills, but within sight of the settlement.[112] The most significant change is in the elaboration of the burial facility, reflecting changing patterns of social organisation. During the Chalcolithic period burials were single inhumations in shaft or pit graves. A new tomb type, the rock-cut chamber tomb used for multiple inhumations, was introduced in the Late Chalcolithic period,[113] and this became the typical tomb type used throughout the Cypriot Bronze Age (Fig. 5.8). It consists of an irregular chamber cut into the bedrock, approached by an open entrance passage (the *dromos*) and entered through a narrow passage or doorway (the *stomion*). The entrance was closed with a stone slab or stone rubble, and it is probable that the *dromos* was closed after successive interments.[114] Presumably the passageway (*dromos*) leading into the tomb chamber was the focus of many of the ceremonies attendant on the funerary ritual, and a single *dromos* frequently served two or more chambers.

The creation of these extramural cemeteries, and in particular the effort involved in the excavation of the chamber and *dromos* from the bedrock, indicates a certain degree of centralised control, at least as far as the allocation and preparation of family burial plots is concerned. The chambers housed multiple inhumations and at Vounous there are some double burials. It is unclear whether individual households or kinship groups had tomb chambers readily prepared for the initial burial. Evidence for widespread secondary treatment of the remains indicates increasing elaboration of funerary ritual beyond the initial deposition of the body in the tomb chamber to an extended multi-phase ritual.[115] The elaboration of funerary ritual, in particular the specialised treatment of human remains in subsequent ceremonies, might support Manning's suggestion that the chamber tombs represent select collective tombs where the emergent elite families were buried.[116] These practices reflect changes in social and economic organisation indicative of the emergence of a kinship-based society rather than household-based social organisation.

Alongside this elaboration of ritual the burials were equipped with increasing quantities of grave goods of increasing diversity. There is a certain degree of uniformity in the range of vessels selected for deposition in tomb groups, suggesting that these were not randomly selected but considered prerequisites for funerary equipment.[117] Knapp suggests that

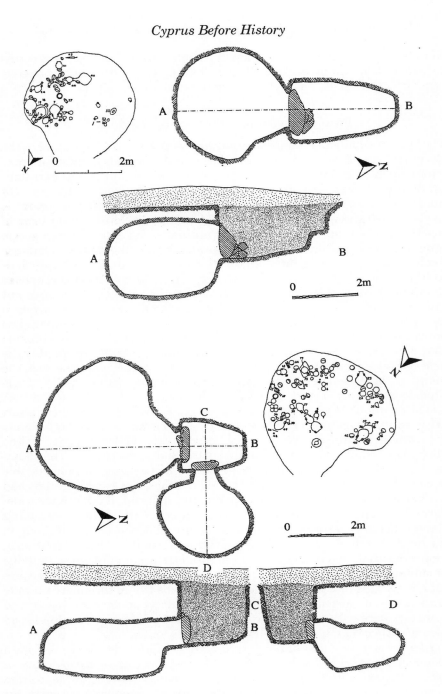

Fig. 5.8. Chamber tombs, Vounous-*Bellapais* T. 11 and T. 3.

some goods might be made specifically for inclusion in graves, suggesting a shift from household production to craft specialisation within workshops. However, more detailed analyses of funerary objects suggest that these had been used within the settlement prior to their deposition in a tomb.[118] Frankel and Webb note that a specific range of household or everyday objects was deliberately removed from the settlement for inclusion in burials, namely decorated pottery, spindle whorls, figurines and jewellery. Other objects more specifically associated with household activities, such as the preparation of food and cooking, were not selected for burial.[119] Typical grave goods therefore include large quantities of ceramics, a limited range of metal objects, especially weapons, but also toiletry articles such as tweezers and ceramic replicas of metal artefacts, such as knives, ceramic combs (Fig. 5.9: 1),[120] spindles and mouth pieces. These models were presumably made specifically for burial. The combination of daggers, spearheads and whetstones in a package is found with a select group of burials, restricted to the coastal cemeteries.[121] While loom weights are not included as grave goods, spindle whorls are a common funerary item and there are examples of model spindles made of clay.[122] Large numbers of whorls are deposited with individual burials, from which it might be possible to infer the presence of a specialised class of textile workers, or at least that these objects were of significance to a select group of individuals. As noted by Crewe, the whorls do not correspond with metal-rich burials, indicating that this activity is not one associated with status.[123]

Although the overall character of the EC and MC settlements suggests a small-scale egalitarian village society, it is possible that the economic changes of this period – namely the introduction of cattle and plough agriculture and the intensification of agriculture – served as the backdrop for the development of social elites. Presumably at this stage elite groups were those households with privileged access to or control over the new resources. However, there appears to have been an innate levelling system within Cypriot society. Manning in particular interprets funerary ritual as the major arena for elite display, as suggested by conspicuous consumption of the new metal artefacts and the development of elaborate burial ritual. He emphasises the appearance of a range of vessels specifically associated with storing, pouring and serving liquids, especially the development of a number of elaborate multi-piece vessels with exaggerated spouts.[124] Manning concludes that these vessels were integral elements of the funerary ritual, specifically the ceremonial consumption of exotic alcoholic drinks as an element of a funerary feast. Further evidence for ceremonial feasting is indicated by the presence of cattle and caprid bones in funerary contexts. This is particularly evident at Vounous, where large joints of meat were found in jars and basins, and the tombs were equipped with elaborate drinking vessels. Herscher suggests such feasting had specifically elite connotations, associated with emphasising membership of an exclusive group being buried in these tombs.[125] The basis for economic control and wealth in EC Cyprus would have been the cattle herds; hence the sacrifice of these animals as part of the funerary ritual and their consumption in ceremonial feasting conveyed powerful ideological messages.

Metal objects are relatively abundant in EC and MC burials, and certain types appear to be very widely distributed, suggesting that these were commonly owned objects and that there were only low levels of control over the circulation of metals, as might be expected from the small-scale copper production within the settlements discussed above.[126] Even so, various scholars have suggested that the distribution of metal artefacts illustrates the emergence of social elites in Cyprus during the EC and MC periods.[127] At Lapithos-*Vrysi tou Barba*, for example, large concentrations of metal artefacts are concentrated in a small number of tomb groups. No metal objects were found in 34 of the 97 tombs excavated, whereas 64% of the metal grave goods were found in a mere nine chambers.[128] These burials clearly stand out from the usual burials in their extraordinary concentration of metal wealth, possibly indicating that certain groups exerted control over the dissemination of metals in EC/MC society. Moreover, certain metal objects with connotations of high status, such as spearheads and axes, tend to be clustered within the wealthiest tombs.[129] Other possible high status grave goods include rare imports, gold, silver and lead trinkets, faience beads, occasional ceramics and impressive large alabaster vessels imported from Old Kingdom Egypt.[130] However, these objects are only sporadically represented, implying that occasional individuals were able to acquire exotic goods from beyond the island, but that these were not systematically incorporated in competitive display within the funerary arena.[131] Other rare grave goods which presumably conveyed specific cultural messages and which might have been incorporated within rare funerary ceremonies are the RP vases with modelled scenes around the shoulder. Their limited distribution and complex imagery suggest that these objects would have been important emblems of identity and prestige, underpinning the new EC/MC ideological system. In particular, the Vounous bowl has been interpreted as a physical manifestation of 'an institutionalised, secular, form of power concentrated in or expressed by a key individual'.[132] In general, while the burial record clearly illustrates the island's changing social and economic organisation, in particular increasing levels of disposable wealth, there is no certain evidence for the emergence of social elites. Instead, the burial record echoes the settlement evidence, and is suggestive of small egalitarian communities with only occasional concentrations of wealth and unusual or exotic grave goods, most notably the unusually large spearheads. Alternatively, the main display of wealth and position may well have been expressed through ceremonial feasting and in particular the slaughter of cattle, the status symbol *par excellence* of these small village communities.

1. Troodos mountains (Kalokhorio-*Zithikionas*).

2. View of the Mesaoria plain.

3. View west along the coast from Kourion.

4. Akrotiri-*Aetokremnos* Site E.

5. Neolithic well, Kissonerga-*Mylouthkia*.

6. Andesite bowl from Khirokitia, aceramic Neolithic.

7. Clay model of head from Khirokitia, aceramic Neolithic.

8. Combed ware bowl from Khirokitia, ceramic Neolithic.

9. Red on White bottle from Sotira, ceramic Neolithic.

10. Reconstruction of Chalcolithic house, Lemba Archaeological Research Centre.

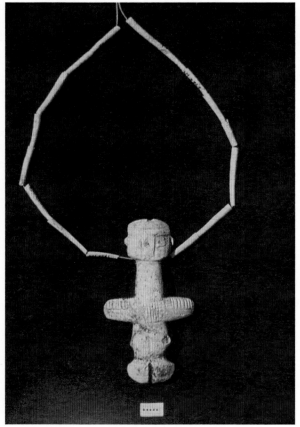

11. Dentalium bead necklace with picro-lite cruciform pendant, Kissonerga-*Mosphilia* Grave 563, Period 3b.

12. Limestone figure,
Lemba-*Lakkous*.

13. Cruciform picrolite figure, Yialia.

14. Building model, Kissonerga-*Mosphilia*, Period 3b.

15. Objects packed in and around building model, Kissonerga-*Mosphilia*, Period 3b.

16. Late Chalcolithic chamber tomb, Kissonerga-*Mosphilia*, Period 4.

17. View of Marki-*Alonia*.

18. Red Polished bull vase, a common image in representations of
the prehistoric Bronze Age.

19. Red Polished ware composite vessel, Vounous, typical of prehistoric Bronze Age funerary ritual.

20. Kotsiatis model of sanctuary, one of a number of scenic compositions dating to the prehistoric Bronze Age.

21. Gold necklace with cylinder seal, Ayios Iakovos, LC IIA.

22. Mycenaean cups, Ayia Irini, LH IIA.

23. Mycenaean chariot krater, Enkomi, LH IIIA (Zeus krater).

24. Mycenaean pictorial krater, Shemishin, LH IIIA.

25. LC terracotta female figurines.

26. Portable bronze hearth, Enkomi, LC IIIA.

27. Bronze wine set, Hala Sultan Tekke, Tomb 23, LC IIIA.

28. Stone model of sanctuary, Hala Sultan Tekke, LC IIIA.

29. Bronze statuette of Horned God, Enkomi, LC IIC-IIIA.

Foreign contacts

The prehistoric Bronze Age saw the initial emergence of Cyprus from her apparent isolation and the development of external contacts, a process that ultimately led to the island's pivotal role in the maritime networks of the East Mediterranean during the later second millennium BC. There was already a tiny trickle of exotica at Late Chalcolithic sites, in particular faience beads. However the period of greatest contact with cultures beyond the island is during the earliest stages of the EC period, in particular the flood of Anatolianising elements that characterise the Philia phase. Whether this represents a population movement or alternative modes of cultural interaction, the effect on Cypriot society was profound and had a lasting impact, and yet Cyprus again appears to revert to internal isolation, even from the closely related cultures of southern Anatolia. Throughout much of the prehistoric Bronze Age Cyprus appears to be largely isolated from the surrounding cultures of the East Mediterranean. This is seemingly a matter of choice, as is reflected by the internal distribution of settlement largely inland and with only two coastal sites, Vasilia and Lapithos both on the north coast. Although there are no natural harbours visible at either site, within the context of early Bronze Age maritime technologies it is possible that small boats were simply dragged up onto the beach. There are occasional imports, including two Minoan ceramic vessels, a jar from Vounous which demonstrates parallels with pottery from Tell Sweyhat,[133] two Egyptian calcite vases, the three tin bronzes from Alambra, and occasional trinkets of lead, silver, gold and faience. The mechanisms by which these objects reached Cyprus are unclear – whether they illustrate direct trading contacts, occasional forays of Cypriots beyond the island, or the appearance of foreign mariners on the island. However, these are exactly the type of exotics that might be invested with prestige value and used in the construction of symbolic ideologies by emergent elites.[134]

By the end of the prehistoric Bronze Age Cyprus had become fully integrated within trade networks operating between Egypt and the Levant which excluded the Aegean. This is especially illustrated by the circulation of small juglets that held small quantities of a precious commodity, possibly a highly coveted luxury perfume.[135] WP juglets are found throughout the Levant and in Egypt, most notable of which is the large deposit of Middle Cypriot pottery found at Tell el-Dab'a in the Nile Delta, capital of the Hyksos rulers of Egypt.[136] The Close Line and Pendent Line styles manufactured in the southeast of the island were those favoured for export. Occasional exotic imports of Yahudiyeh ware juglets, with their distinctive punctured decoration, occur on Cyprus. No longer isolated from outside contact, either through choice or through inertia, in the later second millennium BC the island's culture was dramatically transformed through contact with and assimilation of external cultural influences.

It is assumed that during the LC period Cypriot copper was the impetus for the island's participation in international maritime trade in the East Mediterranean, and the island has frequently been equated with the state of Alashiya known from Near Eastern and Egyptian documents.[137] It is surely no accident that the earliest references to Alashiya and her copper resources date to the eighteenth to seventeenth centuries BC, from Mari, Babylon, and Alalakh,[138] and are therefore contemporary with both the intensification of Cypriot copper production and the island's initial contacts with the cultures of the East Mediterranean. If the equation between Cyprus and Alashiya can be substantiated, this textual evidence pushes external interest in the island's copper resources back to the earliest centuries of the second millennium BC. Even so, it is unlikely that the necessary infrastructure for large-scale exploitation and exchange of copper existed prior to the LC period, and these early textual references are exceptional rather than evidence for Cypriot participation in the international metals trade during the prehistoric Bronze Age.

Representations

The Cypriot prehistoric Bronze Age is particularly rich in terms of its representational art, an area that has been at the forefront of recent research. This material stands apart from the earlier ceramic Neolithic and Chalcolithic figured representations, and the development of a completely new repertoire points to the adoption of a new ideology. There are two main forms of figured representations, both using the medium of fired clay: three-dimensional representations on RP pottery and plank figurines. Although there is an apparent *floruit* of figurative art on the pottery, most RP vessels are in fact undecorated and those that are decorated tend to have simple incised or relief geometric or linear motifs. Consequently, the figurative material is exceptional within its context. It is moreover weighted towards the RP corpus from the north coast cemeteries of Vounous-*Bellapais* and Lapithos-*Vrysi tou Barba*.[139]

Herscher divides the decorated RP into three subgroups on chronological grounds.[140] The earliest group, dating to EC I, comprises large beak-spouted jugs with knobbed 'eyes', possibly a ceramic imitation of a rivet. On some of these vases the knob is extended down into a vertical wavy band to form a snake motif. By EC III/MC I quadrupeds adorn a variety of vessels, usually spouted jugs but also amphorae and bowls. These are very schematic and it is not always possible to identify the species, but stags and cattle are prominent. This indicates the continued importance of the hunting ethos within Cypriot society and the economic importance derived from cattle, which were presumably the major indicator of wealth within the small village communities. Also included in this group are relief animal heads often combined with wavy band motifs, possibly indicating snakes. The so-called shrine models belong in this group. Human representations are very rare. By the MC period large open vessels emerge as the main vehicle for complex display, both relief scenes and representations in the round. Human figures, usually depicted in the round, are depicted engaged in a variety of activities. Apart from a bowl from Kalavasos (Panayia Church Tomb 36), these are largely without firm context.

Scenic compositions in the round are very rare. These include scenes balanced around the rim of a bowl,[141] groups of modelled figures protruding from the shoulder of RP jugs and amphorae, such as the deer-milking scene,[142] and six models depicting figures conducting activities on a flat terracotta slab.[143] Morris interprets these representations as scenes of everyday life in a prehistoric village, but the significance of these scenes and the identification of the specific activities that they depict are difficult to assess and remain elusive. Their rarity and funerary use might indicate that they were commissioned to commemorate the funerary ritual of particular individuals or specific events of great import for the immediate community. The implication is that whatever the choice of scene it would be one of significance for the attendant community and presumably also for the funerary ritual in which it played a part. The famous ploughing scene, for example, might plausibly refer to the wealth of the individual being buried or of his/her family. Common activities depict figures placed around troughs, which Morris interprets as women involved in a variety of activities associated with the preparation of food, such as grinding corn, kneading bread, shaping loaves. Separated from these scenes by the morphology of the vessel there are scenes of individuals associated with circular enclosures containing lumps. These Morris interprets as male figures and bread ovens. An alternative explanation is of a metallurgy scene, depicting copper leaching in special troughs.[144] Most recently, Herscher suggested that the scenes refer to the newly introduced production of alcohol used in ceremonial funerary feasting. Specifically, she interprets the circular enclosures as basins for treading grapes and the trough/basin on the other side as a device for the separation of the wine from the residue.[145] However, the identification and subsequent gendering of these activities is highly problematic, not least because the sex of the figures perched on the side of these bowls tends not to be represented. Other common motifs are of pairs of figures,[146] commonly interpreted as couples and possibly even as marriage scenes, and individuals holding infants. The implication is that these figures illustrate a new social order, emphasising the nuclear household and parenting as the basis for social organisation, a shift from earlier representations of the individual, which Bolger interprets within the framework of the emergence of the patriarchal family.[147]

A number of representations appear to belong to the realm of ceremonial activity rather than scenes of everyday life. The Vounous bowl[148] is the most unusual and complex of the scenic compositions and is unique on a number of counts, including its composition with the scene being placed inside the bowl rather than around its rim. This form is undoubtedly significant, denoting a conscious decision not to use the usual format, such as a terracotta plaque, the rim of a bowl or the shoulder of a jug. The scene on the Vounous bowl is usually interpreted as a religious ceremony taking place within a sacred enclosure, and the tendency has been to place the assumed cult within the framework of a 'Mediterranean' fertility cult with the snake motif illustrating a chthonic deity, very much based on classical associations of the bull and snake. Some interpretations emphasise the undoubted funerary connotations of the scene, possibly an idealised funerary ceremony within the tomb *dromos* or perhaps the physical representation of an ancestor cult.[149] Morris, however, criticises these interpretations, noting that they contradict the general rule of scenic compositions, which is that they illustrate scenes of everyday life and tasks.[150] Instead he suggests that the scene represents a simple village scene, the sides of the bowl representing the walls of the village houses. This reading, however, ignores several important features of the scene: its structured composition, the exclusion of an individual peering over the side of the bowl at the activities within, the different sizes of the participants, the distinct gestures made by certain figures, and the distinction between standing, kneeling, seated and enthroned individuals. All of these are common devices for illustrating the relative importance of individuals in prehistoric art. Other analyses of the Vounous bowl have contextualised it within the wider changes affecting Cypriot village communities, such as the development of social hierarchies and the emergence of an elite group whose wealth was based on ownership of cattle.[151] One possibility is that the scene illustrates an idealised scene of prosperity (indicated by the penned cattle), presided over by the elite class, the enthroned figure representing power invested in or expressed by a figure of authority.

Two plank models from Kotsiatis, depicting a female figure in front of a large jar in front of a triple bucrania motif, are interpreted as abbreviated ceremonial or sanctuary scenes (see Plate 20), which pick up on some of the themes implicit in the Vounous bowl.[152] The interpretations of these scenes as the expression of religious activity within specialised cult locations have enormous implications for our understanding of prehistoric Bronze Age society in Cyprus. At present there is no physical evidence for 'sanctuaries' or specialised cult places of this date. One possibility is that these scenes refer to outdoor locations with ephemeral wooden architecture, which would leave no trace in the archaeological record. Alternatively, these scenes might refer to activities that took place in the *dromoi* of the chamber tombs. Bucrania certainly do have religious or symbolic significance in later Cypriot Bronze Age ritual, but the question remains whether this symbolism can be extrapolated back to the EC period. If the answer is yes, then the Vounous bowl and the Kotsiatis models are evidence of a profound shift in the construction of the metaphysical world at the beginning of the Bronze Age.[153]

5. Cattle, Anatolian Migrants, and the Prehistoric Bronze Age

A new type of portable human representation appears in the prehistoric Bronze Age, the so-called plank figurine made in the RP ware (Fig. 5.9: 2).[154] These figurines may represent another element of material culture that exhibits Anatolian influence.[155] The body is flat, as though carved from a piece of wood. Gender is rarely depicted, arms are indicated by incised lines or in relief, legs are not usually indicated, facial features are indicated by relief and incision. Sometimes the figures have double heads, as though depicting a couple. This might refer back to the representations of couples in the round on RP vases.[156] The emphasis is not on representing the human form, but rather on providing a medium for representing human apparel,[157] either elaborately woven textiles or body tattoos. This might give us some insight into the importance of dress for non-verbal communication of identity and status in prehistoric Bronze Age Cyprus. The bodies and faces are elaborately decorated with incised geometric motifs, which might refer to a variety of modes of personal decoration such as tattoos, jewellery, or woven textiles, possibly referring to the social position of the individual.[158] Frequently the figurines have oblique incised lines on the front of the body in addition to applied clay arms. Washbourne suggests that these represent large toggle pins used to fasten garments. More specifically she relates these to the *tudittu* of ancient Near Eastern texts, jewellery (possibly to be identified as toggle pins) that was given to a woman at her wedding.[159] Certainly the toggle pins found in EC tomb groups tend to be in pairs, supporting Washbourne's interpretation. Occasionally the figure holds an infant and there are also cradle figures, in

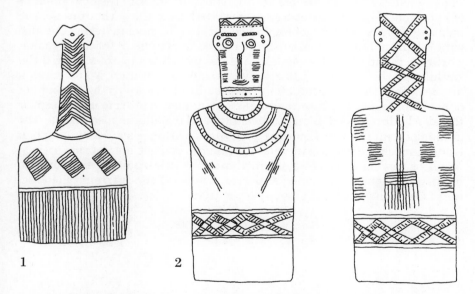

1   2

Fig. 5.9. (1) Black Polished model of 'comb'; (2) Red Polished plank figure from Vounous.

147

which the plank has become the stiff board of the cradle. These specific representations indicate that certain social roles have acquired specific importance within Cypriot society, in particular parenting, which might be expected within the context of the emergence of a hereditary society in which family ties are pre-eminent in the negotiation of identity.[160] Although the best preserved examples have a funerary context, these figurines are not pre-requisites for funerary ritual and are found in less than 10% of burials.[161] They are, moreover, represented in settlement contexts at Alambra-*Mouttes*, Ambelikou-*Aletri*, Episkopi-*Phaneromeni* and Marki-*Alonia*, although not at Sotira-*Kaminoudhia*. The actual function(s) of these figurines remains elusive, although traditional interpretations of such objects within the parameters of traditional figurine studies, as idols, servants for the afterlife and fertility charms, appear unconvincing. Alternative interpretations, which view these figurines as an expression of individuality, are attractive within the context of the social and economic transformations of the prehistoric Bronze Age and the posited rise of lineage groups.[162] A Campo argues that the emphasis on the body markings implies that an important function of the figurines was to express differentiation (status, social roles). She suggests that these were possibly used as exchange tokens, perhaps in marriage contracts, as a means of underpinning the prehistoric Bronze Age social system.[163]

The prehistoric Bronze Age: an overview

The prehistoric Bronze Age marks an important stage in the development of Cypriot society, representing a major break from the earlier prehistoric habitation of the island, not only in cultural and economic terms but also with regard to human relationship with the landscape. Particularly noteworthy is the increased exploitation of the metalliferous zone around the foothills of the Troodos. Ultimately, human exploitation would have a dramatic impact on the landscape, especially clearance of the forests not only to fuel copper and bronze production but also to provide more land for the newly introduced plough agriculture. This phase also marks the gradual integration of Bronze Age Cyprus within East Mediterranean trading mechanisms, again with a dramatic impact on Cypriot society. Many of the changes presaged in these developments did not come to fruition until the subsequent LC period, which is very different in character to the earlier cultural phases on the island.

148

6

Cyprus in the Late Bronze Age

The Late Bronze Age settlement of Cyprus is distinct from that of earlier periods on a number of counts, indicative of substantive social and economic transformations as the island emerged from its prehistoric occupation. There was a massive increase in population and expansion of settlement into new, previously unoccupied areas (Fig. 6.1). Alongside this there is evidence for an increasingly complex hierarchical settlement pattern, culminating in the rise of urban complexes along the southern coast by the thirteenth century BC. During the LBA, in particular during the fourteenth and thirteenth centuries BC, the island was the nexus of wide-ranging international trade networks around the eastern basin of the Mediterranean, incorporating Egypt, Syro-Palestine and the Aegean. The Cypriot role in this trade appears to have been based upon increased

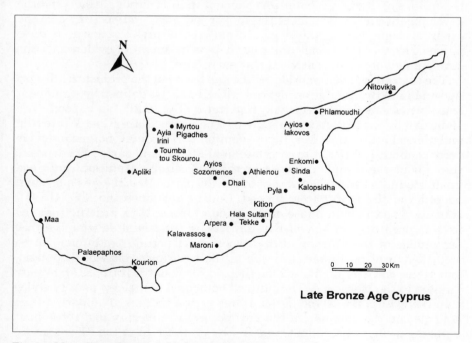

Fig. 6.1. Map of Late Bronze Age settlement on Cyprus.

exploitation of the island's copper resources. The copper trade allowed the emergence of an economic and possibly political elite, which controlled access to luxury imports and prestige goods. Although the LC period remains one of the more intensively researched aspects of Cypriot prehistory, in particular the metal trade and evidence for foreign relations especially with the Aegean, numerous issues remain unresolved. In particular the socio-political organisation underpinning these changes remains elusive, not least whether there was a single unified state or a series of polities at the level of a state or a chiefdom. The identification of Cyprus in the texts of the literate societies of the Near East likewise remains intangible.

Origins

The transition between the prehistoric Bronze Age and the Late Bronze Age occupation of Cyprus was a period of major social upheaval, during which the foundations for the development of the Cypriot LBA were laid. This phase is characterised by regionalism, massive social instability, and a major shift in settlement pattern, in particular the establishment of new sites on the south and east coasts. Alongside these changes several new factors illustrate the quickening pulse of LC society. These include the beginnings of literacy, greater involvement in international trade and the development and expansion of the copper industry, and possibly also the export of copper beyond the island. Initially, social organisation appears to be based around the village unit and there is no apparent evidence for the development of urban centres at this early date.

The transitional period bridging the gap between the prehistoric Bronze Age and Late Bronze Age on Cyprus (MC III-LC I) is defined by significant transformations in the ceramic repertoire (Fig. 6.2). LC deposits are identified by the presence of a suite of type wares: Base Ring, White Slip and Monochrome. However, their adoption is a gradual, non island-wide process and it is difficult to correlate final MC III and early LC I deposits throughout the island. In all areas the MC ceramic tradition continued unaffected into the earliest phase of the LC period, but there is a gradual adoption of the new wares. Indeed, Catling redefines the MC III-LC I transition as the final phase of the Middle Bronze Age, arguing that the initial appearance of Mycenaean imports on the island denotes the true beginnings of the Cypriot LBA.[1] Two distinct pottery traditions can be identified: a monochrome tradition in the west and centre of the island, and in the east a painted tradition (Red on Black in the Karpass and White Painted in the Mesaoria). The cultural homeland of the new pottery styles is in the west of the island. Even in this region there is an apparent time lag between the adoption of the new pottery in funerary and settlement contexts, perhaps best illustrated by the evidence from the coeval settlement and cemetery of Myrtou-*Pigadhes* and Myrtou-*Stephania*. Within

150

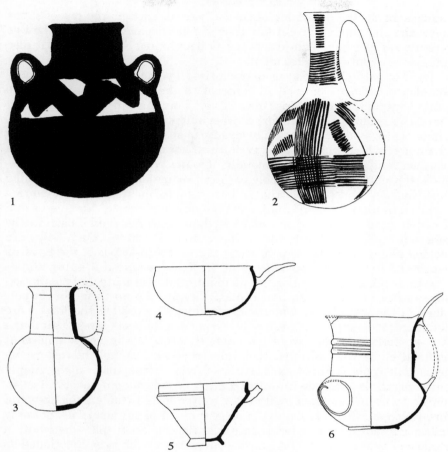

Fig. 6.2. MC III-LC I pottery: (1) Black Slip Reserved Slip amphora from
Myrtou-*Stephania*; (2) Red on Black jug; (3) Red Slip jug; (4) Monochrome bowl;
(5) Base Ring I cup; (6) Base Ring I tankard.

the settlement the MC wares persist and are predominant throughout
Periods I and II (into LC I), whereas in the cemetery the novel LC wares
predominate and the MC wares are in the minority from the very beginning of the LC period.[2] The very abrupt transition in the cemetery is in
contrast to the gradual transformation of the pottery repertoire within the
settlement. This might reflect a hiatus in the archaeological record (possibly a gap in the sequence of burials). Alternatively, it might illustrate a
distinctive cultural use of the new wares, that initially in the northwest
part of the island the new pottery styles had a specifically funerary
function. In the eastern part of the island the MC pottery tradition persists
well into the LC I period, although certain technological and morphological

151

changes signal the beginning of the LC period, such as the use of softer clays and the appearance of flat bases.[3] The disparity between the two ceramic regions has been attributed to geographic distance, but it also illustrates regional cultural identities.

The MC III-LC I period is characterised by the emergence of a more complex settlement pattern in contrast to the pervasive small village settlements of the prehistoric Bronze Age. There is a two-tiered settlement hierarchy, comprising small fort centres and outlying villages or hamlets. There is also evidence for the appearance of specialised sites, the primary function of which was neither agricultural nor defensive. These include a possible religious site at Phlamoudhi-*Vounari*,[4] copper mining sites, specialised production sites, namely pottery production at Morphou-*Toumba tou Skourou*,[5] and possibly the earliest establishment of coastal centres involved in international trade, most notably at Enkomi.[6] Fortresses and fortified sites are one of the more striking features that illustrate the inherent social instability during this period (Fig. 6.3).[7] These sites are located along the Karpass peninsula, the southern slopes of the Kyrenia range and the northeastern slopes of the Troodos massif. Catling argues that their inland distribution points to internal insecurity and population stress rather than an external threat.[8] Despite the *floruit* of forts, their place in the MC III-LC I landscape is unclear. Possibly the forts were simply refugee sites that were only occupied in times of stress,[9] although it is possible that they were permanently occupied by newly emergent political elites who initiated their construction. Frankel, however, suggests that some fortified sites, such as Ayios Sozomenos, might simply have served as corrals within the context of a developing pastoral economy.[10] An economic function for many of the forts is undeniable. Several forts, such as Nitovikla, housed a large number of storage jars,[11] possibly indicating that they were local centres for the collection and redistribution of agricultural surplus. Their large courtyards might have functioned as assembly points for the distribution of staples.[12]

Many fortified sites were strategically placed along the route from the copper-rich region of the Troodos massif and the coastal centre of Enkomi, suggesting that they were built to protect the movement of copper to the island's new economic centres.[13] This is further developed by Peltenburg,[14] who suggests that the forts are an expression of early state formation in Cyprus. He argues that these structures were associated with centralised exploitation of copper (its procurement, processing and distribution) under the control of emergent coastal polities. Enkomi was pre-eminent in this process, hence the cluster of forts at strategic communication points between Enkomi and the Troodos mines. Peltenburg argues that the LC I fort at Enkomi is a physical manifestation of the power of the emergent elite at the site, which was dependent on the growing copper trade. In this respect the concentration of high status burials, richly furnished with prestige objects, in the area of the fort is noteworthy.[15] Keswani, however,

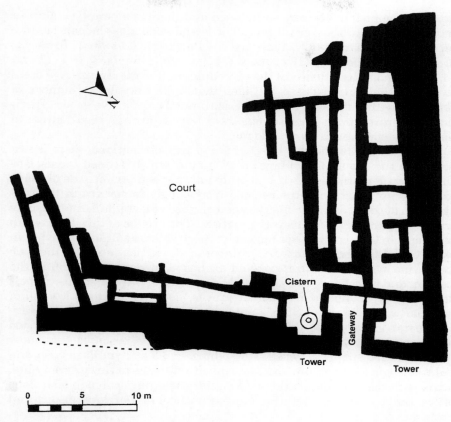

Court

Cistern

Gateway

Tower

Tower

0   5   10 m

Fig. 6.3. Plan of the fort at Nitovikla.

comments that links between the forts and the newly emergent urban centres have yet to be established.[16]

Also indicative of social upheaval at the Middle/Late Bronze Age transition are the destruction horizons, the abandonment of prehistoric Bronze Age sites and apparent mass burials. The destruction horizons at Kalopsidha, Episkopi-*Phaneromeni* and Morphou-*Toumba tou Skourou* in MC III and the fortresses at Nitovikla and Enkomi at the end of LC IA, have also been viewed as evidence for the unsettled conditions on the island during this transitional phase. Keswani suggests that these destructions represent a generalised practice of raiding to obtain livestock (possibly the main signifier of wealth and status), agricultural produce, valuables and human captives, noting in particular the scarcity of valuables, especially metal objects, in LC I settlements such as Episkopi-*Phaneromeni*.[17] Alternatively, the destruction horizons might refer to the competition between emergent rival polities over access to resources and land. While many sites

153

were re-occupied, a few were abandoned and there is a perceived shift in settlement toward the coastal zone. The island-wide mass burials characteristic of this phase,[18] such as at Pendayia-*Mandres* Tomb 1, Myrtou-*Stephania* Tomb 12 or Ayios Iakovos-*Melia* Tombs 8, 10A, 12 and 14, are without precedence in the preceding prehistoric Bronze Age occupation of the island. These are identified by a very large number of skeletons with a disproportionately small number of grave goods. Traditional interpretations suggest that these burials are the result either of human agency (warfare) or of plague.

Concurrent with the MC III-LC I social transformations, there is evidence for the emergence of new social groups which defined themselves through preferential access to elaborate military equipment. The physical expression of warrior status became increasingly important in the construction of social identity and the symbolic use of metal in formal display was central to early LC funerary practices. The origins of this display can be sought in the rare 'warrior burials' of the prehistoric Bronze Age, but in the MC III-LC I phase elite warrior status made explicit reference to exotic Levantine symbols. Bronze socketed axeheads, of a type common in the Levant, and maceheads were adopted as symbols of warrior status.[19] Their deposition in a limited number of graves, such as at Dhali-*Kafkallia*, together with a bronze belt,[20] is particularly striking as there were very few metal grave goods during this period. In general metal was too precious to be removed from circulation, and it is probable that most weapons were simply recycled. Horse burials, as at Ayia Paraskevi and Politiko-*Chomazoudia*, are another explicit reference to this warrior elite, again with oriental connotations. Alongside these physical manifestations of warrior burials are the first representations of warriors on pictorial pottery.[21]

Traditional interpretations of the very apparent social and economic changes at the beginning of the LBA were correlated with contemporary social upheaval in Egypt and the Near East, in particular the expulsion of the Hyksos from Egypt.[22] Although such simplistic correlations have fallen out of vogue, there is certainly considerable evidence for increasing Cypriot participation in the economic and social spheres of the East Mediterranean from the beginning of the LBA. Most notable is the ceramic evidence, illustrating the development of increasingly complex trade networks between Cyprus and the Levant in the sixteenth and fifteenth centuries BC.[23] Large quantities of Levantine pottery imports are found in Cyprus,[24] there is clear evidence for the development of common ceramic styles, such as the Bichrome ware,[25] and increasing quantities of LC pottery (the Base Ring, White Slip and Monochrome wares) were exported to the Levant.[26] Of particular note is the concentration of Proto White Slip and White Slip I at Tell el-'Ajjul, an important nexus of trade between Egypt, southern Palestine and Cyprus in the earlier part of the LBA.[27] Alongside the evidence for maritime trade, the MC III-LC I burials

Fig. 6.4. Impressions of cylinder seals from Ayia Paraskevi.

demonstrate increasing consumption of Near Eastern elite paraphernalia, especially in the central part of the island adjacent to the copper-mining zone.[28] In addition to the warrior equipment discussed above there were small ornaments of precious metal and an Old Babylonian seal in Tomb 1884 at Ayia Paraskevi (Fig. 6.4).[29] From the earliest part of the LC period, therefore, there is clear evidence for the manipulation of luxury imported exotica in the negotiation of elite identity, underlining the close relationship between trade and status in LBA Cyprus.

Landscape and settlement

The LC period is characterised by expansion in settlement and diversified use of the Cypriot landscape. There is more widespread occupation throughout the island, the number of settlements increases and the new sites tend to be larger than the villages of the prehistoric Bronze Age.[30] There is also a marked shift in the location of settlements away from the hinterland toward the coast, reflecting the island's gradual emergence from isolation. The LC inhabitants of Cyprus, or at least those from the coastal sites, looked outwards and chose to negotiate their identity with reference to oriental and Aegean exotica. Urban expansion into the southern coast is one of the most marked facets of the LC settlement pattern, while the previously important sites of the north coast continue to be occupied but are of lesser economic importance and do not appear to be prominent within the LC socio-political arena.[31] Particularly prominent is the group of LC sites around the bay of Larnaca, most notably Hala Sultan Tekke and Kition, both of which appeared to have preferential access to imported exotica from the Aegean, the Near East and Egypt. Few LC IIA-B deposits have been excavated, and the nature of settlement in this period is unclear, but by the thirteenth century BC there is clear development of a hierarchical settlement pattern.

Originally Catling ordered the LC settlement pattern into a tripartite framework: coastal urban centres, mainly situated along the southern coast, inland agricultural settlements, and copper production centres in the metalliferous zone of the Troodos massif.[32] Increasing survey work in the hinterland has further elucidated the nature of LC exploitation of the landscape, in particular subtle differences between the inland sites, reflecting economic specialisation. Knapp suggests a four-tiered settlement hierarchy: (1) primary coastal centres (the main urban sites); (2) secondary inland centres with storage and administrative functions; (3) tertiary inland centres; and (4) specialised economic sites, for agricultural and/or pottery production or copper procurement.[33] Knapp also identifies four major coastal urban polities, Enkomi (Fig. 6.5), Morphou-*Toumba tou Skourou*, Hala Sultan Tekke, and Kourion-*Bamboula*, which he suggests rose to prominence as early as the MC III-LC I transition.[34] These were centres of specialised economic and ceremonial activities, and Knapp

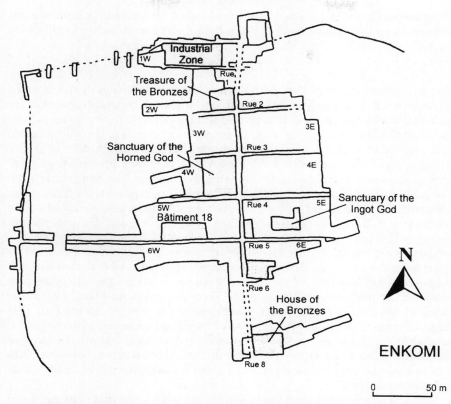

Fig. 6.5. Plan of Enkomi, illustrating grid plan and location of major buildings of the thirteenth and twelfth centuries BC.

suggests that they were the dominant economic and political force within the surrounding landscape. By the fourteenth and thirteenth centuries BC the number of southern urban centres had expanded, including a number of locales around Maroni, and the major settlements at Kalavasos-*Ayios Dhimitrios*, Alassa and Palaepaphos. The thirteenth and twelfth centuries are characterised by major urban reorganisation. This includes spatial reorganisation of the urban centres on grid plans and monumental construction programmes with extensive use of ashlar (cut stone) masonry. The secondary and tertiary inland centres functioned as local redistribution centres for agricultural produce and controlled the movement of copper from the mining sites to the coastal centres. Knapp suggests that these included a number of apparently religious or ceremonial centres, for example at Athienou, Myrtou-*Pigadhes* and perhaps Ayios Iakovos.[35] At the lower end of the settlement hierarchy are the smaller, specialised production centres.[36] These include sites for the procurement of copper, as at Apliki and Politiko-*Phorades*,[37] specialised production of pottery, such

157

as Sanidha-*Moutti tou Ayiou Serkou,* and small farmsteads or agricultural centres, such as Analiondas,[38] Aredhiou-*Vouppes* and possibly Ayia Irini.[39]

Economy

The LC period is characterised by increasing exploitation of the island's mineral wealth, namely copper, both for internal consumption and for external trade, and during this period the island rose to economic prominence in the East Mediterranean. Cyprus was also rich in timber (cypress, pine, and oak),[40] which was used in shipbuilding, mining, and the metallurgy and ceramic industries. Moreover, the evidence for increasing LC participation in maritime trade indicates that for the first time the islanders took full advantage of their privileged geographical position, commanding the sea routes between the Aegean and the Levant. Based on his reading of the LC settlement pattern, Catling argued for a threefold economy.[41] The economic basis was dependent on agriculture at the smaller rural settlements, located in prime arable land near water courses, and stock-rearing. The major innovation of the LC period was the large-scale exploitation of the island's copper resources at the interface between the mountainous zone of the Troodos massif and the lower lying land. Mining sites and primary smelting centres were located in this metalliferous region, usually in areas of poor land unsuited to agricultural production. The urban centres that flourished along the southern coast of the island during the fourteenth and thirteenth centuries (between Enkomi in the east and Palaepaphos in the west) were primarily involved in international trade.[42]

The island's agricultural basis continued with very little change from the prehistoric Bronze Age. Faunal remains indicate that sheep, goat, cattle and pig were all bred. According to LC iconography, cattle and horses were potent symbols of wealth and status. Sheep, goat, cattle and small quantities of fallow deer comprise the typical faunal assemblage in sanctuaries. By the LC period, however, fallow deer was no longer a staple element of the LC diet and seems to have had purely elite connotations associated with hunting practices.[43] Agriculture was based on cultivation of cereals (wheat and barley) and lentils. There is also the first clear evidence for the introduction of orchard husbandry to Cyprus, specifically the cultivation of olives and grapes. At Apliki-*Karamallos*, in House A, charred archaeobotanical remains were uncovered in what appears to have been a storeroom. These included barley, bread wheat, horsebean, lentils, grapes, and olives.[44] Helbaek suggests that the remains of coriander and almond at the site might have been exotic imports from the Near East.[45] The archaeobotanical remains from Kalavasos-*Ayios Dhimitrios* suggest a similar agricultural base. Alongside the cultivation of cereals and lentils there is evidence that either the olive, grape and fig were cultivated or the wild fruits were being collected.[46] A large concentration of olive pits was found in Building IX (A51), associated with pithos sherds, but there was no archaeological evidence to suggest that this was an oil-pressing area.[47] Even so, gas chromatography suggests that the facilities in Building XI (A185) and storerooms in Building X were specifically associated with the production and distribution of olive oil.[48] A particularly rich botanical deposit was found in a possible latrine in Building X (A173), together with meat-bearing bones of sheep/goat, apparently the debris from a feast.[49] The archaeobotanical remains comprised lentils, grapes, peas, figs, and olive, reflecting the typical cultigens found elsewhere on the site, and members of the squash/cucumber/gourd family.[50]

Keswani has argued for two parallel redistribution systems in operation alongside each other and underpinning the LC economy: the staple finance and wealth finance systems.[51] Staple finance is dependent on centralised accumulation of agricultural produce and utilitarian artefacts, which will be redistributed to support members of the elite, the official and bureaucratic classes, and craft specialists. In contrast, the wealth finance model substitutes portable wealth and prestige objects for basic subsistence commodities. There is an obvious parallel between the operation of the wealth finance system and the social storage system advocated for the Bronze Age Aegean,[52] which argues for the substitution of tokens or crafted goods in local exchange systems, which can be reconverted back to agricultural produce in times of shortfall. Interaction between the two redistributive systems argues for increasingly sophisticated use of the Cypriot landscape during the LC period, with the development of primary and secondary centres. There would have been intensified agricultural production and a complex system of subsistence and specialised production that integrated the urban sites and smaller village settlements. An agricultural support village, where produce above the needs of the local inhabitants was processed and stored, might have been identified at Analiondas-*Palioklichia*.[53] Finds include numerous pithos sherds, one of which was impressed, and quantities of querns, implying large-scale processing and storage of cereals at the site. Local redistribution centres have also been suggested for Apliki-*Karamallos*, Athienou[54] and Ayia Irini. Fifteen pithoi were found in the storeroom of House A at Apliki, with an estimated capacity of 7500 litres, beyond the immediate subsistence requirements of the household.[55] Likewise, the facility at Ayia Irini was equipped with extensive storage facilities, and other elements suggestive of local production, such as pestles, grinders and spindle whorls.[56] However, there is rather less evidence for centralised redistribution centres within the primary urban settlements along the coast. Possibly the best example is the LC IIC town at Kalavasos-*Ayios Dhimitrios* (Fig. 6.6).[57] Excavations in the North-East area of the town have uncovered a large tripartite building with an imposing ashlar façade, and equipped with two extensive storage areas: the Pithos Hall and the North Pithos Magazine. These storage areas housed more than 50 large pithoi up to 2 m in height,

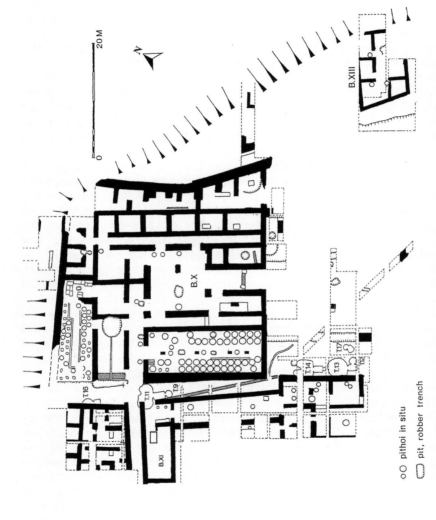

Fig. 6.6. Plan of the North-East area at Kalavasos-*Ayios Dhimitrios*, showing the storage facilities of Building X and the adjacent oil production area in Building XI.

160

and the facility as a whole has an estimated storage capacity of approximately 50,000 litres.[58] There is virtually no archaeobotanical evidence that these stores housed cereal crops[59] and instead it has been suggested that Building X was used for centralised storage of olive oil, based on analyses of the pithoi using gas chromatography.[60] A possible oil production facility has been identified in the adjacent Building XI.[61] Other ashlar structures apparently associated with central administration have been identified at Alassa-*Palaeotaverna* (Building II) and Maroni-*Vournes*.[62]

By the thirteenth century, therefore, there is some evidence for centralised storage of agricultural produce. This implies sufficient agricultural production to allow the removal of the surplus to support economic specialisation and craft production. However, with the exception of Kalavasos, this operated largely at the level of the secondary inland centres and was not directly controlled by the primary urban sites along the south coast. The absence of a developed bureaucratic system to control the movement of agricultural produce, raw materials and prestige goods is striking. In particular, there is no evidence for a systematic sealing system, and where seals are used they appear largely to have had a prestige, ornamental function.[63] However, the standardisation inherent in the storage systems, as has been demonstrated for the large pithoi made specifically for large-scale central storage at Kalavasos-*Ayios Dhimitrios*,[64] and the development of the Cypro-Minoan script illustrate the development of a basic, two-tiered redistribution system. Furthermore, the limited distribution of the impressed pithoi, most notably at Alassa-*Palaeotaverna* (exclusively large, non-domestic pithoi), is suggestive, particularly as they are contemporary with the development of centralised storage.[65] It has been suggested that these impressions made explicit reference to elite Aegean and Near Eastern iconography (chariot scenes, processions of bulls and people, combat between warriors and griffons, a warrior slaying a lion) and denoted special ownership.[66]

Craft specialisation

Craft specialisation is an important characteristic of urban activity. During MC III-LC I there was an apparent move away from domestic production in small villages to large-scale production in specialised centres. As the LC period progressed there is increasing evidence for the intensification of craft production associated with the establishment of the large urban centres along the south coast, and within these two distinct types of craft specialisation can be identified. These are the production of everyday utilitarian household objects and the manufacture of luxury, prestige goods for the elite. The latter used labour intensive, technologically sophisticated techniques and exotic resources. Craft specialisation implies that an element of the labour force was not involved in primary production of agricultural produce, but was maintained by the rest of the community. It

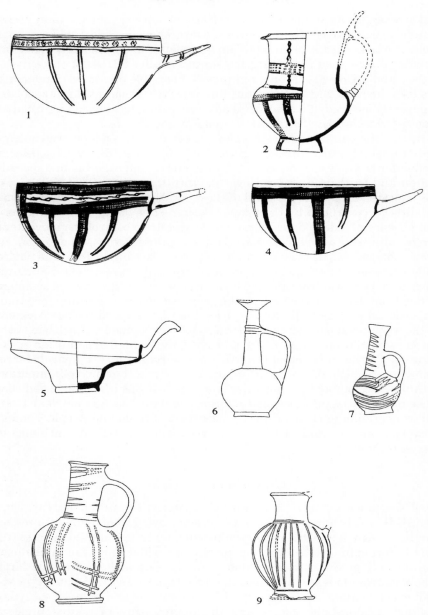

Fig. 6.7. LC pottery: (1) White Slip I hemispherical bowl; (2) White Slip II tankard; (3) White Slip II Normal Style hemispherical bowl; (4) White Slip II Normal Style hemispherical bowl; (5) Base Ring II carinated cup; (6) Base Ring I juglet (bilbil); (7) Base Ring II juglet with painted decoration; (8) Base Ring II jug with painted decoration; (9) Bucchero jug.

also implies at least a rudimentary system of redistribution and social organisation. Whereas Frankel and Webb have argued for household production of handmade wares in the MC period,[67] the evidence for the LC period suggests the establishment of specialist workshops. The typical LC wares (Fig. 6.7) – Base Ring, White Slip, Plain ware and Monochrome – were established and in common use throughout the island by LC II. Specific styles demonstrate the considerable technical skill of specialist potters, most notably the Base Ring ware, which was made from a very plastic clay and formed into elaborate shapes with very thin walls. Likewise the technological information for White Slip production suggests a considerable investment of time and resources, beyond the capabilities of small-scale domestic production.[68]

Specialised LC ceramic production centres have been identified at Morphou-*Toumba tou Skourou* and Sanidha-*Moutti tou Ayiou Serkou*. There was very little evidence for domestic activity at *Toumba tou Skourou* (Fig. 6.8), and the excavators have interpreted it as a specialised industrial quarter for the production of bricks, fine ware pottery and pithoi.[69] The initial occupation of the site dates to LC I and is denoted by the construction of a terrace wall along the north side of the site, against which a series of workshops and large quantities of ceramics were excavated. Physical evidence for a pottery workshop comprises pits filled with potters' clay, a clay dump and sacks of clay, misfired pottery, a basin apparently used for processing clay, benches, and kilns.[70] The site specialised in the production of White Painted bottles, bowls and tankards, and Proto White Slip and White Slip I pottery. The only building with any evidence of residential activity is Building B, where there is evidence for the domestic use of the LC fine wares on the upper floors. Building B was also equipped with large storage facilities and pithoi in the large west hall (room 3) and in room 4, perhaps indicating centralised accumulation of agricultural produce to support craft specialists and thereby some level of centralised elite control over ceramic production.[71] Sanidha, located in the southern foothills of the Troodhos massif, dates to LC IIB and is a specialised White Slip production centre.[72] Here pottery production appears to be more autonomous, although the site's relationship with nearby urban centres, especially Kalavasos-*Ayios Dhimitrios*, is unclear. Abundant timber and clay resources are locally available and the configuration of the site argues for a pottery workshop. There is an overwhelming quantity of White Slip – an abnormal representation of pottery types within LC settlement contexts – which includes unslipped White Slip sherds. Also found at the site were numerous wasters, the fragments of burnt bricks, probably from a kiln, and numerous pebbles that were probably used in ceramic production.

By LC IIC there is increasing evidence for large-scale mass production of pottery in Cyprus. The more elaborate White Slip and Base Ring forms disappear,[73] and the repertoire becomes dominated by simple hemispherical and carinated bowls, and small Base Ring juglets. In addition, there is

163

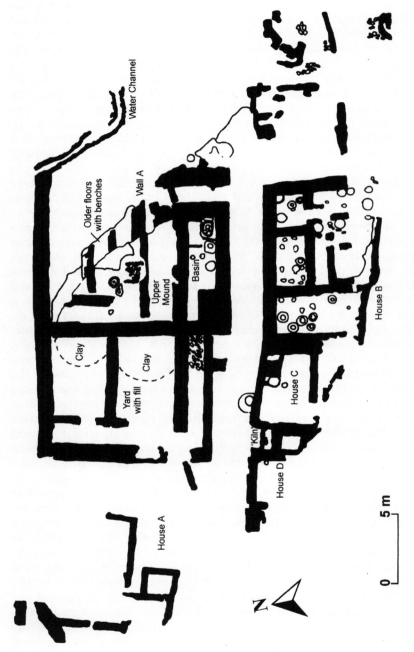

Fig. 6.8. Plan of Morphou-*Toumba tou Skourou*.

164

apparent deterioration of surface treatment, typified by the careless application of paint to White Slip bowls and the matt washy slip of the Base
Ring cups. Moreover, there appears to be a certain degree of standardisation in vessel size, in particular in the utilitarian wares.[74] Sherratt
argues for increasing standardisation of the ceramic industry in LC IIC-
IIIA, particularly illustrated by the pervasive use of the potter's wheel and
the decline of the indigenous handmade fine wares.[75] This process is
largely associated with local production of Mycenaean-style pottery (White
Painted Wheelmade III), in particular to make components of drinking
sets – bell kraters, shallow bowls and, by LC IIIA, deep bowls. Sherratt
relates the mass production of highly standardised ceramics to increasing
urbanisation and administrative centralisation in the thirteenth and
twelfth centuries BC. She argues that by the end of the LBA Cypriot pottery
production was homogeneous throughout the island, subsuming regional
traditions, indicative of centralised control over pottery production.[76]

The relationship between emergent elite groups and luxury craft production is a well documented phenomenon, and it has been argued that
these elites actively employed craft specialists to manufacture luxury
worked goods as a conscious strategy to maintain or increase their political
authority.[77] These prestige goods are frequently made from rare and
imported materials and exhibit exclusive or exotic iconographies as a
means of investing status symbols with greater power.[78] There are rich
archaeological data illustrating elite craft specialisation during the LC
period (Fig. 6.9). These specialists produced plate metal vases,[79] gold
jewellery,[80] ivory objects,[81] faience vases[82] and bronzes.[83] The syncretic
nature of LC society is clearly illustrated by the external referents for
these prestige goods. Aegeanising iconography is particularly prominent,
and yet Cypriot craft specialists were equally influenced by Near Eastern
and Egyptianising images. A particularly intriguing axis of interaction
operated between Mycenaean Greece, Ugarit and Cyprus, and is most
clearly seen in the common style of ivory carving in the three areas. By the
LC IIC-IIIA period there is significant evidence for metallurgical production: bronze hemispherical bowls are the most common, but these are part
of a wide range of metal vessels. Most striking, however, are the cast
bronze statuettes[84] and the tripod and four-sided stands.[85] These prestige
goods were primarily used in display, presumably in competition between
local elites, and many of the prestige goods in circulation in LBA Cyprus
were eventually deposited in religious and funerary contexts. One of the
richest such deposits of exotica, with a high incidence of imported luxuries,
was found in the LC IIA ceremonial structure at Ayios Iakovos-*Dhima*.[86]
The finds included sets of specialised, ritual ceramic vessels, especially the
Red Lustrous wheelmade arm vessels[87] and a Mycenaean krater, a concentration of gold and silver jewellery (see Plate 21), bronze weapons, four
haematite cylinder seals,[88] a glass juglet, an alabaster jar and a small
bronze lion.[89]

Fig. 6.9. (1) Faience vase; (2) incised ivory disc (lid of cylindrical box), both from Kition-*Bamboula*.

Metallurgy

Copper production played a central role in the development of the LBA economy of Cyprus.[90] Indeed, exploitation of Cypriot copper is commonly cited in models of secondary state formation for LBA Cyprus[91] and there is clear evidence for a dramatic increase in bronze-working in the centuries between *c.* 1600 and 1200 BC. Copper and tin were the basis of the LBA metals trade in the East Mediterranean. Although the origins of tin remain elusive,[92] a variety of possible sources have been identified for copper. Most commonly cited is Cyprus, but copper ores are also found in Spain, Sardinia, Tuscany, Attica (at Lavrion), and in Anatolia. Typically, copper was traded in the form of standardised ingots in the shape of an oxhide, weighing between 25 and 28 kg.[93] These ingots have a wide distribution throughout the Mediterranean,[94] between Sardinia and Sicily in the west, mainland Greece and Crete, Cyprus, and Syria in the east, and even as far north as Bulgaria[95] on the Black Sea coast. The largest deposits of copper ingots are from two shipwrecks along the south coast of Turkey at Cape Gelidoniya and Ulu Burun,[96] sites which illustrate the maritime nature of the LBA metals trade. Based on lead isotope analysis of these copper ingots it appears that much of the copper in circulation during the thirteenth century came from the Cypriot (Late Cretaceous) copper sources, from mines such as Apliki-*Karamallos*,[97] supporting Stech's contention that Cyprus was the major copper producer of the East Mediterranean.[98] Copper ingots found in sixteenth-century Crete (Late Minoan I) have a different, non-Mediterranean source. This source has yet to be identified, but was a pre-Cambrian ore from central Asia, possibly Afghanistan.[99] The implication is that Cyprus had yet to become fully integrated within the trading networks of the Near East in the sixteenth century, and it was not until possibly as late as the thirteenth century that Cypriot copper was widely traded beyond the island. Intriguingly, although the ingots were of Cypriot copper, lead isotope analyses of metal artefacts from the Greek mainland and Sardinia suggest the use of local copper sources to manufacture tools and weapons.[100] Possibly this illustrates a high status gift exchange of copper in the form of ingots within the Mediterranean, which was entirely parallel to local metallurgical production. The ingots were simply intended for elite exchange and were not a convertible raw material.

Within Cyprus the social and economic importance of copper as a trade item and in prestige display is evident from the formative phase of the LBA, represented by the series of elite burials from the central copper-mining zone of the island, equipped with bronze socketed axes that reference a Near Eastern package of elite symbols.[101] If Cyprus is to be equated with the kingdom of Alashiya, recorded in ancient Near Eastern texts,[102] it is surely significant that the earliest references to Alashiya in the Mari archives are largely contemporary with the internal development of the Cypriot copper industry in the seventeenth and sixteenth centuries BC.[103] Very little is known about the earliest phase of the LBA copper industry on Cyprus, between LC I and IIB. Most evidence is from the earlier deposits at Enkomi,[104] supplemented by data from Kalopsidha-*Koufos* and Morphou-*Toumba tou Skourou*. Based on the metallurgical debris and associated equipment, Muhly argues that the entire complex of copper-smelting technology can be identified at Enkomi from the initial occupation of the site in MC III/LC IA. This was located within the fortress at the northern limits of the site.[105] Although the extent to which Enkomi exerted control over the procurement and distribution of copper during this period is still under debate,[106] it is probable that the finds from the LC I levels in the fortress represent the earliest attempts to centralise metallurgical production.

As far as can be inferred from the archaeological record, however, the height of the Cypriot copper industry dates to the thirteenth and twelfth centuries BC. The expansion of the copper industry is contemporary with the major phase of urbanisation on Cyprus and the development of the Mediterranean-wide trade in Cypriot copper. There is clear evidence for copper production at both large coastal urban centres and smaller inland sites.[107] Based on detailed analyses of the metallurgical debris found at these sites, Stech has developed a detailed picture of the LC copper industry, which was common throughout the island and appears to have remained constant from the initial development of the copper industry in Enkomi during LC IA until the final stages of the LBA.[108] Essentially, Stech identifies two main phases, which were carried out in two very different production centres. The small mining villages, such as Apliki-*Karamallos* and Politiko-*Phorades*, located in the lower reaches of the Troodos mountains, were involved in both the procurement of copper and the primary smelting of the sulphide ores. The debris of this stage of production is furnace conglomerate, found as plano-convex blocks of slag. This furnace conglomerate was then transported to the coastal urban centres for further refining, which took place within small furnaces. A pool of copper collected in the bottom with prills of copper in the lower outer portion. The slag was then crushed to extract the prills of copper. Subsequent craft production of tools, weapons and luxury items, such as metal vessels, statuettes and stands, presumably also took place within the urban centres and was closely controlled by the LC urban elite. Given the absence of a centralised palatial authority on Cyprus during the LBA, the standardisation of the LC copper industry is significant. Stech argues for a degree of centralisation in the hands of the urban elite, who ensured the production of standardised ingots in an internationally recognised form.[109] Possibly the elite legitimised their control of the copper industry through sophisticated exploitation of religious symbolism. Hence, as argued by Knapp, external demand for Cypriot copper played a significant role in the rise of the coastal urban centres.[110] It is notable that even though Cyprus is copper-rich, the Cypriot elite did not tend to remove substantial quantities of copper from circulation for deposition in tombs or in religious contexts until the latter stages of the LBA, in LC IIC-IIIA. Instead, the local preference for elite display was for imported luxuries from Egypt, the Near East and the Aegean, and copper appears to have been largely intended for export.

Trade and exchange

There have been extensive studies of international trade in the Mediterranean during the LBA. These have largely focused on the movement of pottery and raw materials, most notably utilitarian metals, especially copper,[111] but also exotics such as ivory. Luxury crafted objects, such as faience and textiles, have also been the focus of recent research.[112] The nature of this trade – whether it functioned at the level of gift exchange in the hands of palace elites or should better be characterised as commodity or mercantile trade – has been particularly contended.[113] The excavation of a number of LBA shipwrecks around the coast of the Eastern Mediterranean basin – most notably the Kaş and Ulu Burun shipwrecks off the southern coast of Turkey, but also the Point Iria wreck in the Aegean – have added an interesting perspective on the movement of traded goods and raw materials, in particular the copper trade.[114] Certainly by the fourteenth and thirteenth centuries Cyprus appears to be playing a pivotal role in long-distance maritime trade between the Aegean, Egypt and the Levant, as is indicated by the movement of Cypriot copper throughout the region[115] and the importation of quantities of Mycenaean pottery to the island.[116] There is substantial evidence from the thirteenth and twelfth centuries that maritime contacts extended as far west as the Italian peninsula and the islands of Sicily and Sardinia, illustrated by the movement of copper ingots and finished bronze artefacts.[117] More localised patterns of trade in the East Mediterranean might be illustrated by the movement of Cypriot pottery to Egypt and the Levant,[118] transport amphorae between Egypt, Cyprus and the Levant,[119] and the possible elite, high status trade in exotic perfumes contained in the Red Lustrous wheelmade vessels, in particular the spindle bottles and arm-shaped vessels.[120]

The initial emergence of Cyprus from isolation at the end of the third millennium BC had enormous impact on indigenous Cypriot cultural traditions.[121] However, it was only during the second millennium that the island became fully integrated into international maritime trade. Indeed, one of the more intriguing aspects of Cypriot participation in external trade is the resulting impact of imported material on the development of the LC cultural repertoire during the LBA. In contrast to the apparent isolation of earlier periods, the LC period is characterised by the assimilation and adaptation of foreign iconography and technologies. Hybridisation is apparent in many aspects of the LC cultural repertoire and there is significant evidence for the manipulation of the exotica used in the construction of elite identities. This was achieved through tight control over the dissemination of rare luxury commodities and the privileged ability to 'read' imported iconographies. This is particuarly evident in the distribution of high status commodities such as faience vessels, ivories, and cylinder seals. Occasional items of gift exchange between rulers can be identified, namely rare inscribed Egyptian or Hittite artefacts.[122]

During the earlier second millennium commercial trading contacts were established with Egypt and the Levant. This can be charted through the localised movement of certain pottery styles within this region. In particular Maguire notes the complex patterns of circulation of small juglets, presumably containers of a prized luxury commodity such as a perfumed oil, between Cyprus, Syro-Palestine and Egypt.[123] During the MC III-LC IA period Cypro-Levantine contacts had a largely eastern orientation. Imported pottery, such as the characteristic grey Tell el-Yahudiyeh ware with punctured decoration, is mainly distributed in the eastern Mesaoria,[124] and appears to shadow the copper route from the Troodos down to Enkomi. From the beginning of the LBA, if not slightly earlier, Cypriot pottery – the Base Ring, White Slip and Monochrome wares – was exported to the Levantine city-states and Egypt, where it is found in seemingly large quantities.[125] Base Ring jugs and juglets are the most popular Cypriot exports, largely found in funerary contexts. There has been substantial debate in the archaeological literature as to whether the Base Ring juglets were manufactured specifically as containers for opium, in particular whether the shape and decoration of these jugs explicitly refers to the seed pod of the opium poppy.[126] To a certain extent this has been supported by recent chemical analyses of the residues found in Base Ring juglets – but the evidence still remains tenuous.[127]

One of the clearest indices for Cypriot participation in long-distance maritime trade is the presence of large quantities of Mycenaean pottery (Fig. 6.10). Before the LBA the archaeological record attests to sporadic contacts between Cyprus and the Aegean world. Only occasional Minoan imports are found on the island, including a Kamares ware cup found at Karmi on the north coast, and similarly few Cypriot objects were exported to Crete.[128] Certainly it appears that Cyprus was excluded from Levanto-Aegean relations during the earlier second millennium BC. Only small quantities of LM I and LH I/II pottery are found on the island, for the most part in the northwest of the island at sites such as Ayia Irini (see Plate 22) and Morphou-*Toumba tou Skourou*.[129] In contrast, during the fourteenth and thirteenth centuries there is every indication that Cyprus played a pivotal role in the procurement and dissemination of Mycenaean pottery throughout the East Mediterranean.[130] The typical Mycenean import was the stirrup jar – a small container for a precious substance usually thought to be a perfumed oil, the production of which was closely controlled by the Mycenaean palaces.[131] The pictorial krater, usually decorated with scenes of chariot processions, is a ceramic type that was specifically targeted at the Cypriot and Ugaritic export markets. Within Cyprus the pictorial krater was incorporated within elite feasting practices and high status funerary display (see Plates 23-4).[132] Mycenaean imports rarely penetrated the Cypriot hinterland, which was largely occupied by small, specialised production sites, but instead is mainly found in the large coastal towns, with particular concentrations at Enkomi and around the

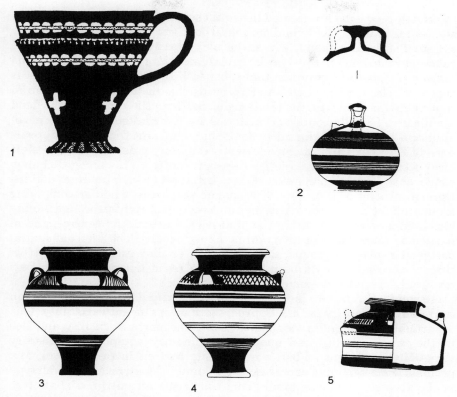

Fig. 6.10. Aegean imported pottery: (1) Kamares ware cup from Karmi; (2) stirrup jar; (3, 4) piriform jars; (5) alabastron.

Bay of Larnaca. Within the coastal sites, however, Mycenaean pottery was fairly widely available, and only the dissemination of the pictorial style was closely controlled by the urban elite.[133] Despite the high incidence of Mycenaean imports found in Cyprus, very few Cypriot ceramic imports have been found in the West Mediterranean. The largest deposit of Cypriot pottery in the Aegean is from Kommos in southern Crete and some Cypriot pottery even penetrated as far west as Italy and Sardinia.[134] For the most part, however, it appears that the major Cypriot export west was its copper.

Funerary practices

The LC period is characterised by a transformation in the funerary arena reflecting the substantial changes in social and economic organisation. Most important is the move from extramural bounded cemeteries typical of the prehistoric Bronze Age to burial within the boundaries of the settlement. At Kalavasos-*Ayios Dhimitrios*, for example, the elite tombs of

171

the North-East area are located beneath the north-south street that runs adjacent to Building X.[135] Similar spatial configuration is evident at other LC sites such as Enkomi, where the many excavated tombs are found below streets and in courtyards, and Alassa-*Pano Mandilaris*.[136] This reflects the spatial location of tombs beneath the courtyard of houses at Ugarit.[137] The social changes underpinning this major transformation in spatial organisation and the relationship between the living and the dead are unclear. Usually bounded cemeteries are interpreted within models of ancestral territorial rights. It is no doubt significant that the disappearance of these extramural cemeteries is contemporaneous with the shift away from rural village societies to urban centres. This societal change would have been accompanied by renegotiation of social status, defined through control of a variety of economic resources. Smaller competing groups might assert their position and economic rights through highly visible funerary ritual within the limits of the new urban centres, and in particular investment in high status luxury exotica. The internal spatial patterning of tomb groups and associated secular and religious structures[138] therefore should be informative in reconstructing the new patterns of LC social and economic organisation.

Although the basic elements of funerary ritual point to a common expression of identity in LBA Cyprus, there is significant variability. This is particularly evident in the construction of the mortuary facility, and also in the range, quality and quantity of funerary equipment. Funerary variability is evident at both an inter-site and an intra-site level, and perhaps is most forcibly expressed at Enkomi.[139] The typical LC tomb type is the rock-cut chamber tomb. This comprises an entrance shaft (the *dromos*), usually a square vertical shaft, a narrow entrance passage or doorway (the *stomion*) leading into the main chamber, and the burial chamber itself cut into the bedrock. This might be oval, elliptical or circular, square or rectangular. A varying number of chambers can open off from the *dromos* (between one and four). Usually a *dromos* services two chambers, either opposite each other (bilobate) or perpendicular to each other. Local topography rather than ritual considerations determined the orientation of the *dromos* and chamber. Internal features include benches, pits cut in the chamber floor, and niches in the *dromos* or chamber. Other tomb types are attested at Enkomi: built tombs and *tholos* tombs. There are five examples of built tombs at Enkomi, all of which were constructed between LC IIA and IIB.[140] These tombs have rectangular chambers lined with fine cut stone (ashlar) blocks and partially corbelled roofs. Although the built tombs were looted in antiquity, the surviving grave goods in British Tombs 162 and 66 are remarkably lavish. Moreover, these tombs are spatially clustered in Quartier 4E and Quartier 3E, which Keswani suggests reflects the establishment of an elite group. The Enkomi ashlar tombs resemble the built tombs of Ugarit,[141] although without the elaborate vaulted roofs, and occasional built tombs are also known in the

172

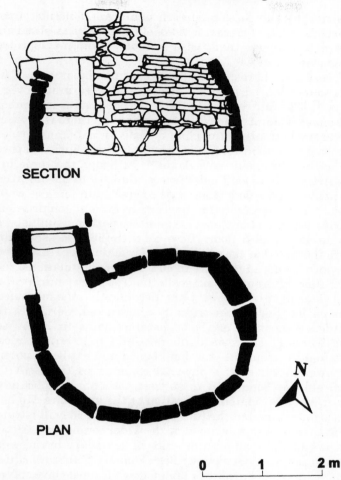

SECTION

PLAN

N

0   1   2 m

Fig. 6.11. Enkomi *tholos* tomb 1336.

Mycenaean world, most notably Tomb Rho at Mycenae. The significance of the dissemination of this tomb type beyond Ugarit is unclear, but close social and cultural ties are signalled by other elements of the cultural repertoire.[142] There are four examples of *tholos* tombs at Enkomi (Fig. 6.11), which were built and used between LC IA and IIA.[143] These tombs comprise small, circular built chamber tombs entered via a small pit-shaped *dromos*. The chamber was built in an oval or circular cutting and had a corbelled superstructure of mudbrick and rough stones capped with large stone slabs. Unlike the built tombs, the *tholos* tombs were not spatially clustered, nor do they appear to have been particularly wealthy. Undoubtedly these tombs are a manifest expression of group identity. It is

173

worth emphasising that these tombs are significantly distinct in construction and form from the Mycenaean *tholoi* of the Greek mainland and there
is no reason to suppose that these funerary monuments refer to an
intrusive Aegean identity.[144]

The LC period is characterised by increasing elaboration of funerary
ritual. The tombs housed multiple burials and were in use over several
generations.[145] The full range of a burying population is represented –
males and females, adults and children – although there is some evidence
to suggest variable treatment of child burials. Infants might be excluded
altogether from formal burial facilities, simply being buried in pots within
the limits of the settlement at Enkomi.[146] Although the three infants in
Kalavasos-*Ayios Dhimitrios* Tomb 11 were admitted to the burial chamber,
they were placed on the floor whereas the three adult females were placed
on benches.[147] The characteristic funerary treatment comprises inhumation, the body being laid out in an extended position, usually on benches
or directly on the chamber floor. However, with the successive interments
deposited in the chamber the earlier burial remains were disturbed and so
were frequently removed to make room for later inhumations. The treatment of the funerary remains suggests that secondary burial was in fact
an integral element of LC funerary practice, and that the movement of the
bones from earlier burials was ritually constructed. Certainly, the carefully recorded disposition of the skeletal remains in Kalavasos-*Ayios
Dhimitrios* Tomb 11 suggests deliberate and preferential recovery of
certain anatomical elements, the long bones and skulls in particular.[148]
Similar manipulation of the physical remains in the EBA tombs of
southern Crete has been used to suggest the social importance of the
ancestors.[149] Whether similar celebration of the ancestors can be posited
for Cyprus is uncertain, but the funerary remains clearly illustrate that in
death the individual was subsumed by the wider community. Although the
protracted use of the tomb and practice of secondary burial were widespread, fumigation was not a prescribed element of funerary ritual. There
are certain instances of burning or laying down a sterile layer of earth, but
these are exceptions.[150]

LC burials were an important arena for competitive display, as is
particularly evident in the varied range of ceramic and non-ceramic grave
goods. Prerequisites include a variety of vessels associated with the serving and consumption of food and drink: jugs, kraters and bowls. Together
with faunal remains,[151] these might indicate that funerary feasts continued to play an important role in funerary ritual. Salient features of elite
display are the restricted ceremonial vases, either ceramic or in other
materials. Pictorial Mycenaean kraters, the focal element of LC drinking
sets, were particularly prominent in wealthier grave groups.[152] Likewise,
vessels made from precious metals or of faience are restricted to wealthier
burial assemblages.[153] By LC IIC bronze vases – hemispherical bowls and
jugs – became the primary medium of high status funerary display.[154]

Small unguent containers, typically imported Mycenaean alabastra or stirrup jars, or less frequently the high status Red Lustrous ware spindle bottles or even arm-shaped vases, are another typical element of LC funerary ritual.[155] In the Bronze Age Aegean Hamilakis has suggested that the perfumed oils and ointments contained in such vases were incorporated within rituals of competitive consumption. They were used to anoint the body and high status textiles, and were a prime commodity in gift exchange and funerary ritual.[156] Similar activities might be extrapolated to Cyprus. Specialised forms, in particular libation vases, are rarely attested and Webb argues that libations played only a minor role in LC funerary ritual.[157] However, the deposition of Base Ring jugs, sometimes with an exaggerated spout, and Base Ring carinated cups illustrates the importance of liquids in funerary ritual and it is very possible that these vases were used in libation ceremonies.[158] Other elements of LC funerary equipment included an array of bronze weapons (knives, daggers, swords, shaft-hole axes, the latter in LC I), toilet articles (pestles and mortars, tweezers, mirrors) and items of personal adornment (a rich array of gold jewellery). Luxury, prestige objects include ivories, alabaster vases, and cylinder seals, which were frequently incorporated in jewellery.[159]

Religion

The nature of religious practices during the prehistoric Bronze Age remains elusive, but at present it appears that the extramural cemeteries served as the main focus of communal ceremonial activity. This appears to continue to be the case in LC I, but during the LC IIA period there is an apparent change in the nature and organisation of communal ritual activities, illustrated by the appearance of demarcated religious sites, or sanctuaries, in the archaeological record. The identification of religious locales and the nature of ancient cult is extremely problematic,[160] but largely rests upon the identification of specialised paraphernalia in deposits that are distinct from typical settlement assemblages[161] and possibly distinctive forms of architecture. Knapp suggests that the LC sanctuaries might be defined by their distinctive architecture, the presence of specialised installations including horns of consecration, altars, and a cult room with restricted access. Moreover, they should house the remains of sacrifice, treasuries for the storage of cult objects or images, and an accumulation of specialised prestige objects and ritual paraphernalia, such as figurines, imported pottery, bucrania.[162] Many aspects of ritual ceremony (feasting, dancing, music, ceremonial processions, libations, prayers, divination) by their very nature remain elusive, and can only be inferred from the material assemblages, iconographic details, and textual data. Accumulations of ash and burnt bone might illustrate animal sacrifice and competitive feasting. Indeed, faunal remains, of sheep, goat, cattle and deer, are a characteristic element of LC cult places.[163] One such example is the

175

accumulation of animal bones and the antlers of at least forty-one individuals of fallow deer associated with the altar at Myrtou-*Pigadhes*.[164]
Pouring and libation ceremonies and feasting might be inferred from
detailed analyses of ceramic deposits. More ephemeral aspects of cult
(music, processions and dance) can only be inferred from iconographic
data, which is fraught with problems of identification and interpretation.
Interpretation of LC religious practices and beliefs is complicated by the
diversity of the evidence, comprising small rural rites and monumental
urban sanctuaries. Moreover, the time span, covering a period of around
400 years, further impedes interpretation.[165]

During the LC I period there is no certain evidence for the construction
of specialised cult buildings at discrete locations and, as in the preceding
prehistoric Bronze Age, focus for communal ceremonial activity appears to
be in the funerary domain. There is a substantive transformation in the
organisation of communal ritual in the LC IIA period, with the construction of a number of specialised cult centres, most notably at Myrtou-
Pigadhes,[166] Athienou[167] and possibly at Ayios Iakovos-*Dhima*.[168] In the LC
IIC-IIIA period there is an apparent explosion in religious architecture at
the urban settlements,[169] most notably at Kition, Enkomi and Palaepaphos, but also represented by the major reorganisation of the sanctuary
at Myrtou-*Pigadhes*.[170] This *floruit* in religious architecture is paralleled
by the apparent reworking of the major urban centres, most notably
Enkomi, during this period, in particular the introduction of monumental
ashlar administrative buildings.[171] Increasing use of ashlar masonry is
likewise apparent in temple construction, both for the temple facades and
for their internal architectural components, such as the built platform or
altar at Myrtou-*Pigadhes* (Fig. 6.12).[172] The urban location of the LC
ceremonial, ritual arena (both funerary and religious) is noteworthy,[173]
beginning with the LC IIA foundation at Myrtou-*Pigadhes*.[174] The single
most striking aspect of LC religious sites is the very great diversity in
architectural form, variability that might reflect the existence of independent local polities.[175] The absence of a consistent, canonical ground
plan and combination of religious elements implies considerable variety in
religious practices throughout the island in the LC period. Even so, Webb
has identified a number of characteristics of LC cult buildings.[176] For the
most part they are freestanding rectangular structures with an enclosed
courtyard (*temenos*). The cult buildings tend to be laid out on an east-west
axis and usually comprise two or three units of rooms: the hall, the *cella*
or *adyton*, and possibly a vestibule. The roof of the hall might be supported
by rows of pillars. Internal installations[177] include benches in the halls (for
storage and display of cult equipment), hearths (frequently with small
quantities of burnt animal bone, suggesting their use in animal sacrifice),
stone podia (for offerings of food and drink and to display votives and cult
equipment), stone platforms topped by stone horns of consecration at
Myrtou-*Pigadhes*, terracotta *larnakes* or bathtubs, pits or *bothroi* (for

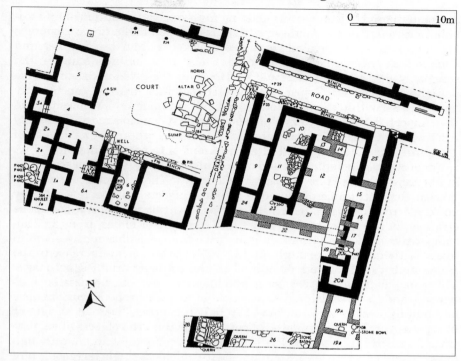

Fig. 6.12. Plan of sanctuary at Myrtou-*Pigadhes*, Periods V-VI.

disposal of discarded cult equipment and debris from sacrifice or feasting), and stepped capitals.

In contrast to the diversity of religious architecture there is considerable uniformity in the range of cult equipment found in LC II sanctuaries, suggesting a certain degree of uniformity of cult practices and religious beliefs. Cult equipment largely comprises a range of ceramics, which were used in a variety of religious activities: libations, feasting, votive offerings. For the most part the range of equipment shadows that found within settlement and funerary contexts, suggesting that there was no specific manufacture of specialised forms for cult purposes. The large deposits of miniature ceramics from Athienou and Kalopsidha-*Koufos*, however, are specific to cult assemblages and might been used for small votive offerings to the deity.[178] Pottery from religious contexts generally comprises indigenous fine wares, with small quantities of imported Mycenaean pottery. The emphasis is on containers for liquid offerings, in particular large numbers of Base Ring carinated cups. These might have been used in feasting, specifically in the consumption of wine, or possibly for pouring libations.[179] Small numbers of kraters, frequently Mycenaean imports, are also commonly found in sanctuary contexts and played an integral role in religious

177

ceremony, possibly competitive feasting involving consumption of an alcoholic beverage. More specialised ritual vessels used in libation ceremonies are rather rare. Mycenaean rhyta are reported at Myrtos-*Pigadhes* and Temple 2 at Kition and a locally-made ivory imitation was found in the sanctuary at Athienou, in stratum III. However, these vessels seem to have a limited impact on Cypriot religious ritual and are not consistently incorporated within the range of Cypriot cult equipment.[180] Webb suggests that imported Mycenaean kylikes and stemmed cups are more commonly used within Cypriot libation ceremonies, based both on the incidence of this form in cult contexts and interpretations of Cypriot iconography.[181] A range of objects, including incised ox scapulae, astragali and worked shells might have been used in divination practices.[182] The religious centres also housed concentrations of valuable prestige objects. In one respect they acted as treasuries for the urban centres, but this was also a conscious strategy by the LC elite. The sanctuaries became a major arena in elite competitive display and removing luxuries from circulation also acted to increase their value. Certainly, by LC IIC-IIIA there is an increase in the range and wealth of votives offered in the affluent urban sanctuaries. These include faience, ivory, glass and alabaster vessels, bronzes such as tripod stands, and sealstones. Occasional bronze anthropomorphic images and bull figures are known from LC religious centres,[183] but these appear to represent the appurtenances of cult, rather than the objects of veneration. Terracotta figures (see Plate 25) are less commonly found, although most LC cult sanctuaries are equipped with at least a single terracotta bull figure, an item of cult equipment rather than a typical votive offering.[184]

It has been suggested that there was a close link between copper production and religion on Cyprus.[185] This is based on the close spatial relationship between bronze-working facilities and religious structures, the importance of crafted goods of bronze in religious sanctuaries, and in particular the interpretations of certain LC representations. There has been extensive discussion of the close proximity of metallurgical installations and religious structures at Enkomi, Kition-*Kathari* (Fig. 6.13), Athienou, Kalopsidha-*Koufos*, and possibly at Myrtou-*Pigadhes*.[186] Large quantities of metallurgical waste were found at Athienou, in a pit in the central courtyard and to the east of the eastern platform.[187] However, there is no evidence for artefacts associated with primary smelting, such as crucibles, tuyères and smelting furnaces, at the sanctuary. Instead it has been argued that the metallurgical waste was the debris of secondary refining and that the preliminary roasting and smelting of ores would have taken place in the area of mines. The assemblage at Kalopsidha-*Koufos* closely parallels that of Athienou. The accumulation of copper ore and slag, together with stone moulds and crucibles, is very suggestive of some form of copper-working at the site.[188] Metallurgical debris, including furnace conglomerate, was identified at the LC IIC-IIIA sanctuary at Myrtou-*Pigadhes*.[189] Particularly noteworthy, however, is the spatial proximity of the

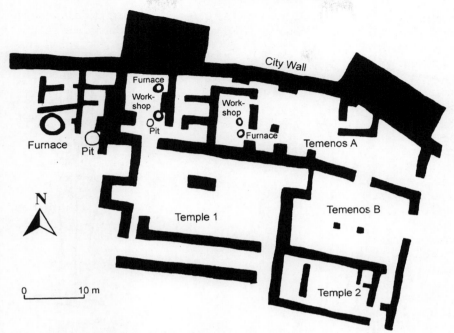

Fig. 6.13. Plan detailing relationship between sanctuaries and metallurgical installations at Kition-*Kathari*.

major copper workshops (rooms 12-15) and the temple complex at Kition-*Kathari*, in particular with Temple 1.[190] There was direct access between the temple structure and the workshops via room 12, underlining the close physical relationship between the religious and material domain at Kition. This data has been used to infer religious control or at least a religious concern in copper production. As one of the centralised forms of authority on Cyprus, it is certainly possible that the temples maintained an interest in copper production but it is difficult to demonstrate that this was dominated by religious authorities in its entirety. Alongside copper production it is possible that the urban temples of LC IIC controlled the manufacture of other prestige commodities, such as textiles; however, temple workshops need not indicate religious control of all areas of such manufacture. Joanna Smith suggests that many of the industrial installations at Kition, such as the basins, are in fact associated with textile production, for example washing and dyeing wool.[191] In this respect it is interesting to note the spindle whorls and loom-weights[192] found in the sanctuaries at Athienou, Myrtou-*Pigadhes*, Ayia Irini and Kition Temples 2, 4, 5, and the quantities of murex shell found in Kition Temple 2.[193] Certainly, it appears as though the LC cult centres were heavily implicated in craft production.

179

Fig. 6.14. Bronze statuettes: (1) 'Ingot God' from Enkomi; (2) Bomford statuette.

The LC III bronze statuette from Enkomi of a warrior in smiting pose (the Ingot God), is one of a pair of statutettes standing on what appears to be a bronze ingot (Fig. 6.14).[194] The Ingot God in particular has been viewed as clear evidence of religious control and divine protection of the LC copper industry.[195] The development of a range of bronze prestige goods, found largely in religious contexts, and possibly also of an exclusive iconography, might have served to underline and indeed to legitimise elite control over copper production. It has been argued that the LC elite exploited religious ceremony and an exclusive range of culturally significant symbols to establish, organise and maintain control of the copper industry.[196] Several scholars have cited a number of representations which they believe to refer to oxhide ingots – the basic unit of exchange for copper throughout the Mediterranean in the LBA. These include apparent miniature votive ingots from Enkomi,[197] several of which were inscribed. There are two four-sided bronze stands which depict individuals carrying copper ingots in apparently ritual processions.[198] Other possible representations of ingots are found on sealstones, objects that were clearly elite paraphernalia used to proclaim status. Knapp lists thirty-three such representations of

180

ingots, usually associated with human figures, trees and bucrania – a common combination of motifs possibly representing the attributes of a specific LC deity.[199] Less convincing are the supposed ingot representations found on Mycenaean chariot kraters, two from Enkomi and a third from Pyla-*Verghi*.[200] Certainly there is a close correlation between religious beliefs, ceremonial practices and the LC copper industry.

Political organisation

The island of Cyprus lies within sight of the littoral of northern Syria (64 miles) and southeast Anatolia (44 miles), both areas that were characterised by complex polities during the LBA. There is, moreover, ample archaeological evidence to illustrate Cypriot participation in the maritime trading networks of the East Mediterranean basin during the second millennium BC. Particularly important is the evidence for exploitation of Cypriot copper resources in the LBA and its transmission beyond Cyprus. Certain elements of the archaeological record might argue for Cypriot integration within the diplomatic framework of the ancient Near East, but this evidence is more tenuous. Internal evidence from Cyprus demonstrates the development of an urbanised society, with inter-site and intra-site differentiation and in particular the emergence of a social and economic elite.[201] Even so, the level of social and political organisation on the island remains elusive, namely whether LBA Cyprus should be characterised as a chiefdom or state.[202] Moreover, it is unclear whether the LC material represents a single island-wide political unit or a collection of geographically defined polities with a common cultural identity. Although on available evidence it appears that Enkomi was pre-eminent in the earlier stages of the LC period, there is no archaeological evidence to support centralised control of the island centred on Enkomi in LC II. Joanna Smith's analysis of inscribed documents – seals and longer texts – suggests that their use throughout the island was regionally diverse.[203] Other economic, architectural and iconographic data argue for centres functioning at similar levels, rather than hierarchical control on the part of a particular urban centre. Architecturally, for example, there is evidence for distinctive local traditions at individual centres rather than a shared expression of architectural symbolism, in contrast to the cultural and architectural homogeneity of Minoan Crete.[204]

It has been suggested that during the LC period Cyprus was organised into smaller regional polities or chiefdoms, rather than being a single unified state.[205] While there is evidence for emergent social complexity – most evident in increasing disparities of wealth and prestige objects deposited in funerary contexts – there is limited corresponding evidence for centralised administrative control of agricultural surplus and copper production. Centralised control of agricultural surplus is only apparent from the LC IIC period, represented by the storage facility in Building X at Kalavasos-*Ayios Dhimitrios*.[206] Other LC IIC storage centres have been identified, such as at Apliki-*Karamallos* (House A) and Athienou,[207] but these are smaller inland, rural settlements. Prior to this only two possible centralised storage facilities have been identified, at Kalopsidha-*Koufos* and Morphou-*Toumba tou Skourou* (House B), although Peltenburg has suggested that the MC III-LC I forts might have served as local redistribution centres.[208] There is limited evidence for centralised authority on an intra-site level, let alone between settlements, and it has not been possible to identify bureaucratic centres and second order sites. Although there is the development of a writing system (the syllabic Cypro-Minoan script) this appears to be used for a rudimentary bureaucratic system.[209] The number of known Cypro-Minoan texts (Fig. 6.15) is small and it is difficult to identify an administrative centre. A similar lack of administrative sophistication can be inferred from the apparent absence of sphragistic seal use. Despite the vast repertoire of cylinder and stamp seals recovered from LC sites there is no physical evidence, namely in the form of seal impressions, that they were actually used in an administrative sphere. Instead it appears that they were used as jewellery or symbols of office.[210] Therefore, rather than being a centralised state with an organised bureaucracy and administrative class, LC society appears to have operated within a two-tier system of authority.[211]

Nonetheless, Peltenburg has argued for secondary state formation in Cyprus as early as the MC III-LC I transition.[212] During this period the island was coming into increasing social and economic contact with the surrounding cultures of the Eastern Mediterranean, which had long functioned at a state level of organisation. Moreover, the archaeological evidence for this period argues for an abrupt and seemingly violent transformation of Cypriot society within a short and clearly defined time period,

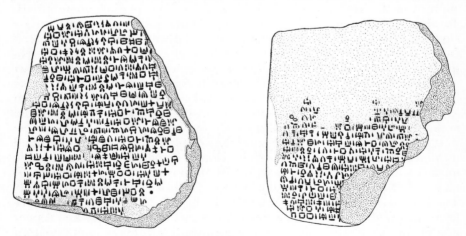

Fig. 6.15. Cypro-Minoan tablet from Enkomi (obverse and reverse).

182

accompanied by a significant increase in the use and manipulation of symbols, especially those associated with a warrior status. These changes denote a period of social reorganisation, in particular the restructuring and renegotiation of power, consistent with state formation. Peltenburg argues that Enkomi occupied a privileged position in the new social order of the MC III-LC I period. This is demonstrated by explicit evidence for large-scale copper-working,[213] the emergence of social stratification and increasing evidence for social organisation, namely the development of literacy[214] and the ability to mobilise a work force to construct monumental buildings. All these elements were spatially associated with the MC III-LC I fort structure at the site.[215] Specifically, Peltenburg argues that the economic development of Enkomi was predicated upon the settlement's involvement in, indeed control of, copper production and exchange, hence the development of fortified sites in the hinterland to protect Enkomi's copper supplies.

Alternatively, Keswani[216] argues that the archaeological record for the LC period cannot simply be forced into anthropologically derived models of state formation, comprising ever-increasing levels of social complexity, passing from chiefdom to state. Instead, Keswani notes considerable regional variation in patterns of social complexity. She suggests that alternative models of social organisation are more appropriate for the north and east of the island, in particular that of the heterarchical polity.[217] Evidence for contemporary competing agnatic groups, each being economically independent, is probably most evident at Enkomi, where it is difficult to identify a discrete elite zone within the urban centre, or indeed any specific activity areas.[218] The posited spatial and economic organisation at Morphou-*Toumba tou Skourou*, an 'urban' site comprising a series of discrete mounds, each identified as a separate production area, also fits a heterarchy.[219] Other sites in the southwest of the island, however, have discrete functional, residential, and elite zones and are characterised by monumental buildings, such as Building II at Alassa-*Palaeotaverna* and Building X at Kalavasos-*Ayios Dhimitrios*, and apparent centralised control over agricultural storage. Certain aspects of Building II in particular are especially grand, as would befit an elite residence. Most notable is the drafted ashlar masonry, and the elaborate stone and sewerage system reminiscent of the palace of Knossos on Crete. Keswani suggests that in these cases the local emergent elites were particularly effective in exerting control over local resources, hence the greater degree of centralisation, and fit more closely into traditional chiefdom models.[220]

The Alashiya question

Pertinent to questions of LC social and political organisation is the identification of the ancient kingdom of Alashiya, known from Near Eastern texts from the eighteenth to the eleventh century BC. Some scholars have argued that this kingdom should be identified with LBA Cyprus, and have used this identification to construct a model of a single unified state on the island, centred on Enkomi.[221] The lynchpin of this model is the increasing exploitation of Cypriot copper resources during the LBA and the evidence for the dissemination of this copper beyond the island. At present it is impossible to demonstrate conclusively that Alashiya and Cyprus (or part thereof) were one and the same. Even so, it is noteworthy that the other surrounding regions are similarly mute and that no convincing arguments have been put forward for an alternative location of Alashiya on the Asiatic mainland.

The earliest references to Alashiya are in Akkadian sources from Mari, Babylon and Alalakh and date to the eighteenth and seventeenth centuries, and possibly even as early the nineteenth century BC. These documents indicate that Alashiya was a town and that its copper sources were in the mountains. Other than this they give no indication as to the political organisation and geographical location of Alashiya. Between the fifteenth and twelfth centuries Alashiya is largely known from Egyptian and Hittite sources. Although these texts place Alashiya within the economic and political spheres of influence of the Hittite and Egyptian empires, there is no precise geopolitical information with which to locate Alashiya. The Annals of Tuthmosis III, recorded on the temple of Amun at Karnak, record that the chief of Alashiya paid tribute to Tuthmosis of lapis lazuli, wood, horses and copper, the last comprising the bulk of the tribute. The Hittite archives of the fifteenth century imply that Alashiya was a vassal state, paying tribute to the Hittite ruler. The extent of Hittite control of Alashiya, however, is unclear. Archaeologically it is difficult to demonstrate any close ties between Cyprus and the Hittite Empire, the latter of which lay very much beyond the periphery of East Mediterranean maritime trade networks. The closest ties are perhaps demonstrated through the dissemination of the Red Lustrous wheelmade ware of possible Cypriot manufacture, in particular the spindle bottles and the arm-shaped vessels, found at sites such as Bogazköy.[222] Hittite objects in Cyprus are rare and are typical items of high status gift exchange. These include two inscribed rings of gold and silver found at Tamassos and Hala Sultan Tekke, and a small silver figure of a male in Hittite dress standing on the back of a deer, found with a child burial at Kalavasos-*Ayios Dhimitrios*.[223]

By the fourteenth century Alashiya was a major player in the diplomatic networks of the East Mediterranean, as is illustrated by the Amarna letters.[224] This correspondence gives a unique insight into the political and economic relations between the rulers of Alashiya and Egypt. Most significantly, the king of Alashiya writes to the king of Egypt as his equal, addressing him as 'brother'. Only the LBA 'super-powers', the pharaoh, the Hittite king, the king of Mitanni and the king of Babylon, addressed each other as 'my brother'. The lesser rulers of the Egyptian vassal city-states in Palestine referred to these powerful rulers as 'father'. More-over, there is every indication that Alashiya was involved in major gift exchange with Egypt. The preferred gifts are copper, horses and timber, and the sheer quantities involved might indicate that the king of Alashiya exerted some control over the production of copper. The physical location of Alashiya remains elusive, although it is possible to surmise that it lies within a copper-rich area. The close integration of Alashiya within the diplomatic networks described in the Amarna archives almost certainly places it within the East Mediterranean. Even so, given its privileged position in these networks it is extremely improbable that Alashiya was located on the Levantine coast. The Hittite archives of the thirteenth century illustrate a close but asymmetrical political relationship between Alashiya and the Hittites, in which Alashiya was very much the lesser partner. A similar asymmetrical relationship is evident between Alashiya and Ugarit in the later thirteenth to twelfth centuries, although in this instance it is Alashiya that is the stronger party.[225]

Alashiya is listed as one of the places sacked by the 'Peoples of the Sea' during year 8 of Rameses III (1189 BC) on his mortuary temple at Medinet Habu.[226] This text has been used to place the LC IIC/IIIA destruction horizon within the wider East Mediterranean picture of socio-economic collapse at the end of the Bronze Age.[227] Although there is no reference to the economic and political situation in Alashiya, the eleventh-century Egyptian tale of Wenamun[228] suggests that Alashiya survived the turmoil of the twelfth century. Here the textual data correlates closely with the archaeological record, which suggests that Cyprus experienced a strong urban and artistic revival during the twelfth century BC, amid the collapse of the surrounding Mediterranean polities.

The information in the Near Eastern archives is very resonant with that of the LC archaeological record. Although it is very important to maintain the temporal aspect of these documents, inferences as to the political and economic and social organisation of Alashiya are possible. Alashiya appears to have been an urban polity ruled by a king who claimed to be the equal of the Egyptian pharaoh. The ruler of Alashiya exercised control over a mountainous hinterland, and in particular over its copper resources, and maintained a naval fleet. Alashiya had scribes versed in Akkadian (from the fourteenth century) and participated in international trade and gift exchange. The archaeological evidence for the correspondingly strong economic and cultural ties between Ugarit and Cyprus reflects the close economic and political links between Ugarit and Alashiya. Most signifi-cantly, although Alashiya only emerges as a copper-producing polity in the eighteenth and seventeenth centuries, it is not until the reign of Tuthmosis III that Alashiya begins to be integrated within Near Eastern trading networks, and Alashiya only emerges as an important diplomatic power in the fourteenth century (Amarna period). This closely shadows the archae-ological evidence for the emergence of Cyprus from 'isolation' to participation in international trade during the second millennium BC. Moreover, there is some evidence that Alashiya, like Cyprus, survived the worst of the twelfth century BC disruptions.[229] However, there is no evidence for a single unified state on Cyprus, which instead appears to have been organised into smaller regional polities.[230] Although each of these polities seems to have had equal access to imported exotica, it is possible that one (possibly to be identified with Alashiya) rose to prominence and played a privileged role in LBA diplomatic exchanges, presumably due to its control over the island's copper resources.

7

Epilogue: The End of the Bronze Age

[Between 1200 and 1050 BC] Cyprus passed through strange and terrible years .... The population of the island withered away, and with it passed its ancient material civilisation. Areas that had long been settled were abandoned for centuries to come; artifacts of a character hallowed by tradition disappeared without trace.[1]

The end of the Bronze Age on Cyprus, traditionally dated to the twelfth and early eleventh centuries BC, witnessed a dramatic reconfiguration of the social, political and economic organisation of the island. This phase (LC III) is characterised by site dislocation and a massive disruption to the island's settlement pattern, apparent depopulation, and by the eleventh century BC a complete transformation of the island's material culture. Many of these changes are frequently attributed to the arrival of a new element of the population from the Aegean and can be paralleled by the apparent influx of a new population group in the southern Levant (the Philistines). Contemporary textual data from Egypt and Ugarit contextualise these changes within a horizon of violent destructions characterising the end of the LBA civilisations of the East Mediterranean around 1200 BC and the Sea Peoples phenomenon.[2] The traditional view of the LC III period is of a Mycenaean colonisation of Cyprus (and the southern Levant) following the collapse of Mycenaean palaces.[3] However, despite increasing 'aegeanisation' of certain elements of the cultural repertoire, most significantly the transformation of the ceramic repertoire, there was no simple imposition of Mycenaean culture on the island. Instead, the LC III material demonstrates a syncretism of influences that reflect the cosmopolitan nature of the LC cultural identity. Mycenaean (or Aegean) culture is not simply transposed from the Aegean to Cyprus but merges with the indigenous Cypriot culture. The modes of transmission and transformation are more complex than a simple demic diffusion.

Twelfth-century settlement

LC IIIA settlement is characterised by a substantial drop in the number of occupied sites, indicative of a decrease in population. Overall, however, there was no substantial change in the pattern of settlement. For the most part the LC IIIA inhabitants rebuilt the towns of LC IIC and continued to bury their dead in the same locales as their LC II predecessors. Indeed, the major innovation of the LC IIIA phase does not appear to be one of settlement but rather the associated cultural package – pottery, domestic architecture, weaponry and prestige symbolism.[4] Even so, the events documented in the archaeological record indicate severe disruption to LC society at the transition between LC IIC and LC IIIA. The end of LC IIC is marked by a wave of destructions throughout the island at sites such as Enkomi, Kition, Maa-*Palaeokastro*, and Pyla-*Kokkinokremos*. Some sites were abandoned, such as Kalavasos-*Ayios Dhimitrios*, Maroni-*Vournes*, Morphou-*Toumba tou Skourou*[5] and Pyla-*Kokkinokremos*.[6] Many other sites, destroyed at the beginning of the twelfth century, were rebuilt. Yet for the most part these LC IIIA settlements illustrate only a brief period of occupation before being finally deserted during the course of the twelfth century, as is clearly the case at Myrtou-*Pigadhes*, Ayia Irini,[7] Athienou,[8] Apliki[9] and Alassa.[10] The only urban centres with clear evidence for continued occupation throughout the twelfth century (and into the initial stages of the eleventh century) are Enkomi, Paphos, Kition and Kourion.[11] Occupation within these urban centres continued at a sophisticated level, and LC IIIA might equally be characterised as a period of cultural *floruit*. At some sites, such as Sinda, there was a second destruction level during the twelfth century, followed by brief 'squatter' reoccupation.[12] At Enkomi the sudden, cataclysmic nature of the twelfth-century destructions is indicated by the remains of children who were trapped and killed by falling mudbrick from the superstructure of the ashlar building in level IIIB.[13]

Significantly, LC IIIA is characterised by the establishment of fortified strongholds and fortification of the surviving urban centres, reflecting the unsettled conditions prevalent during the twelfth century BC. Most notable are the constructions of Cyclopean fortifications at Kition, Maa-*Palaeokastro*, Enkomi and Sinda. In fact, however, the initial construction of apparent defensive outposts predates the destruction horizon at the end of LC IIC.[14] Possibly one of the earliest such outposts is at Pyla-*Kokkinokremos* (Fig. 7.1), a naturally defensive settlement located on a rocky plateau overlooking the route between the bay of Larnaca and the inland Mesaoria plain.[15] Karageorghis emphasises the possible Aegean connections for Pyla-*Kokkinokremos* and clearly states that it is one of the earliest settlements established by Aegean colonists.[16] However, the evidence seems better to support a local stronghold established to ensure movement of goods, in particular metals, between the harbour towns of the Larnaca bay and the Cypriot hinterland. Certainly the inhabitants of the settlement prospered from their control over the route inland from one of the major trading centres of LBA Cyprus, as is indicated by the wealth of prestige imports at the site, including Egyptian alabaster vases, imported Aegean pottery, and raw metals – copper and silver ingots and sheet gold for jewellery cut-outs.[17]

Karageorghis suggests that a similar military outpost was established

7. Epilogue: The End of the Bronze Age

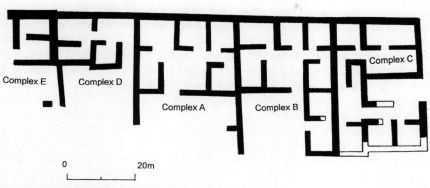

Fig. 7.1. Plan of Pyla-*Kokkinokremos*.

at Maa-*Palaeokastro*,[18] on the west coast of Cyprus. The site is located on a small promontory with only a small strip of land to fortify across the head of the promontory and steep sides down to sea. On either side of the promontory there were two wide bays with sandy beaches, on which small craft could easily dock, and on the eastern bay there was a perennial spring, thereby securing the headland a water supply. The location was therefore easily defensible, but the excavators argue that the site would be too easily cut off from the Cypriot mainland and moreover that the choice of locale indicated a lack of familiarity with the Cypriot hinterland. Consequently, they argue that the site was established by an intrusive, Aegean population rather than a displaced Cypriot population.[19] The earliest occupation at Maa-*Palaeokastro* (floor II) dates to the final phase of LC IIC, and is characterised by the construction of Cyclopean fortifications across the mouth of the promontory with a dogleg entrance. This was protected by a massive construction, presumably a tower or fortress, with a commanding aspect over the Cypriot hinterland and sea approaches to the settlement. A second massive wall was constructed along the southern, seawards limits of the promontory. Within the settlement there was a number of large buildings with a variety of economic functions, including facilities for oil production, metallurgical production and storage. Building II had an ashlar façade of a type that has been demonstrated to be typical of LC IIC architecture. Two buildings, II and IV, were equipped with communal halls for gatherings around a central hearth. Certain aspects of the associated cultural package are indigenous to LC IIC Cyprus. The local ceramics (White Slip and Base Ring) were used, and agricultural produce was stored in typical LC pithoi.[20] The site was destroyed by fire at the end of LC IIC and the subsequent reconstruction and reoccupation in LC IIIA (floor I) is characterised by small, hurriedly constructed buildings. This

189

phase was short-lived and the site was abandoned early in LC IIIA. The conventional interpretation of Maa-*Palaeokastro* as an early Aegean stronghold has yet to be rigorously tested. Certainly the occupation phases are very resonant with the unsettled conditions of the transitional LC IIC-IIIA period. Even so, the occupation and economic activities of the site appear very similar to those of a number of LC IIC-IIIA settlements throughout the island. Moreover, aspects of internal settlement dislocation and population upheaval during this period have not been fully explored. Sites such as Maa-*Palaokastro* and Pyla-*Kokkinokremos* might illustrate indigenous Cypriot strongholds analogous to the LM IIIC defensive settlements, such as Palaikastro-*Kastri*, identified throughout Crete.[21]

Overall, therefore, the LC IIIA occupation of Cyprus is characterised by *synoecism*, the gathering of the population within a smaller number of apparently defensible settlements. The Cypriot hinterland was gradually abandoned. There was an apparent decrease in population, and the survivors of the LC IIC destructions tended to group together in the large and newly fortified urban settlements along the southern coast for protection. However, the continuity of occupation at copper-producing sites such as Apliki-*Karamallos*[22] into the LC IIIA period, suggests that for a time at least the island's copper supply was secured. Indeed, it is possible that the settlement at Sinda was rebuilt and fortified to guard the route between the inland copper mines and Enkomi,[23] which still presumably acted as a major trading port. Although there is an apparent gradual economic decline during the course of LC IIIA, resulting in the eventual abandonment of sites, the final abandonment of the prosperous LC trading ports at Enkomi and Hala Sultan Tekke appears to be economic rather than the result of violent social upheavals. In both cases it appears that the town's harbour became silted and that the local population moved to nearby locales, laying the foundations for the Iron Age cities of Kition and Salamis.[24]

Mycenaean colonisation

The major debate concerning the final phase of the LBA on Cyprus focuses on population movements associated with the collapse of the palatial level of organisation throughout the East Mediterranean. Within this context many scholars have argued that there was a massive influx of Mycenaean settlers on Cyprus during the twelfth century BC. It is believed that these settlers were responsible for the LC IIC destructions and subsequent reconstruction of the sites in LC IIIA, and that they brought with them many facets of their own cultural tradition, which had a major impact on the archaeological record of Cyprus in this period (summarised in Table 7.1).[25] This includes transformations in the ceramic record, new funerary customs, certain changes in religious practices and changes in domestic architecture, culminating in the eleventh century BC with a massive disruption to the traditional LC use of the landscape.[26]

Class	Date	Element	Cultural impact	Mycenaean influence
ARCHITECTURE	LC IIC LC IIIA	Ashlar masonry	Use of space; prestige display	No
	LC IIC LC IIIA	Ceremonial halls with central hearth	Use of space; elite feasting & prestige display	Possibly
	LC IIIA	Cyclopean fortifications	Use of space; defence	Possibly
	LC IIC LC IIIA	Horns of Consecration	Religious display; ideology	Possibly
POTTERY	LC IIC LC IIIA	Locally made Mycenaean pottery (WPWM III)	Diet; elite feasting; technology	Yes
	LC IIIA	Cooking pots	Diet: preparation of food; technology	Yes
	LC IIIA	HBW	Diet: preparation and storage of food; technology	Yes
	LC IIIB	Terracotta figurines: 'goddess with upraised arms'	Religious practices; ideology	Possibly
METALLURGY	LC IIIA	Fibulae	Dress; social communication	Yes
	LC IIIB	Dress pins	Dress; social communication	Yes
	LC IIIA	Naue II swords	Military, prestige display; warfare?	Yes
	LC IIIA	Greaves	Military, prestige display; warfare?	Yes
	LC IIIA	Socketed spears	Military, prestige display; warfare?	Yes
	LC IIIB	Shield bosses/corselet bosses	Military, prestige display; warfare?	Probably

Table 7.1. Summary of 'Mycenaeanising' elements found in Cyprus at the end of the Late Bronze Age.

Mycenaean pottery

The cornerstone of the evidence used to argue for a Mycenaean migration to Cyprus in LC IIIA is the apparent transformation of the Cypriot ceramic repertoire following the LC IIC destructions. The whole issue of whether pottery can be used as a marker of ethnicity has not been made explicit. Certainly, certain elements of the ceramic repertoire appear to illustrate changes in diet – both the preparation and consumption of food – but whether these are the result of internal change, acculturation or population change remains elusive. Moreover, changes in vessel form have not been related to economic data (faunal and botanical remains) that might illustrate novel additions to the LC diet. The ceramic evidence itself is contradictory, with evidence for both continuity and change. The indigenous LC wares (Base Ring, White Slip and Monochrome), representing a ceramic tradition stretching back to the sixteenth century, continue to be used in LC IIIA, but form a much smaller percentage of the ceramic assemblage.[27] There is also a transformation in the cooking wares – the typical LC forms being replaced by new shapes of apparent Aegean derivation.[28] Most significant, however, is the dramatic increase in locally manufactured Mycenaean style pottery (Fig. 7.2), which becomes the predominant LC IIIA tableware, comprising up to 90% of the pottery from some contexts at Enkomi.[29] The largest corpus of locally made Mycenaean pottery so far published is from Enkomi. Here Dikaios identified Mycenaean IIIC:1b pottery (i.e. post-palatial Mycenaean-style pottery) in Level IIIA, associated with the post-LC IIC reconstruction of the site.[30] Similar Mycenaean IIIC:1b pottery has also been identified in post-LC IIC destruction levels at Sinda,[31] Maa-*Palaeokastro*, Palaepaphos,[32] Hala Sultan Tekke and Kition.[33] The style is primarily associated with the consumption of food and drink and open shapes predominate. The bulk of the repertoire comprises two-handled deep bowls (*skyphoi*),[34] but bell kraters,[35] used to serve wine, were also popular. Although the skyphos is a new element in the Cypriot repertoire, the bell krater was imported from the Aegean and

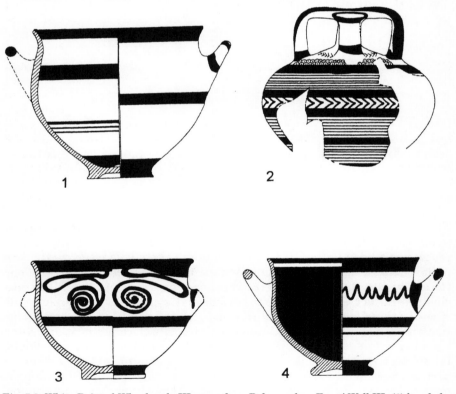

Fig. 7.2. White Painted Wheelmade III vases from Palaepaphos-*Evreti* Well III: (1) banded skyphos; (2) stirrup jar; (3) skyphos with spiral decoration; (4) skyphos with wavy line decoration.

was also copied locally from the thirteenth century.[36] Other drinking vessels are attested, including a type of goblet (the *kylix*) and carinated bowls. Jugs, for pouring liquids, are the most popular closed shapes, but other forms include the stirrup jar[37] (a shape which had been the most commonly imported Mycenaean vessel type to Cyprus and the Levant in the fourteenth and thirteenth centuries), and the side-spouted strainer jug.[38] The latter shape was particularly popular in East Greece and is also a common component of the Philistine ceramic repertoire, where it is usually believed to be associated with the consumption of beer.

The conventional cultural-historical interpretation of the changing pattern of pottery production in Cyprus during the twelfth century BC relates the advent of the Mycenaean IIIC:1b style to the arrival of a significant Aegean population element.[39] However, it has become increasingly apparent that the ceramic record cannot be forced into such a convenient framework.[40] The issue is clouded by the apparent complexity of the LC IIC-IIIA ceramic repertoire, which is dominated by a confusion of terminologies for the wheelmade, matt-painted wares: the Rude or Pastoral Style, Mycenaean IIIC:1b, Decorated LC III, and Late Mycenaean IIIB.[41] This plethora of ceramic styles in fact appears to be a construct of modern archaeology; more recently scholars have proposed grouping these styles together under the umbrella term White Painted Wheelmade III (WPWM III).[42] Once these wares have been deconstructed, it becomes evident that local production of Mycenaean-style pottery in fact can be traced back to the thirteenth century, prior to the LC IIC destructions. It is, moreover, almost impossible to distinguish between certain forms, such as the shallow conical bowl (FS 296), of LC IIC and LC IIIA date.[43] Kling's analysis of the LC IIIA ceramic data demonstrates that the conventional historical framework for the LC IIC-IIIA transition is untenable. The apparent distinctions between wares are not clearly defined and would no doubt have been meaningless to a contemporary user of these wares. Moreover, rather than a single intrusive ceramic tradition, there is in fact a fusion of indigenous, Aegean and Levantine elements,[44] a form of hybridisation which surely is a typical characteristic of Late Cypriot craftsmanship. The LC IIC destruction horizon did not signal the complete submersion of the indigenous cultural tradition by a new Aegean cultural tradition.[45] Rather than signalling a change in population, locally produced Mycenaean pottery instead illustrates the internal dynamics and changing trends in LC ceramic production. This reinterpretation of the ceramic record allows for a more sophisticated reading of social technologies both before and after the LC IIC destructions. One of the most striking aspects of the WPWM III ware is its internal standardisation. Indeed, this class of pottery was particularly suited to centralised mass production, and seems rather to reflect ever-increasing intensification in Cypriot ceramic production throughout the thirteenth and twelfth centuries BC, concomitant with the development of urbanisation and increased craft specialisation through-

193

out the island.[46] Throughout this period, there is evidence for increasing use of the wheel to manufacture a variety of wares,[47] culminating in the production of wheelmade Plain ware carinated cups used in the Sanctuary of the Ingot God in LC III,[48] which imitate the canonical LC II Base Ring form. That the Mycenaean ceramic tradition had an important influence over Cypriot pottery production cannot be denied, but the modes of inter-action are far more complex than would appear in conventional cultural histories.

Handmade Burnished ware

Another novel feature in the LC IIIA ceramic repertoire is a class of coarse handmade pottery used to make a variety of jars, bowls and cups – the Handmade Burnished ware (HBW), otherwise known as 'Barbarian ware' (Fig. 7.3).[49] Similar handmade pottery is attested in the Aegean in post-LH IIIB2 destruction contexts, although at Tiryns it occurs in LH IIIB contexts.[50] It has a very short period of use and does not survive past LH IIIC. In the Aegean HBW has been identified at eighteen sites, including the citadel centres of Mycenae, Tiryns, Athens, and also sites such as the Menelaion and Perati on the Greek mainland, and Khania and Kommos on Crete. The ware appears intrusive within the indigenous wheelmade ceramic industry that characterised the Bronze Age Aegean. This includes the production technique (handmade and use of grog as a temper) and the range of forms. Some scholars have argued that the ware represents an external tradition of pottery production, indicative of an intrusive ethnic element within the population. Others have argued that the ware devel-oped internally within the Aegean, possibly as a response to the collapse of the supra-organisation of the palaces and in particular disruption to the centrally organised ceramic industry affecting distribution of household kitchen wares.[51]

HBW is attested in Cyprus in LC IIIA contexts. The ware was first identified at Maa-*Palaeokastro*,[52] but subsequently has been recognised at Sinda, Hala Sultan Tekke, Enkomi and in greatest quantities at Kition.[53] Derivatives of this ware continue to be used into the earliest phase of the Iron Age (CG I) in the later eleventh century.[54] Two distinct fabric types have been identified, related to vessel type. Large jars and deep bowls with applied decoration were made in a soft fabric with large inclusions, and smaller shapes such as cups and bowls were made in a harder fabric and might have incised, grooved or punctured decoration.[55] Significantly, the initial appearance of this ware in Cyprus post-dates the earliest use of the HBW in the Aegean. Moreover, the appearance of HBW is contemporary with the influx of locally made LH IIIC painted pottery on Cyprus;[56] consequently this ware is a cultural trait that archaeologists have chosen to attribute to elements of a displaced Aegean population settled in Cy-prus. However, it is important to emphasise that HBW comprises only a

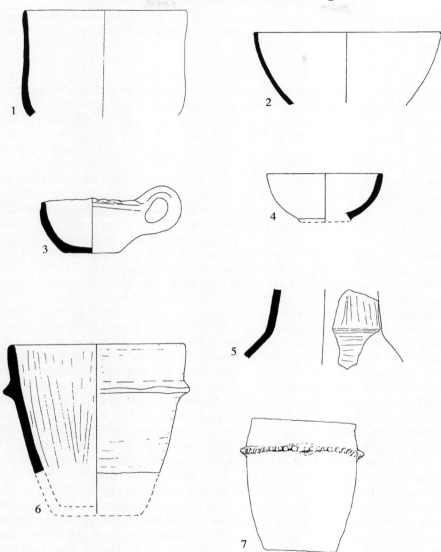

Fig. 7.3. Handmade Burnished ware: (1) jar from Enkomi; (2) hemispherical bowl from Kition; (3) cup from Kourion-*Kaloriziki*; (4) bowl from Kition; (5) bottle/closed jar from Enkomi; (6) deep bowl/jar from Sinda; (7) jar from Maa-*Palaeokastro*.

small percentage of the overall ceramic repertoire recovered from these sites. The economic and social function of HBW in Cyprus remains elusive. Possibly it relates to small-scale household production. It cannot, however, be associated with breakdown in ceramic manufacture on Cyprus, as has been suggested for the Greek mainland,[57] as its initial use is contemporary with intensification of the Cypriot ceramic industry.[58]

New metal types

The LC IIIA archaeological repertoire is also characterised by the appearance of novel metal types, which further illustrate contact with the Aegean.[59] These include dress ornaments and a suite of military equipment. Although these metal types apparently reached Cyprus from the Aegean, it appears that they were not indigenous to the Aegean but instead ultimately derived from northern Europe.[60] Consequently, their assimilation into the Mycenaean (and subsequently the Cypriot) cultural repertoire has been used to argue for the presence of a northern ethnic element within Mycenaean society from LH IIIB. The violin-bow fibula, found in LC IIIA contexts at Enkomi and Maa-*Palaeokastro*,[61] is clear evidence for the introduction of a new style of clothing to the island in the twelfth century. The fibula was designed to fasten large quantities of cloth at the shoulder of a garment, suggestive of clothing developed for a colder climate. By the eleventh to tenth centuries the fibula had become a standard Cypriot dress accessory. Clothing conveys culturally specific, social messages and is intrinsically linked to statements of identity. Thus the spread of a new clothing style certainly reflects close cultural contact between Cyprus and the Aegean during the twelfth century, although it is unclear to what extent this denotes the infiltration of a new element in the population. The introduction of a complex of warrior equipment from the Aegean might simply reflect the Cypriot response to changing military tactics at the end of the Bronze Age. Alternatively, it could be read as the Cypriot elite appropriating exotic status goods within a new complex of prestige symbolism. The new equipment comprises the cut-and-thrust (or Naue II) sword (Fig. 7.4),[62] found together with socketed spears (Fig. 7.5)[63] and, as the new sword type necessitated some sort of leg protection, bronze greaves. The complement of LC IIIA military equipment is found in Enkomi, in British Tomb 15 and Swedish Tomb 18. It appears that the LC IIIA elite identified itself on grounds of its military prowess and external elite references, in much the same way as the elite burials of LC I referred to a Near Eastern warrior package.[64] The militaristic society underpinning the development of this new warrior equipment in the Aegean is illustrated by the new style of vase-painting in LH IIIC, which focuses on warrior processions.[65] A similar taste in militaristic iconography is developed in Cyprus in the pictorial style of the eleventh century BC.[66]

Architecture

It has been argued that the LC IIIA period is characterised by a number of architectural innovations. Traditionally the introduction of ashlar ma-

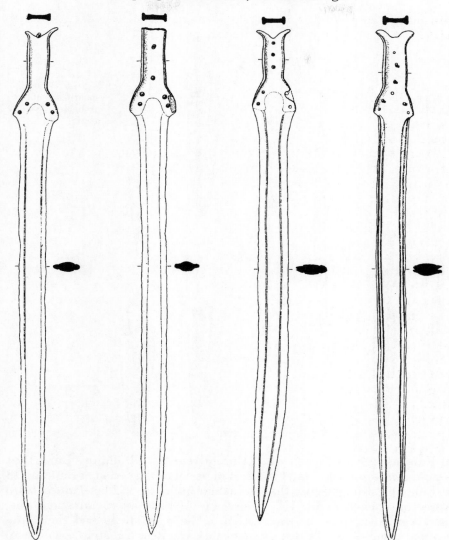

Fig. 7.4. Bronze Naue II swords from Enkomi Well 212.

sonry to Cyprus was attributed to Mycenaean colonists, based on the finds from Enkomi.[67] Following the destructions at the end of LC IIC, the LC IIIA reconstruction of the site was typified by monumental buildings with an ashlar façade, namely the sanctuaries of the Horned God[68] and the Ingot God.[69] The use of ashlar masonry on Cyprus, however, can be traced back to LC IIA-B at Enkomi, in the construction of the built tombs.[70] By LC IIC it was being extensively used in the construction of public buildings

197

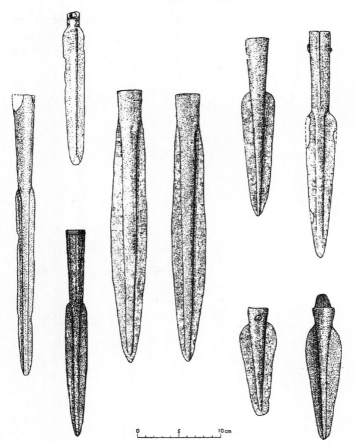

Fig. 7.5. Bronze
spearheads of
probable Aegean
origin.

at Kalavasos-*Ayios Dhimitrios*,[71] Maroni-*Vournes*,[72] Buildings I and II at
Alassa-*Palaeotaverna*,[73] and the first phase of construction of Building 18
at Enkomi.[74] Kling argues that the ashlar buildings at Maa-*Palaeokastro*
were constructed in LC IIC, before any Mycenaean colonisation. She,
moreover, attributes the destruction of these buildings and their subsequent rebuilding 'in a less sophisticated architectural style' to newcomers who brought the Mycenaean IIIC:1b pottery to the site.[75] Moreover, the
use of ashlar masonry in Cyprus is very different to that in mainland
Greece during the LBA, where it was largely restricted to the construction
of *tholos* tombs or reinforcing the weak points of citadel architecture (the
lintels and jambs of the massive gateways for example), rather than the
construction of impressive building façades. In contrast, in Cyprus ashlar
masonry was used extensively as a building material, for monumental
façades, internal pillars and pilasters. The character of this construction
is rather more oriental than Aegean and points to the close cultural

198

contacts between Cyprus and Ugarit.[76] The continued use, refurbishment and construction of such buildings in Cyprus during the twelfth century illustrate the cultural *floruit* experienced on the island subsequent to the destructions at the end of the thirteenth century.[77]

The LC IIIA towns and settlements were protected by fortification walls built in the Cyclopean technique: two faces of massive uncut stone blocks with a rubble core and a mudbrick superstructure. These fortifications have been attested at Maa-*Palaeokastro*, Enkomi, Kition, Sinda and Lara.[78] This form of military architecture is a new feature in Cyprus and has been attributed to Aegean immigrants. Certainly, the development of military architecture is intrusive to the island, but whether it should be attributed to an immigrant element of the population in preference to the consideration of other internal factors has yet to be fully explored in the literature. Another architectural innovation in LC IIIA is paralleled in contemporary southern Anatolia (at Tarsus) and the Philistine sites of the southern Levant (Ashdod, Ashkelon, Tel Qasile and Tel Miqne). This is the large communal hall with a central hearth, used for elite gatherings and communal feasting.[79] This architectural unit appears to relate to Aegean domestic architecture such as the central megaron element of the Mycenaean palace. The typical Mycenaean megaron unit, comprising porch, vestibule and hall, is not, however, found in Cyprus in LC III. Several central hearths have been identified at Enkomi in LC IIC[80] and LC IIIA levels,[81] in a LC IIC/IIIA context at Alassa-*Palaeotaverna* in Building II,[82] and associated with the LC IIIA temples at Kition.[83] Hearths are also attested at Maa-*Palaeokastro* in LC IIIA, in Buildings II and IV, associated with large quantities of drinking vessels and in close proximity to rooms associated with the preparation of food,[84] illustrating their function as a location for feasting. At Enkomi the hearths in rooms 77 and 89A are directly associated with platforms or benches, which Dikaios interpreted as seats or thrones, very much in the tradition of the Mycenaean megaron unit. The form and construction of the hearths is variable. Some are square, others are semi-circular. At Enkomi, room 77, the hearth is built of slabs of sandstone covered with a mud mortar, whereas the hearths at Maa-*Palaeokastro* are built using pithos sherds within a mudbrick border.[85] Another related novel element of material culture, also apparently derived from the Aegean, comprises occasional portable hearths made of bronze. These are also found in LC IIIA contexts, at Enkomi (see Plate 26)[86] and Sinda.[87] The social transformation associated with the use of these halls and hearths remains elusive. Karageorghis views them as an element of a Mycenaean cultural package introduced to Cyprus at the transition between LC IIC and LC IIIA,[88] in much the same way that hearth rooms were introduced to Crete from the Greek mainland in LM IIIA/B.[89] Their use certainly illustrates new social customs. Thus it is particularly interesting to note their explicit association with the new range of locally produced Mycenaean drinking equipment, comprising deep bowls and kraters.

Funerary ritual

The profound social and economic changes experienced during the twelfth century BC are particularly evident in transformations in the funerary record. The typical tomb type in LC IIIA is the shaft grave, a rectangular shallow cutting in the ground, which might be lined with loose stones.[90] It housed between one and three burials, in itself a major break from the traditional LC burial customs discussed in the previous chapter. The traditional LC rock-cut chamber tombs do continue to be used, and some were still constructed as late as the twelfth century,[91] but the ancestral chamber tombs used over generations that did survive the twelfth century were short-lived. Even so, the continuity of certain aspects of LC IIIA burial ritual, namely location and on occasion burial facility, suggest that the occupants of the towns rebuilt in this period felt no aversion to re-using the tombs of the earlier inhabitants.[92] The practice of secondary burial of the physical remains of the deceased was abandoned, possibly illustrating abbreviated funerary ritual or else indicative of changes in ideologies of death.[93] Keswani has argued that the shaft graves are a factor of the unsettled situation in Cyprus during this period, specifically referring to displaced elements of the population group that had no family tomb group. This might refer to internal population shifts subsequent to the destructions at the end of LC IIC, or even intrusive ethnic elements.[94]

Although minimal effort was involved in the construction of the burial facility, the actual grave goods deposited in the tombs might be quite valuable. This is amply illustrated by the wealthy shaft grave from Hala Sultan Tekke, Tomb 23. This burial was furnished with a number of prestige exotica, such as a pair of a faience bowls (once containing an organic substance), a bronze wine set (see Plate 27), an ivory gaming board, gold pendants, lapis lazuli, a silver ring with a Hittite motif on the bezel, and a gold-mounted scarab marked with the cartouche of Rameses II.[95] Niklasson argues for some specialised ritual treatment of the grave goods in this shaft grave. One faience bowl had been deliberately broken and placed in the other, and both were upturned. Moreover, a murex shell had been placed on the chest of the male buried in the grave.[96] The wealthiest tomb excavated at Alassa-*Pano Mandilaris* – Tomb 3, an indigenous type chamber tomb – has been attributed to LC IIIA. The burials were equipped with gold jewellery, bronzes and a haematite cylinder seal,[97] indicating the continued use of luxury, prestige artefacts on Cyprus into the twelfth century. However, the richest tomb of this period is Evreti Tomb VIII. The grave goods included a profusion of gold jewellery – six elaborately worked finger rings decorated with cloisonné enamelling, 14 earrings (boat-shaped, with simple loops, and with bull's head pendants), bracelets, a diadem – four bronze bowls and two silver bowls, four daggers, two iron knives and various ivories.[98] This range of grave goods represents a significant display of disposable wealth, not only in terms of raw materials but also of the craftsmanship involved in their manufacture, comparable with the funerary display of the earlier LC II period.

For the most part, however, LC IIIA shaft graves were modestly furnished. The standard provision of grave goods comprised a pottery jug and a bronze bowl, interpreted by Niklasson as sustenance for the afterlife. At Enkomi Keswani has noted a decline in the quantity of gold deposited in tombs.[99] Similarly the range of artefact type decreases, and exotics, such as faience and glass, become rarer. There is, however, substantial evidence for a major ivory-working industry in the twelfth century and ivories continued to be highly valued luxury grave goods. Particularly popular were the carved ivory boxes and mirror handles found in the British Museum excavations at Enkomi.[100] The iconography used to decorate these ivories – lion and bull fights, hunting, warriors, mythical beasts such as sphinxes and griffons – refers to Near Eastern ideologies of kingship.[101] Moreover, a wealth of bronzes was deposited in tombs, primarily drinking sets comprising bowls and jugs.[102] Keswani suggests that the standardised hemispherical bronze bowls had an exchange value in Cyprus, within the LC IIIA wealth-finance system. Bronze was also used to manufacture high status, prestige goods, primarily used within funerary display, most notably the characteristic LC IIIA tripods and four-sided stands, found for example in British Tombs 15, 58 and 97 at Enkomi.[103] Stone grave goods, including vases and pestles and mortars as part of a cosmetic kit, were increasingly common in the twelfth century.[104] Although there is an overall decrease in wealth, there is still pronounced variability between tomb groups and Keswani argues for the continued existence of an elite group in LC IIIA, which controlled the circulation of exotics, valuables and metals. However, the funerary arena was no longer the primary location for competition and display.[105]

Religion

For the most part LC IIIA cult activity demonstrates significant cultural continuity from the preceding LC IIC period and it is in fact very difficult to make a coherent division between the practices of the thirteenth and twelfth centuries. As has already been noted in Chapter 6, there was a dramatic increase in the construction of urban cult buildings in the LC IIC-IIIA period.[106] This phenomenon is concurrent with the reworking of the major urban centres and the extensive use of ashlar masonry to construct and adorn monumental buildings, including the new sanctuaries (see Plate 28). The salient characteristics of LC IIIA cult are, therefore, its urban location[107] and its monumentality. New temple constructions dating to the LC IIC-IIIA horizon include the reconfiguration of Myrtou-*Pigadhes*

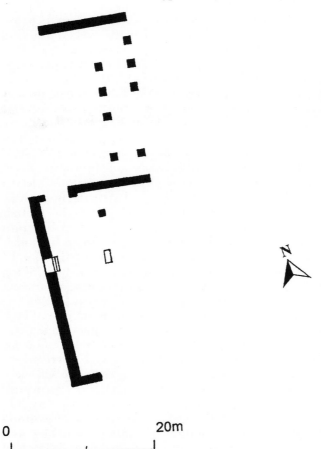

Fig. 7.6. Plan of the LC
III sanctuary at
Palaepaphos.

0   20m

(Period V),[108] Idalion-*Ambelleri*,[109] Sanctuary I at Palaepaphos (Fig. 7.6),[110] the construction of Temples 1-5 at Kition-*Kathari*,[111] and three temple constructions at Enkomi – the Sanctuary of the Horned God,[112] the Sanctuary of the Ingot God (Fig. 7.7),[113] and the Sanctuary of the Double Goddess.[114] The LC IIIA sanctuaries all share the typical components of LC cult buildings: an outer court (possibly where the participants of the cult gathered), and more restricted spatial zones, the covered hall and inner room, which presumably were accessed only by the religious hierarchy. Possibly the most elaborate of the cult buildings of this period is the sanctuary at Palaepaphos. This comprises a large open court (*temenos*) enclosed by a wall of huge limestone orthostats and at its northern end a large colonnaded hall, built using ashlar masonry.[115] The religious complex built at Kition-*Kathari* in LC IIIA likewise is an impressive, monumental building endeavour. The economic aspect of the temples continues to be

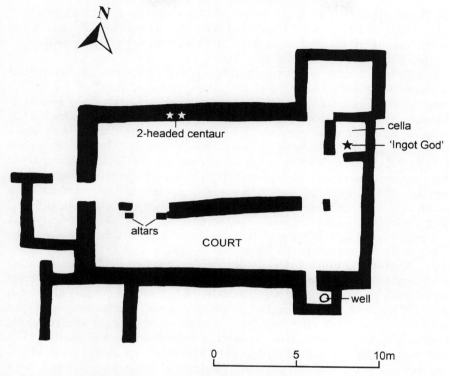

Fig. 7.7. Plan of the LC III Sanctuary of the 'Ingot God' at Enkomi.

important in LC IIIA. There is evidence for textile production within the sacred area at Kition, in the western workshops, to the west of Temple 1.[116] The close relationship between metallurgical production and the sacred domain appears to continue to be significant. Metallurgical debris was found in the courtyard and the so-called 'priest's house' at Idalion-*Ambelleri*[117] and the major urban sanctuaries at Enkomi[118] and Kition[119] were in close proximity to metallurgical workshops.

Novel elements in LC (IIC-)IIIA cult furniture include the so-called horns of consecration,[120] apparently the representation of bull's horns in stone, standing between 0.43 and 1.15 m high. These have been identified at Kition (Temenos A and B),[121] Palaepaphos[122] and Myrtou-*Pigadhes*.[123] Many scholars have attributed the introduction of this piece of cult furniture to Aegean immigrants,[124] but Webb notes that the Cypriot horns in fact differ significantly from their Aegean counterparts in having flat square terminals rather than inward curving and pointed horns.[125] Albeit, the importance of the bull was an indigenous and ancient aspect of Cypriot spiritual beliefs as is indicated by EC representations illustrating the totemic use of bucrania in Cypriot cult practices from the earliest part of the Bronze Age.[126] The stone horns of consecration in fact illustrate a salient characteristic of LC social and religious practices – external referencing and hybridisation of Aegean and Near Eastern iconography and equipment.

Debris of cult activity, or cult equipment, includes bucrania and incised ox scapulae, further illustrating the importance of the bull in LC III religion. Bucrania are found in the sanctuaries at Enkomi and Kition.[127] Karageorghis suggested that the bucrania were used as masks within religious ritual, in analogy to later cult practices in the Phoenician temple at Kition-*Kathari*.[128] There is, however, no evidence that the bucrania were modified for attachment as masks; instead the masks all demonstrate clear signs of burning. Consequently, Nys has concluded that they are the remains of bull sacrifice that had possibly been selectively retrieved to adorn the sanctuaries, being placed on benches or hung on walls.[129] Scapulae, incised with regularly spaced parallel lines, are found in wells and bothroi and on the floors of Temples 4 and 5 at Kition,[130] on the north bench of the Sanctuary of the Ingot God,[131] and in the LC IIC-IIIA sanctuary at Myrtou-*Pigadhes*.[132] Originally Webb suggested that these scapulae were used in the practice of divination.[133] More recently Karageorghis has suggested that they served an alternative purpose, as a musical instrument.[134] As with the bucrania, the scapulae were retrieved from the carcasses of animals that had been sacrificed as part of the religious ceremony at these sanctuaries. Incised scapulae continue to be an important element of cult material in Cypriot sanctuaries into the Iron Age.[135] The use of the triton shell (*Charonia*) in liminal religious contexts is well attested in the Aegean during the LBA and appears to be an aspect of Aegean cult equipment that was transmitted to the East Mediterranean during the twelfth century.[136] It is interesting, therefore, to note their appearance amongst LC III cult equipment in Temple 2 at Kition[137] and in a possible cult building at Hala Sultan Tekke.[138] The Cypriot examples had been worked to form a trumpet, from which it is possible to infer the use of music as part of LC III ritual performance.[139]

A new element of LC III cult equipment, attested at Enkomi and Kition, is the terracotta mask. These are slightly smaller than life-size and can be divided into two types, the anthropomorphic mask and the demonic mask.[140] Nys identifies eight anthropomorphic masks, all representing a bearded male with a closed mouth and cut-out eyes, and possibly with additional painted decoration.[141] In addition there are three demonic masks, two from Enkomi and a third from Kition, which are distinguished by their deeply grooved face. These demonic masks have been variously related to the Babylonian demon Humbaba and the Egyptian god Bes, although Nys prefers to interpret them within an indigenous framework of religious beliefs.[142] The function of the masks is unclear. It is however worth noting their limited number and restricted distribution at the urban sanctuaries of Enkomi and Kition. Their limited distribution does not appear to support their use as votive offerings, suggesting that they were instead used by specific participants within the context of LC religious ritual. An intriguing possibility, which takes into account the small size of the masks, has been put forward by Nys. She suggests that the masks were worn as part of the ritual associated with the initiation of children into the world of adults. In this respect she argues that the human and demonic images of the masks might have been a deliberate juxtaposition symbolising the individual's transition from the wild, uncivilised state of childhood into the tamed adult community.[143] Alternatively, Webb suggests that the masks were used in ceremonies involving mythological re-enactments, possibly associated with metal-working given their close proximity to the metallurgical installations at Enkomi and Kition.[144]

Although anthropomorphic clay figurines are not a typical element of LC cult equipment in LC II or LC III,[145] bull figures are found in some quantity in all the LC IIC-IIIA cult buildings, excepting Kition Temple 2 and the Sanctuary of the Double Goddess at Enkomi.[146] These include large quantities of small, solid handmade bull figures from Enkomi, Kition and Idalion-*Ambelleri*, and occasional larger hollow wheelmade bulls with incised, stamped or painted decoration, attested at Myrtou-*Pigadhes*, Enkomi and possibly Ayia Irini. Webb notes that the bull terracottas were found on the floors of the sanctuaries rather than being deposited in bothroi or wells, indicating their use as cult equipment rather than votive offerings by the participants of cult. Moreover, there is no apparent association of these objects with the debris of religious sacrifice.[147] These figures, however, emphasise the importance of the bull in LC IIIA religious practices. This is particularly evident in the cult practised at the Sanctuary of the Horned God at Enkomi, as illustrated by the finds of numerous cattle bones, including 15 skulls, and numerous bronze and terracotta figurines.[148] The cult equipment also might also have included a bull's head rhyton of Aegean type, only the gold leaf horns of which have survived.[149] In LBA Aegean contexts Rehak has suggested that bull's head rhyta served as a simulacrum for animal sacrifice,[150] but the large quantities of cattle bones from the sanctuary indicate that actual animal sacrifice occurred on a regular basis as an integral element of LC IIIA cult practices.

The focus of LC cult and the nature of the deities worshipped in the LC sanctuaries remain elusive. Only two possible cult images have been identified, both bronze statuettes of male warriors found in sanctuaries at Enkomi. These are the Horned God (see Plate 29) and Ingot God,[151] both apparently defined as 'warrior' deities by their attributes: a horned helmet, and the shield and spear held in striking pose by the Ingot God. Most discussion of these images has sought to place them within either a Near Eastern or Aegean artistic and religious tradition, according to the archaeological training and academic prejudices of individual scholars.[152] However, the eclectic style of both pieces is characteristically Cypriot and reflects the cultural and ideological syncretism of LC society. It is unclear whether these images were actual cult statues and the focus of veneration,[153] or were elements of cult paraphernalia used in re-enactment ceremonies or revealed as part of an epiphany ceremony. However, both figures have tenons, suggesting permanent attachment. Neither image was found *in situ*; instead they had both been deposited in apparent closure ceremonies, possibly signalling an end to the cult practices for which they were intended. Later representations of the cult centre at Palaepaphos[154] indicate that the focus of the Paphian cult was aniconic – a baetyl or conical stone. Certainly, the greyish-green conical stone that was the focus of later cult activity at the site has survived,[155] but it is not clear whether its religious significance can be extrapolated back to the LC III period.

Metal hoards

A small number of metal hoards have been identified in Cyprus, dating to the LC IIC/LC IIIA transition (Table 7.2).[156] These have a very restricted distribution both temporally and spatially. Very few hoards have been recognised in LC IIC contexts and there is an apparent peak in the practice of depositing bronzes in hoards during LC IIIA.[157] For the most part the hoards are found in the southeast part of the island; there is a particular concentration at Enkomi,[158] although this might be an artificial attribute resulting from the very intensive archaeological fieldwork at the site since the latter part of the nineteenth century. Knapp, however, argues that the apparent concentration of hoards at Enkomi reflects the town's privileged position in metallurgical production stretching back to the beginning of the LBA.[159] The hoards contain a wide variety of metal objects. These include a range of tools, weapons, metal vessels and stands, cast bronze figurines, ingots, weights and scales, scrap metal and castings.

Possibly the hoards were utilitarian and simply represent scrap metal for recycling or otherwise precious objects hidden before the settlement was abandoned and never retrieved.[160] Alternatively, the hoards might represent ceremonial foundation or votive deposits, which were deliberately made to remove prestige items from circulation, thereby enhancing the status of the individual or group making the deposit.[161] Certainly, the pair of ploughshares and single bronze peg placed under the foundations of the reconstructed Temple 4 at Kition can be interpreted as a deliberate foundation deposit,[162] as it was not found in a retrievable context. Other possible ceremonial hoards have been identified at Enkomi. These include the rich foundation deposit from the so-called Maison des Bronzes, comprising portable hearths, a basin and a situla,[163] and the pit in room 9 of the Sanctuary of the Horned God, containing the cast bronze figure of the Horned God, a miniature bronze sickle and a bronze pin.[164] Although this is usually interpreted as a closure deposit, Webb argues that the statuette was not in fact ritually buried or concealed but instead placed in an open

Hoard	Date	Tools	Weapons	Vessels & stands	Figurines	Ingots	Castings	Weights & scales	Scrap metal
Enkomi 'foundry'		•	•	•		•	•	•	•
Enkomi 'Gunnis'		•							
Enkomi 'maison des bronzes'	LC IIIA	•		•					
Enkomi 'tresors des bronzes'	LC IIIA	•	•		•			•	•
Enkomi 'Stylianou'		•		•	•		•		•
Enkomi 'miniature'	LC IIIB		•	•	•		•	•	•
Enkomi 'weapon'	LC IIIA	•	•	•					•
Enkomi quartier 3W P.438	LC II	•			•				
Enkomi quartier 3W P.783	LC IIIA		•			•	•		•
Enkomi quartier 6W P.1458	LC IIIA	•		•	•	•	•		•
Enkomi well 212	LC IIIA	•	•	•	•	•		•	•
Enkomi 'Ingot'		•		•		•			•
Enkomi Sanctuary of the Horned God	LC III	•			•				•
Kition Temple 4 (floor III)	LC IIIA	•							•
Mathiati		•	•			•	•		•
Pyla-Kokkinokremos Gold Hoard	LC IIC				•		•		
Pyla-Kokkinokremos Silver Hoard	LC IIC			•		•			
Pyla-Kokkinokremos Bronze Hoard	LC IIC	•	•	•	•	•			•
Sinda		•		•	•				•
Kalavasos Building III A.219	LC IIC				•			•	
Myrtou-*Pigadhes*	LC IIC-LC IIIA	•		•					•
Hala Sultan Tekke	LC IIC				•				•
Nitovikla?		•	•						
Alassa-Pano Mandilaris Room B	LC IIIA		•						

Table 7.2. Late Cypriot metal hoards (after Knapp 1988, table 2).

pit, the head and horns visible from the doorway into Room 9.[165] Other hoards, however, appear to have an economic or utilitarian value. Knapp, for example, suggests that the group of eleven bronze weights, found together with a haematite weight and a single haematite cylinder beneath the floor of Building III at Kalavasos-*Ayios Dhimitrios*,[166] represents a merchant's hoard that had been concealed but never retrieved, as is emphasised by the clear economic value of its contents.[167] The contents of the hoards also distinguish between utilitarian hoards and ceremonial deposits. Mixed deposits, containing scrap metal together with a range of tools, weapons, ingots, vessels and statuettes, might indicate hoards that are only of economic, utilitarian value. Discrete groups of high status prestige objects are more likely to denote the deliberate removal of wealth from circulation.[168]

The practice of hoarding metal should be interpreted within the social and economic context of LC IIC-IIIA, a period characterised by a breakdown in the political and economic superstructure of the East Mediterranean, caused by the collapse of the Bronze Age palatial economies across the region and resulting in major disruptions to long-distance trade. There is a significant increase in the number of scrap metal hoards in LC IIIA, suggesting that many of the Cypriot hoards were simply buried for safe-keeping and never subsequently retrieved. Yet these hoards also include prestige goods, such as vessels, tripod stands and figurines. Alongside the increasing emphasis on bronze grave goods in LC IIC-IIIA,[169] these hoards appear to reflect a deliberate strategy of elite competition,[170] with the removal of both large quantities of metal and high status craft objects from circulation. This would not only maintain the exclusivity of these objects and remove them from the reach of rivals, but also increase the social standing and political power of the giver.[171]

Cultural floruit

Despite the very apparent signs of internal stress and social upheaval, LC IIIA might equally be viewed as the culmination of urbanisation on Cyprus and a period of great economic and cultural prosperity. Compared to other areas in the East Mediterranean, Cyprus was in fact relatively stable and prosperous during the twelfth century. The earlier part of LC IIIA can be characterised as a period of urbanisation. Several large towns flourished along the southern coast – Palaepaphos, Kition, Hala Sultan Tekke, Enkomi – and were still participating in international trade. These towns are characterised by massive building programmes, in particular the construction or reconfiguration of religious structures, with extensive use of ashlar masonry. LC IIIA was correspondingly a prosperous and cosmopolitan period, as is illustrated by the horizon of wealthy burials, most notably at Palaepaphos.[172] The elite buried in these tombs were able to procure luxury commodities such as gold and ivory and moreover to support a number of highly skilled craft specialists. Indeed, a prime characteristic of the LC IIIA archaeological record is the evidence for craft specialisation, illustrated by intensification of pottery production,[173] and also by elite craft production, such as ivories, bronzes and gold jewellery. Some of the clearest evidence for craft specialisation is found at Palaepaphos, in particular the carved ivory fragments and 1.5 kg of debris from ivory workshops found in the wells at Evreti.[174] The products of the Cypriot ivory workshops, found in tombs at Enkomi and Palaepaphos, include gaming boxes, mirror handles, and circular pyxis lids.[175] In many respects LC IIIA was the height of metallurgical production, not least for bronze-working.[176] Prestige bronzes include tripods (Fig. 7.8) and open-work four-sided stands with elaborate figural decoration,[177] a variety of cast bronze figures,[178] and drinking sets. These objects are found in sanctuaries, bronze hoards and tomb groups, and were also exported beyond Cyprus to the Central Mediterranean, where they turn up in EIA contexts in Italy.[179] It is unclear whether this tradition of bronze-working survived the twelfth century. Certainly some fine displays of wealth in the form of bronze drinking sets and tripod stands are found in eleventh-century tomb

Fig. 7.8. Bronze stands: (1, 2, 3) tripod stands from Myrtou-*Pigadhes*; (4, 5) ring stands from Myrtou-*Pigadhes*; (6) tripod stand from Pyla-*Kokkinokremos*; (7) tripod stand from Enkomi British Tomb 15; (8) tripod stand, of unknown provenance.

groups at Kourion and Palaepaphos,[180] but whether these objects were the products of contemporary bronze workshops or were twelfth-century 'heir-looms' is a matter of some debate.[181] The tombs from Evreti indicate the skill of the goldsmiths, in particular the six rings with decoration using the innovative technique of enamelled cloisonné.[182] Another twelfth-century innovation is iron metallurgy, which was first used to manufacture small knives with bone or more rarely ivory handles and bronze rivets,[183] which are found in both tomb and settlement contexts at the main urban centres. Sherratt argues that these objects can be used to chart shifting patterns of trading contacts between Cyprus and the southern Levant during the twelfth and eleventh centuries.[184]

It appears therefore that Cyprus continued to flourish both economically and culturally during the twelfth century, despite the disappearance of the palaces from around the East Mediterranean basin. Although the Aegean largely disappears from international trading networks, there is certainly no evidence for the collapse of maritime trade in this period in the East Mediterranean. Eriksson[185] has recently identified Egyptian transport jars in LC IIC-IIIA deposits at Hala Sultan Tekke, Pyla-*Kokkinokremos*, Maa-*Palaeokastro* and Canaanite jars are found in large quantities at Maa-*Palaeokastro*. Luxuries such as ivory, faience and gold are still in circulation and there is substantial evidence for the existence of wide-ranging trading networks associated with the movement of metals, between Cyprus and Italy.[186] Given the extremely limited data for the LC IIIB period it is uncertain whether these trade routes were disrupted at the beginning of the eleventh century. There is, however, increasing evidence for Cypriot and Levantine trade in the later eleventh and early tenth centuries, illustrated by the presence of large quantities of Phoenician ceramic imports at Palaepaphos-*Skales* and more occasional Cypriot ceramic imports to the Levant.[187] These earliest Iron Age contacts are the foundations for the development of the Phoenician maritime trade networks of the first millennium BC.

A brave new world: the advent of the Iron Age

Although the conventional cultural-historical framework applied to the Cypriot Late Bronze Age argues for a major disruption at the LC IIC-IIIA transition, attributed to an influx of Aegean settlers, it has become increasingly apparent that there was in fact a large degree of cultural continuity between the two phases.[188] In fact the major discontinuity in the archaeological record is at the LC IIIA/IIIB interface.[189] The totality of the archaeological record argues for a complete cultural break at the end of LC IIIA, and the subsequent LC IIIB phase effectively marks the beginning of the Iron Age. Despite the apparent cultural *floruit* that marks LC IIIA there was a gradual decline during this period, resulting in the eventual abandonment of the LC IIIA settlements by the end of the twelfth century.[190] Continuity into the eleventh century has only been demonstrated for a few sites, and this appears to be confined to sacred areas and moreover to be short-lived. LC IIIB material has been identified at Enkomi, in the area of the Ingot God Sanctuary, but there is no evidence for continued urban occupation around this structure.[191] Instead settlement moved to the nearby, newly established settlement of Salamis, possibly due to silting of the harbour at Enkomi.[192] Similarly, there was continued activity in the area of the temples at Kition.[193] The LC IIIB period is characterised by a complete transformation in settlement pattern and the introduction of new modes of burial within newly established extramural cemeteries.[194] The settlements of LC IIIB for the most part are not archaeologically visible. This is partly because the earliest settlements were rather simple in construction, but also due to the centuries of continuous occupation that have obliterated the earliest habitation remains.[195] However, the evidence from the cemeteries suggests that many LC IIIB settlements were short-lived, and that this was a period of site dislocation.

Within the surviving settlements there appears to be some continuity of religious activity. Indeed the clearest evidence for LC IIIB settlement activity is at the location of the cult areas at Kition and the Sanctuary of the Ingot God at Enkomi.[196] There is, however, a significant change in the practice of cult, indicated by the deposition of large numbers of small terracotta figurines, usually female but on occasion male, especially in the Sanctuary of the Ingot God (Sols I-II).[197] The small figures might represent votives and thereby illustrate a dramatic change in the nature of worship at these sanctuaries at the beginning of the eleventh century. Occasional larger wheelmade figures, some standing to an estimated height of 25-30 cm, are more probably representations of deities.[198] It is usually accepted that these figures, the so-called goddess with up-raised arms, were introduced to the island from Crete, along with shrine models.[199] There are also a number of terracotta wheelmade zoomorphic models of probable Aegean inspiration, including bulls and horses. Most significant is the model of a double-headed animal from the Sanctuary of the Ingot God at Enkomi (Fig. 7.9). Although commonly referred to as a centaur, this is more plausibly a model of a two-headed sphinx.[200]

Burial practices underpin a very different relationship between the living and the dead from that illustrated by the very close spatial proximity typical of LC intramural tombs. Throughout the LC period (into LC IIIA) the communities that built and used the intramural chamber tombs, and subsequently the shaft graves, appeared to have no aversion to proximity to the dead. Indeed, the arena of the living and the dead was closely integrated. In the Iron Age, however, from LC IIIB, the living made a conscious decision to remove the dead from the boundaries of their settlements. Alongside the establishment of the new burial grounds, a new burial facility was introduced to the island – the chamber tomb approached by a long narrow *dromos*, a type apparently derived from the

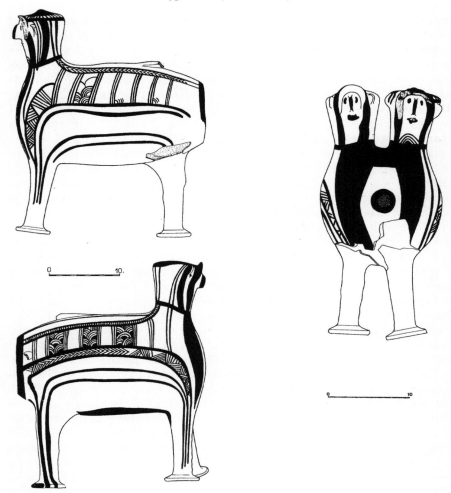

Fig. 7.9. Double-headed animal model from the Ingot God Sanctuary, Enkomi.

Mycenaean chamber tomb.[201] The LC IIIB tombs housed only a small number of burials, between one and three individuals, and there is no evidence for extended funerary ritual, secondary burial, or specialised treatment of any of the bones. These abbreviated rites, in contrast to the more complex funerary ritual of LC I-II, might refer to the unsettled social and economic climate of LC IIIB. The unsettled conditions of LC IIIB are similarly reflected by a near breakdown in international exchange and the apparent poverty of the LC IIIB burials. With only a few exceptions, most notably Kourion-*Kaloriziki* Tomb 40 which is furnished with a suite of bronze vessels and tripods,[202] it is not until the subsequent CG I period that the local elite was prepared to remove valuables such as bronzes and gold from circulation, depositing them in tombs.[203] Despite the unsettled conditions and the very elusive nature of the evidence, it is clear that during LC IIIB the foundations of Iron Age Cyprus were established. This is most clearly illustrated by the changing pattern of settlement, foreshadowing the distribution of the Iron Age city kingdoms[204] and the development of a new funerary ideology, but also in a transformation of the cultural repertoire of Cypriot households.

Notes

1. The Island of Cyprus

1. Gjerstad 1980, p. 11.

2. The application of theoretical perspectives in Cypriot archaeology remains haphazard, and for the most part the material has been evaluated according to a cultural-historical framework. Only recently have social archaeologies been applied to the archaeological record, and predominantly to the earlier prehistory. See discussion in Knapp *et al.* 1994, pp. 430-1.

3. Steel 1993; Catling 1994; Iacovou 1999.

4. Ward & Joukowsky (eds) 1992.

5. For example, Susan and Andrew Sherratt (1993) explore the changing economic basis of exchange throughout the East Mediterranean during the first millennium BC.

6. For example Held 1993, pp. 28-9.

7. Constantinou 1982, p. 15.

8. Constantinou 1982, p. 15.

9. Constantinou 1982, fig. 1 gives a clear stratigraphy of the Troodos massif rock formation.

10. Peltenburg, 1982a, p. 54, also notes the presence of pockets of serpentine in the Akamas peninsula and the western flanks of the Paphos plateau. See Peltenburg 1982a, fig. 3a for the distribution of serpentine sources in Cyprus.

11. Apliki: du Plat Taylor 1952; Cyprus Survey: Catling 1962.

12. Frankel & Webb 1996.

13. Todd & Hadjicosti 1991; Todd & Pilides 1993.

14. Given *et al.* 1999.

15. Knapp 1994, pp. 271-2.

16. Knapp 1994, p. 271.

17. Swiny 1982, p. 1.

18. Frankel 1974b, p. 10.

19. Stanley-Price 1977a, pp. 27-8, fig. 1; Held 1989, p. 12, fig. 1. Sea level changes during the Pleistocene (the last Ice Age) suggest a maximum regression of around 130 m and that the distance between Cyprus and the Asiatic mainland (southern Turkey) would have been at least 60 km.

20. Swiny 1988, p. 3.

21. Myres 1914, p. xxvii.

22. Merrillees 1978, p. 6; Knapp 1994, p. 273; both quoting Holmboe 1914, pp. 1-3.

23. Strabo (*Geographica* 14.6.5) reports that Eratosthenes had once described the island's forest-covered plains. Merrillees 1978, p. 6; Raptou 1996, pp. 254-6, discusses the use of timber in the Iron Age and Roman economy of the island.

24. Halstead 1977, p. 267.

25. Merrillees 1978, p. 7; Tsintides 1998, p. 11.
26. Tsintides 1998, p. 31.
27. Tsintides 1998, p. 103.
28. Merrillees 1978, pp. 6-7; Knapp 1994, p. 273; Tsintides 1998, pp. 12-14.
29. Tsintides 1998, p. 14.
30. Merrillees 1978, p. 7.
31. Tsintides 1998, pp. 15-17. Most endemics are located in the Troodos Forest, the Paphos Forest, the Kyrenia mountains (Pentadaktylos), and in the Akamas peninsula; Tsintides 1998, p. 21. The cedar is the only endemic tree on the island.
32. Held 1989, p. 15.
33. Broodbank 2000, p. 110.
34. Cherry 1990, pp. 194-6; see discussion in Vigne 1996.
35. Swiny 1982, p. 4.
36. Possibly already present prior to the Pleistocene, see Held 1989, p. 15.
37. Guilaine *et al.* 2000, p. 80. Discussed in depth in Chapter 2.
38. Caubet 2001, p. 143; Severis 2001, p. 32.
39. Given 1998, p. 11; Severis 2001, p. 34.
40. Given 1998, p. 11.
41. Balandier 2001, p. 4; Caubet 2001, pp. 141-2.
42. The term Eteo-kyprier (true Cypriot) was coined by Johannes Friedrich in 1932 to denote the indigenous population of the island and it is also used to refer to their language. Gjerstad 1948, pp. 429-31, 444; Reyes 1994, pp. 13-17. See summary in Given 1998, pp. 18-20, on the historiography of the Eteocypriots and pp. 20-4 for a discussion of the archaeology of the Eteocypriots. A number of inscriptions written in the Phoenician alphabet illustrate the third language spoken on the island during the Iron Age; Gjerstad 1948, pp. 436-44; Reyes 1994, pp. 18-21.
43. These include de Saulcy, Guillaume-Rey, and de Vogüé. See discussion in Caubet *et al.* 1992; Caubet 1993, 2001; Masson 1993.
44. Caubet 1993, p. 28; 2001, p. 144; Masson 1993, p. 19; Bonato 2001.
45. Caubet 2001, p. 144, my translation.
46. Caubet 1993, pp. 24-5; 2001, p. 144. Many pieces are illustrated in Caubet *et al.* 1992.
47. Ulbrich 2001, p. 93, fig. 8.1, Appendix 1.
48. Ulbrich 2001, pp. 95-6; see Lang 1878.
49. Cesnola 1877 (reprint 1991).
50. Swiny 1991, p. 5; Balandier 2001, pp. 6-8.
51. Ulbrich 2001, pp. 97-8.
52. Cesnola 1877 (reprint 1991), pp. 302-87. Cesnola claims to have found the 'Treasure' in a large chamber below a mosaic at the acropolis of Kourion. In fact, this comprises finds from a series of tombs in the Kourion area ranging in date from the final phase of the LBA to the Roman period. Swiny 1991, p. 4. See also E. McFadden 1971.
53. Balandier 2001, p. 8.
54. Given 1998, p. 11. See for example Taylor's (2001) discussion of the exploits of Lady Brassey in 1878, who used archaeology to elevate her social position back in fashionable society in England.
55. Ohnefalsch-Richter 1893.
56. Ohnefalsch-Richter 1893; Ulbrich 2001, pp. 98-102.
57. Gardner *et al.* 1888, pp. 193-258.
58. Steel 2001; Enkomi: Murray *et al.* 1900, pp. 1-54; Kourion Site D: Murray *et*

al. 1900, pp. 57-86; Hala Sultan Tekke: D.M. Bailey 1972; Maroni: Manning & Monks 1998, pp. 303-07.

59. Kourion Sites A-C, E: Murray *et al.* 1900, pp. 57-86; Amathus: Murray *et al.* 1900, pp. 89-126.

60. Sandwith 1880; Merrillees 2001, pp. 222-3.

61. Steel 2001.

62. Myres & Ohnefalsch-Richter 1899.

63. Myres 1914, p. xxx; Given 1998, p. 12; Steel 2001, pp. 163-4. See for example Gjerstad 1948, pp. 428-35.

64. The organisation of pottery styles into a typological sequence or series, illustrating the development of the ceramic styles through time.

65. Gjerstad *et al.* 1934, 1935, 1937. See also Gjerstad 1980 for an account of the history of these excavations.

66. These had been excavated by Markides, curator of the Cyprus Museum, in the early years of the twentieth century.

67. Gjerstad completed the synthesis of the Iron Age material in 1948, in *SCE* IV.2. Other syntheses of the Neolithic, Chalcolithic and Bronze Age remains were completed within the same series, but by other archaeologists working on the relevant material (see below).

68. Given 1998, pp. 16-17.

69. Dikaios 1953, 1961, 1969-71.

70. Stewart & Stewart 1950; Stewart 1962a.

71. See for example Dikaios 1962.

72. Knapp & Antoniadou 1998.

73. See however the survey work that has been carried out in the north by Sevketoglu (2000).

74. See discussion in Chapter 2.

75. See Knapp & Cherry 1994 for summary of scientific techniques that have been applied to Cypriot archaeological data.

76. Knapp 1997a, pp. 21-7.

77. Catling 1962; Knapp 1997a, pp. 29-30.

78. See discussion in Knapp 1997a, pp. 33-45.

79. See for example Knapp 1990; Manning 1993; Peltenburg 1996.

80. Most important is the work of Keswani (1989b, 1993, 1994, 1996) and Bolger (1992, 1994, 1996).

81. See for example Frankel & Webb 1996; Peltenburg *et al.* 1998.

82. A relative chronology simply organises archaeological material into a chronological sequence, based either on a site's stratigraphy or on a typological sequence of artefacts, usually pottery. The underlying principle of the typological sequence is that objects change through time and can be ordered sequentially: i.e. Neolithic, Chalcolithic, Bronze Age, Iron Age. Although a relative chronology is the archaeologist's primary tool in ordering archaeological data, it does not provide calendrical dates. These dates, the absolute chronology, can be determined through the recovery of datable objects (for example coins) in sealed contexts, or more commonly using scientific dating techniques, in particular radiocarbon dating.

83. Sandwith 1880; Merrillees 1978, p. 29; 2001, pp. 223-4. The wares listed below are referred to according to the terminology in current use, based on Myres' and Gjerstad's typology.

84. Sandwith 1880, p. 131.

85. Myres & Ohnefalsch-Richter 1899; Myres 1914; Merrillees 1978, pp. 15-17.

86. Gjerstad 1926.
87. The Three Age system is based upon antiquarian thought of the eighteenth century and organises early prehistory into a unilinear tripartite sequence: the Stone Age, the Bronze Age and the Iron Age. The three ages were further subdivided into three subphases, e.g. Early, Middle and Late Bronze Age, and these might be subdivided, e.g. EBA I, II, III. With the adaptation of evolutionary theory to the development of past human societies in the nineteenth century, the tripartite system was forced into a cyclical framework of growth, maturity, decay, overtones of which permeate the cultural histories written about the newly discovered Bronze Age societies of the Aegean and Cyprus in the early twentieth century.
88. Stewart 1962a, pp. 208, 210-11; Catling 1973b, pp. 165-6; Knapp 1990, pp. 148-9; 1994, pp. 274-6.
89. Barlow 1991, p. 51.
90. Barlow 1985; 1991, pp. 51-2.
91. Barlow 1991, pp. 53-5.
92. Dikaios 1962, pp. 192-203.
93. Knapp 1990, p. 148.
94. See Chapters 2 and 4.
95. Stanley-Price 1979a, pp. 1-4; Knapp 1990, 148-9.
96. Alambra: Coleman *et al.* 1996; Marki: Frankel & Webb 1996.
97. Knapp 1994, p. 276.
98. Knapp 1990, p. 154.
99. Catling 1973b, p. 166.
100. Simmons 1991; 1998; Simmons *et al.* 1999.
101. Cherry 1990, pp. 151-2.
102. See discussion in Peltenburg *et al.* 2000; 2001.
103. Peltenburg *et al.* 2000; 2001.
104. Following a conference on the Cypriot Neolithic held in Nicosia in May 2001.
105. Merrillees 1977; 1978, pp. 34-6.
106. See Chapter 2.
107. Simmons and Wigand 1994, p. 252.
108. Manning *et al.* 2001, p. 339. The upper limits of the LC IIC period were fixed by radiocarbon determinations taken from roof beams from Kalavasos-*Ayios Dhimitrios* and Alassa-*Palaeotaverna*, dating to a LC IIB-C building phase, Manning *et al.* 2001, p. 334. These indicated a likely felling date within the fourteenth century for the beams used in the construction of Building X at Kalavasos. The close of the LC IIC period was dated by short-life samples from Maroni-*Tsaroukkas* Building 2 (final LC IIC) and Apliki-*Karamallos* (transitional LC IIC-IIIA), Manning *et al.* 2001, pp. 337-8.
109. See Manning *et al.* 2001, fig. 6.
110. Kling 1989b, pp. 2-4; Merrillees 1992; Manning *et al.* 2001, p. 340.
111. Merrillees 1977; 1978, pp. 34-6; 1992; 2002; Åström 1987; Maguire 1992.
112. The king lists are ancient Egyptian records detailing the reigns of Egyptian rulers from the unification of Egypt *c.* 3100 BC, their dates, and important events that occurred during their reigns.
113. The date of deposition of the object will be at least the date recorded on the object or more probably later.
114. Maguire 1992, p. 115.
115. Manning & Swiny 1994, p. 150.

116. Coleman *et al.* 1996, p. 340; these date to between *c.* 1900 and 1700 BC.

117. Ancient Avaris, capital of the Asiatic Hyksos rulers of Egypt, occupied during the Second Intermediate Period (MBA) and early Eighteenth Dynasty (early LBA). See discussion of Cypriot pottery in Maguire 1992.

118. Merrillees 2002, p. 2.

119. Maguire 1992, p. 117.

120. Manning 1999, fig. 23. Maguire, 1992, p. 118, argues for a span of deposition from *c.* 1770-1530 BC, whereas Merrillees (2002, p. 6) dates the WP Pendent Line style export horizon to *c.* 1675-1550 BC.

121. Maguire 1992, pp. 115-16; Merrillees 2002, p. 5.

122. Maguire 1992, p. 118.

123. Manning 1999, pp. 119-22. LC IA material (Proto White Slip, WP V/VI) is found in stratum D/2 at Tell el-Dab'a and a Base Ring I jug is found at Memphis in a SIP tomb; Manning 1999, p. 120.

124. Vermeule & Wolsky 1990, pp. 287-307.

125. Dikaios 1969-1971, p. 541, no. 2283/1.

126. Vermeule & Wolsky 1990, pp. 159-243, with an LM IA import.

127. Manning 1999, pp. 129-35.

128. Manning 1999, pp. 117-18, lists a number of LC IA imports to Crete that are consistently found in mature LM IA deposits: a Red on Black bowl fragment from Mallia, a WP Pendent Line sherd from Zakros, and a variety of wares from Kommos – handmade Red Slip, a Proto White Slip sherd, Proto Base Ring or Monochrome sherds. There is also an early White Slip I bowl, belonging to a style common at LC IA Morphou-*Toumba tou Skourou*, found in the pre-eruption (i.e. LM IA) deposits at Thera, Manning 1999, pp. 150-60.

129. Cadogan 1973; 1993; Steel 1998.

130. See concordance of dates in Åström 1972a, p. 760.

131. Åström 1972b, p. 761; Manning *et al.* 2001, p. 337.

132. Maguire 1992, p. 115.

133. Maguire 1992, pp. 118-19.

2. The Colonisation of Cyprus

1. Eriksen 1993, pp. 133-4.

2. MacArthur & Wilson 1967, p. 3; Evans 1973.

3. See discussion in Rainbird 1999, pp. 222-6.

4. However, it should be noted that cultural islands and geographical islands are separate concepts. Eriksen (1993, p. 135, n.2) notes that in many respects island communities might well be less isolated than other geographically bounded communities, such as mountain villages. In this respect Broodbank, 2000, p. 16, distinguished between analytical islands, where insularity is an important consideration when undertaking analyses, and perceived islands, whose insularity was experienced by the inhabitants.

5. Evans 1973, pp. 517-18.

6. Evans 1973, p. 519.

7. Stoddart *et al.* 1993; Patton 1996.

8. Patton 1996, p. 137.

9. See for example the discussion in Broodbank 1992.

10. Held 1993, p. 28.

11. Held 1993, p. 29.

12. Most recently Webb & Frankel 1999.

13. For example Sjöqvist 1940; Maier 1973; Karageorghis 1990a.
14. van Dommelen 1999, p. 249.
15. Rainbird 1999, p. 228; Broodbank 2000, p. 19.
16. Broodbank 2000, p. 20.
17. Rainbird 1999; Broodbank 2000.
18. Rainbird 1999; Broodbank 2000, p. 17.
19. Rainbird 1999, pp. 222-5, 230; Broodbank 2000, p. 17, notes that the degree of maritime activity exhibited by a culture will depend upon its attitude to the sea, viewing it either as an isolating medium or as a powerful medium for contact and exchange.
20. Rainbird 1999, p. 230.
21. Horden & Purcell 2000, p. 133.
22. Eriksen 1993, p. 135; Rainbird 1999, p. 223.
23. See discussion of seafaring in Broodbank 2000, pp. 96-106; Rainbird 1999, p. 227.
24. Rainbird 1999, p. 227.
25. Broodbank 1999, p. 238.
26. Helms 1988.
27. Held 1989, p. 17.
28. Swiny 1988, p. 3.
29. Held 1989, p. 21.
30. Swiny 1988, p. 7.
31. Held 1989, p. 19.
32. Simmons *et al.* 1999, p. 168.
33. Held 1989, p. 16.
34. Simmons *et al.* 1999, p. 303.
35. Swiny 1988, p. 9; Simmons *et al.* 1999, p. 315.
36. Swiny 1988, p. 8.
37. Simmons *et al.* 1999, p. 304.
38. Akanthou-*Arkosyko* and Xylophagou-*Spilia tis Englezou*: Reese 1996, p. 111.
39. The possibility that pockets of the *Phanourios* population survived in isolated geographical zones such as Akrotiri as late as the aceramic Neolithic has been examined by Swiny (1988, p. 10). However, he argues that it is unlikely that these early farming communities, which were also dependent on herding and hunting, would have ignored such a valuable meat resource.
40. For example Mallorca: Cherry 1990, pp. 147-8. See however Vigne's 1996 discussion of the material from Corsica. At most he feels that the evidence is insufficient to eliminate some overkill of endemic fauna on Corsica, but that on balance it argues against human involvement in insular faunal extinction in the Mediterranean context.
41. Evans 1977, p. 13; Cherry 1990, p. 146; Simmons *et al.* 1999, p. 18.
42. Broodbank & Strasser 1991.
43. Cherry 1990, pp. 147-8, 184.
44. Stanley-Price 1977b, pp. 67-9.
45. Stanley-Price 1977b, p. 69.
46. Cherry 1990, pp. 151-2.
47. Adovasio *et al.* 1975, 1978.
48. Stockton 1968.
49. Vita-Frinzi 1973.
50. Badou & Englemark 1983.
51. The flints from Kyrenia, comprising scrapers, blades, knives, backed flake

tools, possible microliths and thumbnail scrapers (Stockton 1968) are surface finds. Simmons suggests that 'these are not compelling' artefacts and that 'Much of the material is so undiagnostic as to even question its human origin' (Simmons *et al.* 1999, p. 21). The flints from Maronou river were dated according to their geological context, but Simmons notes that they are undiagnostic and suggests that they are natural geofacts rather than anthropogenic material (Simmons *et al.* 1999, p. 22). Todd, 1987, attributes the tools from Ayia Anna-*Perivolia* to the aceramic Neolithic.

52. Held 1989, p. 7. See also Stanley-Price 1977b, pp. 69-70.
53. Cherry 1981, pp. 45-64; 1990, pp. 198-9.
54. Broodbank 2000, p. 114.
55. Broodbank 2000, p. 108.
56. Cherry 1990, p. 153.
57. Simmons *et al.* 1999, p. 1.
58. Simmons *et al.* 1999, pp. 10-11.
59. Simmons *et al.* 1999, p. 33.
60. Simmons *et al.* 1999, p. 4.
61. Stanley-Price 1977b, p. 69; Swiny 1988, pp. 9-10.
62. Simmons *et al.* 1999, p. 93.
63. Bunimovitz & Barkai 1996, pp. 89-90.
64. Simmons & Wigand 1994, p. 252.
65. Manning (1991) attempted to calibrate the radiocarbon determinations from Akrotiri-*Aetokremnos*, and proposed a date range of late eleventh to early tenth millennium BC as a *terminus post quem* for the cultural deposits.
66. Simmons *et al.* 1999, p. 153.
67. Simmons *et al.* 1999, p. 156.
68. See discussion in Swiny 1988; Cherry 1990, p. 155, and further references.
69. Simmons *et al.* 1999, p. 161.
70. Simmons *et al.* 1999, p. 161.
71. Simmons *et al.* 1999, pp. 161-2.
72. Vigne and Poplin disagree with the identification of the fallow deer, suggesting pig instead. The inference of function remains the same. Simmons *et al.* 1999, p. 167, n. 1.
73. Simmons *et al.* 1999, p. 167.
74. Simmons *et al.* 1999, p. 186.
75. Simmons *et al.* 1999, pp. 170-8.
76. Simmons *et al.* 1999, pp. 188-91.
77. 18% of *Monodonta* and 40% of limpet (*Patella*) are burnt, Simmons *et al.* 1999, p. 189.
78. Simmons *et al.* 1999, p. 102.
79. Simmons *et al.* 1999, pp. 106-7.
80. Simmons *et al.* 1999, p. 134.
81. Simmons *et al.* 1999, pp. 137-9.
82. Simmons *et al.* 1999, p. 129.
83. Simmons *et al.* 1999, pp. 149-51.
84. Simmons *et al.* 1999, pp. 147-8.
85. Bunimovitz & Barkai 1996, pp. 92-4. Instead, they suggested that the site represented a natural die-off site, although this does not explain why the bone bed lay directly on a clean (swept) floor, nor the mixing of artefacts, hearths, and burnt bones within stratum 4.

86. Simmons *et al.* 1999, pp. 292-8.
87. Simmons *et al.* 1999, p. 158.
88. Simmons *et al.* 1999, pp. 318, 323-8.
89. Stanley-Price 1977b.
90. Guilaine 2000, p. 77.
91. Bar-Yosef 1995, p. 190. The dates proposed for the PPNA in the Levant are as early as 10,300/10,000 BP.
92. McCartney 1999, p. 10.
93. Rainbird 1999, p. 228.
94. Peltenburg *et al.* 2000, 2001 have proposed the term Cypro-PPNB, clearly signalling the supposed Levantine origins of this culture. However, at a recent conference on the Neolithic in Cyprus (Nicosia 2001) it was agreed to term this newly identified phase as the early aceramic Neolithic, thereby placing it within the local Cypriot cultural sequence rather than applying terminology derived from an external framework.
95. Guilaine 2000; Peltenburg *et al.* 2000; Sevketoglu 2000, pp. 72-9, 117; Todd 1987.
96. Site 23, identified on the southern coast of the Akrotiri peninsula, 1 km east of Akrotiri-*Aetokremnos*, possibly belongs to the early aceramic Neolithic phase, based on the presence of a possible Byblos point and a backed tanged blade among the chipped stone assemblage and two radiocarbon determinations. Swiny 1988, pp. 10-11, figs 4.1, 4.2; Simmons *et al.* 1999, 254-8, fig. 10.6.
97. McCartney 1998, p. 85.
98. Halstead (1987, p. 75) notes that deer is very unsuitable to close herding because of its territoriality and violent male conflicts and suggests that distance hunting is a more viable strategy for exploitation of deer as a meat resource.
99. Guilaine *et al.* 1998, p. 603: water basins (St. 115, 118, 167), well/cistern (St. 2).
100. Guilaine *et al.* 1995, pp. 20-4; Guilaine *et al.* 1997, p. 825.
101. Guilaine *et al.* 1998, p. 603.
102. Guilaine *at al.* 1997, p. 825.
103. B. Boyd, personal communication, 7.12.00.
104. Todd 1989, p. 4, fig. 1.2.
105. Peltenburg *et al.* 2001, pp. 41-2, fig. 4.
106. Peltenburg *et al.* 2001, p. 47.
107. Peltenburg *et al.* 2000, pp. 846-8, fig. 4; 2001, pp. 46-8. St. 66 (dating to the earliest use of Parekklisha-*Shillourokambos*) is a similar cylindrical well, with hand and foot holes cut into its walls; Guilaine *et al.* 1998, p. 604.
108. Guilaine *et al.* 1998 p. 604; 2000, p. 78.
109. Peltenburg *et al.* 2000, p. 849; 2001, p. 54.
110. Peltenburg *et al.* 2000, fig. 6.
111. Peltenburg *et al.* 2001, p. 54.
112. Bender, 1978, and Hayden, 1990, argue for the emergence of socio-economic inequalities specifically within the realm of competitive feasting and consumption of resources from as early as the epi-Palaeolithic, within hunter-gatherer societies. Possibly the deposit of animal bones from Kissonerga-*Mylouthkia* Well 133 should be interpreted within a similar such social context.
113. Briois *et al.* 1997; Guilaine *et al.* 1997, p. 825; McCartney 1999; Peltenburg *et al.* 2000, p. 878. See also Swiny's discussion of the projectile point from Akrotiri Site 23, 1988, pp. 10-11.
114. McCartney 1999, p. 10; Peltenburg *et al.* 2000, p. 878.

115. Guilaine *et al.* 1997, pp. 827-30; 1998, p. 606; 2000, p. 79, n. 4.
116. Peltenburg *et al.* 2001, p. 42. See discussion in Peltenbug 1979, pp. 24-5.
117. Peltenburg *et al.* 2001, p. 42.
118. McCartney, 1999, p. 7, suggests that the naviform technology either demonstrates the Asiatic mainland to be the point of origin of the Cypriot colonists or possibly illustrates the existence of maritime and cultural interconnections between the island and the mainland during the earliest colonisation phase of the Cypriot Neolithic.
119. McCartney 1999, pp. 7-8.
120. Guilaine *et al.* 1995, p. 16; 2000, p. 79, fig. 3.5-7; Peltenburg *et al.* 2000, p. 848.
121. Peltenburg *et al.* 2000, p. 848.
122. Guilaine *et al.* 1997, p. 827.
123. Guilaine *et al.* 2000, p. 79.
124. Guilaine *et al.* 1998, p. 609.
125. Guilaine *et al.* 1995, p. 14; 1997, p. 827; 1998, p. 606; 2000, pp. 79-80.
126. Peltenburg *et al.* 2001, pp. 48-9.
127. Guilaine *et al.* 2000, p. 79.
128. See for example a Campo 1994.
129. Guilaine *et al.* 2000, p. 79.
130. Guilaine *et al.* 1998, p. 605, fig. 1. See discussion in Guilaine *et al.* 1999, pp. 5-7, 9-10.
131. Peltenburg *et al.* 2000, p. 845.
132. Peltenburg *et al.* 2000, pp. 851-2.
133. Guilaine *et al.* 1997, p. 830; 2000, p. 80.
134. Guilaine *et al*, 2000, p. 80.
135. Halstead 1987, p. 75.
136. Guilaine *et al*, 2000, p. 80.
137. Based on the three radiocarbon determinations from the site, Kritou Marattou-*Ais Yiorkis* should not be placed within the early aceramic Neolithic horizon: 7867 ± 106 BP, 7540 ± 169 BP, and 7658 ± 105 BP, Simmons 1998, p. 237. In this respect, the apparent late exploitation of *Bos* that is documented at the site (economically a characteristic of the early rather than the late aceramic Neolithic) needs to be explained.
138. Guilaine *et al.* 1997, p. 830.
139. Simmons 1998, p. 239.
140. Peltenburg *et al.* 2000, p. 849; 2001, p. 43.
141. Peltenburg *et al.* 2001, p. 46.
142. Peltenburg *et al.* 2000, p. 849-50.
143. Peltenburg *et al.* 2001, p. 55.
144. Broodbank 2000, p. 110.
145. Bar-Yosef & Meadows 1995, p. 41.
146. Peltenburg *et al.* 2001, p. 56.
147. van Andel & Runnels 1995; Peltenburg *et al.* 2001, p. 56.
148. Broodbank & Strasser 1991; Broodbank 2000, discussion in ch. 4.
149. See discussion in Peltenburg *et al.* 2001.

3. Early Farming Communities

1. So called because the inhabitants did not make and use ceramic containers for storing, serving, and consuming food.

2. Peltenburg *et al.* 2000; Peltenburg *et al.* 2001.

3. Stanley-Price 1977b, p. 76. The economic package introduced by the early aceramic Neolithic settlers is virtually identical to that used by the late aceramic farmers, with the exception of cattle, a strong argument for continuity of population.

4. Gjerstad 1934, pp. 1-13.

5. Todd 1989, p. 4.

6. Todd 1989, p. 5.

7. Dikaios 1962, p. 5.

8. Todd 1985a, p. 6, fig. 3; 1985b, p. 7; 1989, p. 4.

9. Helms, 1988, discusses the prestige attached to control of esoteric knowledge derived from other cultures and the attendant material goods, especially within the context of geographical distance and the unknown. The widespread association between political and religious elites and foreign goods and information can be demonstrated by numerous anthropological examples from different cultural contexts, and Helms argues that these are explicitly exploited by these elites in the construction of their mystique, aura and authority.

10. Todd 1989, p. 4.

11. Le Brun 1997, 20, fig. 13.

12. Dikaios 1962, p. 7.

13. Dikaios 1962, p. 5, named these so-called circular domed structures *tholoi.*

14. Le Brun 1997, pp. 19-20, figs 11-12.

15. Dikaios 1962, p. 7.

16. Peltenburg *et al.* 2001, p. 42.

17. Todd 1981, pp. 48-51, fig. 3. Structure 11 is close to the series of concentric structures (17 and 36) crowning the summit of the hill, and with the enigmatic red plastered floors. The physical location of the structure might indicate its special status; moreover the symbolic content of the painting is inferred from its subsequent treatment. During later use of the structure the representation was covered by a layer of undecorated plaster, which in some way symbolically 'killed' it, Todd 1981, p. 50.

18. Dikaios 1962, pp. 7-9. He suggests that the basin was used to store water.

19. Le Brun 1997, pp. 21-4, fig. 18.

20. Todd 1989, p. 6; Le Brun 1997, p. 24.

21. Todd 1985b, p. 7; 1987, p. 102, pl. XXXI:2. Le Brun suggests that a similar small structure at Khirokitia (Structure 99) was also a granary, Le Brun 1984, p. 63, pl. VIII/4-5.

22. Todd 1989, p. 4, fig. 1.2.

23. Radiocarbon determinations for the 'top of site' at *Tenta* are 8480 ± 110 BP, 8020 ± 90 BP and 8010 ± 260 BP, Peltenburg *et al.* 2001, p. 41 fig. 3. See discussion in Chapter 2.

24. Broodbank, 2000, suggests a similar shift in social organisation in the Final Neolithic (Grotta-Pelos culture) of the Cyclades, with an emphasis on the individual rather than the community, from the *floruit* of anthropomorphic figures and single primary inhumations.

25. Dikaios 1962, pp. 13-14; Le Brun 1989, p. 71.

26. Todd 1985a, p. 7; 1989, p. 6.

27. Le Brun 1989, p. 72.

28. Le Brun 1989, p. 74, fig. 11.2. As noted by Le Brun, the southwest orientation for the cranium was specifically avoided for male burials.

29. Le Brun 1989, p. 77, fig. 11.3.

30. Le Brun 1989, p. 77.

31. Niklasson 1991, p. 109.

32. Broodbank, 2000, pp. 170-1, notes that the deceased's immediate relatives in the Grotta-Pelos culture were in effect his/her community.

33. Dikaios 1953, pp. 219, 230; 1962, p. 14; Le Brun 1989, p. 75.

34. Angel 1953, p. 416.

35. Peltenburg *et al.* 2000, fig. 6.

36. Tattoos in the Cycladic EBA context are believed to have been important in the construction of individual identities, Broodbank 2000, p. 248. See Broodbank 2000, ch. 8, for further discussion of the social importance of tattooing, and archaeological evidence to substantiate this practice within the EBA Cyclades.

37. Dikaios 1962, figs 30-1.

38. Le Brun 1996, p. 4.

39. Dikaios 1962, figs 28-9.

40. Dikaios 1962, figs 16, 17 and 23/998, 988, 49, 607, 1232, 31, 1193.

41. Dikaios 1962, figs 23/950, 1171, 785, 1137, 642, 328, 616, 727, 24/698, 979, 1190, 277, 276.

42. Dikaios 1962, figs 5-15.

43. The most famous of the decorated bowls is from Khirokitia, Dikaios 1962, fig. 11/813. This spouted bowl had been broken and mended in antiquity.

44. Dikaios 1962, pp. 14-15.

45. Dikaios 1962, figs 26-7; Le Brun 1997, fig. 33.

46. Peltenburg *et al* 2001, p. 42. Picrolite ornaments are found at *Kastros*, illustrating the extent of these inter-island contacts. At Khirokitia it was 'imported' in raw form, or otherwise the inhabitants went themselves to the Kouris river to procure the stone, as some 20 unworked pieces were found together in one building at the site, Le Brun 1997, 35.

47. Dikaios 1962, figs 26/906, 564, 740, 1282, 1118 and 26/70, 1110, 754, 965, 941, 110, 1009, 17, 1022.

48. Dikaios 1962, flat pebbles: fig. 19/445, 14, 827, 23 and conical stones: fig. 19/32, 1193, 12, 1240, 1005, 1161, 1071, 739, 145, 1152. See also Le Brun 1997, figs 34-5.

49. Most recently discussed in Broodbank 2000, pp. 84, 166-7. Social storage would bind early subsistence communities together in a system of mutual obligation, and presumably would have been critical to survival within the economic landscape of the Cypriot Neolithic.

50. J. Clarke, personal communication.

51. Dikaios 1953, pls XCVIII, CXLIV.1063; 1962, fig. 25/1063. See also a Campo 1994, pp. 46-50. Other representations are too infrequently attested in the archaeological record to allow any meaningful discussion. These include the figures on the wall paintings from *Tenta* (Todd 1981, pp. 48-51, fig. 3) and the andesite bowl from Khirokitia with a relief figure of an individual with upraised arms (Le Brun 1989, fig. 11.4). It is interesting to note, however, that all these figures are depicted with upraised arms, a deliberate and culturally significant gesture, possibly of symbolic import.

52. Schematic figurines include Le Brun 1997, fig. 23. More detailed figures include Dikaios 1962, fig. 25/967; Le Brun 1997, fig. 25; and with flat discoid heads Dikaios 1962, fig. 25/1, 1068, 1404; Le Brun 1997, fig. 26.

53. Dikaios 1953, pls XCV, CXLIII.680; 1962, fig. 24/680.

54. Le Brun 1989, p. 80.

55. Hamilton *et al.* 1996; Tringham and Conkey 1998, pp. 22-9.

56. Le Brun 1989, p. 79.
57. Le Brun 1996, fig. 2.
58. Le Brun 1996, p. 5.
59. Le Brun 1996, p. 3.
60. Peltenburg *et al.* 2000, pp. 849-50; 2001, pp. 43-6.
61. Le Brun 1996, p. 6.
62. Le Brun 1996, p. 4.
63. A. Sherratt, 1981, argues that the earliest use of animals by the hunter/herders of the Neolithic made use only of the primary products of animals, such as their meat or skins, and that these were a non-renewable resource. However, in the fourth millennium BC in Mesopotamia, there is representational and archaeological evidence that animals were being reared for their secondary products, as a renewable resource, for example for milk, wool, and for animal traction. From Mesopotamia, these farming techniques were subsequently transmitted, by cultural diffusion, to the EBA cultures of the Mediterranean during the third millennium BC.
64. Barber 1991, pp. 20-30, especially pp. 23-4, for the early use of wool as a textile and the woolliness of sheep.
65. Guilaine *et al* 2000, p. 80; Peltenburg *et al.* 2001, p. 46.
66. Le Brun 1996, p. 7.
67. See Le Brun 1996, pp. 7-8, for details.
68. Le Brun 1996, p. 9.
69. Le Brun 1996, p. 9 and references.
70. Todd 1985b, p. 10.
71. Stanley-Price 1977a, pp. 34-7.
72. Watkins 1973, p. 50.
73. Knapp *et al.* 1994, p. 381.
74. Dikaios 1962, p. 180. Some of the earliest Neolithic pottery has been identified at Dhali-*Agridhi*. This Dark Burnished pottery is dated by radiocarbon determinations to 4465 ± 310 BP. Lehavy 1989, pp. 203, 210-11.
75. Watkins 1973, p. 50.
76. Peltenburg 1982b, p. 49.
77. Dikaios 1962, p. 168.
78. Dikaios 1962, pp. 180-7.
79. Watkins 1972.
80. Peltenburg 1982b, p. 39; Knapp 1990, pp. 148-9.
81. Peltenburg 1978.
82. Clarke 2001, p. 66.
83. At *Tenta* and Khirokitia the remains are too eroded to comment as to the type of settlement. There is a clear occupational hiatus between the aceramic and ceramic Neolithic remains at *Troulli*, best seen in Pit A where a sterile layer separates Periods I and II, Peltenburg 1979, p. 26.
84. Clarke 2001, p. 71.
85. Peltenburg 1978, p. 70.
86. The area around *Vrysi* was forested with pine, oak and olive, as is indicated by identification of charcoal from the settlement, Peltenburg 1982b, p. 20. Peltenburg's identification of two major regional styles identifies the Troodos mountains as a major impediment to inland communications, 1978, p. 68.
87. Legge 1982, p. 15.
88. Peltenburg 1978, pp. 66-8.
89. Clarke 2001, pp. 72-8, especially pp. 77-8. Emblemic style: a conscious and

clear statement of identity aimed at a specific target group; symbolic style: formal variation in material culture conveying personal information about individual identity; Clarke 2001, p. 72.

90. Important ceramic Neolithic settlements are currently being excavated at Nysia-*Paralimni* and Kantou-*Kouphovounos*: Mantzorani 1994, 1996; Flourentzos 1997.

91. Dikaios 1962, figs 37, 38; Stanley-Price 1979b, p. 46.

92. Peltenburg 1978, p. 62.

93. This follows the architectural phases for the site established by Stanley-Price 1979b.

94. Stanley-Price 1979b, pp. 62, 65-6 fig. 4.

95. Compare Stanley-Price 1979b, fig. 5 (Phase 1 plan) and fig. 6 (Phase 2 plan).

96. Stanley-Price 1979b, p. 66.

97. Peltenburg 1982b, p. 22. To the north of the ridge the hollow occupied an area of 10 x 15 m and was constructed to a depth of 6 m. On the southern side the hollow was excavated over an area of 25 x 10 m and to a depth of 4 m. See also discussion in Peltenburg 1982c, p. 104.

98. Peltenburg 1982b, pp. 23-5; 1982c, pp. 38-9, 56-7.

99. Peltenburg 1982b, pp. 25-7.

100. Peltenburg 1982b, p. 25; 1982c, p. 103.

101. Dikaios 1962, p. 62; Peltenburg 1979, p. 26.

102. Peltenburg 1985, pp. 58-62; 1993, p. 10.

103. Peltenburg 1982c, pp. 25-6; 1989, pp. 110-11, fig. 15.2; 1993, p. 11.

104. Dikaios 1962, figs 32-3.

105. Peltenburg 1979, pl. II.1.

106. Peltenburg 1982c, p. 102.

107. Peltenburg 1982c, p. 103.

108. Dikaios 1962, pp. 73-81; Peltenburg, 1978, pp. 56-8; 1982b, pp. 41-2; 1982c, pp. 96-8.

109. Peltenburg 1978, p. 57.

110. Peltenburg 1982c, p. 96.

111. Peltenburg 1978, pp. 57-8; 1985, pp. 54-5.

112. Peltenburg 1978, p. 62.

113. Stanley-Price 1979b, p. 79.

114. Peltenburg 1978, p. 62; 1982b, p. 98.

115. Peltenburg 1982c, p. 97, fig. 9.

116. Peltenburg 1982c, p. 97; 1985, pp. 55-6.

117. Dikaios 1962, p. 82; Stanley-Price 1979b, p. 76.

118. Peltenburg 1978, p. 61; Stanley Price 1979b, pp. 76-7.

119. Stanley-Price 1979b, p. 78; Peltenburg 1985, p. 57.

120. A bead-worker's toolkit was found in *Vrysi* House 2A, comprising partly finished bone beads and chert blades; Peltenburg 1982b, p. 29.

121. Dikaios 1962, figs 45-51; Peltenburg 1978, pp. 58-9, fig. 3.

122. These include rare examples of chisels hafted in antler from Sotira, *Troulli*, and Kalavasos; Dikaios 1961, pl. 106; Peltenburg 1979, pl. III.1, 2.

123. Peltenburg 1982b, p. 29, pl. 5.

124. See Peltenburg 1982b, pp. 30-3; Peltenburg 1982c, pp. 61-75; Peltenburg & Spanou 1999; Clarke 2001, pp. 68-9.

125. Peltenburg 1978, p. 66; Clarke 2001, p. 68.

126. Clarke 2001.

127. See for example Talalay 1994 for the Aegean and Hamilton 1996 for Çatalhöyük.

128. Dikaios 1962, fig. 48; Peltenburg 1982b, fig. 5.15; a Campo 1994, p. 48.

129. Swiny & Swiny 1983, fig. 1, pl. VI.1-4; Knapp & Meskell, 1997, pp. 193-4, fig. 2, suggest that the figurine might date to the subsequent Chalcolithic period.

130. Peltenburg 1982b, pl. 4; 1985, fig. 4.

131. Peltenburg 1989, pp. 110-12.

132. Peltenburg 1989, p. 113.

133. Dikaios 1962, pp. 82-4, fig. 42. A single chamber tomb was excavated at Philia, immediately outside the habitation area. There is no clear dating evidence for this tomb and it appears unlikely that it should date to the Neolithic period, but might more plausibly be associated with the nearby Chalcolithic settlement at Philia-*Drakos* (B). See discussion in Niklasson 1991, pp. 117-18.

134. Peltenburg suggests that the sherds and flints found in grave fills are accidental inclusions rather than intentional funerary offerings, 1978, p. 62, n. 27. See also Niklasson 1991, p. 116.

135. Definitions of rubbish and its disposal are culturally constructed, an aspect that has been explored in ethnographical studies. Moore's 1986 study of Endo compounds, for example, clearly illustrates complex spatial and gender divisions involved in the disposal of debris.

136. Peltenburg 1978, p. 64.

137. Peltenburg 1982c, pp. 76, 78. However, bones are found on the site on floor deposits, in the fill between floor deposits and in collections of debris that are interpreted as middens.

138. Ducos 1965; Peltenburg 1982c, p. 87; Croft 1991; Clarke 2001, pp. 70-1.

139. Peltenburg 1982c, p. 82.

140. Peltenburg 1978, p. 64.

141. Barber 1991, pp. 11-19.

142. Clarke 2001, pp. 70-1.

143. For example Halstead, 1977, suggests that the fallow deer from LBA Palaepaphos were hunted.

144. Peltenburg 1982c, p. 92.

145. Peltenburg 1982c, p. 86.

146. Peltenburg 1978, p. 74; 1982a, p. 49.

147. Pelteburg 1982b, p. 51.

148. Peltenburg 1993; for example the occupants of the northern sector of *Vrysi*.

4. The Age of Copper

1. Peltenburg 1982b, p. 51; 1993.

2. The radiocarbon determinations from Kissonerga-*Mylouthkia* have a date range of 3630-3560 at one standard deviation. There are three determinations from Kissonerga-*Mosphilia*, which place the Early Chalcolithic between 4320 and 3530 BC at one standard deviation; Peltenburg *et al.* 1998, p. 16, table 2.3. Kalavasos-*Ayious* is dated to between 5040 ±110 to 4700 ± 310 BP; Todd 1991, p. 11.

3. Dikaios 1936, p. 50; Peltenburg 1982b, p. 63, pl. 9; Maier & Karageorghis 1984, fig. 25.

4. Peltenburg 1982b, pp. 62-5.

5. See Peltenburg 1982b, pp. 65-6.

6. Peltenburg 1993, p. 12. Kalavasos-*Kokkinoyia* and Kalavasos-*Pamboules*: Dikaios 1962, pp. 106-40; Peltenburg 1982b, pp. 54-6; Kalavasos-*Ayious*: Todd

1991, pp. 4-11; 1996, pp. 325-9; Kissonerga-*Mylouthkia*: Peltenburg 1982b, pp. 56-63; Kissonerga-*Mosphilia*: Peltenburg 1991a, p. 21; Peltenburg *et al.* 1998, pp. 240-1.

7. Peltenburg *et al.* 1998, p. 240.

8. Todd 1991, pp. 4-11; 1996, pp. 325-9.

9. See discussion of fragmentation theory in Chapman 2000.

10. Peltenburg 1989, p. 113.

11. Bolger, 1989, examines the evidence for stylistic differences and similarities of the pottery from different Chalcolithic sites.

12. Croft 1991.

13. Peltenburg 1991b, p. 108.

14. Held 1993, p. 28.

15. Held 1993, p. 29.

16. See discussion in Broodbank 2000, p. 20.

17. Peltenburg refers to small quantities of obsidian, carnelian, calcite, marble and ivory; 1991b, p. 109.

18. Peltenburg *et al.* 1998, p. 232.

19. The Lemba Archaeological Project has constructed a series of Chalcolithic houses, following the same floor plan and according to probable technical limitations.

20. Peltenburg *et al.* 1998, pp. 235-40, fig. 14.2.

21. Peltenburg *et al.* 1998, pp. 28, 190-2, 242.

22. Peltenburg *et al.* 1998, p. 243.

23. Broodbank suggests that the critical population threshold for organisational change lies somewhere between 150 and 400 individuals, 1992, p. 42.

24. Peltenburg *et al.* 1998, pp. 242-3.

25. Peltenburg *et al.* 1998, pp. 27-8, 242.

26. Peltenburg *et al.* 1998, pp. 244-8.

27. The areas of these buildings vary from around 50 m^2 (B4), to 64 m^2 (B2) and up to 133 m^2 (B206).

28. Peltenburg 1982b, pp. 77-8. Discussed below.

29. Broodbank 1992, p. 42.

30. Broodbank 1992, p. 46.

31. Croft 1991, p. 70.

32. Croft 1991, pp. 72-3.

33. Halstead 1977; Croft 1988.

34. Croft 1991, p. 73.

35. Croft 1991, p. 74. Barber has also argued that in early prehistoric societies textile production was based on plant fibres rather than wool; 1991 pp. 11, 20, 23-5.

36. Peltenburg *et al.* 1998, p. 252.

37. Peltenburg *et al.* 1998, pp. 214-23.

38. Runnels & Hansen 1986; Hamilakis 1996.

39. Peltenburg *et al.* 1998, p. 222.

40. Bolger 1991b, p. 82.

41. Bolger 1991b, pp. 84-90.

42. Bolger 1991b, p. 92.

43. Bolger 1994, p. 13.

44. Peltenburg *et al.* 1998, p. 243.

45. Peltenburg 1991b, p. 117.

46. This is paralleled in fourth- to third-millennium BC Egypt and the Near East; the colour blue was encoded for the first time and was attributed magical or

symbolic properties, as is illustrated by the increasing decorative use of blue (turquoise or lapis lazuli) in high status contexts, Sagona 1996, pp. 151-4. This argument is based upon Berlin and Kaye's categorisation of colour coding within an evolutionary framework, along seven stages. They argue that as societies increase in complexity (and increasingly manipulate their environment) they will undergo paradigm shifts to accommodate new concepts of colour. Early societies will encode only white, black and subsequently red. At Stage III societies will proceed to encode green or blue, which are interchangeable, and yellow. For a critique of the cultural evolutionary perspective of this model, see Chapman 2002.

47. Peltenburg 1982a, p. 55.

48. Peltenburg 1991b, p. 116; Bolger, 1994, argues for household production of picrolite objects and suggests that there is no reason to exclude women from either the production of picrolite artefacts or from the procurement of the raw material.

49. Peltenburg 1982a, p. 55, figs 3a & 3b illustrates the close geographical association of these two resources.

50. Peltenburg 1982a, p. 55.

51. Chalcolithic copper objects: to the six copper artefacts listed in Peltenburg 1982a, pp. 41, 44, we can add six artefacts from *Mosphilia*, Peltenburg *et al.* 1998, p. 189, fig. 97.1-5.

52. Nakou 1995, p. 4.

53. Curation refers to strategies used for caring for, maintaining, reworking and repairing artefacts within the settlement over a long period, rather than a simple strategy of use and discard.

54. Nakou 1995.

55. Peltenburg 1982b, p. 59.

56. Todd 1991, p. 6.

57. 67% of the burials from the Middle Chalcolithic levels at Kissonerga-*Mosphilia* are infants below the age of three and neonates, reflecting partly the differential burial practices at the site, but also the high level of infant mortality. Peltenburg *et al.* 1998, p. 75.

58. Peltenburg 1992, p. 32.

59. Peltenburg *et al.* 1985, pp. 43-4; 1998, pp. 68-70, fig. 4.1: Types 1 and 2.

60. Maier & Karageorghis 1984, p. 24, fig. 1; Christou 1989, p. 85, fig. 12.3.

61. Peltenburg *et al.* 1998, p. 65.

62. Peltenburg 1992, p. 31.

63. Peltenburg *et al.* 1998, p. 73.

64. Peltenburg *et al.* 1998, pp. 245-6.

65. Christou 1989, p. 84.

66. Peltenburg 1982b, pp. 77-8, pl. 13. The prominent and isolated position of this building, set apart from the habitation structures, is typical of early prehistoric sacred buildings, Peltenburg 1989, p. 122.

67. Peltenburg 1992, pp. 32-3.

68. See discussion in South 1985; Goring 1991a, p. 155; a Campo 1994, pp. 51-60.

69. Goring 1991a, p. 155.

70. Todd 1991, p. 8, figs 5-7.

71. Vagnetti 1974; Goring 1991a, p. 155.

72. Morris 1985, p. 122; Peltenburg 1992, p. 32.

73. Goring 1991b, p. 41.

74. Maier & Karageorghis 1984, p. 26, fig. 3.

75. For a review of figurine studies look at Hamilton *et al.* 1996. Bolger, 1996, examines the Cypriot Chalcolithic and Early Bronze Age material from the perspective of a shift from a matriarchical to a patriarchical society.

76. D. Bailey 1994; see for example Broodbank 2000, pp. 170-4, for the Cyclades.

77. See also Knapp & Meskell 1997, p. 194.

78. Bolger suggests that this is the only possible candidate for an image of a Chalcolithic goddess; 1992, p. 155.

79. Maier & Karageorghis 1984, p. 34, fig. 16.

80. Vagnetti 1974, p. 29, pl. VI.2.

81. Hamilton 1994, fig. 1.

82. Morris 1985, p. 135.

83. Hamilton 1994.

84. Peltenburg 1991a, pp. 23-7; Peltenburg *et al.* 1991, in particular the chapters by Bolger and Goring; Bolger 1992; Peltenburg 2001.

85. Bolger 1991c, pp. 14-15.

86. Peltenburg 2001, p. 126. See Boriç 2002, pp. 26-8, on the apotropaic use of colour and geometric designs.

87. Peltenburg 1989, p. 120; Bolger 1991d, pp. 32-3; Bolger 1992, pp. 146-52.

88. Goring 1991b, pp. 52-3; Bolger 1992, pp. 154-5.

89. Goring, 1991b, p. 52; Bolger 1992, p. 155.

90. Bolger 1992, pp. 156-9.

91. Peltenburg 1993, pp. 12-14; 2001, pp. 129-33.

92. Peltenburg *et al.* 1998, p. 249.

93. The Late Chalcolithic occupation of *Mosphilia* is estimated to cover the period between *c.* 2700 and 2400 BC, based on 10 radiocarbon assays. Peltenburg *et al.* 1998, pp. 18-20.

94. Peltenburg *et al.* 1998, p. 249.

95. Peltenburg *et al.* 1998, pp. 37-43.

96. Peltenburg *et al.* 1998, pp. 250-1.

97. Peltenburg *et al.* 1998, p. 251.

98. Peltenburg *et al.* 1998, p. 251.

99. Peltenburg *et al.* 1998, p. 251.

100. Peltenburg *et al.* 1998, p. 252.

101. Peltenburg *et al.* 1998, p. 213.

102. Peltenburg *et al.* 1998, p. 253.

103. Peltenburg *et al.* 1998, pp. 252-3.

104. Peltenburg *et al.* 1998, p. 254.

105. Peltenburg *et al.* 1998, pp. 42-3, figs 3.9-10.

106. Hamilakis 1999, p. 44.

107. Runnels & Hansen 1986, pp. 302-3; Hamilakis 1996; 1999, pp. 41-5.

108. Hamilakis 1999, pp. 43-5.

109. Halstead 1981, 1988, 1994; Halstead & O'Shea 1982.

110. Broodbank 2000, chs 7 and 8; Nakou 1995, p. 22.

111. Peltenburg *et al.* 1998, p. 120.

112. Bolger 1994, p. 13.

113. Bolger 1994, p. 13.

114. Peltenburg *et al.* 1985, pp. 121-2, 328; Keswani 1994, pp. 266-7.

115. Peltenburg *et al.* 1998, pp. 188-9.

116. Peltenburg *et al.* 1998, pp. 70-2, Type 3.

117. Peltenburg *et al.* 1998, p. 72, Type 5.

118. Peltenburg *et al.* 1998, p. 46, figs 31.4, 47.

119. Goldstein 1981, p. 61.
120. Peltenburg *et al.* 1998, p. 188.
121. Peltenburg *et al.* 1998, p. 91.
122. Peltenburg *et al.* 1998, p. 91.
123. Peltenburg *et al.* 1998, p. 257.
124. Peltenburg *et al.* 1998, pp. 256-8.
125. Peltenburg *et al.* 1985, pl. 33/10.
126. Bolger 1991b, p. 32; Peltenburg 1991; Peltenburg *et al.* 1998, pp. 120-1.
127. Peltenburg *et al.* 1985, pl. 35/7; Peltenburg 1996, fig. 3/3. This mimics a well known anthropomorphic vessel from Karatas, Peltenburg 1996, fig. 3/4.
128. Mellink 1991, p. 170.
129. Peltenburg *et al.* 1998, p. 257.
130. Helms 1988.
131. Peltenburg *et al.* 1998, pp. 256-8.

5. Cattle, Anatolian Migrants, and the Prehistoric Bronze Age

1. Frankel 1988; p. 52, n.1; Swiny 1989, p. 16; Knapp 1990, pp. 154-5; Knapp 1994, p. 276. Recent excavations at Marki-*Alonia* and excavations at Sotira-*Kaminoudhia* have illustrated the primary characteristics of EC settlement, but at present it is still preferable to lump the EC and MC periods together in general discussions of the society and the economy, as the overall data base is still too limited.

2. Ten radiocarbon determinations from Sotira-*Kaminoudhia* suggest a date range between *c.* 2300 and 2100 BC, Manning & Swiny 1994, p. 162.

3. This vase allowed Schaeffer to correlate the Cypriot Early Bronze Age with the EB III-IV period in Syro-Palestine, suggesting a date in the later third millennium BC (Manning & Swiny 1994, p. 150). Other synchronisms are provided by rare Minoan imports – a MM IA bridge-spouted jug from Lapithos T. 806A and a MM II cup from Karmi-*Palealona* (Coleman *et al.* 1996, p. 340). Such correlations, however, are very vague and do not allow archaeologists to construct a firm chronological framework, particularly as it is unclear how long such objects would have remained in circulation before being deposited in tomb groups. They only allow a general correspondence between cultural phases in different geographical areas.

4. Herscher 1984, p. 23; 1991, pp. 45-50: north coast types include Red Polished bottles; south coast types include Brown Polished juglets, the Red Polished punctured ware and the Drab Polished Blue Core ware.

5. Manning 1993, p. 39.
6. Peltenburg *et al.* 1998.
7. Swiny 1985b; 1997, pp. 177-85.
8. Dikaios 1962, pp. 191-2; Stewart 1962a, p. 210; Bolger 1983, p. 60.
9. Webb & Frankel 1999, especially p. 4. *Facies* indicates that this group of material is distinct from the EC assemblage on the basis of its appearance or its internal composition. This has no loaded significance for the chronological or spatial relationship between the assemblages.

10. Webb & Frankel 1999, pp. 42-3.

11. Webb & Frankel 1999, p. 5. A single radiocarbon determination from Marki-*Alonia* was between 2440 and 2120 BC (2 standard deviations). One radiocarbon determination was taken from Kissonerga-*Mosphilia* Period 5, albeit from a re-used timber, possibly derived from Period 4 (the Late Chalcolithic occupation

at the site). Based on this reading Peltenburg suggests a date range of *c.* 2500-2400 for Kissonerga Period 5 and the Philia culture; Peltenburg *et al.* 1998, pp. 20-1, figs 2.6, 2.12.

12. Webb & Frankel list nineteen Philia sites; 1999, pp. 8-12.

13. Stewart 1962a, pp. 288-9.

14. Such as identified at Sotira-*Kaminoudhia* and Marki-*Alonia* Phase D: Swiny 1985a, pp. 15-16; Webb & Frankel 1999, fig. 26.

15. Dikaios 1962, pp. 174-6: Red Polished ware, Band Burnished ware, Black Slip and Combed ware. Stewart 1962a, pp. 223-5: Red Polished I (Philia) ware, Red Polished I (Philia coarse ware), Red Polished I (Philia) Stroke Burnished ware, White Polished (Philia), White Painted I (Philia). See also discussion of Philia pottery in Bolger 1991a.

16. Webb & Frankel 1999, pp. 14-31.

17. Webb & Frankel 1999, pp. 14-23.

18. Bolger 1991a, p. 34. This is homogeneous, fine textured and medium fired. The skill involved in the procurement and treatment of the clay resources, and its homogeneity, might indicate centralised production moving away from the household.

19. Bolger 1983, p. 72.

20. Mellink 1991, pp. 172-3.

21. Webb & Frankel 1999, pp. 28-9.

22. Webb & Frankel 1999, pp. 24-5, fig. 16.

23. Peltenburg 1982b, p. 96; Mellink 1991, pp. 170-1. Webb & Frankel 1999, pp. 25-8.

24. Dikaios 1962, fig. 84/10-12; Webb & Frankel 1999, p. 21.

25. Dikaios 1962, fig. 84/1-9; Stewart 1962a, fig. 99/1-11, 14; Webb & Frankel 1999, pp. 21-2.

26. Dikaios 1962, fig. 84/18-24 (pendants); Webb & Frankel 1999, fig. 25 (spindle whorls).

27. Swiny 1985a, p. 18; 1989, p. 23; Croft 1996, pp. 217-22.

28. Knapp 1990, pp.155-6. This is based on A. Sherratt's secondary products model; 1981.

29. Peltenburg 1996, p. 23.

30. Helms 1988.

31. Manning 1993, p. 48.

32. Lemba Period 3, Building 2; Kissonerga Period 4, Building 3 (Pithos House). Peltenburg 1982b, p. 79; Peltenburg *et al.* 1998, pp. 41-2.

33. Knapp 1990, p. 157.

34. Knapp 1990, p. 157.

35. Peltenburg *et al.* 1985, pl. 35/7; Peltenburg 1996, fig. 3/3.

36. Peltenburg 1996, p. 24.

37. Dikaios 1962, p. 190; Swiny 1985a, pp. 21-2; Mellink 1991, pp. 172-3; Frankel *et al.* 1996; Webb & Frankel 1999.

38. Dikaios 1962, pp. 202-3; see also Peltenburg 1982b, pp. 98-101.

39. Mellink 1991, p. 173.

40. Manning 1993; Peltenburg 1996.

41. Frankel *et al.* 1996 p. 41.

42. Frankel *et al.* 1996, p. 41.

43. Frankel *et al.* 1996, pp. 42-5; Frankel & Webb 2000, p. 764.

44. This custom is a common feature of Anatolian burial practices from the Chalcolithic period but there are only four examples of the pot or urn burials

attested in Philia contexts on Cyprus, one at Philia-*Laksia tou Kasinou*, one at Marki-*Alonia* and two at Kissonerga-*Mosphilia*. Despite rarity of this burial Frankel *et al.*, 1996, p. 46, suggest that it 'is sufficient to indicate the importation of this custom [from Anatolia]'; see Frankel & Webb 2000, p. 764.

45. Frankel *et al.* 1996, p. 47.
46. Frankel *et al.* 1996, pp. 43-4.
47. Frankel *et al.* 1996, pp. 48-9; Webb & Frankel 1999, p. 40.
48. Frankel *et al.* 1996, pp. 49-50.
49. Swiny 1989, p. 16, fig. 2.1.
50. Swiny 1981, p. 79; 1989, p. 16.
51. Such as the concentration of EC-MC settlement and cemetery in the Alykos valley, comprising the Marki cluster, Frankel & Webb 1996, p. 9.
52. Todd attributes the high density of MC settlement along the Vasilikos valley, and in particular the position of Kalavasos-*Laroumena* to the movement of copper from the Kalavasos copper mines down to the coast, 1988, p. 140; 1993, p. 83.
53. Swiny 1981, p. 78.
54. As for example suggested for the chain of MC settlement in the Vasilikos Valley, Todd 1988; 1993, p. 81.
55. Swiny 1981, pp. 80-1, 86; 1989, p. 17.
56. Peltenburg 1996, p. 32.
57. Peltenburg 1996, p. 30, and references.
58. Merrillees 1982, p. 375; Peltenburg 1996, pp. 31-5.
59. Frankel 1974b, p. 11.
60. Frankel & Webb 1996, pp. 53-4.
61. Frankel & Webb 2000, p. 763.
62. Discussed most fully by Swiny 1989, pp. 20-1, figs 2.2-4.
63. Frankel & Webb 1996, pp. 53-4.
64. Frankel & Webb 1996, pp. 54-5.
65. Apparently introduced to Cyprus as part of the Philia package from Anatolia, based on their occurrence with Philia pottery at Marki. See Frankel & Webb 1996, p. 183.
66. Swiny 1989, p. 20 (Sotira-*Kaminoudhia*).
67. Swiny 1989, p. 20.
68. Frankel & Webb 1996, p. 49. Unit L-1 was identified as a textile production area on the basis of two spindle whorls, four loom weights and two needles. XII-1 and XXX-1 are interpreted as cooking areas. Two hobs, three cooking pots and a hearth were found in XII-1 and a hob associated with cooking pot fragments in XXX-1. They also note the association of small work benches and bins in rooms, which they suggest were specifically designed as areas for food preparation, p. 55.
69. Frankel & Webb 2000, p.764.
70. Frankel & Webb 1996, p. 48.
71. Webb (1998) has examined the curation and discard patterns of the ground stone tools used at Marki.
72. Frankel & Webb 2000, p. 764.
73. Swiny 1989, p. 23.
74. Frankel & Webb 1996, p. 223, table 9.14.
75. Swiny 1989, p. 23.
76. Knapp 1990, p. 157.
77. Croft 1996, pp. 217-23. The percentages given are derived from table 9.1,

but have been adjusted for comparison with Swiny 1989, only to give percentages for the three main domesticates and the fallow deer.

78. Croft 1996, p. 221.

79. Croft 1996, pp. 218. The new breed resembles the wild *Capra aegagrus* of western Asia.

80. Coleman *et al.* 1996, pp. 476-9.

81. Croft 1996, p. 222; Coleman *et al.* 1996, p. 479. Equid bones occur occasionally in Neolithic and Chalcolithic contexts.

82. Sherratt 1981, fig. 10.11; Morris 1985, pl. 327.

83. Frankel & Webb 1996, p. 110.

84. Frankel & Webb 1996, pp. 130-3. There is some evidence for the use of trays at Chalcolithic sites on the Akrotiri peninsula, Swiny, personal communication.

85. Frankel & Webb 1996, pp. 117-48.

86. Barlow 1991, pp. 52-5.

87. Frankel & Webb 1996, pp. 202-5, figs 8.7, 8.9, pls 34a-d.

88. Morris 1985, pls 154-97, 169-72, 290-2, 298.

89. Morris 1985, p. 78.

90. See discussion in Frankel 1988, pp. 29-33; see also Coleman *et al.* 1996, pp. 238-9.

91. Frankel & Webb 1996, p. 111.

92. Coleman *et al.* 1996, p. 266.

93. Coleman *et al.* 1996, p. 254.

94. Coleman *et al.* 1996, p. 255.

95. Frankel 1974a, pp. 204-5; 1974b, pp. 48, 51.

96. See discussion in Maguire 1995.

97. Frankel *et al.* 1996, p. 43.

98. Webb & Frankel 1999, pp. 31-3.

99. Coleman *et al.* 1996, p. 344.

100. Gale *et al.* 1996, p. 361; Frankel & Webb 1996, pp. 213-15, fig. 8.10, pl. 35c-d: needles, pins and ornamental spirals.

101. Frankel & Webb 1996, pp. 102-9. Cores, flakes and waste (debitage) have been identified, made using the local chert supplies. Tools include sickle blades (pp. 106-7, fig. 6.16, 6.17, pl. 27a-b), scrapers (pp. 107-8, fig. 6.18, pl. 27c) and borers (p. 109, fig. 6.18, pl. 27c).

102. Frankel & Webb 1996, p. 213.

103. Gale *et al.* 1996, pp. 360-2, table 2.1.

104. Todd 1993, p. 93.

105. Craddock 1986, pp. 153-5.

106. Gale *et al.* 1996, p. 400.

107. Gale *et al.* 1996, pp. 400-1.

108. Gale *et al.* 1996, p. 362, table 2.1.

109. Belgiorno 2000, p. 3.

110. Belgiorno 2000, pp. 8-10, fig. 1.

111. Giardino 2000, p. 23.

112. At Sotira-*Kaminoudhia*, for example, the cemetery lies 100 m to the north east of the settlement; Manning & Swiny 1994, p. 155. At Marki five separate cemeteries have been identified in the hills circling the site, at about 800 m distance; Frankel & Webb 1996, p. 11. Likewise the settlement at Alambra-*Mouttes* is surrounded by clusters of tombs; Coleman *et al.* 1996, p. 341.

113. Peltenburg *et al.* 1998, pp. 70-2, 257, Type 3.

114. Stewart 1962a, pp. 215-16.

115. Keswani 1989a, pp. 491-9.
116. Manning 1993, p. 45.
117. Frankel 1988, p. 41.
118. See discussion in Dugay 1996. See also Frankel 1988, pp. 41-2.
119. Frankel & Webb 1996, p. 48, for example querns, grinders, cooking pots, hobs.
120. Washbourne, 1997, suggests that the ceramic combs in fact are representations of a counterweight worn with heavy multiple necklaces.
121. Manning 1993, p. 45.
122. Crewe 1998, p. 8, fig. 2.2.
123. Crewe 1998, pp. 36-7.
124. Manning 1993, p. 45.
125. Keswani 1994, pp. 270-1. Herscher 1997, pp. 31-4.
126. Keswani 1989a, p. 509; Peltenburg 1996, p. 20.
127. Keswani 1989a, pp. 508-10; Swiny 1989, p. 27; Knapp 1990, p. 158.
128. Swiny 1989, p. 27.
129. Keswani 1989a, pp. 509-10.
130. Keswani 1989a, pp. 507, 509; Knapp 1994, p. 281: pottery imports include the EB III-IV Syro-Palestinian jug from Vounous, a Middle Minoan IA bridge-spouted jug from Lapithos and a Middle Minoan II cup from Karmi-*Palealona*; Stewart 1962b, fig. 8.
131. Peltenburg 1996, pp. 20-1.
132. Manning 1993, p. 45.
133. Peltenburg 1982b, p. 95.
134. See Helms' 1988 discussion of the political use of the exotic (tangible goods and esoteric knowledge).
135. Maguire 1995, pp. 55, 63, fig. 12.
136. Maguire 1992, pp. 117-18.
137. Knapp 1996b.
138. Knapp 1996b.
139. Herscher 1997, p. 25, n. 1.
140. Herscher 1997, pp. 25-7.
141. Morris lists four from Marki, one from Kalavasos, and one without provenance, 1985, p. 264.
142. Morris 1985, pp. 265-9, pls 290, 291.
143. Morris 1985, p. 264.
144. Morris 1985, pp. 272-4.
145. Herscher 1997, pp. 29-30.
146. Such as a couple on the shoulder of a jug from Lapithos Tomb 823, Morris 1985, p. 288.
147. Bolger 1996, p. 372.
148. Found in Tomb 22, Vounous-*Bellapais*. Dikaios 1940, 118-25, 173, pls VII, VIII.
149. Frankel & Tamvaki 1973; See discussion in Åström 1988.
150. Morris 1985, pp. 281-3. This is, however, dependent on Morris's own interpretation of the scenes and constitutes a circular argument.
151. Manning 1993, p. 45-6; Peltenburg 1994, pp. 159-62; Bolger 1996, pp. 371-2.
152. Karageorghis 1970; Frankel & Tamvaki 1973; Åström 1988.
153. Peltenburg 1989, p. 123.

154. Morris 1985, pp. 135-62; a Campo 1994, pp. 164-9; Bolger 1996, p. 369; Knapp & Meskell 1997, pp. 183-204.
155. Bolger 1996, p. 370.
156. Morris 1985, p. 145; a Campo 1994, pp. 164-5.
157. a Campo 1994, p. 166.
158. Knapp & Meskell 1997, p. 196.
159. Washbourne 2000, pp. 97-9.
160. Bolger 1996, p. 369.
161. Webb 1992b, p. 90; a Campo 1994, p. 167.
162. Knapp & Meskell 1997, pp. 198-9.
163. a Campo 1994, pp. 168-9.

6. Cyprus in the Late Bronze Age

1. Catling 1973b, pp. 165-6.
2. Merrillees 1971, pp. 56-61.
3. Merrillees 1971, p. 62; see also discussion of eastern ceramic tradition in Herscher 1984, p. 25.
4. al-Radi 1983. More recently, however, Webb has argued against the identification of Phlamoudhi-*Vounari* as a religious structure, suggesting instead a possible defensive function; Webb 1999, pp. 135-40.
5. Vermeule & Wolsky 1990.
6. Dikaios 1969-71.
7. Merrillees 1971, p. 75.
8. Catling 1962, p. 141.
9. Catling 1973b, p. 168.
10. Frankel 1974b, p. 11.
11. Hult 1992, pp. 34, 75, in the northern casemates.
12. Peltenburg 1996, p. 35.
13. Merrillees 1982, p. 375; Keswani 1996, p. 219.
14. Peltenburg 1996, pp. 30-4.
15. Peltenburg 1996, pp. 29-30.
16. Keswani 1996, p. 219.
17. Swiny 1986, p. 87; Keswani 1989a, p. 136.
18. Merrillees 1971, p. 75.
19. E. Masson 1976, pp. 153-7, fig. 6; Keswani 1989a, p. 513; Peltenburg 1996, p. 35.
20. Overbeck & Swiny 1972, pp. 7-24. Socketed axeheads are also recorded at Ayia Paraskevi, Alambra, Pera and Politiko.
21. Merrillees 1971, p. 76; Peltenburg 1996, p. 30.
22. Sjöqvist 1940, p. 199; Merrillees 1971, p. 77.
23. Maguire 1995.
24. E. Masson 1976, pp. 143-50.
25. Epstein 1966.
26. See discussion in Oren 1969.
27. Bergoffen 2001.
28. Courtois 1986; Keswani 1989a, p. 513.
29. Merrillees 1989, figs 19.1-19.3.
30. Catling 1962, p. 143.
31. Catling 1962, pp. 142-3.
32. Catling 1962, pp. 142-3.

33. Knapp 1997a, pp. 56-61; 1997b, pp. 156-8.

34. Knapp 1997a, p. 56.

35. Knapp 1997a, p. 58. The facility at Ayios Iakovos-*Dhima* (Gjerstad *et al.* 1934, pp. 356-7) does not really fit the profile of a rural sanctuary. Webb, 1992b, pp. 94-6, suggests that the structure might be more plausibly identified as a cenotaph or specialised funerary facility rather than a sanctuary, as there is no convincing evidence for continued ritual activity at the site over an extended period.

36. Knapp 1997a, pp. 59-61.

37. Apliki-*Karamallos*: du Plat Taylor 1952; Politiko-*Phorades*: Knapp *et al.* 1999.

38. Webb & Frankel 1994.

39. Identified by Gjerstad as a sanctuary and dated to LC III, but a non-ritual function and LC IIC date appear more likely. Gjerstad *et al.* 1935, pp. 667-8, 820-1.

40. Cyprus was heavily forested in antiquity, as is recorded by Strabo (14.6.5), quoting Eratosthenes. See also Raptou 1996, pp. 254-6.

41. Catling 1962, pp. 144-5.

42. Cadogan 1972, 1993; Steel 1998.

43. Halstead 1977, pp. 270-3.

44. Helbaek 1962.

45. Helbaek 1962, p. 186.

46. South *et al.* 1989, pp. 92-3.

47. South *et al.* 1989, p. 89.

48. Keswani 1992, pp. 141-6.

49. South 1988, p. 227.

50. South 1991, pp. 131-2.

51. Keswani 1993, pp. 76-80.

52. Halstead 1981, 1988; Halstead & O'Shea 1982.

53. Webb & Frankel 1994.

54. Keswani 1993, pp. 77-8.

55. Keswani 1993, p. 77.

56. Gjerstad *et al.* 1935, pp. 820-1. This structure is usually interpreted as a cult building (most recently Webb 1999, pp. 53-8), largely based on the later, Iron Age, religious function of the site. However, the only unusual attribute of the site is the concentration of coloured pebbles associated with a Base Ring bull figure and a Plain White ware fruitstand/offering stand. See discussion in Webb 1999, p. 188.

57. Keswani 1993, pp. 76-7.

58. Keswani 1992, p. 141.

59. South *et al.* 1989, p. 92.

60. Keswani 1992, pp. 141-5.

61. South 1992, pp. 137-9.

62. Maroni: Cadogan 1984; 1989. Finds included an olive press, Cadogan 1984, p. 8. Alassa Building II is one of the largest LC buildings to be excavated, and was constructed using elaborate drafted stone masonry. A long rectangular storeroom holding two rows of pithoi ran along the north side of the structure. Finds included a large number of pithos sherds, some with impressed chariot scenes, Hadjisavvas 2001, pp. 212-13.

63. Webb 1992a, pp. 114-16; Smith 1994.

64. Group III pithoi, South *et al.* 1989, pp. 16-17.

65. Most recently discussed by Hadjisavvas 2001, pp. 213-18.
66. Webb & Frankel 1994, pp. 18-19.
67. Frankel & Webb 1996, p. 111.
68. Todd & Pilides 2001. Of particular interest is the small percentage of wasters (1%) from Sanidha, implying that the potters had considerable control over production and firing.
69. Vermeule & Wolsky 1990, p. 20.
70. Vermeule & Wolsky 1990, pp. 55, 76-8, 142.
71. Vermeule & Wolsky 1990, p. 101.
72. Todd & Hadjicosti 1991; Todd *et al.* 1992; Todd & Pilides 1993, 2001.
73. Steel 1998, p. 292; Steel in press: the large White Slip spouted bowls, large Base Ring jugs (both round-mouthed and with elaborate pinched spouts) and tankards and kraters in both wares all disappear from the ceramic repertoire.
74. Steel, in press.
75. E. Sherratt 1991.
76. E. Sherratt 1991, p. 193.
77. See discussion in Peregrine 1991.
78. Helms 1988.
79. Courtois *et al.* 1986, pp. 100-6. Most notable is a silver cup with inlaid decoration of bucrania in silver and niello, Schaeffer 1952, pl. CXVI. This resembles a cup found in a tomb at Dendra, on the Greek mainland, and is possibly of Aegean workmanship.
80. Courtois *et al.* 1986, pp. 107-22.
81. Pierides 1973; Caubet 1985b, pp. 82-7; Courtois *et al.* 1986, pp. 127-36.
82. See discussion in Peltenburg 1972; Caubet 1985a, pp. 61-73; Courtois *et al.* 1986, pp. 138-56; Caubet & Kaczmarczyk 1989.
83. Catling 1964; Matthäus 1985, 1988.
84. For discussion of the hybrid style of the Ingot God, for example, see Hulin 1989, and references.
85. Catling 1964, pp. 191-223; Matthäus 1985, 1988; Courtois *et al.* 1986, pp. 84-100; Papasavvas 2001.
86. Gjerstad *et al.* 1934, pp. 356-61, pls LXVI-LXVII; Webb 1999, pp. 29-35.
87. Eriksson 1993, pp. 257-9.
88. Webb 1999, pp. 33, 244, fig. 82.5-7.
89. Catling 1964, p. 249.
90. Many scholars have emphasised the importance of the development of the Cypriot copper industry. See for example Stech 1982; Muhly 1982, p. 251; 1989.
91. Knapp 1986b; Keswani 1996; Peltenburg 1996.
92. Muhly 1982, p. 257. There is some evidence for the development of a 'tin route' in the West Mediterranean during the later second millennium, Lo Schiavo 1995, p. 47.
93. Stos-Gale *et al.* 1997, p. 84.
94. Gale 1991, pp. 200-1, fig. 2.
95. Although typologically the ingot from Apollonia, Bulgaria, appears to belong to the horizon represented by the Cretan ingots recovered at Ayia Triadha, Gale notes that it is marked with a sign similar to that found on an ingot from Enkomi; Gale 1991, p. 200.
96. Bass 1986; Puluk 1988; 1997.
97. For example the Sardinian copper oxhide ingots, Gale 1991, pp. 216-19; Lo Schiavo 1995, pp. 47-9; the Mycenaean copper oxhide ingots, Gale 1991, p. 227; and the ingots from the Ulu Burun and Cape Gelidonya shipwrecks, Gale 1991, pp.

228-9. See also discussion in Stos-Gale *et al.* 1997, pp. 109-17. There has been a significant debate on the efficacy of lead isotope analysis for sourcing copper/copper alloy objects, for example Budd *et al.* 1995a and 1995b. For full references see Stos-Gale *et al.* 1997.

98. Stech 1982, p. 111.

99. Gale 1991, pp. 225-6.

100. The nuragic bronzes are made from Sardinian ores, Gale 1991, p. 217; the Mycenaean bronze artefacts are made from copper from the Lavrion mines in Attica, Gale 1991, p. 231.

101. E. Masson 1976, pp. 153-7, fig. 6; Keswani 1989a, p. 513.

102. Knapp 1986b, p. 35.

103. See for example the discussion of metallurgical production at Alambra in Gale *et al.* 1996, and the early production of copper at Enkomi in LC I, Muhly 1989, p. 299.

104. Muhly 1989, p. 298. See also the review of Cypriot copper production in Stech 1982, pp. 105-9. The importance of Enkomi as a copper-producing centre is illustrated in particular by the high incidence of tuyères (blow-pipes, ensuring a constant air supply to the furnace) at the site. Muhly has identified over 400 fragments, the single largest deposit of tuyères from a Bronze Age Mediterranean centre, Muhly 1989, p. 299.

105. Muhly 1989, p. 299. See also Courtois 1982, pp. 155-8, fig. 1, the 'zone industrielle du rempart nord'. Finds from the LC I levels of the fortress include crucibles, tuyères, hearths and areas of charcoal. Notably this metallurgical debris is associated with one of the earliest examples of a clay tablet written in the Cypro-Minoan script, found in room 103, Dikaios 1969-71, pp. 22-3.

106. See Peltenburg 1996, pp. 29-30.

107. Muhly (1989, pp. 301-2) lists the following sites as having evidence for copper production during the thirteenth and twelfth centuries: urban centres, Enkomi, Kition, Hala Sultan Tekke, Maroni-*Vournes*, Kalavasos-*Ayios Dhimitrios*, Kourion-*Bamboula*, Alassa-*Pano Mandilaris*, and Myrtou-*Pigadhes*; inland settlements, Athienou, Apliki-*Karamallos*, to which can be added Politiko-*Phorades*, Knapp *et al.* 1999. Also the establishments at Maa-*Palaeokastro* and Pyla-*Kokki-nokremos*.

108. Stech 1982, pp. 111-13; see also Muhly 1989, pp. 302-3.

109. Stech 1982, pp. 112-13.

110. Knapp 1986b.

111. Gale 1991; Stos-Gale *et al.* 1997; Mangou & Ioannou 2000.

112. Faience: Peltenburg 1991c; textiles: Barber 1991.

113. One of the clearest discussions is A. Sherratt and E.S. Serratt 1991. See also Knapp 1991. For analyses of the mechanics of elite gift exchange in the East Mediterranean see Zaccagnini 1987.

114. Bass 1986; Puluk 1988, 1997; Vichos & Lolos 1997.

115. See discussion in Gale 1991, Stos-Gale *et al.* 1997.

116. Most recently, see Steel 1998.

117. Vagnetti & Lo Schiavo 1989; Lo Schiavo *et al.* 1985; Lo Schiavo 1995.

118. Merrillees 1968; Gittlen 1981; Bergoffen 1991.

119. For example Egyptian amphorae have been identified in LC IIC-IIIA levels at sites such as Pyla-*Kokkinokremos* and Maa-*Palaeokastro*, Eriksson 1995.

120. Eriksson 1993.

121. See discussion of the Late Chalcolithic period in Chapter 4 and the Philia material in Chapter 5.

122. Egyptian: a faience sceptre-head with the cartouche of Horemheb, the last ruler of the Eighteenth Dynasty from Hala Sultan Tekke, Åström 1979; Hittite: a silver ring from Hala Sultan Tekke, gold ring from Tamassos, possibly also the silver figure from Kalavasos-*Ayios Dhimitrios*, Todd 2001, pp. 205-6. Also a lion-hunt scarab dating to the reign of Amenophis III (Eighteenth Dynasty) was found in an EIA tomb at Palaepaphos-*Skales*, Clerc 1983, pp. 389-91, fig. 7. This is a typical item of gift exchange and might plausibly have reached the island during the fourteenth century. The process by which it only entered the archaeological record during the eleventh century is unclear.

123. Maguire 1995, pp. 55, 63, fig. 12.

124. Merrillees 1971, p. 73; E. Masson, 1976, p. 148.

125. Gittlen 1981; Merrillees 1968. Maguire, 1995, discusses the earlier, MC trade of WP juglets in the East Mediterranean; see also Gittlen 1981, pp. 49-50, and discussion in Chapter 5.

126. Merrillees 1962, pp. 287-92; 1968, pp. 145-57; 1969b, pp. 167-71; Gittlen 1981, p. 55; Knapp 1991, pp. 23-5.

127. Bisset *et al.* 1996, pp. 203-4; Koschel 1996, pp. 159-66.

128. Stewart 1962b, p. 202, fig. 8, pl. VII. The few Cypriot objects found in LM IA-B contexts on Crete were possibly hospitality gifts (drinking vessels) exchanged in occasional meetings between trading partners, Manning 1999, p. 128. Manning lists the pottery found in LM IA-B contexts, 1999, pp. 117-18, fig. 34.

129. Pecorella 1973, p. 20, pl. V; Vermeule 1973, pp. 30, 31, pls VI.1, 3, VII; Portugali & Knapp 1985, pp. 71-2, cat. nos 4-29.

130. Cadogan 1973, 1993; Steel 1998.

131. Shelmerdine 1985, pp. 7, 41, 63. Leonard has commented that the two types of speciality oil indicated in the Mycenaean palace archives corresponds closely to the two types of Mycenaean closed vessel imported in large quantities to Cyprus and the Levant: the *po-ro-ko-wa* (pouring oil) in the narrow-mouthed flasks and stirrup jars, and the *we-a-re-pe* (more viscous unguent) in the wide-mouthed piriform jars and alabastra. Leonard 1981, pp. 94-6.

132. Steel 1998, pp. 291-4.

133. Steel 1998.

134. Lo Schiavo *et al.* 1985, pp. 4-9; Vagnetti & Lo Schiavo 1989, pp. 219-20.

135. South 2000.

136. Hadjisavvas 1989, pp. 35, 39, fig. 3.3; 1991, fig. 17.3.

137. Salles 1995, p. 173; fig. 18.1; Marchegay 2000, pp. 209-10.

138. This is particularly well illustrated by the elite tombs from the North-East area of Kalavasos, discussed in South 2000.

139. Keswani 1989b, pp. 52-6.

140. Courtois *et al.* 1986, pp. 24-6; Keswani 1989b, pp. 54-5.

141. Salles 1995, figs 18.2-18.4.

142. Of particular note is the common artistic school of the three areas, especially evident in the ivory workshops. Close cultural ties are similarly expressed by the adoption of the Mycenaean chariot krater as the central element of the Ugaritic and LC drinking sets.

143. Gjerstad *et al.* 1934, pp. 570-3; Johnstone 1971; Courtois *et al.* 1986, pp. 49-50; Keswani 1989b, pp. 53-4.

144. Pelon 1973, pp. 249-53.

145. Keswani 1989b, p. 53; Webb 1992b, p. 88.

146. Dikaios 1969-71, pp. 109, 115-16, 518, pls 65/10, 254; Keswani 1989b, p. 52.

147. Goring 1989, p. 101.

148. Goring 1989, p. 100.

149. See for example the discussion by Branigan (1987) on manipulation of the physical funerary remains in the tombs of the Mesara.

150. A layer of ash in Hala Sultan Tekke T. 20 and Enkomi Swedish T. 12 might illustrate fumigation; Webb 1992b, p. 91.

151. Sheep, goat, fish and bird bones are reported from tombs at Kalavasos-*Ayios Dhimitrios*; South 2000, p. 361. Pyres with sheep, goat and deer bone, charcoal, ash and fine ware pottery were found at Morphou-*Toumba tou Skourou*, above Ts. I and II; Vermeule & Wolsky 1990, pp. 158, 169 and 245.

152. Steel 1998, pp. 291-2.

153. Keswani 1989b, pp. 58-9; South 2000, p. 355.

154. Keswani 1989b, p. 65; Steel 1998, p. 291, n. 43.

155. Steel 1998, pp. 294-6.

156. Hamilakis 1999, 45-7.

157. Webb 1992b, p. 89.

158. Vaughan for example has suggested that Base Ring cups, a common shape in funerary and sanctuary contexts, were typically associated with libation ceremonies; Vaughan 1991, p. 124.

159. Webb 1992a, p. 117.

160. Knapp 1996a, p. 75; Webb 1999, pp, 10-15.

161. Webb notes that the curation and deposition of ritual paraphernalia will be distinct from the continual process of use, breakage and replacement that is charted in domestic contexts (1999, p. 12). In particular, she notes that the deliberate deposition of valuable artefacts, such as the bronze statuettes in sanctuaries at Enkomi is in stark contrast to the removal of similar valuables from settlement areas as part of the process of abandonment.

162. Knapp 1996a, pp. 75-6.

163. Webb 1999, pp. 250-2.

164. Webb 1999, pp. 47, 53. Webb suggests that these remains represent the accumulation of an annual sacrifice of deer over a number of years.

165. Webb 1999, p. 15.

166. du Plat Taylor *et al.* 1957, pp. 8-10, 114, fig. 6.

167. Dothan & Ben-Tor *et al.* 1983.

168. Gjerstad *et al.* 1934, pp. 356-61, plan XIII. See discussion in Webb 1992b, pp. 94-6; 1999, pp. 29-35.

169. This is most clearly illustrated by Webb's chart illustrating the chronology of the LC cult sites; 1999, table 1, pp. 18-19. Knapp suggests that this reflects increasing economic and political power invested in the LC elite during this period, and that LC religion was specifically used within an ideology of power; Knapp 1996a, p. 45.

170. Periods V-VII, du Plat Taylor *et al.* 1957, figs 4, 12.

171. See discussion in Hult 1983.

172. Gray, in du Plat Taylor 1957, pp. 104-7.

173. Merrillees 1973; Knapp 1996a, p. 89.

174. Periods III-IV, du Plat Taylor *et al.* 1957, pp. 8-10, 114, fig. 6.

175. Keswani 1993, p. 74. An overview of the LC religious sites that have been identified in the archaeological record, detailing their architecture and finds, is provided by Webb (1999, pp. 21-134).

176. Webb 1999, pp. 157-8.

177. Webb 1999, pp. 166-88.

178. Webb 1999, p. 198.

179. Vaughan 1991, p. 124; Steel 1998, p. 292.

180. This is in stark contrast to the situation in Ugarit, where imported Mycenaean rhyta are integrated within local cult practices and are also imitated locally; see Yon 1987.

181. Webb 1999, pp. 193-6.

182. Webb 1999, pp. 249-50.

183. Webb 1999, pp. 229-36.

184. Webb 1999, p. 219, table III.

185. Catling 1971; Knapp 1986a, 1988b.

186. For example Catling 1971; Stech 1982; Knapp 1986a, pp. 43-56.

187. Dothan & Ben-Tor *et al.* 1983, pp. 132-8.

188. See discussion in Webb 1999, pp. 113-16.

189. Muhly 1989, p. 302.

190. Karageorghis & Demas 1985, pp. 81-4, 115-20, 135-8, plans XXVIII-XXX; Stech *et al.* 1985; Webb 1999, p. 74, fig. 27.

191. Smith, personal communication; see also Karageorghis & Demas 1985, p. 37.

192. Webb 1999, p. 248.

193. Reese 1985. Murex was commonly used in various cultural contexts in the East Mediterranean for the manufacture of a purple dye.

194. Courtois 1971, pls XII-XIVA. The other figure, of a naked female, is the Bomford figurine in the Ashmolean Museum; Catling 1971, pp. 15-32, figs 3-4.

195. Catling 1971, p. 17; see discussion in Knapp 1986a, pp. 1-2, 10-12; 1988b, p. 144; Webb 1999, p. 225.

196. The most important review of these arguments is in Knapp 1986a.

197. Catling 1971, p. 29; O. Masson 1971, p. 449; Knapp 1986a, pp. 25-9, table 1, pls 4-5.

198. Catling 1971, p. 30; 1984; Knapp 1986a, pp. 30-4, pls 6-7.

199. Knapp 1986a, p. 37, table 2, fig. 2, pl. 10.

200. Dikaios 1969-71, pp. 918-25; Knapp 1986a, pp. 35-7, pls 8, 9, 11; Knapp 1988b, p. 145.

201. Keswani 1989b, 1993 and Knapp 1986b.

202. Smith 1994, pp. 33-6.

203. Smith 1994.

204. Keswani 1993, p. 74; 1996, p. 234; Cherry 1986, pp. 27-9.

205. Smith 1994, pp. 33-6.

206. South 1989, p. 321; 1992, pp. 133-5; Keswani 1993, pp. 76-7.

207. Keswani 1993, pp. 77-8. Apliki: du Plat Taylor 1952; Atheniou: Dothan & Ben-Tor *et al.* 1983.

208. Peltenburg 1996, p. 35.

209. Keswani 1993, p. 75.

210. Webb 1992a, p. 114.

211. See discussion in Smith 1994, pp. 33-6.

212. Peltenburg 1996, pp. 27-37.

213. Dikaios 1969-71, pp. 16-24. Finds include slag, tuyères and numerous crucible fragments.

214. Dikaios 1969-71, pp. 22-3. A single Cypro-Minoan tablet.

215. Peltenburg 1996, pp. 29-30.

216. Keswani 1996.

217. Keswani 1996, p.219. Rather than a single hierarchical organisation, a heterarchy is organised into several competing social groups, each with differential

control over a variety of economic, political and religious institutions. The ascendancy of particular groups will vary over time. Instead of centralised control expressed through discrete architectural zones, heterarchies are characterised by dispersed economic, administrative, religious and elite activity areas within one urban centre.

218. Keswani 1996, pp. 221-6.

219. Vermeule & Wolsky 1990, pp. 14-16; Keswani 1996, pp. 220-1.

220. Keswani 1996, pp. 236-7.

221. Dussaud 1952. Knapp, 1996b, argues for a unified island-wide kingdom on Cyprus during the LBA, possibly centred at Enkomi. This position is also supported by Muhly 1989, p. 299. Merrillees, 1969a; 1987, is the most vigorous opponent of the Alashiya historical model. See also discussion in Smith 1994, pp. 10-26.

222. Eriksson 1993, pp. 129-34.

223. Todd 2001, pp. 205-6.

224. Petrographic analysis of the Amarna tablets indicates that the clay used for the Alashiya tablets is Cypriot. Its source has been pinpointed to the Troodos massif, significantly from the copper-producing region of Cyprus, and it has chemical similarities with the clays used to make the pottery at Kalavasos-*Ayios Dhimitrios*, Palaepaphos and Alassa-*Paliotaverna*, Goren *et al.* 2003, pp. 242-5.

225. Sandars 1985, pp. 142-3.

226. Sandars 1985, p. 119; Muhly 1984, pp. 38-9.

227. Muhly 1984; Kling 1989b, pp. 2-4. For discussion of disruptions to East Mediterranean polities in early 12th century BC see Ward and Joukowsky (eds) 1992.

228. Åström 1989, pp. 202-3.

229. See discussion in Ch. 7.

230. See Keswani 1993.

7. Epilogue: the End of the Bronze Age

1. Catling 1973a, p. 37.

2. For example this association has been made very explicit for sites such as Sinda; Furumark 1965. The destruction horizons throughout the East Mediterranean are discussed in Ward & Joukowsky (eds) 1992. See also Kling 1989b, pp. 2-4. Specifically for the correlation of the Cypriot archaeological record and the Egyptian textual accounts, see discussion in Muhly 1984.

3. The archaeological evidence and cultural-historical framework is comprehensively reviewed in Kling 1989b, pp. 6-87.

4. Patterns of LC IIIA settlement are summarised in Iacovou 1989, pp. 52-3. See also Iacovou 1994, for a discussion of shifting patterns of settlement over the twelfth and eleventh centuries BC.

5. Iacovou 1994, p. 151.

6. Karageorghis 1990a, pp. 9-10. The suddenness of the abandonment at Pyla-*Kokkinokremos*, where much portable wealth was left *in situ* on the settlement floors, is in marked contrast to Kalavasos-*Ayios Dhimitrios*, where most portable wealth was removed before the abandonment of the site.

7. Gjerstad 1935, p. 671.

8. Dothan & Ben-Tor *et al.* 1983, p. 140.

9. du Plat Taylor 1952.

10. Hadjisavvas 1991, 1994.

11. The degree of continuity of settlement at Kourion has in fact been over-emphasised in the archaeological literature, based on erroneous ceramic identifications. There was in fact a significant disjuncture between the final LBA settlement at *Bamboula* and the establishment of the Iron Age settlement on the acropolis associated with the cemetery at the locality of *Kaloriziki*. See discussion in Steel 1996.

12. Furumark 1965, pp. 101-3, 107.

13. In level IIIB Dikaios notes the remains of a single child in room 8 of the ashlar building, trapped beneath fallen mudbrick and pisé from the superstructure. The remains of two other children had been cleared out from the collapsed building and thrown in with other debris into room 2. Dikaios 1969-71, pp. 193-4.

14. The destruction of the fortified town of Sinda, for example, dates to the final phase of LC IIC; Furumark 1965, p. 105.

15. Karageorghis & Demas 1984, pp. 3-5.

16. Karageorghis 2001, p. 3.

17. Karageorghis 1990a, p. 9.

18. Karageorghis & Demas 1988; Karageorghis 1990a, pp. 21-6; 2001, p. 3.

19. Karageorghis & Demas 1988, pp. 262-3.

20. Pilides 2000, pp. 40-4, 79-80 (nos 174-184).

21. Nowicki 2001.

22. du Plat Taylor 1952.

23. Karageorghis 1990a, pp. 12-13.

24. Hala Sultan Tekke: Karageorghis 1990a, p. 16; Enkomi and Salamis: Yon 1980, pp. 75-7; Iacovou 1994, p. 153.

25. This thesis was initially developed by Sjöqvist 1940, pp. 186-90, 207-9. See also Dikaios 1969-71, pp. 509-23; Catling 1975, pp. 207-8. See also Karageorghis 1990a, p. 28.

26. Iacovou 1994.

27. Kling 1989a, pp. 167-8; 1991, p. 182.

28. LC IIC cooking ware forms are best illustrated by the assemblage at Kalavasos-*Ayios Dhimitrios*, South *et al.* 1989, pp. 6-7, fig. 10. The new forms are apparent in the LC IIIA assemblage at Athienou, Dothan & Ben-Tor *et al.* 1983, fig. 50: 7-8, pl. 33. These resemble Mycenaean cooking forms, from sites such as Midhea and Mycenae. See Tzedakis & Martlew 1999, pp. 126-7 (nos 106, 108), 131 (nos 112-13), 135 (nos 120-1). Unfortunately, it is not yet possible to demonstrate any technological changes associated with the introduction of these new forms, using chemical component analyses (see for example the work that has been done on Philistine cooking pots, Killebrew 1999).

29. Kling 1984, pp. 29-30; 1989a, p. 165.

30. Dikaios 1969-71, pp. 260-2, 514-23.

31. Furumark 1965, pp. 107-8, fig. 6, pls I-II; Kling 1984, pp. 31-2.

32. See discussion in Maier 1973.

33. Kling 1984, pp. 29, 32-3.

34. Kling 1989b, pp. 106-7, 108, figs 3a-b.

35. Kling 1989b, p. 126, fig. 3c.

36. Kling 1989a, p. 167.

37. Kling 1989b, p. 165, figs 18a-d.

38. Kling 1984; 1989b, p. 158, figs 16a-b.

39. Explored for example by Maier, 1973. See also Kling 1984, pp. 37-8; 1989a, p. 165; 1991, p. 182.

40. E. Sherratt 1991, pp. 185-90.

41. Kling 1984, pp. 34-6; 1991.
42. South *et al.* 1989, pp. 8-9; Kling 1989a, 1989b, 1991; E. Sherratt 1991.
43. Kling 1989a, 1991; E. Sherratt 1991; Hadjisavvas 1991.
44. Kling 1989b, p. 175.
45. Kling 1989b, pp. 174-6.
46. E. Sherratt 1991, p. 191. See also discussion in Steel, in press.
47. Base Ring and White Slip: Artzy 1985, pp. 96-8; Vaughan 1991, p. 125. Plain ware: Keswani 1991.
48. Courtois 1971, pp. 254-5.
49. Pilides 1994, pp. 69-74.
50. Pilides 1994, pp. 1, 11.
51. Pilides gives a clear summary of the alternative hypotheses put forward by different scholars; 1994, pp. 1-9.
52. Karageorghis & Demas 1988, p. 249: restored jar found in Area II on floor 1.
53. Pilides 1994, pp. 49-67.
54. Pilides 1994, p. 67.
55. Pilides 1994, pp. 70-1: Fabrics A and B.
56. Pilides 1994, p. 107.
57. See discussion in Pilides 1994, pp. 4-5.
58. See E. Sherratt 1991, Steel in press.
59. Iacovou 1989, p. 53; Pilides 1994, pp. 99-106.
60. Desborough 1964, pp. 47-72; Muhly 1984, p. 42.
61. Pilides 1994, pp. 103-5.
62. Sandars 1961, 1963.
63. Catling 1964, pp. 117-25.
64. E. Masson 1976, pp. 153-7, fig. 6; Keswani 1989a, p. 513.
65. Rutter 1992, p. 63.
66. The pictorial style of the eleventh century in Cyprus depicts males engaged in a number of aristocratic pursuits, such as hunting (Iacovou 1988, figs 10, 11), horse-riding (Iacovou 1988, figs 19, 21, 50) and drinking (Iacovou 1988, figs 34, 36). E. Sherratt suggests that this style was a means of marking membership of a warrior elite, which based status upon the military prowess and hunting skills of its male members, 1992, p. 333.
67. Dikaios 1969-71, pp. 260-2, 514-23. The best discussion and rebuttal of this issue is in Hult 1983.
68. Dikaios 1969-71, pp. 194-205; Courtois *et al.* 1986, pp. 16-18.
69. Coutois 1971, pp. 273-9; Courtois *et al.* 1986, pp. 35-40.
70. Courtois *et al.* 1986, pp. 24-30.
71. South 1988, p. 223, fig. 1.
72. Cadogan 1984, pp. 8-9; 1989, pp. 43-9, fig. 4.2.
73. Hadjisavvas 1994, pp. 107-14; Hadjisavvas 2001, pp. 211-12.
74. Dikaios 1969-71, p. 201, pl. 36/4; Courtois *et al.* 1986, pp. 18-20.
75. Kling 1984, p. 37.
76. Muhly 1984, p. 45.
77. Muhly 1992, p. 14.
78. Maier & Karageorghis 1984, p. 110; Karageorghis 2001, p. 4.
79. Karageorghis & Demas 1988, pp. 60-1; Mazar 1991; Dothan 1992; Karageorghis 1998.
80. Ashlar building, Area I, Dikaios 1969-71, p. 175; Area III, room 3, Dikaios 1969-71, p. 48.
81. Area III, rooms 77 and 89A, Dikaios 1969-71, pp. 106, 112-13.

82. Hadjisavvas 1994, p. 110.
83. Karageorghis 1998, p. 277.
84. Karageorghis & Demas 1988, p. 61.
85. Karageorghis 1998, pp. 277-8.
86. Catling 1964, pp. 155-6.
87. Karageorghis 1998, p. 280, fig. 4.
88. Karageorghis 1998.
89. Central hearths have been attested in Late Minoan IIIA buildings at Khania and Mallia on Crete, Driessen 1994, pp. 76, 78.
90. Niklasson 1987; Keswani 1989b, pp. 54-5.
91. Niklasson 1987, p. 219; Iacovou 1989, p. 52; Keswani 1989b, p. 53.
92. Iacovou 1989, p. 53.
93. Niklasson 1987, p. 222-3.
94. Keswani 1989b, p. 70.
95. Niklasson 1983, pp.169-213, especially 176-8.
96. Niklasson 1987, pp. 223-4.
97. Hadjisavvas 1991, p. 173.
98. Catling 1968; Maier & Karageorghis 1984, pp. 67-71; figs 49-53, 55-8.
99. Keswani 1989b, p. 66.
100. Murray *et al.* 1900, pls I, II; Courtois *et al.* 1986, pp. 127-34, 137-8.
101. Keswani 1989b, p. 68.
102. Keswani 1989b, p. 65.
103. Murray *et al.* 1900, pp. 17, 31; Catling 1964, 1984; Courtois *et al.* 1986, pp. 84-100; Matthäus 1988; Keswani 1989b, p. 67; Papasavvas 2001.
104. Niklasson 1987, p. 223, n. 26; Keswani 1989b, p. 67.
105. Keswani 1989b, p. 68.
106. This is most clearly illustrated by Webb's chart illustrating the chronology of the LC cult sites, 1999, table 1, pp. 18-19. Knapp suggests that this reflects increasing economic and political power invested in the LC elite during this period, and that LC religion was specifically used within an ideology of power; Knapp 1988b; 1996a, p. 45.
107. Merrillees 1973; Knapp 1996a, p. 89.
108. du Plat Taylor *et al.* 1957, figs 4, 12.
109. Gjerstad *et al.* 1935, pp. 460-628, fig. 242, pls XVI-XVIII.
110. Maier 1979, pp. 230-4, figs 2, 3.
111. Karageorghis & Demas 1985.
112. Dikaios 1969-71, pp. 194-9.
113. Courtois 1971.
114. Dikaios 1969-71, pp. 199-200.
115. Maier 1979, pp. 230-3, figs 2, 3, pls XXXIV/3, 4; Maier & Karageorghis 1984, pp. 91-8, figs 81, 82.
116. Karageorghis & Demas 1985, pp. 77-81, 112-15, 132-5.
117. Webb 1999, p. 91.
118. Webb 1999, pp. 101, 113.
119. Karageorghis & Demas 1985, pp. 81-4, 115-20, 135-8.
120. It is interesting to note the occasional occurrence of Mycenaean pictorial pottery with representations of horns of consecration in earlier LC II tombs at Enkomi and Kalavasos-*Ayios Dhimitrios*; Murray *et al.* 1900, fig. 67.3; Steel 1994. The latter illustrates a chariot procession to a sanctuary housing a seated female figure, presumably a goddess.
121. Karageorghis & Demas 1985, pl. 42.3.

122. Maier 1979, p. 233, pl.XXXV/3; Maier & Karageorghis 1984, fig. 85.
123. du Plat Taylor *et al.* 1957, pp. 104-7.
124. Loulloupis 1973, p. 242; Papadopoulos 1997, p. 176.
125. Webb 1999, p. 179.
126. See for example the Vounous bowl and the Kotsiatis models discussed in Ch. 5. Dikaios 1940, pp. 118-25, 173, pls VII, VIII; Karageorghis 1970; Frankel & Tamvaki 1973; Åström 1988.
127. Nys 1995, p. 26.
128. Karageorghis & Demas 1985, p. 260.
129. Nys 1995, pp. 26-7.
130. Webb 1985, pp. 317-28.
131. Courtois 1971, pp. 109-14, 277-80, figs 97, 109-10, 113.
132. du Plat Taylor *et al.* 1957, pp. 21, 99-100, pl. Vd.
133. Webb 1985.
134. Karageorghis 1990b, p. 67.
135. Webb 1999, p. 249.
136. Åström & Reese 1990, pp. 8-11.
137. Reese 1985.
138. Åström & Reese 1990, pp. 5-6.
139. Åström & Reese 1990, pp. 6, 8, 11-12.
140. Courtois *et al.* 1986, pp. 165-6, pl. XXIX.6, 8, 9; Nys 1995, pp. 19-25; Webb 1999, pp. 219-22, fig. 77.
141. Nys 1995, pp. 20-1.
142. See discussion in Nys 1995, pp. 23-5; Webb 1999, p. 220.
143. Nys 1995, pp. 30-1.
144. Webb 1999, p. 222.
145. Webb 1999, p. 215.
146. Webb 1999, pp. 216-19.
147. Webb 1999, p. 219.
148. Webb 1999, p. 99.
149. Dikaios 1969-71, pl. 136.
150. Rehak 1995, pp. 450-4.
151. Horned god: Dikaios 1969-71, p. 295, pls 139-44; Ingot god: Courtois 1971, pls XII-XXIVA.
152. For summary of the discussion and references see Hulin 1989.
153. As advocated by Webb, 1999, p. 223.
154. Coins and gold medallions of the Roman period depict a sacred cone within a tripartite shrine. Maier 1979, p. 233, pl. XXXIV/1; Maier & Karageorghis 1984, pp. 85, 98-9, figs 65-7, 87.
155. Maier & Karageorghis 1984, p. 99, fig. 83.
156. Catling 1964, pp. 297-8; Lagarce 1971; Knapp 1988a; Hadjisavvas 1994, pp. 112-13.
157. Knapp 1988a, p. 164.
158. Knapp 1988a, p. 159, fig. 2. See for example Lagarce 1971.
159. See the discussion of metallurgy in the previous chapter. Knapp 1988a, pp. 159-61.
160. As suggested by Hadjisavvas for the Alassa hoard, 1994, p. 112.
161. Knapp 1988a, p. 152.
162. Karageorghis & Demas 1985, pp. 133-4.
163. Courtois *et al.* 1986, p. 40.
164. Dikaios 1969-71, pp. 196-9.

165. Webb 1999, p. 99.
166. Courtois 1983; South *et al.* 1989, pp. 26-7, figs 24-5, pls I, IX, X.
167. Knapp 1988a, p. 155.
168. Knapp 1988a, pp. 156-9.
169. Keswani 1989b, p. 65.
170. Knapp 1988a, pp. 167-71.
171. A similar phenomenon is well documented throughout Bronze Age Europe where it is interpreted as high status competition for political power, Bradley 2000, pp. 37-8.
172. For example Evreti T. VIII: Catling 1968. Also Teratsoudhia: Karageorghis 1990b.
173. E. Sherratt 1991.
174. Maier & Karageorghis 1984, p. 70.
175. Murray *et al.* 1900, pls I, II; Pierides 1973; Maier & Karageorghis 1984, figs 54-60; Courtois *et al.* 1986, pls XXIV-XXV.
176. Courtois *et al.* 1986, pl. XVIII.
177. Catling 1964, pp. 191-223; Matthäus 1985, 1988; Courtois *et al.* 1986, pp. 84-100.
178. Courtois *et al.* 1986, pp. 68-84.
179. Lo Schiavo *et al.* 1985.
180. Coldstream 1989, pp. 328-9.
181. Catling 1984; Matthäus 1988.
182. Maier & Karageorghis 1984, p. 68, figs 50, 53.
183. E. Sherratt 1994, pp. 69-71, Appendix I, pp. 86-7.
184. E. Sherratt 1994, pp. 69-75.
185. Eriksson 1995. Similar Egyptian pottery has also been identified in LC IIC deposits at Kalavasos-*Ayios Dhimitrios* and Maroni-*Tsaroukkas*.
186. Lo Schiavo *et al.* 1985; Vagnetti & Lo Schiavo 1989.
187. Bikai 1987, pp. 58-62, 68-9: the so-called Kouklia horizon; Gilboa 1989.
188. Kling 1989a; Hadjisavvas 1991; E. Sherratt 1991.
189. Catling 1994; Iacovou 1989, p. 56; Steel 1996, p. 287.
190. Catling 1994, p. 136; Iacovou 1989, pp. 53-4; 1994.
191. Catling 1994, p. 136; Iacovou 1994, p. 153; Steel 1996, p. 287.
192. Yon 1980, pp. 75-7; Iacovou 1994, p. 153.
193. Karageorghis & Demas 1985, pp. 266-7.
194. Steel 1995, pp. 199-200.
195. Iacovou 1989, p. 54; 1994, p. 150.
196. Courtois 1971; Karageorghis & Demas 1985, pp. 266-7.
197. Courtois 1971, pp. 326-56, figs 141-54; Webb 1999, pp. 213-15.
198. Webb 1999, p. 215, and further references.
199. See discussion of the diffusion of Aegean religious paraphernalia in Hägg 1991.
200. Courtois 1971, pp. 280-308, figs 114-27; Courtois *et al.* 1986, pp. 169-70; Webb 1999, p. 218.
201. Steel 1995, pp. 199-200.
202. G. McFadden 1954. The attribution of the so-called Kourion sceptre to this tomb group remains extremely problematic. The object looks out of place in the context of LC prestige paraphernalia, and its provenance is by no means secure. For a full discussion of its discovery, technology, and possible dating see Goring 1995.
203. Coldstream discusses the nature of status symbols (military equipment,

metal vessels, gold jewellery) deposited in tombs during the eleventh century: 1989, pp. 325-35.

204. Iacovou 1989, p. 54; Steel 1993.

Bibliography

a Campo, A.L. 1994 *Anthropomorphic Representations in Prehistoric Cyprus: A Formal and Symbolic Analysis of Figurines, c. 3500-1800 BC.* SIMA Pocketbook 109. Jonsered: P. Åströms Förlag.

Adovasio, J., Fry, G., Gunn, J. & Maslowski, R. 1975 Prehistoric and historic settlement patterns in western Cyprus (with a study of Cypriot Neolithic stone tool technology). *World Archaeology* 6: 339-64.

Adovasio, J., Fry, G., Gunn, J. & Maslowski, R. 1978 Prehistoric and historic settlement patterns in western Cyprus: an overview. *RDAC*: 39-57.

Angel, J.L. 1953 The human remains from Khirokitia. In Dikaios 1953, 416-30.

Artzy, M. 1985 Supply and demand: a study of second millennium Cypriote pottery in the Levant. In A.B. Knapp & T. Stech (eds), *Prehistoric Production and Exchange: The Aegean and Eastern Mediterranean.* Monograph 25. Los Angeles: Institute of Archaeology, University of California, 93-9.

Åström, P. 1972a *The Swedish Cyprus Expedition* IV. 1c. *The Late Cypriote Bronze Age. Architecture and Pottery.* Lund: Swedish Cyprus Expedition.

Åström, P. 1972b *The Swedish Cyprus Expedition* IV. 1d. *The Late Cypriote Bronze Age. Relative and Absolute Chronology, Foreign Relations, Historical Conclusions.* Lund: Swedish Cyprus Expedition.

Åström, P. 1979 A faience sceptre with a cartouche of Horemhab. In V. Karageorghis (ed.), *Studies Presented in Memory of Porphyrios Dikaios.* Nicosia: Lions Club, 46-8.

Åström, P. 1987 The chronology of the Middle Cypriote Bronze Age. In P. Åström (ed.), *High, Middle or Low? Acts of an International Colloquium on Absolute Chronology held at the University of Gothenburg 20th-22nd August 1987.* Part 3. SIMA Pocketbook 80. Göteborg: P. Åströms Förlag, 57-66.

Åström, P. 1988 A Cypriote cult scene. *Journal of Prehistoric Religion* 2: 5-11.

Åström, P. 1989 Trade in the Late Cypriot Bronze Age. In E. Peltenburg (ed.), *Early Society in Cyprus.* Edinburgh: University of Edinburgh Press, 202-08.

Åström, P. & Reese, D.S. 1990 Triton shells in East Mediterranean cults. *Journal of Prehistoric Religion* 3-4: 5-14.

Badou, E. & Engelmark, R. 1983 The Tremithos Valley Project: a preliminary report for 1981-1982. *RDAC*: 1-8.

Bailey, D.M. 1972 The British Museum excavations at Hala Sultan Tekke in 1897 and 1898. The material in the British Museum. In D.M. Bailey & V. Karageorghis, *Hala Sultan Tekke* 1. *Excavations 1897-1971.* SIMA 45.1. Göteborg: P. Åströms Förlag.

Bailey, D. 1994 Reading prehistoric figurines as individuals. *World Archaeology* 25: 322-31.

Balandier, C. 2001 Cyprus, a new archaeological frontier in the XIXth century: the struggle of European museums for Cypriot antiquities. In V. Tatton-Brown

Bibliography

(ed.), *Cyprus in the 19th Century AD: Fact, Fancy and Fiction. Papers of the 22nd British Museum Classical Colloquium*. Oxford: Oxbow Books, 3-12.

Barber, E.J.W. 1991 *Prehistoric Textiles: The Development of Cloth in the Neolithic and Bronze Age*. Princeton: Princeton University Press.

Barlow, J.A. 1985 Middle Cypriot settlement evidence. A perspective on the chronological foundations. *RDAC*: 47-54.

Barlow, J.A. 1991 New light on Red Polished ware. In J.A. Barlow, D.L. Bolger & B. Kling (eds), *Cypriot Ceramics: Reading the Prehistoric Record*. University Museum Monograph 74. Philadelphia: University of Pennsylvania, 51-7.

Bar-Yosef, O. 1995 Earliest food producers – Pre-pottery Neolithic (8000-5500). In T.D. Levy (ed.), *The Archaeology of Society in the Holy Land*. Leicester: Leicester University Press, 190-201.

Bar-Yosef, O. & Meadows, R. 1995 The origins of agriculture in the Near East. In T. Douglas Price & A. Gebauer (eds), *Last Hunters, First Farmers: New Perspectives on the Prehistoric Transition to Agriculture*. Sante Fe: School of American Research Press, 39-94.

Bass, G. 1986 A Bronze Age shipwreck at Ulu Burun (Kaş): 1984 campaign. *AJA* 90: 269-96.

Belgiorno, M.R. 2000 Project 'Pyrame' 1998-1999. Archaeological, metallurgical and historical evidence at Pyrgos (Limassol). *RDAC*: 1-17.

Bender, B. 1978. Gatherer-hunter to farmer: a social perspective. *World Archaeology* 10: 204-22.

Bergoffen, C.J. 1991 Overland trade in northern Sinai: the evidence of the Late Cypriot pottery. *BASOR* 284: 59-76.

Bergoffen, C.J. 2001 The Proto White Slip and the White Slip I pottery from Tell el-'Ajjul. In V. Karageorghis (ed.), *The White Slip Ware of Late Bronze Age Cyprus*. Vienna: Verlag der Österreichischen Akademie der Wissenschaften, 145-55.

Bikai, P.M. 1987 *The Phoenician Pottery of Cyprus*. Nicosia: A.G. Leventis Foundation.

Bisset, N.G., Bruhn, J.G. & Zeuk, M.H. 1996 The presence of opium in a 3,500-year-old Cypriote Base Ring juglet. *Egypt and the Levant. International Journal for Egyptian Archaeology and Related Disciplines* 6: 203-4.

Bolger, D.L. 1983 Khrysiliou-Ammos, Nicosia-Ayia Paraskevi and the Philia culture of Cyprus. *RDAC*: 60-73.

Bolger, D.L. 1989 Regionalism, cultural variation and the culture-area concept in Later Prehistoric Cypriot studies. In E. Peltenburg (ed.), *Early Society in Cyprus*. Edinburgh: Edinburgh University Press, 142-52.

Bolger, D.L. 1991a Early Red Polished ware and the origin of the Philia culture. In J.A. Barlow, D.L. Bolger & B. Kling (eds), *Cypriot Ceramics: Reading the Prehistoric Record*. University Museum Monograph 74. Philadelphia: University of Pennsylvania, 29-36.

Bolger, D.L. 1991b The evolution of the Chalcolithic painted style. *BASOR* 282/283: 81-93.

Bolger, D.L. 1991c The building model. In Peltenburg *et al.* 1991, 12-27.

Bolger, D.L. 1991d Other ceramics. In Peltenburg *et al.* 1991, 28-38.

Bolger, D.L. 1992 The archaeology of fertility and birth: a ritual deposit from Chalcolithic Cyprus. *Journal of Anthropological Research* 48: 145-64.

Bolger, D.L. 1994 Engendering Cypriot archaeology: female roles and statuses before the Bronze Age. *Opuscula Atheniensia* 20: 9-17.

Bibliography

Bolger, D.L. 1996 Figurines, fertility, and the emergence of complex society in prehistoric Cyprus. *Current Anthropology* 37: 365-73.

Bonato, L. 2001 Melchior de Vogüé *et alii* and Cyprus. In V. Tatton-Brown (ed.), *Cyprus in the 19th Century AD: Fact, Fancy and Fiction. Papers of the 22nd British Museum Classical Colloquium.* Oxford: Oxbow Books, 189-97.

Borić, D. 2002 Apotropaism and the temporality of colours: colourful Mesolithic-Neolithic seasons in the Danube Gorges. In A. Jones & G. MacGregor (eds), *Colouring the Past: The Significance of Colour in Archaeological Research.* Oxford & New York: Berg, 23-43.

Bradley, R. 2000 *An Archaeology of Natural Places.* London & New York: Routledge.

Branigan, K. 1987 Ritual interference with human bones in the Mesara tholoi. In R. Laffineur (ed.), *Thanatos: Les Coutumes Funéraires en Egée à l'Age du Bronze.* AEGAEUM 1 Annales d'archéologie égéenne de l'Université de Liège et UT-PASP: 41-51.

Briois, F. Gratuze, B. & Guilaine, J. 1997 Obsidiennes du site Néolithique Précéramique de Shillourokambos (Chypre). *Paléorient* 23/1: 95-112.

Broodbank, C. 1992 The Neolithic labyrinth: social change at Knossos before the Bronze Age. *JMA* 5: 39-75.

Broodbank, C. 1999 The insularity of island archaeologists: comments on Rainbird's 'Islands out of Time'. *JMA* 12: 235-9.

Broodbank, C. 2000 *An Island Archaeology of the Early Cyclades.* Cambridge: Cambridge University Press.

Broodbank, C. & Strasser, T. 1991 Migrant farmers and the Neolithic colonization of Crete. *Antiquity* 65: 233-45.

Budd, P. *et al.* 1995a Oxhide ingots, recycling and the Mediterranean metals trade. *JMA* 8: 1-32.

Budd, P. *et al.* 1995b Lead isotope analysis and oxhide ingots, a final comment. *JMA* 8: 70-5.

Bunimovitz, S. & Barkai, R. 1996 Ancient bones and modern myths: ninth millennium BC hippopotamus hunters at Akrotiri-*Aetokremnos*, Cyprus. *JMA.* 9: 85-96.

Cadogan, G. 1973 Patterns of the distribution of Mycenaean pottery in the Eastern Mediterranean. In *Acts of the International Symposium: The Mycenaeans in the Eastern Mediterranean.* Nicosia: Department of Antiquities, 166-72.

Cadogan, G. 1984 Maroni and the Late Bronze Age of Cyprus. In V. Karageorghis & J.D. Muhly (eds), *Cyprus at the Close of the Late Bronze Age.* Nicosia: A.G. Leventis Foundation, 1-10.

Cadogan, G. 1989 Maroni and the monuments. In E. Peltenburg (ed.), *Early Society in Cyprus.* Edinburgh: University of Edinburgh Press, 43-51.

Cadogan, G. 1993 Cyprus, Mycenaean pottery, trade and colonisation. In C. Zerner *et al.* (eds), *Wace and Blegen. Pottery as Evidence for Trade in the Aegean Bronze Age 1939-1989.* Amsterdam: J.C. Gieben, 91-9.

Catling, H.W. 1962 Patterns of settlement in Bronze Age Cyprus. *Opuscula Atheniensia* 4: 129-69.

Catling, H.W. 1964 *Cypriot Bronzework in the Mycenaean World.* Oxford: Clarendon Press.

Catling, H.W. 1968 Kouklia: Evreti Tomb 8. *BCH* 92: 162-9.

Catling, H.W. 1971 A Cypriot bronze statuette in the Bomford collection. In C.F.A. Schaeffer (ed.), *Alasia* I. Mission d'Archéologie d'Alasia 4. Paris: Klincksiek, 15-32.

253

Bibliography

Catling, H.W. 1973a The Achaean settlement of Cyprus. In *Acts of the International Symposium: The Mycenaeans in the Eastern Mediterranean*. Nicosia: Department of Antiquities, 34-9.

Catling, H.W. 1973b Cyprus in the Middle Bronze Age. In I.E.S. Edwards, C.J. Gadd & N.G.L. Hammond (eds), *Cambridge Ancient History* II, part 1. Cambridge: Cambridge University Press, 165-75.

Catling, H.W. 1975 Cyprus in the Late Bronze Age. In I.E.S. Edwards, C.J. Gadd & N.G.L. Hammond (eds), *Cambridge Ancient History* II, part 2. Cambridge: Cambridge University Press, 188-216.

Catling, H.W. 1984 Workshop and heirloom: prehistoric bronze stands in the east Mediterranean. *RDAC*: 69-91.

Catling, H.W. 1994 Cyprus in the 11th century BC – an end or a beginning? In V. Karageorghis (ed.), *Proceedings of the International Symposium 'Cyprus in the 11th Century BC'*. Nicosia: University of Cyprus and Leventis Foundation, 133-40.

Caubet, A. 1985a Matières vitreuses. In M. Yon & A. Caubet, *Kition Bamboula* III. *Le Sondage L-N 13 (Bronze Récent et Géométrique I)*. Paris: Editions Recherche sur les Civilisations, 61-82.

Caubet, A. 1985b Matières dures animales. In M. Yon & A. Caubet, *Kition Bamboula* III. *Le Sondage L-N 13 (Bronze Récent et Géométrique I)*. Paris: Editions Recherche sur les Civilisations, 83-93.

Caubet, A. 1993 Les antiquités chypriotes au musée du Louvre et dans les collections publiques françaises. In M. Yon (ed.), *Kinyras: l'Archéologie française à Chypre*. Lyon: Maison de l'Orient, 23-37.

Caubet, A. 2001 Les antiquités de Chypre au Louvre: entre l'Orient et l'Occident. In V. Tatton-Brown (ed.), *Cyprus in the 19th Century AD: Fact, Fancy and Fiction. Papers of the 22nd British Museum Classical Colloquium*. Oxford: Oxbow Books, 141-8.

Caubet, A., Hermary, A. & Karageorghis, V. 1992 *Art Antique de Chypre au Musée du Louvre, du Chalcolithique à l'époque romaine*. Athens: A.G. Leventis Foundation & Réunion des musées nationaux.

Caubet, A. & Kaczmarczyk, A. 1989 Trade and local production in Late Cypriot faience. In Peltenburg (ed.), *Early Society in Cyprus*. Edinburgh: University of Edinburgh Press, 209-16.

Cesnola, L.P. di 1877 *Cyprus, its Cities, Tombs and Temples*. London: John Murray (reprint 1991, Nicosia: Star Graphics).

Chapman, J. 2000 *Fragmentation in Archaeology. People, Places and Broken Objects in the Prehistory of South-Eastern Europe*. London & New York: Routledge.

Chapman, J. 2002 Colourful prehistories: the problem with the Berlin and Kay colour paradigm. In A. Jones & G. MacGregor (eds), *Colouring the Past: The Significance of Colour in Archaeological Research*. Oxford & New York: Berg, 45-72.

Cherry, J.F. 1981 Pattern and process in the earliest colonisation of the Mediterranean islands. *PPS* 47: 41-68.

Cherry, J.F. 1986 Polities and palaces: some problems in Minoan state formation. In C. Renfrew & J.F. Cherry (eds), *Peer Polity Interaction and Socio-Political Change*. Cambridge: Cambridge University Press, 19-45.

Cherry, J.F. 1990 The first colonisation of the Mediterranean islands: a review of recent research. *JMA* 3: 145-221.

Christou, D. 1989 The Chalcolithic Cemetery at Souskiou-*Vathyrkaks*. In E.J.

Bibliography

Peltenburg (ed.), *Early Society in Cyprus*. Edinburgh: Edinburgh University Press, 82-94.

Clarke, J.T. 2001 Style and society in Ceramic Neolithic Cyprus. *Levant* 33: 65-80.

Clerc, G. 1983 Aegyptiaca de Palaepaphos-*Skales*. In V. Karageorghis (ed.), *Palaepaphos-Skales: An Iron Age Cemetery in Cyprus. Ausgrabungen in Alt-Paphos auf Cypern 3*. Konstanz: Universitätsverlag, 375-95.

Coldstream, J.N. 1989 Status symbols in Cyprus in the eleventh century BC. In E. Peltenburg (ed.), *Early Society in Cyprus*. Edinburgh: University of Edinburgh Press, 325-35.

Coleman, J.E. *et al.* 1996 *Alambra: A Middle Bronze Age Settlement in Cyprus. Archaeological Investigations by Cornell University 1974-1985*. SIMA 118. Jonsered: P. Åströms Förlag.

Constantinou, G. 1982 Geological features and ancient exploitation of the cupriferous sulphide orebodies of Cyprus. In J. Muhly, R. Maddin & V. Karageorghis (eds), *Early Metallurgy in Cyprus*. Larnaca: Pierides Foundation, 13-24.

Courtois, J.-C. 1971 Le sanctuaire du dieu au lingot d'Enkomi-Alasia. In C.F.A. Schaeffer (ed.), *Alasia* I. Mission d'Archéologie d'Alasia 4. Paris: Klincksiek, 151-362.

Courtois, J.-C. 1982 L'activité métallurgique des bronzes d'Enkomi au Bronze Récent (1650-1100 avant J.-C.). In J.D. Muhly, R. Maddin & V. Karageorghis (eds), *Early Metallurgy in Cyprus, 4000-500 BC*. Nicosia: Pierides Foundation, 155-74.

Courtois, J.-C. 1983 Le trésor de poids de Kalavasos-*Ayios Dhimitrios* 1982. *RDAC*: 155-76.

Courtois, J.-C. 1986 A propos des apports orientaux dans la civilization du Bronze Récent à Chypre. In V. Karageorghis (ed.), *Acts of the International Archaeological Symposium 'Cyprus between the Orient and the Occident'*. Nicosia: Department of Antiquities, 69-87.

Courtois, J.-C., Lagarce, J. & Lagarce, E. 1986 *Enkomi et le Bronze Récent à Chypre*. Nicosia: Leventis Foundation.

Craddock, P.T. 1986 Report on the composition of bronzes from a Middle Cypriot site at Episkopi-*Phaneromeni* and some comparative Cypriot Bronze Age metalwork. In S. Swiny 1986, 153-8.

Crewe, L. 1998 *Spindle Whorls: A Study of Form, Function and Decoration in Prehistoric Bronze Age Cyprus*. SIMA Pocketbook 149. Jonsered: P. Åströms Förlag.

Croft, P. 1988 Animal remains from Maa-*Palaeokastro*. In V. Karageorghis & M. Demas 1988, 449-57.

Croft, P. 1991 Man and beast in Chalcolithic Cyprus. *BASOR* 282/283: 63-79.

Croft, P. 1996 Subsistence economy: animal remains. In Frankel & Webb 1996, 217-23.

Desborough, V.R.d'A. 1964 *The Last Mycenaeans and their Successors: An Archaeological Survey*. Oxford: Clarendon Press.

Dikaios, P. 1936 Excavations at Erimi 1933-1935. *RDAC*: 1-75.

Dikaios, P. 1940 Excavations at Vounous-*Bellapais* in Cyprus, 1931-2. *Archaeologia* 83: 1-168.

Dikaios, P. 1953 *Khirokitia*. Oxford: Oxford University Press.

Dikaios, P. 1961 *Sotira*. Philadelphia: University of Pennsylvania.

Dikaios, P. 1962 The Stone Age. In P. Dikaios & J.R. Stewart, *Swedish Cyprus Expedition* IV.1A. *The Stone Age and Early Bronze Age*. Lund: Swedish Cyprus Expedition.

Bibliography

Dikaios, P. 1969-71 *Enkomi: Excavations 1948-1958.* Mainz am Rhein: Verlag Philipp von Zabern.

Dothan, T. 1992 Social dislocation and cultural changes in the 12th century BCE. In W.A. Ward & M.S. Joukowsky (eds), *The Crisis Years: The Twelfth Century BC.* Dubuque, Iowa, 93-8.

Dothan, T. & Ben-Tor, A. *et al.* 1983 *Excavations at Athienou, Cyprus, 1971-1972.* QEDEM 16. Jerusalem: Hebrew University.

Driessen, J. 1994 La Crète mycénienne. *Les Dossiers d'archéologie* 195: 66-83.

Ducos, P. 1965 Le daim à Chypre aux époques préhistoriques. *RDAC*: 1-10.

Dugay, L. 1996 Specialized pottery production on Bronze Age Cyprus and pottery use-wear analysis. *JMA* 9: 167-92.

du Plat Taylor, J. 1952 A Late Bronze Age settlement at Apliki, Cyprus. *Antiquaries Journal* 32: 133-67.

du Plat Taylor, J. *et al.* 1957 *Myrtou-Pigadhes: A Late Bronze Age Sanctuary in Cyprus.* Oxford: Ashmolean Museum.

Dussaud, R. 1952 Note préliminaire. Identification d'Enkomi avec Alasia. In Schaeffer 1952, 1-10.

Epstein, C. 1966 *Palestinian Bichrome Ware.* Leiden: E.J. Brill.

Eriksen, T. 1993 In which sense do cultural islands exist? *Social Anthropology* 1: 133-47.

Eriksson, K. 1993 *Red Lustrous Wheel-made Ware.* SIMA 103. Jonsered: P. Åströms Förlag.

Eriksson, K. 1995 Egyptian amphorae from Late Cypriot contexts in Cyprus. In S. Bourke & J.-P. Descoeudres (eds), *Trade, Contact, and the Movement of Peoples in the Eastern Mediterranean. Studies in Honour of J. Basil Hennessy.* Sydney: Mediterranean Archaeology Supplement 3, 199-205.

Evans, J.D. 1973 Islands as laboratories for the study of culture process. In A.C. Renfrew (ed.), *The Explanation of Culture Change: Models in Prehistory.* London: Duckworth, 517-20.

Evans, J.D. 1977 Island archaeology in the Mediterranean: problems and opportunities. *World Archaeology* 9: 12-26.

Flourentzos, P. 1997 Excavations at the Neolithic site of Paralimni, a preliminary report. *RDAC*: 1-10.

Frankel, D. 1974a Inter-site relationships in the Middle Bronze Age of Cyprus. *World Archaeology* 6: 190-208.

Frankel, D. 1974b *Middle Cypriot White Painted Pottery. An Analytical Study of the Decoration.* SIMA 42. Göteborg: P. Åströms Förlag.

Frankel, D. 1988 Pottery production in prehistoric Bronze Age Cyprus: assessing the problem. *JMA* 1: 27-55.

Frankel, D. & Tamvaki, A. 1973 Cypriote shrine models and decorated tombs. *Australian Journal of Biblical Archaeology* 2: 39-44.

Frankel, D. & Webb, J.M. 1996 *Marki Alonia. An Early and Middle Bronze Age Town in Cyprus. Excavations 1990-1994.* SIMA 123. Jonsered: P. Åströms Förlag.

Frankel, D. & Webb, J.M. 2000 Marki-*Alonia*: a prehistoric Bronze Age settlement in Cyprus. *Antiquity* 74: 763-4.

Frankel, D., Webb, J.M. & Eslick, C. 1996 Anatolia and Cyprus in the third millennium BCE. A speculative model of interaction. In G. Bunnens (ed.), *Cultural Interaction in the Ancient Near East.* Louvain: Peeters Press, 37-50.

Furumark, A. 1965 The excavations at Sinda. Some historical results. *Opuscula Atheniensia* 6: 99-116.

Bibliography

Gale, N.H. 1991 Copper ingots: their origin and their place in the Bronze Age metals trade in the Mediterranean. In N.H. Gale (ed.), *Bronze Age Trade in the Mediterranean*. SIMA 100. Jonsered: P. Åströms Förlag, 197-239.

Gale, N., Stos-Gale, Z. & Faschnact, W. 1996 Copper and copper working at Alambra. In Coleman *et al.* 1996, 359-402.

Gardner, E.A. *et al.* 1888 Excavations in Cyprus 1887-8. *JHS* 9: 149-271.

Giardino, C. 2000 Prehistoric copper activity at Pyrgos. *RDAC*: 19-31.

Gilboa, A. 1989 New finds at Tel Dor and the beginning of Cypro-Geometric pottery import to Palestine. *Israel Exploration Journal* 39: 204-18.

Given, M. 1998 Inventing the Eteocypriots: imperialist archaeology and the manipulation of ethnic identity. *JMA* 11: 3-29.

Given, M. *et al.* 1999 The Sydney Cyprus Survey Project: an interdisciplinary investigation of long-term change in the north central Troodos, Cyprus. *Journal of Field Archaeology* 26:19-39.

Gittlen, B.M. 1981 The cultural and chronological implications of the Cypro-Palestinian trade during the Late Bronze Age. *BASOR* 241: 49-59.

Gjerstad, E. 1926 *Studies in Cypriot Prehistory*. Uppsala: Uppsala Universitets Årsskrift.

Gjerstad, E. *et al.* 1934 *The Swedish Cyprus Expedition* I. *Finds and Results of the Excavations in Cyprus 1927-1931*. Stockholm: The Swedish Cyprus Expedition.

Gjerstad, E. *et al.* 1935 *The Swedish Cyprus Expedition* II. *Finds and Results of the Excavations in Cyprus 1927-1931*. Stockholm: The Swedish Cyprus Expedition.

Gjerstad, E. *et al.* 1937 *The Swedish Cyprus Expedition* III. *Finds and Results of the Excavations in Cyprus 1927-1931*. Stockholm: The Swedish Cyprus Expedition.

Gjerstad, E. *et al.* 1948 *The Swedish Cyprus Expedition* IV.2. *The Cypro-Geometric, Cypro-Archaic and Cypro-Classical Periods*. Stockholm: The Swedish Cyprus Expedition.

Gjerstad, E. *et al.* 1980 *Ages and Days in Cyprus*. SIMA Pocketbook 12. Göteborg: P. Åströms Förlag.

Goldstein, L. 1981 One-dimensional archaeology and multi-dimensional people: spatial organisation and mortuary analysis. In R. Chapman, I. Kinnes & K. Randsborg (eds), *The Archaeology of Death*. Cambridge: Cambridge University Press, 95-105.

Goren, Y., Bunimovitz, S., Finkelstein, I and Na'aman, N. 2003 The location of Alashiya: new evidence from petrographic investigation of Alashiyan tablets. *AJA* 107: 233-55.

Goring, E. 1988 *A Mischievous Pastime: Digging in Cyprus in the Nineteenth Century*. Edinburgh: National Museums of Scotland/Bank of Cyprus Cultural Foundation.

Goring, E. 1989 Death in everyday life: aspects of burial practice in the Late Bronze Age. In E. Peltenburg (ed.), *Early Society in Cyprus*. Edinburgh: University of Edinburgh Press, 95-105.

Goring, E. 1991a Pottery figurines: the development of coroplastic art in Chalcolithic Cyprus. *BASOR* 282-3: 39-60.

Goring, E. 1991b The anthropomorphic figures. In Peltenburg *et al.* 1991, 39-60.

Goring, E. 1995 The Kourion sceptre: some facts and factoids. In C. Morris (ed.), *Klados: Essays in Honour of J.N. Coldstream*. Bulletin of the Institute of Classical Studies Supplement 63. London: University of London, Institute of Classical Studies, 103-10.

Bibliography

Guilaine, J. *et al.* 1995 L'Etablissement néolithique de Shillourokambos (Parekklisha, Chypre). Premiers résultats. *RDAC*: 11-31.

Guilaine, J. *et al.* 1997 Chroniques et rapports. Rapports sur les travaux de l'Ecole Française d'Athènes. Shillourokambos (Chypre). *BCH* 121: 825-30.

Guilaine, J. *et al.* 1998 La site néolithique précéramique de Shillourokambos (Parekklisha, Chypre). *BCH* 122: 603-10.

Guilaine, J. *et al.* 1999 Tête sculptée en pierre dans le néolithique pré-céramique de *Shillourokambos* (Parekklisha, Chypre). *RDAC*: 1-11.

Guilaine, J. *et al.* 2000 Découverte d'un néolithique précéramique ancien chypriot (fin 9e, debut 8e millénaires cal. BC) apparenté au PPNB ancien/moyen. *Earth and Planetary Sciences* 300: 75-82.

Hadjisavvas, S. 1989 A Late Cypriot community at Alassa. In E. Peltenburg (ed.), *Early Society in Cyprus*. Edinburgh: University of Edinburgh Press, 32-42.

Hadjisavvas, S. 1991 LC IIC to LC IIIA without intruders: the case of Alassa-*Pano Mandilaris*. In J.A. Barlow, D.L. Bolger & B. Kling (eds), *Cypriot Ceramics: Reading the Prehistoric Record*. University Museum Monograph 74. Philadelphia: University of Pennsylvania, 173-80.

Hadjisavvas, S. 1994 Alassa Archaeological Project 1991-1993. *RDAC*: 107-14.

Hadjisavvas, S. 2001 Crete and Cyprus: religion and script. The case of Alassa. In H.G. Buchholz (ed.), *Kreta und Zypern: Religion und Schrift. Von der Frühgeschichte bis zum Ende der archaischen Zeit.* Herausgeber: Weilheim, 205-28.

Hägg, R. 1991 Sacred horns and naïskoi. Remarks on Aegean religious symbolism in Cyprus. In V. Karageorghis (ed.), *The Civilisations of the Aegean and their Diffusion in Cyprus and the Eastern Mediterranean*. Larnaca: Pierides Foundation, 78-83.

Halstead, P. 1977 A preliminary report on the faunal remains from Late Bronze Age Kouklia, Paphos. *RDAC*: 261-75.

Halstead, P. 1981 From determinism to uncertainty: social storage and the rise of the Minoan palace. In A. Sheridan & G.F. Bailey (eds), *Economic Archaeology*. Oxford: British Archaeological Reports. International Series 96: 187-213.

Halstead, P. 1987 Man and other animals in later Greek prehistory. *BSA* 82: 71-83.

Halstead, P. 1988 On redistribution and the origins of Minoan-Mycenaean palatial economies. In E. French & K. Wardle (eds), *Problems in Greek Prehistory*. Bristol: Bristol Classical Press, 519-30.

Halstead, P. 1994 The north-south divide: regional paths to complexity in prehistoric Greece. In C. Mathers & S. Stoddart (eds), *Development and Decline in the Mediterranean Bronze Age*. Sheffield: J.R. Collis Publications, 195-219.

Halstead, P. & O'Shea, J. 1982 A friend in need is a friend indeed: social storage and the origins of social ranking. In C. Renfrew & S. Shennan (eds), *Ranking, Resource, and Exchange*. Cambridge: Cambridge University Press, 92-9.

Hamilakis, Y. 1996 Wine, oil and the dialectics of power in Bronze Age Crete: a review of the evidence. *OJA* 15: 1-32.

Hamilakis, Y. 1999 Food technologies/technologies of the body: the social context of wine and body, production and consumption in Bronze Age Crete. *World Archaeology* 31: 38-54.

Hamilton, N. 1994 A fresh look at the 'seated gentleman' in the Pierides Foundation Museum, Republic of Cyprus. *CAJ* 4: 302-12.

Hamilton, N. 1996 Figurines, clay balls, small finds, and burials. In I. Hodder (ed.), *On the Surface: Çatalhöyük 1993-95*. Cambridge: Macdonald Institute Monographs & British Institute of Archaeology at Ankara.

Hamilton, N. *et al.* 1996 Can we interpret figurines? *CAJ* 6: 282-285.

Bibliography

Hayden, B. 1990 Nimrods, piscators, pluckers and planters: the emergence of food production. *Journal of Anthropological Archaeology* 9: 31-69.

Helbaek, H. 1962 Late Cypriote vegetable diet at Apliki. *Opuscula Atheniensia* 4: 171-86.

Held, S.O. 1989 Colonization cycles on Cyprus: the biogeographic and paleontological foundations of Early Prehistoric settlement. *RDAC*: 7-28.

Held, S.O. 1993 Insularity as a modifier of culture change: the case of prehistoric Cyprus. *BASOR* 292: 25-33.

Helms, M.W. 1988 *Ulysses Sail: An Ethnographic Odyssey of Power, Knowledge and Geographical Distance*. Princeton: Princeton University Press.

Herscher, E. 1984 The pottery of Maroni and regionalism in Late Bronze Age Cyprus. In V. Karageorghis & J.D. Muhly (eds), *Cyprus at the Close of the Late Bronze Age*. Nicosia: A.G. Leventis Foundation, 23-8.

Herscher, E. 1991 Beyond regionalism: toward an islandwide Early and Middle Cypriot sequence. In J.A. Barlow, D.L. Bolger & B. Kling (eds), *Cypriot Ceramics: Reading the Prehistoric Record*. University Museum Monograph 74. Philadelphia: University of Pennsylvania, 45-50.

Herscher, E. 1997 Representational relief on Early and Middle Cypriot pottery. In V. Karageorghis, R. Laffineur & F. Vandenabeele (eds), *Four Thousand Years of Images on Cypriote Pottery*. Brussels – Liège – Nicosia: Leventis Foundation, 25-36.

Holmboe 1914 *Studies on the Vegetation of Cyprus*. Bergens Museums Skrifter. Ny Raekke 1, No. 2. Bergen: Griegs.

Horden, P. & Purcell, N. 2000 *The Corrupting Sea: A Study of Mediterranean History*. Oxford: Blackwell Publishers.

Hulin, L. C. 1989 The identification of Cypriot cult figures through cross-cultural comparison: some problems. In E. Peltenburg (ed.), *Early Society in Cyprus*. Edinburgh: University of Edinburgh Press, 127-39.

Hult, G. 1983 *Bronze Age Ashlar Masonry in the Eastern Mediterranean. Cyprus, Ugarit, and Neighbouring Regions*. SIMA 66. Göteborg: P. Åströms Förlag.

Hult, G. 1992 *Nitovikla Reconsidered*. Stockholm: Medelhavsmuseet, Memoir 8.

Iacovou, M. 1988 *The Pictorial Pottery of Eleventh Century BC Cyprus*. SIMA 78. Göteborg: P. Åströms Förlag.

Iacovou, M. 1989 Society and settlements in Late Cypriot III. In E. Peltenburg (ed.), *Early Society in Cyprus*. Edinburgh: University of Edinburgh Press, 52-9.

Iacovou, M. 1994 The topography of eleventh century BC Cyprus. In V. Karageorghis (ed.), *Cyprus in the 11th Century BC*. Nicosia: A.G. Leventis Foundation & University of Cyprus, 149-65.

Iacovou, M. 1999 *Excerpta Cypria Geometrica*: materials for a history of Geometric Cyprus. In M. Iacovou & D. Michaelides (eds), *Cyprus: The Historicity of the Geometric Horizon*. Nicosia: Archaeological Research Unit, University of Cyprus, 141-61.

Johnstone, W. 1971 A Late Bronze Age tholos tomb at Enkomi. In C.F.A. Schaeffer (ed.), *Alasia* I. Mission d'Archéologie d'Alasia 4. Paris: Klincksiek, 51-122.

Karageorghis, V. 1970 Two religious documents of the Early Cypriote Bronze Age. *RDAC*: 10-13.

Karageorghis, V. 1990a *The End of the Late Bronze Age in Cyprus*. Nicosia: Pierides Foundation.

Karageorghis, V. 1990b *Tombs at Palaepaphos: 1. Teratsoudhia, 2. Eliomylia*. Nicosia: Leventis Foundation.

Karageorghis, V. 1998 Hearths and bathtubs in Cyprus: a 'Sea Peoples' innovation? In S. Gitin, A. Mazar & E. Stein (eds), *Mediterranean Peoples in Transition. Thirteenth to Early Tenth Century BCE*. Jerusalem: Israel Exploration Society, 276-82.

Karageorghis, V. 2001 Patterns of fortified settlements in the Aegean and Cyprus c. 1200 BC. In V. Karageorghis & C. Morris (eds), *Defensive Settlements of the Aegean and the Eastern Mediterranean after c. 1200 BC*. Nicosia: Trinity College Dublin & A.G. Leventis Foundation, 1-10.

Karageorghis, V. & Demas, M. 1984 *Pyla-Kokkinokremos. A Late 13th Century BC Fortified Settlement in Cyprus*. Nicosia: Department of Antiquities.

Karageorghis, V. & Demas, M. 1985 *Excavations at Kition* V.1. *The Pre-Phoenician Levels. Areas I and II*. Nicosia: Department of Antiquities.

Karageorghis, V. & Demas, M. 1988 *Excavations at Maa-Palaeokastro 1979-1986*. Nicosia: Department of Antiquities.

Keswani, P.S. 1989a *Mortuary Ritual and Social Hierarchy in Bronze Age Cyprus*. Unpublished PhD Dissertation, Department of Anthropology, University of Michigan. University Microfilms, Ann Arbor.

Keswani, P.S. 1989b Dimensions of social hierarchy in Late Bronze Age Cyprus: an analysis of the mortuary data from Enkomi. *JMA* 2: 49-86.

Keswani, P.S. 1991 A preliminary investigation of systems of ceramic production and distribution in Cyprus during the Late Bronze Age. In J.A. Barlow, D.L. Bolger & B. Kling (eds), *Cypriot Ceramics: Reading the Prehistoric Record*. University Museum Monograph 74. Philadelphia: University of Pennsylvania, 97-118.

Keswani, P.S. 1992 Gas chromatography analyses of pithoi from Kalavasos-*Ayios Dhimitrios*: a preliminary report. In A.K. South 1992, 141-6.

Keswani, P.S. 1993 Models of local exchange in Late Bronze Age Cyprus. *BASOR* 292: 73-83.

Keswani, P.S. 1994 The social context of animal husbandry in early agricultural societies: ethnographic insights and an archaeological example from Cyprus. *Journal of Anthropological Archaeology* 13: 255-77.

Keswani, P.S. 1996 Hierarchies, heterarchies, and urbanisation processes: the view from Bronze Age Cyprus. *JMA* 9: 211-250.

Killebrew, A.E. 1999 Late Bronze and Iron I cooking pots in Canaan: a typological, technological, and functional study. In T. Kapitan (eds), *Archaeology, History and Culture in Palestine and the Near East. Essays in Memory of Albert E. Glock*. Atlanta: Scholars Press. ASOR Books 3, 83-126.

Kling, B. 1984 Mycenaean IIIC:1b pottery in Cyprus: principal characteristics and historical context. In V. Karageorghis & J.D. Muhly (eds), *Cyprus at the Close of the Late Bronze Age*. Nicosia: A.G. Leventis Foundation, 20-38.

Kling, B. 1989a Local Cypriot features in the ceramics of the Late Cypriot IIIA period. In E. Peltenburg (ed.), *Early Society in Cyprus*. Edinburgh: University of Edinburgh Press, 160-70.

Kling, B. 1989b *Mycenaean IIIC:1b and Related Pottery in Cyprus*. SIMA 87. Göteborg: P. Åströms Förlag.

Kling, B. 1991 A terminology for the matte-painted wheelmade pottery of Late Cypriot IIC-IIIA. In J.A. Barlow, D.L. Bolger & B. Kling (eds), *Cypriot Ceramics: Reading the Prehistoric Record*. University Museum Monograph 74. Philadelphia: University of Pennsylvania, 181-4.

Knapp, A.B. 1986a *Copper Production and Divine Protection: Archaeology, Ideology and Social Complexity on Bronze Age Cyprus*. SIMA Pocketbook 42. Göteborg: P. Åströms Förlag.

Bibliography

Knapp, A.B. 1986b Production, exchange and socio-political complexity on Bronze Age Cyprus. *OJA* 5: 53-60.

Knapp, A.B. 1988a *Hoards d'oeuvres*: of metals and men on Bronze Age Cyprus. *OJA* 7: 147-76.

Knapp, A.B. 1988b Ideology, archaeology and polity. *Man* 23: 133-63.

Knapp, A.B. 1990 Production, location and integration in Bronze Age Cyprus. *Current Anthropology* 31: 147-76.

Knapp, A.B. 1991 Spice, drugs, grain and grog: organic goods in Bronze Age East Mediterranean trade. In N.H. Gale (ed.), *Bronze Age Trade in the Mediterranean*. SIMA 90. Jonsered: P. Åströms Förlag, 21-68.

Knapp, A.B. 1994 Emergence, development and decline on Bronze Age Cyprus. In C. Mathers & S. Stoddart (eds), *Development and Decline in the Mediterranean Bronze Age*. Sheffield Archaeological Monographs 8: J.R. Collis Publications, 271-304.

Knapp, A.B. 1996a The Bronze Age economy of Cyprus: ritual, ideology, and the sacred landscape. In V. Karageorghis & D. Michaelides (eds), *The Development of the Cypriot Economy from the Prehistoric Period to the Present Day*. Nicosia: Leventis Foundation, 71-106.

Knapp, A.B. 1996b *Sources for the History of Cyprus* II. *Near Eastern and Aegean Texts from the Third to the First Millennium* BC. Greece and Cyprus Research Centre.

Knapp, A.B. 1997a *The Archaeology of Late Bronze Age Cypriot Society: The Study of Settlement, Survey and Landscape*. Glasgow: Department of Archaeology, University of Glasgow.

Knapp, A.B. 1997b Mediterranean maritime landscapes: transport, trade and society on Late Bronze Age Cyprus. In S. Swiny, R.L. Hohlfelder & H.W. Swiny (eds), *Res Maritimae. Cyprus and the Eastern Mediterranean from Prehistory to Late Antiquity*. Cyprus American Archaeological Research Institute. Monograph Series 1. Atlanta: Scholars Press, 153-61.

Knapp, A.B. & Antoniadou, S. 1998 Archaeology, politics and the cultural heritage of Cyprus. In L. Meskell (ed.), *Archaeology Under Fire: Nationalism, Politics and heritage in the Eastern Mediterranean and Middle East*. London & New York: Routledge, 13-43.

Knapp, A.B. & Cherry, J.F. 1994 *Provenience Studies and Bronze Age Cyprus: Production, Exchange and Politico-Economic Change*. Monographs in World Archaeology 21. Madison: Prehistory Press.

Knapp, A.B., Held, S. & Manning, S.W. 1994 The prehistory of Cyprus: problems and prospects. *Journal of World Prehistory* 377: 377-453.

Knapp, A.B., Kassianidou, V. & Donnelly, M. 1999 Excavations at Politiko-*Phorades* 1998. *RDAC*: 125-46.

Knapp, A.B. & Meskell, L. 1997 Bodies of evidence on prehistoric Cyprus. *CAJ* 7: 183-204.

Koschel, K. 1996 Opium alkaloids in a Cypriote Base-Ring I vessel (bilbil) of the Middle Bronze Age from Egypt. *Egypt and the Levant. International Journal for Egyptian Archaeology and Related Disciplines* 6: 159-66.

Lagarce, J. 1971 La cachette de fondeur aux épées (Enkomi 1967) et l'atelier voisin. In C.F.A. Schaeffer (ed.), *Alasia* I. Mission d'Archéologie d'Alasia 4. Paris: Klincksiek, 381-432.

Lang, H.R. 1878 Narrative of excavations in a temple at Dali (Idalium) in Cyprus. *Transactions of the Royal Society of Literature* 2nd series XI, 30-79.

Bibliography

Le Brun, A. 1984 *Fouilles récentes à Khirokitia*. Paris: Editions Recherches sur les Civilisations.

Le Brun, A. 1989 Le Traitement des morts et les représentations des vivants à Khirokitia. In E. Peltenburg (ed.), *Early Society in Cyprus*. Edinburgh: Edinburgh University Press, 71-81.

Le Brun, A. 1996 L'économie néolithique de Chypre. In V. Karageorghis & D. Michaelides (eds), *The Development of the Cypriot Economy from the Prehistoric Period to the Present Day*. Nicosia: Leventis Foundation, 1-15.

Le Brun, A. 1997 *Khirokitia: A Neolithic Site*. Nicosia: Bank of Cyprus Cultural Foundation.

Le Brun, A. and Evin, J. 1991 De nouvelles datations 14C pour l'établissement précéramique de Khirokitia. *Reports of the Department of Antiquities, Cyprus*, 15-18.

Legge, A.J. 1982 Ayios Epiktitos: the recent farming economy. In Peltenburg 1982c, 14-20.

Lehavy, Y.M. 1989 Excavations at Dhali-*Agridhi*: 1972, 1974, 1976. Dhali-*Agridhi*: the Neolithic by the river. In L.E. Stager & A.M. Walker (eds), *American Expedition to Idalion, Cyprus 1973-1980*. Oriental Institute Communications 24. Chicago: Oriental Institute of the University of Chicago, 203-43.

Leonard Jr., A. 1981 Considerations of morphological variation in the Mycenaean pottery from the southeastern Mediterranean. *BASOR* 241: 87-101.

Lo Schiavo 1995 Cyprus and Sardinia in the Mediterranean trade routes toward the west. In V. Karageorghis & D. Michaelides (eds), *Cyprus and the Sea. Proceedings of the International Symposium*. Nicosia: University of Cyprus, 45-59.

Lo Schiavo, F., MacNamara, E. & Vagnetti, L. 1985 Late Cypriot imports to Italy and their influence on local bronzework. *Papers of the British School at Rome* 53: 1-71.

Loulloupis, M. 1973 Mycenaean 'horns of consecration' in Cyprus. In *Acts of the International Archaeological Symposium 'The Mycenaeans in the Eastern Mediterranean'*. Nicosia: Department of Antiquities, 225-44.

MacArthur, R.H. & Wilson, E.O. 1967 *The Theory of Island Biogeography*. Monographs in Population Biology 1. Princeton: Princeton University Press.

McCartney, C. 1998 Preliminary report on the chipped stone assemblage from the aceramic Neolithic site of Ayia Varvara Asprokremnos. *Levant* 30: 85-90.

McCartney, C. 1999 Opposed platform core technology and the Cypriot Aceramic Neolithic. *Neo-Lithics* 1: 7-10.

Maguire, L. 1992 A cautious approach to the Middle Bronze Age chronology of Cyprus. *Egypt and the Levant. International Journal for Egyptian Archaeology and Related Disciplines* 3: 115-20.

Maguire, L. 1995 Tell el-Dab'a. The Cypriot connection. In W. Vivian Davies & L. Schofield (eds), *Egypt, the Aegean and the Levant. Interconnections in the Second Millennium BC*. London: British Museum Press, 54-65.

Maier, F.G. 1973 Evidence for Mycenaean settlement at Old Paphos. In *Acts of the International Symposium: The Mycenaeans in the Eastern Mediterranean*. Nicosia: Department of Antiquities, 68-78.

Maier, F.G. 1979 The Paphian shrine of Aphrodite and Crete. In *Acts of the International Archaeological Symposium: The Relations between Cyprus and Crete, c. 2000-500 BC*. Nicosia: Department of Antiquities, 228-34.

Maier, F.G. & Karageorghis, V. 1984 *Paphos: History and Archaeology*. Nicosia: A.G. Leventis Foundation.

Bibliography

Mangou, H. & Ioannou, P.V. 2000 Studies of the Late Bronze Age copper-based ingots found in Greece. *BSA* 95: 207-17.

Manning, S.W. 1991 Approximate calendar date for the first human settlement of Cyprus? *Antiquity* 65: 870-8.

Manning, S.W. 1993 Prestige, distinction and competition: the anatomy of socio-economic complexity in 4th-2nd millennium BCE Cyprus. *BASOR* 292: 35-58.

Manning, S.W. 1999 *A Test of Time. The Volcano of Thera and the Chronology and History of the Aegean and East Mediterranean in the Mid Second Millennium BC.* Oxford: Oxbow Books.

Manning, S.W. & Monks, S.J. 1998 Late Cypriot tombs at Maroni-*Tsaroukkas*, Cyprus. *BSA* 93: 297-351.

Manning, S.W. & Swiny, S. 1994 Sotira-Kaminoudhia and the chronology of the Early Bronze Age in Cyprus. *OJA* 13: 149-72.

Manning, S.W. *et al.* 2001 Absolute age range of the Late Cypriot IIC period on Cyprus. *Antiquity* 75: 328-40.

Mantzourani, E. 1994 Ekthese apotelesmaton tis anaskaphes sti these KANTOU-KOUPHOVOUNOS. *RDAC*: 1-38.

Mantzourani, E. 1996 Ekthese apotelesmaton tis anaskaphes sti these KANTOU-KOUPHOVOUNOS kata tis periodos 1994-1996. *RDAC*: 1-24.

Marchegay, S. 2000 The tombs. In 'The mysteries of Ugarit: history, daily life, cult', *Near Eastern Archaeology* 63: 209-10.

Masson, E. 1976 A la recherche des vestiges proche-orientaux à Chypre, fin du bronze moyen et début du bronze récent. *Archäologischer Anzeiger* 2: 139-65.

Masson, O. 1971 Deux petits lingots de cuivre inscrits d'Enkomi (1953). In C.F.A. Schaeffer (ed.), *Alasia* I. Mission d'Archéologie d'Alasia 4. Paris: Klincksiek, 449-55.

Masson, O. 1993 Les archéologues et voyageurs du XIXe siècle. In M. Yon (ed.), *Kinyras: l'Archéologie française à Chypre*. Lyon: Maison de l'Orient, 17-37.

Matthäus, H. 1985 *Metallgefässe und Gefäsuntersatze der Bronzezeit, der geometrischen und archaischen Periode auf Cypern*. Munich: Prähistorische Bronzefunde II.8.

Matthäus, H. 1988 Heirloom or tradition? Bronze stands of the second and first millennium BC in Cyprus, Greece and Italy. In E. French & K.A. Wardle (eds), *Problems in Greek Prehistory*. Bristol: Bristol Classical Press, 285-300.

Mazar, A. 1991 Comments on the nature of the relations between Cyprus and Palestine during the 12th-11th centuries BC. In V. Karageorghis (ed.), *Proceedings of an International Symposium 'The Civilizations of the Aegean and their Diffusion in Cyprus and the Eastern Mediterranean, 2000-600 BC'*. Larnaca: Pierides Foundation.

McFadden, E. 1971 *The Glitter and the Gold: A Spirited Account of the Metropolitan Museum of Art's First Director, the Audacious and High-Handed Luigi Palma di Cesnola*. New York: The Dial Press.

McFadden, G.H. 1954 A Late Cypriote III tomb from Kourion, *Kaloriziki* no. 40. *AJA* 58: 131-42.

Mee, C. & Steel, L. 1998 *Corpus of Cypriote Antiquities* 17. *The Cypriote Collections in the University of Liverpool and the Williamson Art Gallery and Museum*. SIMA 20/17. Jonsered: P. Åströms Förlag.

Mellink, M. 1991 Anatolian contacts with Chalcolithic Cyprus. *BASOR* 282: 165-75.

Merrillees, R.S. 1962 Opium trade in the Bronze Age Levant. *Antiquity* 36: 287-92.

Merrillees, R.S. 1968 *The Cypriot Pottery Found in Egypt*. SIMA 18. Lund: P. Åströms Förlag.

Bibliography

Merrillees, R.S. 1969a Alasia. In V. Karageorghis (ed.), *The First International Congress of Cypriot Studies*. Nicosia: Etaireia Kypriakon Spoudon.

Merrillees, R.S. 1969b Opium again in antiquity. *Levant* 11: 167-71.

Merrillees, R.S. 1971 The early history of Late Cypriote I. *Levant* 3: 56-79.

Merrillees, R.S. 1973 Settlement, sanctuary and cemetery in Bronze Age Cyprus. *Australian Studies in Archaeology* 1: 44-57.

Merrillees, R.S. 1977 The absolute chronology of the Bronze Age in Cyprus. *RDAC*: 33-50.

Merrillees, R.S. 1978 *Introduction to the Bronze Age Archaeology of Cyprus*. SIMA Pocketbooks 9. Göteborg: P. Åströms Förlag.

Merrillees, R.S. 1982 Early metallurgy in Cyprus 4000-500 BC. Historical summary. In J.D. Muhly, R. Maddin & V. Karageorghis (eds), *Early Metallurgy in Cyprus, 4000-500 BC*. Nicosia: Pierides Foundation, 371-6.

Merrillees, R.S. 1987 *Alashiya Revisited*. Cahiers de la Revue Biblique 22. Paris: J. Gabalda.

Merrillees, R.S. 1989 The glyptics of Bronze Age Cyprus: 'through a glass darkly'. In E.J. Peltenburg (ed.), *Early Society in Cyprus*. Edinburgh: Edinburgh University Press, 153-9.

Merrillees, R.S. 1992 The absolute chronology of the Bronze Age in Cyprus: a revision. *BASOR* 288: 47-52.

Merrillees, R.S. 2001 T.B. Sandwith and the beginnings of Cypriote archaeology. In V. Tatton-Brown (ed.), *Cyprus in the 19th Century AD: Fact, Fancy and Fiction. Papers of the 22nd British Museum Classical Colloquium*. Oxford: Oxbow Books, 222-35.

Merrillees, R.S. 2002 The relative and absolute chronology of the Cypriote White Painted Pendent Line style. *BASOR* 326: 1-9.

Moore, H. 1986 *Space, Text and Gender*. Cambridge: Cambridge University Press.

Morris, D. 1985 *The Art of Ancient Cyprus*. Oxford: Phaidon.

Muhly, J.D. 1982 The nature of trade in the LBA eastern Mediterranean. In J.D. Muhly, R. Maddin & V. Karageorghis (eds), *Early Metallurgy in Cyprus, 4000-500 BC*. Nicosia: Pierides Foundation, 251-66.

Muhly, J.D. 1984 The role of the Sea Peoples in Cyprus during the LC III period. In V. Karageorghis & J.D. Muhly (eds), *Cyprus at the Close of the Late Bronze Age*. Nicosia: A.G. Leventis Foundation, 39-56.

Muhly, J.D. 1989 The organisation of the copper industry in Late Bronze Age Cyprus. In E. Peltenburg (ed.), *Early Society in Cyprus*. Edinburgh: University of Edinburgh Press, 298-314.

Muhly, J.D. 1992 The crisis years in the Mediterranean world: transition or cultural disintegration? In W.W. Ward & M.S. Joukowsky (eds), *The Crisis Years: The 12th Century BC from beyond the Danube to the Tigris*. Dubuque, Iowa, 10-26.

Murray, A.S., Smith, A.H. & Walters, H.B. 1900 *Excavations in Cyprus (Bequest of Miss E.T. Turner to the British Museum)*. London: British Museum.

Myres, J.L. 1914 *Handbook of the Cesnola Collections of Antiquities from Cyprus*. New York: Metropolitan Museum of Art.

Myres, J.L. & Ohnefalsch-Richter, M. 1899 *A Catalogue of the Cyprus Museum*. Oxford: Clarendon Press.

Nakou, G. 1995 The cutting edge: a new look at early Aegean metallurgy. *JMA* 8: 1-32.

Niklasson, K. 1983 A shaft-grave of the late Cypriote III period. In P. Åström *et al.* (eds), *Hala Sultan Tekke* 8. SIMA 45/8. Göteborg: P. Åströms Förlag, 169-87.

Bibliography

Niklasson, K. 1987 Late Cypriote III shaft graves: burial customs of the last phase of the Bronze Age. In R. Laffineur (ed.), *Thanatos: Les Coutumes Funéraires en Egée à l'Age du Bronze.* AEGAEUM 1. Annales d'archéologie égéenne de l'Université de Liège et UT-PASP: 219-25.

Niklasson, K. 1991 *Early Prehistoric Burials in Cyprus.* SIMA 96. Jonsered: P. Åströms Förlag.

Nowicki, K. 2001 Sea-raiders and refugees: problems of defensible sites in Crete *c.* 1200 BC. In V. Karageorghis & C. Morris (eds), *Defensive Settlements of the Aegean and the Eastern Mediterranean after c. 1200 BC.* Nicosia: Trinity College Dublin & A.G. Leventis Foundation, 23-40.

Nys, K. 1995 The use of masks in Cyprus during the Late Bronze Age. *Journal of Prehistoric Religion* 9: 19-34.

Ohnefalsch-Richter, M. 1893 *Kypros, the Bible and Homer: Oriental Civilization, Art and Religion in Ancient Times.* London: Asher.

Oren, E. 1969 Cypriot imports in the Palestinian Late Bronze I context. *Opuscula Atheniensia* 9: 127-50.

Overbeck, J. & Swiny, S. 1972 *Two Cypriote Bronze Age Sites at Kafkallia (Dhali).* SIMA 33. Göteborg: P. Åströms Förlag.

Papadopoulos, Th.J. 1997 Cyprus and the Aegean world: links in religion. In *Cyprus and the Aegean in Antiquity from the Prehistoric Period to the 7th Century AD.* Nicosia: Department of Antiquities, 171-84.

Papasavvas, G. 2001 *Chalkinoi Ypostates apo tin Kypro kai tin Krete. Tripodikoi kai Tetrapleuroi ypostates apo tin Ysteri Epoche tou Chalkou eos tin Proimi Epoche tou Siderou.* Nicosia: Leventis Foundation.

Patton, M. 1996 *Islands in Time: Island Sociogeography and Mediterranean Prehistory.* London: Routledge.

Pecorella, P.E. 1973 Mycenaean pottery from Ayia Irini. In *Acts of the International Symposium: The Mycenaeans in the Eastern Mediterranean.* Nicosia: Department of Antiquities, 19-24.

Pelon, O. 1973 Les 'tholoi' d'Enkomi. In *Acts of the International Symposium: The Mycenaeans in the Eastern Mediterranean.* Nicosia: Department of Antiquities, 246-53.

Peltenburg, E.J. 1972 On the classification of the faience vases from Late Bronze Age Cyprus. In *Praktika tou Protou Diethnous Kyprologikou Synedriou* I. *Archaion Tmema.* Nicosia: Leventis Foundation, 129-36.

Peltenburg, E.J. 1978 The Sotira Culture: regional diversity and cultural unity in Late Neolithic Cyprus. *Levant* 10: 55-74.

Peltenburg, E.J. 1979 Troulli reconsidered. In V. Karageorghis (ed.), *Studies Presented in Memory of Porphyrios Dikaios.* Nicosia: Lion's Club, 21-45.

Peltenburg, E.J. 1982a Early copperwork in Cyprus and the exploitation of picrolite; evidence from the Lemba Archaeological Project. In J.D. Muhly, R. Maddin & V. Karageorghis (eds), *Early Metallurgy in Cyprus, 4000-500 BC.* Nicosia: Pierides Foundation, 41-61.

Peltenburg, E.J. 1982b *Recent Developments in the Later Prehistory of Cyprus.* SIMA Pocketbooks 16. Göteborg: P. Åströms Förlag.

Peltenburg, E.J. 1982c *Vrysi: A Subterranean Settlement in Cyprus.* Warminster: Aris and Phillips.

Peltenburg, E.J. 1985 Pattern and purpose in the prehistoric Cypriot village of Ayios Epiktitos Vrysi. In Y. de Sike (ed.), *Chypre: la vie quotidienne de l'antiquité à nos jours.* Actes de Colloque. Paris: Musée de l'Homme, 46-64.

Bibliography

Peltenburg, E.J. 1989 The beginnings of religion in Cyprus. In E.J. Peltenburg (ed.), *Early Society in Cyprus*. Edinburgh: Edinburgh University Press, 108-26.

Peltenburg, E.J. 1991a Kissonerga-*Mosphilia*: a major Chalcolithic site in Cyprus. *BASOR* 282/283: 17-35.

Peltenburg, E.J. 1991b Local exchange in prehistoric Cyprus: an initial assessment of picrolite. *BASOR* 282-3: 107-26.

Peltenburg, E.J. 1991c Greeting gifts and luxury faience: a context for orientalising trends in Late Mycenaean Greece. In N.H. Gale (ed.), *Bronze Age Trade in the Mediterranean*. SIMA 90. Jonsered: P. Åströms Förlag, 162-179.

Peltenburg, E.J. 1992 Birth pendants in life and death: evidence from Kissonerga grave 563. In G. Ioannides (ed.), *Studies in Honour of Vassos Karageorghis*. Nicosia: Leventis Foundation, 27-36.

Peltenburg, E.J. 1993 Settlement discontinuity and resistance to complexity in Cyprus, *c.* 4500-2500 BC. *BASOR* 292: 9-23.

Peltenburg, E.J. 1994 Constructing authority: the Vounous enclosure model. *Opuscula Atheniensia* 20: 157-62.

Peltenburg, E.J. 1996 From isolation to state formation in Cyprus, *c.* 3500-1500 BC. In V. Karageorghis & D. Michaelides (eds), *The Development of the Cypriot Economy from the Prehistoric Period to the Present Day*. Nicosia: Leventis Foundation, 17-43.

Peltenburg, E.J. 2001 A ceremonial model: contexts for a prehistoric building model from Kissonerga, Cyprus. In B. Muller & D. Vaillancourt (eds), *'Maquettes architecturales' de l'antiquité. Regards croisés. (Proche-Orient, Egypte, Chypre, bassin égéen et Grèce, du Néolithique à l'époque hellénistique)*. Paris: Boccard, 123-41.

Peltenburg, E.J. & Spanou, S. 1999 Neolithic painted pottery from Agios Epiktitos-*Vrysi*. *RDAC*: 13-34.

Peltenburg, E.J. *et al.* 1985 *Lemba Archaeological Project* I. SIMA 70/1. Göteborg: P. Åströms Förlag.

Peltenburg, E.J. *et al.* 1991 *Lemba Archaeological Project* 2:2 *A Ceremonial Area at Kissonerga*. SIMA 70/3. Göteborg: P. Åströms Förlag.

Peltenburg, E.J. *et al.* 1998 *Lemba Archaeological Project* 2:1A *Excavations at Kissonerga-Mosphilia 1979-1992*. SIMA 70/2. Jonsered: P. Åströms Förlag.

Peltenburg, E.J. *et al.* 2000 Agro-pastoralist colonization of Cyprus in the 10th millennium BP: initial assessments. *Antiquity* 74: 844-53.

Peltenburg, E.J. *et al.* 2001 Neolithic dispersals from the Levantine corridor: a Mediterranean perspective. *Levant* 33: 35-64.

Peregrine, P. 1991 Some political aspects of craft specialization. *World Archaeology* 23: 1-11.

Pierides, A. 1973 Observations on some Mycenaean ivories from Cyprus. In *Acts of the International Symposium: The Mycenaeans in the Eastern Mediterranean*. Nicosia: Department of Antiquities, 274-7.

Pilides, D. 1994 *Handmade Burnished Wares of the Late Bronze Age in Cyprus*. SIMA 105. Jonsered: P. Åströms Förlag.

Pilides, D. 2000 *Pithoi of the Late Bronze Age in Cyprus*. Nicosia: Department of Antiquities.

Portugali, Y. & Knapp, A.B. 1985 Cyprus and the Aegean: spatial analysis of interaction in the seventeenth to fourteenth centuries BC. In A.B. Knapp & T. Stech (eds), *Prehistoric Production and Exchange. The Aegean and Eastern Mediterranean*. Los Angeles: Monograph XXV, University of California, 44-78.

Bibliography

Pulak, C. 1988 The Bronze Age shipwreck at Ulu Burun, Turkey: 1985 campaign. *AJA* 92: 1-37.

Pulak, C. 1997 The Ulu Burun shipwreck. In S. Swiny, R.L. Hohlfelder & H. Wylde Swiny (eds), *Res Maritimae: Cyprus and the Eastern Mediterranean from Prehistory to Late Antiquity*. Cyprus American Archaeological Research Institute Monograph Series, volume 1. Atlanta: Scholars Press, 233-62.

al-Radi, S.M.S. 1983 *Phlamoudhi Vounari: a sanctuary site in Cyprus*. SIMA 65. Göteborg: P. Åströms Förlag.

Rainbird, P. 1999 Islands out of time: towards a critique of island archaeology. *JMA* 12: 216-34.

Raptou, E. 1996 Contribution to the study of the economy of ancient Cyprus: copper – timber. In V. Karageorghis & D. Michaelides (eds), *The Development of the Cypriot Economy from the Prehistoric Period to the Present Day*. Nicosia: Leventis Foundation, 249-59.

Reese, D.S. 1996 Cypriot hippo hunters no myth. *JMA* 9: 107-12.

Reese, D.S. 1985 The Late Bronze Age to Geometric shells from Kition. In Karageorghis (ed.), *Excavations at Kition V.2. The Pre-Phoenician Levels. Areas I and II*. Nicosia: Department of Antiquities, 340-72.

Rehak, P. 1995 The use and destruction of Minoan stone bull's head rhyta. In R. Laffineur & W.D. Niemeier (eds), *Politeia: Society and State in the Aegean Bronze Age*. Proceedings of the 5th International Aegean Conference, University of Heidelberg, Archäologisches Institut, 10-13 April 1994. AEGAEUM 12. Annales d'archéologie égéenne de Université de Liège et UT-PASP, 435-459.

Reyes, A.T. 1994 *Archaic Cyprus: A Study of the Textual and Archaeological Evidence*. Oxford: Clarendon Press.

Runnels, C.N. & Hansen, J. 1986 The olive in the prehistoric Aegean: the evidence for domestication in the Early Bronze Age. *OJA* 5: 299-308.

Rutter, J. 1992 Cultural novelties in the post-palatial Aegean world: indices of vitality or decline? W.W. Ward & M.S. Joukowsky (eds), *The Crisis Years: The 12th Century BC from beyond the Danube to the Tigris*. Dubuque, Iowa, 61-78.

Sagona, C. 1996 Red to blue: colour symbolism and human societies. In G. Bunnens (ed.), *Cultural Interaction in the Ancient Near East*. Louvain: Peeters Press, 145-54.

Salles, J-F. 1995 Rituel mortuaire et rituel social à Ras Shamra/Ougarit. In S. Campbell & A. Green (eds), *The Archaeology of Death in the Ancient Near East*. Oxbow Monograph 51. Oxford: Oxbow Books, 171-84.

Sandars, N.K. 1961 The first Aegean swords and their ancestry. *AJA* 65: 17-29.

Sandars, N.K. 1963 Later Aegean Bronze Age swords. *AJA* 67: 117-53.

Sandars, N.K. 1985 *The Sea Peoples: Warriors of the Ancient Mediterranean*. London: Thames and Hudson (revised edition).

Sandwith, T.B. 1880 On the different styles of pottery found in ancient tombs in the island of Cyprus. *Archaeologia* 45: 127-42.

Schaeffer, C.F.A. 1952 *Enkomi-Alasia*. Paris: Klinckseick.

Severis, R.C. 2001 Edmond Duthoit: an artist and ethnographer in Cyprus, 1862, 1865. In V. Tatton-Brown (ed.), *Cyprus in the 19th Century AD: Fact, Fancy and Fiction. Papers of the 22nd British Museum Classical Colloquium*. Oxford: Oxbow Books, 32-49.

Sevketoglu, M. 2000 *Archaeological Field Survey of the Neolithic and Chalcolithic Settlement Sites in Kyrenia District, North Cyprus: Systematic Surface Collection and the Interpretation of Artefact Scatters*. BAR International Series 834. Oxford: Archaeopress.

Bibliography

Shelmerdine, C.W. 1985 *The Perfume Industry of Mycenaean Pylos*. SIMA Pocketbook 34. Göteborg: P. Åström's Förlag.

Sherratt, A. 1981 Plough and pastoralism: aspects of the secondary products revolution. In I. Hodder *et al.* (eds), *Pattern of the Past: Studies in Memory of David Clarke*. Cambridge: Cambridge University Press, 261-305.

Sherratt, A. & Sherratt, E.S. 1991 From luxuries to commodities: the nature of Mediterranean Bronze Age trading systems. In N.H. Gale (ed.), *Bronze Age Trade in the Mediterranean*. SIMA 90. Jonsered: P. Åströms Förlag, 351-86.

Sherratt, E.S. 1991 Cypriot pottery of Aegean type in LC II-III: problems of classification, chronology and interpretation. In J.A. Barlow, D.L. Bolger & B. Kling (eds), *Cypriot Ceramics: Reading the Prehistoric Record*. University Museum Monograph 74. Philadelphia: University of Pennsylvania, 185-98.

Sherratt, E.S. 1992 Immigration and archaeology: some indirect reflections. In P. Åström (ed.), *Acta Cypriot 1.2. Acts of an International Congress on Cypriote Archaeology Held in Göteborg on 22-24 August*. SIMA Pocketbook 117. Göteborg: P. Åströms Förlag, 316-46.

Sherratt, E.S. 1994 Commerce, iron and ideology: metallurgical innovation in 12th-11th century Cyprus. In V. Karageorghis (ed.), *Cyprus in the 11th Century BC*. Nicosia: Leventis Foundation & University of Cyprus, 59-106.

Sherratt, E.S. & Sherratt, A. 1993 The growth of the Mediterranean economy in the early first millennium BC. *World Archaeology* 24: 361-78.

Simmons, A.H. 1991 Humans, island colonisation and Pleistocene extinctions in the Mediterranean: the view from Akrotiri *Aetokremnos*, Cyprus. *Antiquity* 65: 857-69.

Simmons, A.H. 1998 Of tiny hippos, large cows and early colonists in Cyprus. *JMA* 11: 232-41.

Simmons, A. & Wigand, P. 1994 Assessing the radiocarbon determinations from Akrotiri *Aetokremnos*, Cyprus. In R. Kraa & O. Bar-Yosef (eds), *Late Quarternary Chronology and Paleoclimates of the Eastern Mediterranean*. Cambridge (Mass), 247-54.

Simmons, A.H. *et al.* 1999 *Faunal Extinction in an Island Society. Pygmy Hippopotamus Hunters of Cyprus*. New York: Kluwer Academic, Plenum Publishers.

Sjöqvist, E. 1940 *Problems of the Late Cypriot Bronze Age*. Stockholm: Swedish Cyprus Expedition.

Smith, J.S. 1994 *Seals for Sealing in the Late Bronze Age*. Unpublished PhD dissertation. Department of Classical and Near Eastern Archaeology, Bryn Mawr College.

South, A.K. 1985 Figurines and other objects from Kalavasos-*Ayious*. *Levant* 17: 65-79.

South, A.K. 1988 Kalavasos-*Ayios Dhimitrios* 1987: an important ceramic group from Building X. *RDAC*: 223-8.

South, A.K. 1989 From copper to kingship: aspects of Bronze Age society viewed from the Vasilikos valley. In E. Peltenburg (ed.), *Early Society in Cyprus*. Edinburgh: University of Edinburgh Press, 315-324.

South, A.K. 1991 Kalavasos-*Ayios Dhimitrios* 1990. *RDAC*: 131-9.

South, A.K. 1992 Kalavasos-*Ayios Dhimitrios* 1991. *RDAC*: 133-46.

South, A.K. 2000 Late Bronze Age burials at Kalavasos-*Ayios Dhimitrios*. In G.K. Ioannides & S. A. Hadjistyllis (eds), *Praktika tou Tritou Diethnous Kyprologikou Synedriou (Nicoisa, 16-20 April 1996)* 1. *Archaion Tmema*. Nicosia: Leventis Foundation, 345-64.

South, A.K. *et al.* 1989 *Kalavasos-Ayios Dhimitrios II. Ceramics, Objects, Tombs,*

Specialist Studies. Vasilikos Valley Project 3. SIMA 71/3. Göteborg: P. Åströms Förlag.

Stanley-Price, N.P. 1977a Colonisation and continuity in the early prehistory of Cyprus. *World Archaeology* 9: 27-41.

Stanley-Price, N.P. 1977b Khirokitia and the initial settlement of Cyprus. *Levant* 9: 66-89.

Stanley-Price, N.P. 1979a On terminology and models in Cypriote prehistory. In V. Karageorghis (ed.), *Studies Presented in Memory of Porphyrios Dikaios*. Nicosia: Lions Club, 1-11.

Stanley-Price, N.P. 1979b The structure of settlement at Sotira in Cyprus. *Levant* 11: 46-83.

Stech, T. 1982 Urban metallurgy in Late Bronze Age Cyprus. In. J.D. Muhly, R. Maddin & V. Karageorghis (eds), *Early Metallurgy in Cyprus, 4000-500 BC*. Nicosia: Department of Antiquities, 105-15.

Stech, T., Maddin, R. & Muhly, J.D. 1985 Copper production at Kition in the Late Bronze Age. In V. Karaeorghis & M. Demas 1985, 105-15.

Steel, L. 1993 The establishment of the city kingdoms in Iron Age Cyprus: an archaeological commentary. *RDAC*: 147-56.

Steel, L. 1994 Representations of a shrine on a Mycenaean chariot krater from Kalavasos-Ayios Dhimitrios, Cyprus. *BSA* 89: 201-11.

Steel, L. 1995 Differential burial practices in Cyprus at the transition from the Bronze Age to the Iron Age. In S. Cambell & A. Green (eds), *Death in the Ancient Near East*. Oxford: Oxbow Monographs, 199-205.

Steel, L. 1996 Transition from Bronze to Iron at Kourion: a review of the tombs from Episkopi-*Bamboula* and *Kaloriziki*. *BSA* 91:287-300.

Steel, L. 1998 The social impact of Mycenaean imported pottery in Cyprus. *BSA* 93: 285-96.

Steel, L. 2001 The British Museum and the invention of the Cypriot Late Bronze Age. In V. Tatton-Brown (ed.), *Cyprus in the 19th Century AD: Fact, Fancy and Fiction. Papers of the 22nd British Museum Classical Colloquium*. Oxford: Oxbow Books, 160-7.

Steel, L. in press Late Cypriot ceramic production: regionalism or standardisation. In B. Boyd & B. Siller (eds), *Embedded Technologies. Reworking Technological Studies in Archaeology*. Lampeter Workshop.

Stewart, E. & Stewart, J.R. 1950 *Vounous 1937-1938*. Lund: Swedish Institute in Rome.

Stewart, J.R. 1962a The Early Cypriote Bronze Age. In P. Dikaios & J.R. Stewart, *Swedish Cyprus Expedition* IV 1A. *The Stone Age and Early Bronze Age*. Lund: Swedish Cyprus Expedition.

Stewart, J.R. 1962b The tomb of the seafarer at Karmi in Cyprus. *Opuscula Atheniensia* 4: 197-204.

Stockton, E. 1968 Pre-Neolithic remains at Kyrenia, Cyprus. *RDAC*: 6-19.

Stoddart, S. *et al.* 1993 Cult in an island society: prehistoric Malta in the Tarxien period. *CAJ* 3: 3-193.

Stos-Gale, Z.A. *et al.* 1997 Lead isotope characteristics of the Cyprus copper ore deposits applied to provenance studies of copper oxhide ingots. *Archaeometry* 39: 83-123.

Swiny, H.W. & Swiny, S. 1983 An anthropomorphic figurine from the Sotira area. *RDAC*: 56-9.

Swiny, S. 1981 Bronze Age settlement patterns in southwest Cyprus. *Levant* 13: 51-87.

Bibliography

Swiny, S. 1982 The environment. In H.W. Swiny (ed.), *Ancient Kourion Area*. Nicosia: Zavallis Press.

Swiny, S. 1985a The Cyprus-American Archaeological Research Institute's excavations at Sotira-*Kaminoudhia* and the origins of the Philia culture. In T. Papadopoulou & S. Hadjistyllis (eds), *Praktika tou Deuterou Diethnous Kyprologikou Synedriou*. Nicosia: Leventis Foundation, 13-26.

Swiny, S. 1985b Sotira-*Kaminoudhia* and the Chalcolithic/Early Bronze Age transition in Cyprus. In V. Karageorghis (ed.), *Archaeology in Cyprus 1960-1985*. Nicosia, 115-24.

Swiny, S. 1986 *The Kent State University Expedition to Episkopi-Phaneromeni 2*. SIMA 74/2. Nicosia: P. Åströms Förlag.

Swiny, S. 1988 The Pleistocene fauna of Cyprus and recent discoveries on the Akrotiri Peninsula. *RDAC*: 1-14.

Swiny, S. 1989 From round house to duplex: a reassessment of prehistoric Cypriot Bronze Age society. In E.J. Peltenburg (ed.), *Early Society in Cyprus*. Edinburgh: Edinburgh University Press.

Swiny, S. 1991 Foreword to reprint of Cesnola 1877, *Cyprus: Its Cities, Tombs and Temples*. Nicosia: Star Graphics.

Swiny, S. 1997 The Early Bronze Age. In *Istoria tes Kyprou. Tomos A. Archaia Kypros*. Nicosia: Makarios Foundation, 117-212.

Talalay, L.E. 1994 *Deities, Dolls, and Devices. Neolithic Figurines from Franchthi Cave, Greece*. Bloomington & Indianapolis: Indiana University Press.

Taylor, L. 2001 Lady Brassey, 1870-1886: traveller, writer, collector, educator, woman of means and the fate of her Cypriot artefacts. In V. Tatton-Brown (ed.), *Cyprus in the 19th Century AD: Fact, Fancy and Fiction. Papers of the 22nd British Museum Classical Colloquium*. Oxford: Oxbow Books, 239-47.

Todd, I.A. 1981 A Cypriote Neolithic wall painting. *Antiquity* 55: 47-51.

Todd, I.A. 1985a The Vasilikos Valley and the chronology of the Neolithic/Chalcolithic periods in Cyprus. *RDAC*: 1-15.

Todd, I.A. 1985b The Vasilikos vallery and the Neolithic/Chalcolithic periods in Cyprus. In *Praktika tou Deuterou Diethnous Kyprologikou Synedriou 1. Archaion Tmema*. Nicosia: Leventis Foundation, 5-12.

Todd, I.A. 1987 *Excavations at Kalavasos-Tenta*, I. SIMA 71.6. Göteborg: P. Åströms Förlag.

Todd, I.A. 1988 The Middle Bronze Age in the Kalavasos area. *RDAC* (part 1): 133-40.

Todd, I.A. 1989 Early prehistoric society: a view from the Vasilikos Valley. In E. Peltenburg (ed.), *Early Society in Cyprus*. Edinburgh: Edinburgh University Press, 2-13.

Todd, I.A. 1991 The Vasilikos valley and the Chalcolithic period in Cyprus. *BASOR* 282/283: 3-16.

Todd, I.A. 1993 Kalavasos-*Laroumena*: test excavation of a Middle Bronze Age settlement. *RDAC*: 81-96.

Todd, I.A. 1996 The Vasilikos Valley: its place in Cypriot and Near Eastern prehistory. In J.E. Coleson & V.H. Matthews (eds), *'Go to the Land that God will show you': Studies in Honour of Dwight W. Young*. Winona Lake: Eisenbrauns, 317-51.

Todd, I.A. 2001 Early connections of Cyprus with Anatolia. In V. Karageorghis (ed.), *The White Slip Ware of Late Bronze Age Cyprus*. Vienna: Verlag der Österrichischen Akademie der Wissenschaften, 203-13.

Todd, I.A. & Hadjicosti, M. 1991 Excavations at Sanidha 1990. *RDAC*: 37-74.

Bibliography

Todd, I.A. & Pilides, D. 1993 Excavations at Sanidha 1992. *RDAC*: 97-146.

Todd, I.A. & Pilides, D. 2001 The archaeology of White Slip production. In V. Karageorghis (ed.), *The White Slip Ware of Late Bronze Age Cyprus*. Vienna: Verlag der Österrichischen Akademie der Wissenschaften, 27-43.

Todd, I.A. *et al.* 1992 Excavations at Sanidha 1991, *RDAC*: 75-112.

Tringham, R. & Conkey, M. 1998 Rethinking figurines: a critical view from archaeology of Gimbutas, the 'goddess' and popular culture. In L. Goodison & C. Morris (eds), *Ancient Goddesses: The Myths and the Evidence*. London: British Museum Press, 22-45.

Tsintides, T.Ch. 1998 *The Endemic Plants of Cyprus*. Nicosia: Bank of Cyprus.

Tzedakis, Y. & Martlew, H. 1999 (eds), *Minoans and Mycenaeans: Flavours of Their Time*. Athens: Kapon Editions.

Vagnetti, L. 1974 Preliminary remarks on Cypriot Chalcolithic figurines. *RDAC*: 24-34.

Vagnetti, L. 1980 Figurines and minor objects from a chalcolithic cemetery at Souskiou-*Vathyrkakas* (Cyprus). *SMEA* 21: 17-72.

Vagnetti, L. & Lo Schiavo, F. 1989 Late Bronze Age long distance trade in the Mediterranean: the role of the Cypriots. In E. Peltenburg (ed.), *Early Society in Cyprus*. Edinburgh: University of Edinburgh Press, 217-43.

Ulbrich, A. 2001. An archaeology of cult? Cypriot sanctuaries in 19th-century archaeology. In V. Tatton-Brown (ed.), *Cyprus in the 19th Century AD: Fact, Fancy and Fiction. Papers of the 22nd British Museum Classical Colloquium*. Oxford: Oxbow Books, 93-106.

van Andel, T. & Runnels, C. 1995 The earliest farmers in Europe. *Antiquity* 69: 481-500.

van Dommelen, P. 1999 Islands in history. *JMA* 12: 246-51.

Vaughan, S. 1991 Material and technical classification of Base Ring ware: a new fabric typology. In J.A. Barlow, D.L. Bolger & B. Kling (eds), *Cypriot Ceramics: Reading the Prehistoric Record*. University Museum Monograph 74. Philadelphia: University of Pennsylvania, 119-130.

Vermeule, E. 1973 Excavations at Toumba tou Skourou, Morphou, 1971. In *Acts of the International Symposium: The Mycenaeans in the Eastern Mediterranean*. Nicosia: Department of Antiquities, 25-33.

Vermeule, E. 1974 *Toumba tou Skourou: Mound of Darkness*. Cambridge (Mass): Harvard University Press.

Vermeule, E. & Wolsky, F. 1990 *Toumba tou Skourou. A Bronze Age Potters' Quarter on Morphou Bay in Cyprus*. Cambridge (Mass): Harvard University Press.

Vichos, Y. & Lolos, Y. 1997 The Cypro-Mycenaean wreck at Point Iria in the Argolid gulf: first thoughts on the origin and the nature of the vessel. In S. Swiny, R.L. Hohlfelder & H.W. Swiny (eds), *Res Maritimae: Cyprus and the Eastern Mediterranean from Prehistory to Late Antiquity*. Cyprus American Archaeological Research Institute Monograph Series, volume 1. Atlanta: Scholars Press, 321-37.

Vigne, J.-D. 1996 Did man provoke extinctions of endemic large mammals on the Mediterranean islands? The view from Corsica. *JMA* 9: 117-26.

Vita-Frinzi, C. 1973 Palaeolithic finds from Cyprus? *PPS* 39: 453-4.

Ward, W.A. & Joukowsky, M.S. (eds), 1992 *The Crisis Years: The Twelfth Century BC*. Dubuque, Iowa.

Washbourne, R. 1997 A possible interpretation of the 'comb figures' of Bronze Age Cyprus. *RDAC*: 27-30.

Bibliography

Washbourne, R. 2000 Cypriot plank figures and the Near Eastern *tudittu*. *RDAC*: 95-100.

Watkins, T.F. 1972 Cypriote Neolithic chronology and the pottery from Philia-*Drakos* A. In *Praktika tou Protou Diethnous Kyprologikou Synedriou* I. *Archaion Tmema*. Nicosia: Leventis Foundation, 167-74.

Watkins, T.F. 1973 Some problems of the Neolithic and Chalcolithic period in Cyprus. *RDAC*: 34-61.

Webb, J.M. 1985 The incised scapula. In V. Karageorghis (ed.), *Excavations at Kition V.2. The Pre-Phoenician Levels. Areas I and II*. Nicosia: Department of Antiquities, 317-28.

Webb, J.M. 1992a Cypriote Bronze Age glyptic: style, function and social context. In R. Laffineur & J.L. Crowley (eds), EIKON. *Aegean Bronze Age Iconography: Shaping a Methodology*. AEGAEUM 8. Annales d'archéologie égéenne de l'Université de Liège et UT-PASP, 113-21.

Webb, J.M. 1992b Funerary ideology in Bronze Age Cyprus: towards the recognition and analysis of Cypriote ritual data. In G. Ioannides (ed.), *Studies in Honour of Vassos Karageorghis*. Nicosia: Leventis Foundation, 87-99.

Webb, J.M. 1998 Lithic technology and discard at Marki, Cyprus. Consumer behaviour and site formation in the prehistoric Bronze Age. *Antiquity* 72: 796-805.

Webb, J.M. 1999 *Ritual Architecture, Iconography and Practice in the Late Cypriot Bronze Age*. SIMA Pocketbook 75. Jonsered: P. Åströms Förlag.

Webb, J.M. & Frankel, D. 1994 Making an impression: storage and surplus finance in Late Bronze Age Cyprus. *JMA* 7: 5-26.

Webb, J.M. & Frankel, D. 1999 Characterizing the Philia facies: material culture, chronology, and the origin of the Bronze Age in Cyprus. *AJA* 103: 3-43.

Yon, M. 1980 La fondation de Salamine. In *Salamine de Chypre: Histoire et Archéologie. Etat des recherches*. Paris: Editions Recherche sur les Civilizations, 71-80.

Yon, M. 1987 Les rhytons du sanctuaire. In *Ras Shamra-Ougarit* III. *Le Centre de la Ville. 38e-44e campagnes 1978-1984*, 343-50. Lyon: Editions Recherche sur les Civilizations.

Zaccagnini, C. 1987 Aspects of ceremonial exchange in the Near East during the late second millennium BC. In M. Rowlands, M. Larsen & K. Kristiansen (eds), *Centre and Periphery in the Ancient World*. Cambridge: Cambridge University Press, 57-65.

Index

Index

Index